THE LOGIC OF CULTURE

CONTRIBUTING AUTHORS

CHARLES ACKERMAN, University of New Brunswick, New Brunswick, Canada

PAUL BOUISSAC, Victoria College, University of Toronto, Ontario, Canada

N. ROSS CRUMRINE, University of Victoria, British Columbia, Canada

MAURICE GODELIER, Ecole des Hautes Etudes en Sciences Sociales, Paris, France

FADWA EL GUINDI, Ain Shams University, Cairo, Egypt
University of California, Los Angeles, United States of America

WOLFGANG G. JILEK, University of British Columbia, Vancouver, Canada

LOUISE JILEK-AALL, University of British Columbia, Vancouver, Canada

KENNETH MADDOCK, Macquarie University, New South Wales, Australia

PIERRE MARANDA, Université Laval, Québec, Canada

ROGER NEICH, National Museum of New Zealand, Wellington, New Zealand

HARVEY ROSENBAUM, American Institute for Research in the Behavioral Sciences, Washington, D.C., United States of America

INO ROSSI (*Editor*), St. John's University, Jamaica, New York, United States of America

R. T. ZUIDEMA, University of Illinois, Urbana–Champaign, Illinois, United States of America

THE LOGIC OF CULTURE
Advances in Structural Theory and Methods

Ino Rossi and Contributors

J. F. BERGIN PUBLISHERS, INC.

To Irene and Paul

Library of Congress Cataloging in Publication Data
Main entry under title:
The Logic of Culture.
  Bibliography: p.
  1. Structuralism—Addresses, essays, lectures.
I. Rossi, Ino.
B841.4.L63   149'.96   81-29
ISBN 0-89789-015-9

First Published in 1982 by
J. F. Bergin Publishers, Inc.
670 Amherst Road
South Hadley, Massachusetts 01075

0123456789   056   987654321

Printed in the United States of America

Contents

Preface

The previous volume I edited on Levi-Strauss' structuralism (*The Unconscious in Culture,* Dutton:1974) dealt with interpretations and refinements of key structural notions, suggestions for more rigorous ethnographic applications, and evaluations of structuralism from the point of view of contrasting theoretical perspectives. Reviews published in professional journals have indicated that the volume has filled an important gap in the literature on structuralism. However, various contributors to that volume have pointed out issues still open and concepts in need of further clarification. Articles and volumes appearing after the publication of that volume have added new fuel to old controversies and brought forward new criticisms—some of which are ethnographic, others theoretical in nature. Hence the reason for this volume. The content and structure of the book have taken shape during numerous sessions I have organized at the annual meetings of the American Anthropological Association and as a result of correspondence, reviews and comments originating from the publication of *The Unconscious in Culture.* Prospective contributors understood that we sought theoretical and methodological refinements rather than mere replications of structural analysis à la Levi-Strauss; I have also solicited chapters which show the applicability of structuralism to a new range of cultural data or, more ambitiously, which add new analytical dimensions to the structural paradigm.

The chapters in Part One and Part Two contain refinements of the structural paradigm as applied by Levi-Strauss and his followers, whereas those in Part Three offer revisions and extensions of the Levi-Straussian paradigm. The objective of Part One is to clarify the premises and precise scope of the structural paradigm (Chapter 1), to offer a more rigorous definition of key theoretical notions (Chapter 2), to eliminate trite misinterpretations (Chapter 3) and to suggest solutions to the vexed question of verification in structural analysis (Chapters 4 and 5). The objective of Part Two is to cope with certain issues encountered in the ethnographic application of structuralism. The first three chapters deal with issues which emerged from the study of myth and ritual (Chapters 6,

7 and 8)—issues concerning the structural analysis of kinship are discussed in the first and last of those three. The last two chapters of Part Two suggest innovative research directions—the structural study of history (Chapter 9) and the utilization of elements of generative-transformational grammar with the intent of proposing a more rigorous and replicable form of structural analysis (Chapter 10). The chapters of Part Three offer examples of the interface between structuralism and other semiotic approaches (Chapters 11 and 12) and between structuralism and Marxism (Chapter 13). In the concluding chapter, I deal with a variety of radical criticisms that have recently appeared in scientific journals—many of which are centered around the presumed untenableness or mentalistic character of the notion of deep structure.

I have made a special effort to select as much ethnographically oriented material as possible — a major part of this work is based on ethnographic data. The reasons for this choice are the following. First of all, the abundant literature on structuralism tends to be overtheoretical, and no theoretical orientation can be effectively tested or refined apart from empirical research. Secondly, and more importantly, one must counteract the widespread notion that structural analysis is based more on gratuitous assumptions than on the close scrutiny of ethnographic data. Many chapters of this volume demonstrate that the analytical power of the structural paradigm emerges more fully whenever the ethnographic information appears so heterogeneous and seemingly contradictory as to make impossible a unified and coherent interpretation by using traditional—i.e., non-structural—perspectives. The majority of the ethnographic chapters are based on data collected through first-hand field experience; this circumstance is particularly important, considering the often-heard criticism that Levi-Strauss bases his analysis on secondary sources rather than on data collected in first-hand fieldwork.

The chapters of this volume will not lay to rest all the criticisms advanced against such an innovative and controversial approach as structuralism. However, the patience of the contributors, and the relentless attempts of the editor, will be adequately rewarded if the volume will eliminate certain repetitious misunderstandings, and help to chart the future course of structuralism.

PART ONE

THEORETICAL
AND METHODOLOGICAL
REFINEMENTS OF THE
STRUCTURAL PARADIGM

1
On the Assumptions of Structural Analysis: Revisiting its Linguistic and Epistemological Premises

Ino Rossi

The "scientific" perspective and the technological mode of functioning are both distinguishing characteristics and marks of achievement of Western society. It is not surprising, then, that the "scientific" mode of thinking has heavily permeated the social sciences at the expense of the humanistic, historical and critical approaches, which have produced such distinguished thinkers as Max Weber, Karl Marx, William I. Thomas, Alfred Schutz, Pitirim A. Sorokin, Jean-Jacques Rousseau, Gian Battista Vico, Robert Redfield and many others. The critical and humanistic approaches are still alive in contemporary social sciences, mainly in the work of phenomenologists, ethnomethodologists, marxists and dialectical anthropologists. However, were one to locate the works of social scientists along a continuum ranging from the humanistic and historical focus to the "hard" scientific focus, the weight would heavily fall on the scientific end of the continuum in terms of the quantity of publications, and session topics discussed at professional meetings. Especially in Anglo-Saxon countries the "scientific" emphasis in social sciences has been construed to imply a stress on the quantitative study of behavior and observable patterns of interaction.

The issue, however, must be raised as to whether this predominant behavioristic orientation is justified by the nature of the scientific

3

method and of the socio-cultural data, or whether it derives from such questionable epistemological views as positivism, empiricism, operationalism, and the like. Humanistically, phenomenologically and critically oriented social scientists argue that the latter explanation is the correct one, and propose their own theoretical orientations as effective antidotes against the "naturalistic attitude" of positivists, behaviorists and operationalists. As we shall shortly explain, the "naturalistic attitude" consists in studying psychic and social phenomena as if they were natural phenomena and with the methods of natural sciences.

Transformational structuralists[1] find objectionable not only the "naturalistic" attitude of behaviorists and positivists but also the humanistic, phenomenological and critical approaches. The difference between behavioral and positivist social scientists, on the one hand, and critical and phenomenological social scientists, on the other hand, is at times rendered as a difference between an "objective" and a "subjective" approach (Natanson 1963:viii). On the one hand, behaviorists and positivists argue that their approach is "objective" because they study observable realities which are documented and analyzed through rigorous, well-defined and replicable procedures. Behaviorists and positivists argue further that the paradigm of critical social scientists is based on personal and ideological preferences, and that this is in violation of the basic canons of a "value free" science. Moreover, behaviorists and positivists find the phenomenological approach too subjective and arbitrary, an intuitive approach which does not permit replication of research procedures and rigorous verification of findings. On the other hand, humanistic, historical and critical social scientists argue that the so-called "objective" approach pursues "objectivity" at the cost of missing or altering what is most unique in psychic and social phenomena; they argue that behaviorists and operationalists reduce psychic and social phenomena—it reduces the latter to their observable manifestations, and neglects to study their "meaning" in its intentional, existential, or historical aspects.

Transformational structuralists understand the difference between the so-called "objective" and "subjective" approaches in a totally different way. They argue that social scientists should be interested not with empirically documentable patterns of interaction, as positivist sociologists are, but with the "meaning" of social phenomena. However, they do not advocate the study of "subjective" meaning; rather, they claim that transformational structuralism goes beyond the scope of the traditional "objective" and "subjective" approaches, avoiding their limitations by placing social sciences back on their right track. This consists in studying the "true meaning" of social phenomena—that is, an "objective meaning" which is beyond the realm of both the observable patterns of interaction and conscious meaning. Transformational structuralists claim that their approach is the only approach which avoids the empiricist shortcomings present in both the "objective" and "subjective" approaches as traditionally understood.

In this opening chapter I will discuss the following points:

(1) In the first part, I will examine in what sense the subjective and objective approaches as traditionally understood are debilitated by empiricist flaws, and how transformational structuralists avoid the empiricist bias;

(2) In the second part, I will systematically discuss the usage made by structuralists of certain linguistic concepts in their attempt to study kinship as a symbolic rather than a "natural" phenomenon;

(3) In the third part, I will show that the structuralists' selective usage of linguistics is not totally arbitrary but based on well-developed epistemological and ontological views.

Structuralism as an Alternative to the Empiricism of the Functional Approach

Transformational structuralists have made an explicit effort to ground their approach on carefully elaborated epistemological assumptions. By "epistemology" I mean a discourse about the source and validity of scientific knowledge. Such a discourse must deal with (1) the scientific definition of the object of analysis and (2) the relationship of scientific activity to the object studied. One might object that if one defines the object of analysis before conducting scientific investigations, he will be inevitably led to alter or twist the data in the direction of his own theoretical orientation. Social scientists of positivistic and behavioristic orientation argue that the term "data" cannot indicate but the "objective" characteristics of what is studied—that is, characteristics which any social scientist can and should perceive regardless of his own theoretical presuppositions. Against this contention transformational structuralists counter-argue that the terms "data" and "objective characteristics" are scientific concepts, and that no scientific concept is independent of theoretical presuppositions. The theoretical orientation of the researcher inevitably determines what kind of data are worth studying and what characteristics can be accepted as "objective" or valid for scientific analysis. For instance, positivist social scientists claim that the notion of "social fact" is the only scientifically valid notion because it entails an "objective"—i.e., "unbiased"—attitude toward the data. On the contrary, we can counter-argue that the notion of "social fact" is a positivist construct based on the notion that social phenomena must be analyzed as if they were "natural" phenomena. As we have already mentioned, such a principle, derived from a positivistic conception of scientific explanation and experimental method, deprives social phenomena of their "meaning."

Transformational structuralists are not against the scientific method, but they are against the empiricist interpretation of the notions of external and internal experience and the related empiricist notion of "subjective" and "objective" approach. Empiricists conceive "experience" as a reading or registering of already organized and immediately discernible characteristics which are presumed to exist in external objects or within the conscious states of the individual (Piaget 1971:336). As I have explained elsewhere, Levi-Strauss has explicitly rejected the "dull" and "naive" objectivism of empiricists who accept as reliable objects of investigation what is immediately given in sensory perception (Rossi 1974:64 ff). Similarly, Levi-Strauss has argued that it is not only naive but also false to accept overt behavior or people's conscious explanations at their face value as "genuine" objects for scientific investigation. In fact, it is well known that verbal explanations and/or actions may hide ideological and material interests, or entail a poor understanding of social processes. Moreover, the explanations and behavior of certain people at times contradict the explanations and behavior of others, and, therefore, the social scientist seems to be left without a guiding criterion for explanation. For these reasons, transformational structuralists argue that we have to go beyond surface structures to find the deep and real structures which alone can account for the variety of observable phenomena or conscious explanations and their apparently contradictory or discrepant properties. This point, to which I shall return at the end of the essay, provides the context within which we have to interpret Levi-Strauss' statement that we must "understand being in relation to itself and not in relation to oneself" (1965:62)—that is, we must forego the subjective approach and follow an objective one.[2]

Levi-Strauss has proposed theoretical critiques of the phenomenological approach in his own autobiographical account (1965), in polemic with Sartre (1966), and in the epistemological manifesto at the end of L'Homme Nu (1971). He has also shown the shortcomings of the empiricist approach—especially in its functional version— in classic ethnographic essays, outstanding among which is Levi-Strauss' explanation of the problem of the avunculate. I select this example not only because of the actuality of the controversy surrounding the structural analysis of kinship (see the third essay in this volume), but also because it was in kinship analysis that Levi-Strauss first broke away from traditional approaches, notably British structural functionalism. Kinship analysis seems an area of study apt to show the differences between the two approaches because kinship has been a central concern of British structural functionalism.

In a 1945 classic paper, Levi-Strauss proposed an alternative explanation of the avunculate to the one proposed by Radcliffe-Brown. The latter maintained that the mother's brother plays two different roles in different cultures, and that the two roles give origin to two antithetic systems of attitudes. When the maternal uncle plays the role of authority, his relationships to his nephew are characterized by respect and obedience, and the relationships between son and father are warm. On the contrary, when the father is an authority figure, the relationship between maternal uncle and nephew are warm, and the relation between father and son are characterized by respect. It is Radcliffe-Brown's contention that the principle of descent determines which one of the systems will occur. The authority role is played by the father in patrilineal societies and by the maternal uncle in matrilineal societies (Levi-Strauss 1963:39-41).

Although Levi-Strauss credits Radcliffe-Brown for having attempted a synthesis based on empirical data rather than *a priori* evolutionary criteria, he finds the proposed explanation inadequate for two reasons. Firstly, the principle of descent cannot offer a universal explanation because various forms of avunculate exist in both patrilineal and matrilineal descent systems. Secondly, and most importantly, the avuncular relationship cannot be understood on the basis of just two terms alone because brother, sister, brother-in-law and nephew are all presupposed by the avuncular relationship (41). In other words, the relationship between uncle and nephew is a function of a larger cluster of relationships. This important point is clearly and succinctly expressed by the following classic law: "The relation between maternal uncle and nephew is to the relation between brother and sister, as the relation between father and son is to that between husband and wife" (42). This formula offers a good example of structural causality and structural prediction which Levi-Strauss offers as an alternative to empirical causality and empirical predictions: "If we know one pair of relations, it is always possible to infer the other" (42). Levi-Strauss illustrates this with various ethnographic examples showing that no matter whether the descent is patrilineal or matrilineal such a predictive law always holds true, whenever the system is at its pure state—that is, when the system is not subjected to outside interferences. Since this structural relationship remains always operative, no matter what the principle of descent is, it must be considered as a more fundamental explanatory principle than the principle of descent. Levi-Strauss shows that when empirically observable kinship systems operate through the juxtaposition of elementary structures, the avuncular relationship is apparent; however, when kinship systems are composed of more complex building blocks, the avuncular relationship is submerged in a differentiated context.

The clause "if the system is at its pure state" has been forgotten by Levi-Strauss' critics, who consequently have produced many misinterpretations and useless criticisms of his position. In polemic with De Heusch, Levi-Strauss has shown that the alleged ethnographic exceptions mentioned by the latter either confirm his own position or are instances of those complex structures which he had already anticipated in 1945 (Levi-Strauss 1973:5-30). Levi-Strauss argues that "the atom of kinship" is the most simple structure—the point of departure of kinship analysis—not only because it is implied in the problem of the avunculate but also because it is the most economic way to articulate the three constitutive relationships of kinship: (1) the relations of consanguinity between siblings; (2) alliance between spouses, and; (3) filiation between parents and children (7; also Levi-Strauss 1963:46).

Levi-Strauss is careful in noticing that his conception of the atom of kinship does not reduce all the relationships between the four terms to one dimension, as might be deduced by the + and − of the illustrative diagram (Levi-Strauss 1963:45). In reality, the relationship among terms may be expressed by one or more of the four fundamental attitudes, two of which are bilateral (mutuality of affection and reciprocity of prestations), and two of which are unilateral (the relationships of debtor and creditor).

The same structural way of thinking is applied to the problem of the cross-cousin marriage. Cross-cousin marriage is composed of four elements, a brother and a sister in the older generation, and a son and a daughter in the next generation; this means that cross-cousin marriage consists of a quartet composed of one man creditor and one man debtor, and one woman given and one woman received (Levi-Strauss 1969:442-443). In purely structural terms we can express this notion by saying that cross-cousin marriage is a by-product of the opposition, or rather distinction, among siblings of the same sex and siblings of opposite sex, and among a creditor and a debtor. Levi-Strauss uses this elemental quartet to illustrate the fundamental differences between the mother's brother's daughter marriage (open structure) and the father's sister's daughter (closed structure), and shows that the first of these two types of marriages produces a greater social integration than the other types. The quartet called by Levi-Strauss "the atom of kinship" is at the core of the alliance principle.

It is by now obvious that the explanation of observed kinship systems in terms of few underlying relational constants is a radical departure from the naturalistic perspective of Radcliffe-Brown. For Radcliffe-Brown the basic kinship structure is the "elementary family" which implies the first-order relationships among siblings (consanguinity), among spouses (affinity), and among parents and children (filiation). Out of the connection between two elementary relations derive second-order relationships—such as relationships among father's father, mother's brother, wife's sister—and third-order relationships—such as relationships among father's brother's son, and mother's brother's wife (Levi-Strauss 1965:2).

Levi-Strauss concedes that no explanation of kinship systems can prescind from biological parenthood, but he argues that the crucial task is to explain why kinship can be established and perpetuated through certain marriage forms and not others, and that this is a cultural, rather than a biological, phenomenon. The essence of kinship as a cultural phenomenon consists not in explaining first-order relationships, or biological relationships, but in explaining what Radcliffe-Brown calls second-order relationships. This is in line with the basic structuralist tenet that the elementary level of kinship must be sought not in isolated terms (families) but in the *relationship* among the terms.

Levi-Strauss claims that only through the structural perspective can one explain why the incest taboo is universal. The incest prohibition establishes a relationship among four terms and these relationships are considered to be the constituent elements of all forms of marriage. The avunculate is a corollary of the incest taboo because, if one cannot marry his own siblings or relatives, he has to find a marriage partner from outside his group. It is clear, then, that the essence of kinship relations cannot reside in the *biological* fact of consanguinity or descent, but only in *consciousness* as it entails an arbitrary system of representations; the structural explanation has the advantage of taking seriously symbolic thought—that which is at the origin of culture. Such a drastic change of perspective has puzzled many anthropologists, who, however, should abandon their perplexity because, far from disregarding empirical data, structuralism utilizes this data to map out underlying (constitutive) symbolic structures.

At this point the question of the sources and validity of Levi-Strauss' orientation arises. In *Tristes Tropiques*, he has expressed his gratitude to his three masters—Freud, Saussure, Geology (1965:59-63). I have dealt elsewhere with the intellectual antecedents of Levi-Strauss' thought (Rossi 1973). Here I elaborate further on the influence of linguistics, an influence crucial both for historical and theoretical reasons. Firstly, Levi-Strauss explicitly states in the 1949 preface of *The Elementary Structures of Kinship* that he owed "a great deal....for theoretical orientation" to Roman Jakobson, "who amicably insisted that the work be finished" (Levi-Strauss 1969:xxvi; also 461). Secondly, the influence of linguistics on the method of Levi-Strauss' kinship analysis has been too greatly overinterpreted or too easily dismissed. Yet, Levi-Strauss claims that the revolution of the semiotic approach was made possible precisely by structural linguistics.

Linguistic Foundations of Levi-Strauss' Methodology In the Study of Kinship

Levi-Strauss begins his kinship analysis from a long-established insight of structural linguistics: the sounds present in the phonological structure of language are only a few among many other possible sounds; moreover, some of these sounds are common to all linguistic systems. In an analagous way, Levi-Strauss argues, a great variety of attitudes and "psychophysiological" elements can be found at the level of interpersonal relationships. Yet, only certain of these elements are retained by kinship systems, and some of these elements are common to a great variety of kinship systems. From this fundamental conceptualization, the following typical structuralist questions arise: (1) Why are only a few psychological elements selected? (2) How are these elements related to each other? (3) What is the law of their combination? The structural approach consists in showing that the few elements which are present in a given system are particular realizations of basic relational constants, realizations which are governed by combinatory and transformational rules.

We have seen that Levi-Strauss has explicitly acknowledged the influence of structural linguistics in the preface to *The Elementary Structures of Kinship* (1949). However, such an influence was already clearly crystallized in Levi-Strauss' mind at least four years earlier, when he wrote a classic essay on the application of Troubetzkoy's method in anthropology; that essay remains a most clear formulation of Levi-Strauss' methodological orientation.

According to Levi-Strauss, structural linguistics has introduced four revolutionary principles in scientific methodology: (1) It has shifted the inquiry from the level of conscious linguistic phenomena to that of their unconscious infrastructure; (2) It has selected as an object of inquiry the relations between terms, rather than the terms considered as independent entities; (3) It has focused on the systematic nature of phonemes and their structure; (4) Its aim has been the formulation of general laws either by induction or deduction (Levi-Strauss 1963:33).

Santerre has characterized the phonological method as a process from the concrete (sounds) to the abstract (phoneme) to the phonological system (unconscious). This formulation perfectly describes the itinerary followed by Levi-Strauss under the influence of Saussure and Jakobson. Two notions are the key elements of such an itinerary: the notion of opposition and that of the phoneme.

The Notion of Opposition

Jakobson and Halle explain that language is studied at a *semantic* level and at a *feature* level. At the *semantic* level, linguists are interested in units of meaning which range from discourse (the most complex unit), to utterance, to morpheme (the smallest semantic unit). At the *feature* level, linguists deal with those sound components which differentiate morphemes from each other. A distinctive feature is a property (feature) conceptualized as a choice between two opposite terms of polar quality—for instance, the presence vs. absence of a given characteristic. The listener has to choose between a high and a low pitch of sound, between grave and acute, between voiced and voiceless, nasalized and non-nasalized, and the like. These polar qualities are called by Jakobson and Halle "oppositions," where the term "opposition" is used in Saussurian terms. An opposition exists whenever only one of two logically correlated alternatives is possible (Jakobson and Halle 1956:4): "two signs, each having a signified and signifier, are not different but only distinct. Between them there is only opposition" (Saussure 1966:121). Opposition here means only distinction among two signs or positive terms, each having its own signifier (sound-image) and signified (concept).

Saussure uses the word "difference" when he compares two signifiers (sound image) or two signifieds (concepts). For him language is a system of merely differential and negative signifiers, and not a system of positive terms or "signs" which are distinct from each other in terms of their own intrinsic properties. Saussure's basic notion is that "the value of each term can be determined only in a system of interdependent terms; only from the relational differences among the terms, we know the value of each term. However, when a signifier (sound image) is combined with its signified (concept) we have a 'positive' linguistic term. At that point we no longer speak of two different but of two distinct or opposite terms" (Saussure 1966:120-121). In other words, two linguistic terms or signs are opposed when they are positively defined and distinct from each other in terms of their own intrinsic properties.

Jakobson and Halle clarify that distinctive features have two physical aspects: for each one of the distinctive features there exists a corresponding opposite distribution of energy at the end of the spectrum and an opposite size and shape in the resonating cavity of the larynx (Jakobson and Halle 1956:4). The notion of distinction among positively identified (constituted) terms and the reference to their objective reality in terms of acoustic measurement enable one to understand what Levi-Strauss means when he states that distinctive features have an "objective existence from the psychological, physiological and even physical points of view" (1963:109). Levi-Strauss' contention that the oppositions he is dealing with refer to objective and concrete aspects of kinship phenomena could not be more explicit and emphatic. This means that structural analysis must be anchored on oppositional properties of the ethnographic data, that is, on oppositions which can be shown to be objective aspects of data. This programmatic principle is antithetical to the criticism of mentalism which is all too often leveled against structuralism, a criticism I shall deal with in the concluding chapter of this volume.

The Notion of Phoneme

The distinctive features are combined into simultaneous or co-occurring bundles called *phonemes*, and phonemes are clustered into sequences according to precise rules. The syllable is the elementary pattern which underlies a group of phonemes, and phonemic elements differentiate morphemes and words, the latter being semantic units (Jakobson and Halle 1956:5, 20). Jakobson proposes a theory of universal features, and Chomsky and Halle even hope to build a universal phonetic theory (1965:120); in a parallel way Levi-Strauss aims at explaining all forms of kinship rules on the basis of a few elementary structures.

The linguistic principles so far discussed can be synthesized in the following elements: (1) First, one must identify the elementary (basic) components; (2) These components must be combined in oppositional pairs, that is, in distinct units having polar characteristics; (4) The oppositional pairs are arranged in bundles (such as the phonemes or the "atom of kinship"); (5) The bundles are recombined into higher units until one has reached the observable level of cultural phenomena; (6) The ultimate aim is to formulate universal explanations on the basis of few elementary structures, or relational constants among oppositional units.

It is precisely by applying this phonological method that Levi-Strauss has been able to show that a great variety of kinship and marriage rules can be reduced to three elementary structures constructed out of two forms of exchange; the two forms of exchange in turn depend on the combination of residence and descent rules (1963:493). Levi-Strauss explicitly states that his approach is "close" to that of the phonologist in terms of method and object studied (1963:492).

Levi-Strauss makes reference also to game theory. As in all combinations with several partners, the game for two is treated as a particular case of the game for three; in an analogous fashion, bilateral marriage is opposed as a particular case of restricted exchange to a general principle (general exchange), even though the latter is composed of two opposite poles, matrilateral and patrilateral marriage (1963:465). This mathematical perspective is common also to Piaget, Chomsky and other thinkers who adopt the mathematical notion of "group."[3] In this sense Josselin De Jong seems correct in asserting that the methodological principles of *The Elementary Structures of Kinship* are clear without reference to linguistics (1952:58). For instance, the Saussurian notions of syntagmatic and paradigmatic analysis, permutation and inversion are absent from *The Elementary Structures of Kinship*, whereas the conceptualization of cultural phenomena as signs within the framework of the theory of communication is explicitly discussed in the first and last chapter of that book and provides the underlying rationale for the whole work. One can go even further and say that there is nothing original in the mathematical and linguistic notions used by Levi-Strauss. However, the originality of Levi-Strauss' contribution must be seen in the analytical insight and methodological leverage he derives from these notions.

One word of caution has to be put forward. The issue of mathematical or linguistic perspective and/or methodologies must not be understood in the sense of literal application of ideas taken from other disciplines,[4] but only as ideas providing generalizations and orientations for the analysis of cultural and symbolic systems which, by their very nature, evade the canons of rigorous replication and verification. Yet, one could still object that anthropologists cannot apply the phonological method because phonologists deal with the following elements: (1) Sound units which are precisely and objectively identifiable through spectrographic analysis; (2) Clusters and patterns of sound units which are not only identifiable with instruments but also subject to quantitative procedures; (3) Phonemes which are clearly distinguishable from each other by their function, which is to oppose different semantic units. On the contrary, anthropologists are concerned only with the semantic level of culture where precise, objective and quantitative criteria to identify elementary units and their clusters are not available. Can one, then, conclude that the parallel between kinship atoms and phonemes is an analogy too vague to serve as the basis for a scientifically valid analysis?

One must interpret this analogy as a methodological hypothesis. Levi-Strauss intends to derive from language a "logical model" to study social life from the point of view of the theory of communication, without implying that culture derives from language or that language and culture can be substituted or reduced to each other (Levi-Strauss 1963:83, 85). Levi-Strauss states that he does not deal with content *per se* but with its formal properties, and he attempts to determine whether the formal properties exhibit homologies (85). An analogy based on content would entail a reductionism, whereas Levi-Strauss is interested in an analogy of structures—that is, in the similarity of the logical organization of kinship and language. Many criticisms raised against Levi-Strauss' analogy automatically vanish once this central point is placed in a very clear focus.

Levi-Strauss, however, is a thorough scholar who justifies his methodological hypothesis with theoretical reasoning. He argues that the relationship between language and culture must be considered at the level of "operational" as well as "substantial" comparability. "Operational comparability" refers to the fact that social life can be studied with the help of methods and concepts used in linguistics. The notion of "substantial comparability" refers to the similarity of the "inmost nature" of language and culture. Levi-Strauss argues that language and culture are comparable at both levels because they are both products of the "human mind" (1963:71). Like any other system of communication, language and kinship are projections of or are caused by identical unconscious structures (59, 62) and, therefore, are built out of the same material—i.e., "logical relations, oppositions, correlations" (69). It follows that the method of kinship analysis can be modeled after "modern research into the problem of phonemics, which have reached beyond the superficial conscious and historical expression of linguistic phenomena to attain fundamental and objective realities consisting of systems of relations which are the products of unconscious thought processes" (58).

One must inevitably conclude that the notions of the symbolizing activity of mind and the structural nature of its functioning are the fundamental notions on which Levi-Strauss' version of the structural method is based.

Theoretical Foundations of Structural Methodology: From the Early Views of *The Elementary Structures of Kinship* to the Epistemological and Mathematical Views of *L'Homme Nu*

Levi-Strauss' semiotic conception of symbolic systems derives not only from the Saussurean perspective but also from Durkheim. Both Durkheim and Levi-Strauss have declined to inquire about the origin of social phenomena due to their disillusionment with diffusionist and evolutionary theories, (although Durkheim has been rather ambivalent on the latter ones). On the contrary, both Durkheim and Levi-Strauss are concerned with explaining social phenomena in terms of their internal determinations (Levi-Strauss 1966a:113) and classificatory principles (1945:575). Throughout Levi-Strauss' book on kinship one can find obvious traces of Durkheimian concepts, such as the notions of social integration, elementary structures, collective and "mental" aspects of social phenomena and so on.[5]

However, Levi-Strauss conceives the mental and collective aspects of social phenomena differently from Durkheim. Levi-Strauss reverses Durkheim's position, by positing the origin of the symbolic aspect of cultural phenomena in the dialectical working of the human mind, and not in the way society is organized. Levi-Strauss argues that symbolism makes social life possible and necessary, and, therefore, symbolism must be taken for granted, as a Kantian *a priori* form.

I have shown elsewhere that Levi-Strauss' kinship theory is based on the notion of reciprocity, which in turn is explained in terms of the dialectic and unconscious functioning of the human mind (Rossi 1974:107-122). The notion of the unconscious is often neglected, or considered a gratuitous philosophical notion, or worst, useless "mumbo jumbo" (Cohen 1977). Such an attitude, which is quite common among many empiricist anthropologists, is erroneous on many counts. To begin with, the notion of the unconscious is not merely a philosophical notion since Levi-Strauss has used not only Kantian, but also linguistic, Freudian, "cybernetic," and "Gestalt psychological" notions to explain it (see Rossi 1973). Secondly, the notion of deep structure finds support in, or at least is consistent with, contemporary scientific research trends. I have discussed some of these trends in another essay (Rossi 1978), and I will discuss a few more in the concluding chapter of this book.

In this section I will first bring to light aspects of the notion of the unconscious contained in *The Elementary Structures of Kinship* which I have not discussed in my 1974 essay (Rossi 1974:107-122), then I will locate this notion in the context of the ontological and epistemological views Levi-Strauss has put forward in the last volume of the *Mythologiques*.

The Unconscious in *The Elementary Structures of Kinship*

There is no doubt about the centrality of the notion of the unconscious in the theoretical framework of *The Elementary Structures of Kinship*. There Levi-Strauss states that the emergence of symbolic thought engenders social life (1969:496) and, therefore, the forms of social life cannot be understood without an inquiry into the fundamental structures of the human mind (75). Levi-Strauss invokes the authority of Boas to state that "all types of social phenomena (language, beliefs, techniques and customs) have in common that their elaboration in the mind is at the level of unconscious thought" (108). The elementary structures of bilateral, matrilateral and patrilateral exchange "are always present to the human mind, at least in an unconscious form" (464). These "logical structures are elaborated by unconscious thought" (268) and, consequently, the social system has an unconscious and collective aspect (110). Underlying a great variety of contingent institutional structures, there is always the same force or principle of reciprocity which is always at work and it is oriented in the same direction.

In *The Elementary Structures of Kinship* Levi-Strauss conceptualizes the activity of the unconscious in dialectical, or at least oppositional, terms. "An internal logic directs the unconscious working of the human mind" (220). The human mind proceeds by perceiving relational properties and, more precisely, oppositional relationships which give origin to a dialectic process and structure of reciprocity (490). Having discussed elsewhere Levi-Strauss' use of the Gestalt perspective (Rossi 1974), I now briefly discuss Levi-Strauss' use of Susan Isaacs' studies on child development to elucidate the role of mental structures in the origin of social phenomena. Levi-Strauss argues that because of the primitive need for security, man wants to possess. Most of the items the child wants to possess are desired because other people are interested in them. There is no objective connection between the object and the person's wants so that the desire to possess cannot be considered an instinct; it is only the object's relationship to persons which makes the object worth possessing; to receive gifts means to be loved. Consequently, the desire to possess is a "social response" and a means to gain security out of the dilemma of power vs. impotence. By becoming aware of the existence of competing interests, the child experiences the "collective" and the basic concept of equality (Levi-Strauss 1969:108-125). The mechanisms of identification and feelings of reciprocity emerge out of the opposition "me-others" (86) and as a mechanism to resolve the opposition (84). Levi-Strauss states that this psychological argument can be backed up with the study of simple cultures, where one can observe similar attitudes. In Levi-Strauss' view this is not surprising because infant thought is the common denominator of all thinking and all cultures. Infant mental structures contain the potentialities of all cultures, potentialities which are developed through enculturation.

Since these mental structures are the product of the unconscious logic of mind, they are by definition unconscious and, therefore, metaempirical; this means that the deep level of culture cannot be studied by using the "subjective" or "objective" approaches as traditionally understood. Consequently, Levi-Strauss' notion about the nature of human mind (ontological notion) dictates a new epistemological and methodological approach. To a French interviewer who had asked Levi-Strauss whether there is a deep opposition between structuralism and existentialism, Levi-Strauss has replied that the two movements differ in the way they apprehend human phenomena. Instead of studying phenomena from the point of view of the subjective experience by which they are lived, structuralism studies them from a point of view which is beyond the awareness or conscious experience of their protagonists (*L'Express*, 15-21 mars, 1971). Such a statement implies that structuralism is fundamentally a theoretical attitude, or more precisely an epistemological orientation. Levi-Strauss has repeatedly rejected the term "philosophy" as an accurate qualification of his approach; in his 1972 visit to the United States he also rejected the term "method" but accepted the label "epistemological approach."[6]

The Epistemological Manifesto of *L'Homme Nu*

In polemics with the subjectivism of phenomenologists and the empiricist objectivism of positivists, behaviorists, functionalists and operationalists, Levi-Strauss has offered in *L'Homme Nu* the most complete discussion of the ontological and epistemological assumptions of his metaempirical objectivism. In particular, Levi-Strauss has there defended his epistemological approach by grounding it on carefully spelled out views on the nature of the human mind as well as natural and cultural reality.

It goes without saying that many anthropologists of empiricist orientation are tempted to raise the following question: Why should we care about the ontological or ideological foundations of the anthropological method? The obvious answer to this question is that the question itself abundantly documents the naiveté of the empiricist position. Empiricists do not seem to realize that their conception of scientific method is based on ideological postulates also, and that those postulates are highly questionable. It is precisely the blatancy of the empiricists' naiveté which makes it necessary to discuss Levi-Strauss' views on the nature of mind and culture, and to show that there lies the crucial difference between the structuralist and the empiricist approaches.

(a) Assumptions About the Organization of Natural and Cultural Reality

As far as natural reality is concerned, Levi-Strauss states that a principle of "discontinuity is intrinsic within nature, including physical and biological classifications (Levi-Strauss 1971:605, 606). The discontinuities between species are related by Levi-Strauss to the discontinuity of the genetic code, which consists of a few discrete chemical units continuously combining and recombining to give new superior life forms (611, 612). The same holds true of phonological structures which are constituted by combinations and recombinations of phonemes. The principle of discontinuity is a fundamental process in nature so that the latter is basically transformational or generative; our present forms continuously give origin to new discontinuities. Levi-Strauss argues that by a series of continuous transitions we pass from one biological form to another, and by an algebraic function we can deduce the sensory details which distinguish one form from another. (Here Levi-Strauss quotes Goëthe, Dürer and the contemporary biologist D'Arcy W. Thompson, p. 606-605).

The same principles of discontinuity and transformation hold true for culture. Myths are "discrete" phenomena because they do not simply state that the world exists but that it exists in the form of asymmetries between high-low, sky-earth, earth-water, and the like. Myths consist in series of interconnected assertions of the following type: (1) There exist sky and earth; (2) Any parity between them is inconceivable; (3) The presence of fire (heavenly element) is a mystery; (4) Consequently, if fire is found on earth as a domestic fire, one must search for its origin in heaven (539). Discontinuities which are intrinsic to reality activate mythical thought, and, more fundamentally, they condition the very existence of the object of our thinking activity (538, 539). Each mythic transformation derives from a dialectic opposition to another transformation, and the very essence of each transformation resides in being "translated" *by* and *for* the opposition (576). Consequently, the "diacritical nature" of mythic thought reveals that "opposition" is first all "given" and that the world consists in a "disparity"—a more precise term than "opposition" (539). The methodological consequence of this conception of culture is clear; if there is an intrinsic discontinuity within physical and cultural reality, structuralists are justified in studying it in terms of oppositions and in searching for constant relational properties among systems of opposition.

(b) Assumptions About the Perceptual Apparatus

Levi-Strauss' bias for the Kantian approach is evident in the following assertions: within human understanding is already built an apparatus of oppositions which is activated by social experiences (539); when empirical experiences occur, the conceptual apparatus extracts meaning and makes of it an object of thought by bending it to the imperatives of its formal organization—"opposition" is a basic law of this organization (539). We do not perceive external objects directly and intuitively in themselves, but rather in the form of a text elaborated by the joint action of the sensory and intellectual apparatus (607). According to Levi-Strauss, reality is inherently structured because logical structures underlie and antedate subsequent sensory perceptions. Mind structurally apprehends what is initially already structured, mind being already structured in itself. There is no opposition (dualism) between ideal-real, abstract-concrete, since the immediate datum is something in between, already encoded by senses and brain. There is a primary coding in physical and chemical process, and a secondary coding in the mind; both of these codings are substantially the same (607).

We can, then, conclude that Levi-Strauss' ontological and epistemological views provide the foundations of the structural method. The anthropologist looks for logical order in empirical cultural phenomena and he can do so because the empirical world and the mind are not heterogeneous but structurally homologous. For this reason structural explanations are not reductionist in the psychological or physiological sense but rather they bring to light homologous and parallel structures which exist at the biological, psychological and cultural levels. As Levi-Strauss says, structural analysis emerges in the mind because it already exists in the body; structural analysis brings up to the level of conscience organic truths (619).

For this reason I have disagreed with Nutini's contention that there is an incongruence, and even a contradiction, between the ontological and epistemological dimension of Levi-Strauss' structuralism (Nutini 1971). However, Nutini wrote his essay before the publication of *L'Homme Nu*, and he has later expressed his agreement (at least verbally) with a reply of mine to his article. In that reply I argued that the thesis opposite to the one expressed by Nutini is more consistent and faithful to Levi-Strauss' position (Ross 1972).

The Isomorphic and Cybernetic Views

What we have so far stated leads us to conclude that the whole of Levi-Strauss' approach is based on the assumption that there exist isomorphic relations between the biological, psychological, and cultural level of reality. "The assertion that the most parsimonious explanation comes closest to the truth rests, in the final analysis, upon the identity postulated between the laws of the universe and those of the human mind" (Levi-Strauss 1963:89). In various places, although at times incidentally, Levi-Strauss has discussed his conception of the relation between nature and culture, the nature of brain and the nature and origin of culture. In the 1960 inaugural lecture at the College of France he stated that "culture was at once the natural result and the social mode of apprehension" of "the structure and functioning of the brain" (in Levi-Strauss 1976:14). In turn "culture created the intersubjective milieu indispensable for the occurrence of transformations, both anatomical and physiological" (14). Culture is based on the way mind structures biological and natural reality: "The transition from nature to culture is determined by man's ability to think of biological relationships as systems of oppositions" (Levi-Strauss 1969:136). Whereas "the natural state recognizes only indivision and appropriation, and their chance admixture," the dialectic activity of mind "ineluctably give(s) rise to the world of reciprocity, as the synthesis of two contradictory characteristics inherent in the natural order. The rules of kinship and marriage are not made necessary by the social state. They are the social state itself, reshaping biological relationships and natural sentiments, forcing them into structures implying them as well as others, and compelling them to rise above their original characteristics" (490). This does not mean that culture is an heterogeneous order, an order based on principles of organization different from the natural ones. On the contrary the natural and cultural orders are bound to be isomorphic because the human mind has the same laws of physical reality, and the structuring activity of mind is what gives origin to culture: "the laws of thought—primitive or civilized—are the same as those which are expressed in physical reality and in social reality, which is itself only one of its aspects" (451). In 1969 Levi-Strauss drew an explicit corollary out of the premises he had laid down in 1947: "Ultimately we shall perhaps discover that the interrelationship between nature and culture does not favour culture to the extent of being hierarchically superimposed in nature and irreducible to it. Rather, it takes the form of a synthetic duplication of mechanisms already in existence but which the animal kingdom shows only in disjointed form and dispersed variously among its members—a duplication, moreover, permitted by the emergence of certain cerebral structures which themselves belong to nature" (xxx). Seen in this context, a famous passage from *The Raw and the Cooked* which has puzzled many commentators becomes clear: "Myths signify the mind that evolves them by making use of the world of which it is itself a part. Thus, there is a simultaneous production of myths by the mind and a production, by the myths, of an image of the world which is already inherent in the structure of mind" (1969a:341). Levi-Strauss' isomorphic conception of nature and culture also clarifies his statement that structural analysis is based on the postulate that a rationality is immanent within the universe even before the advent of consciousness—that is, before man becomes aware of its existence. Were this not the case we could never understand cultural data through our cognitive apparatus. Levi-Strauss forcefully expresses this point by stating that within the universe there exists an "objectified" thought which functions rationally even before man becomes aware of its existence.

Precisely because of the isomorphic hypothesis Levi-Strauss can claim that structuralism offers an epistemological model which is superior to the ones previously offered by anthropologists for at least two reasons. (1) First, structuralist anthropologists discover the unity and coherence behind cultural phenomena by studying the relationships among phenomena rather than the phenomena themselves, which are more complex and difficult to penetrate than their reciprocal relationships. (2) Secondly, structuralists reintegrate man with nature because they study man objectively, as if man were nature, by putting aside subjective consciousness and intentionality. In Levi-Strauss' opinion, the "subject" has for too long a time attracted all the attention of social scientists and has prevented serious scientific progress (Levi-Strauss 1971:614-615).

There are some social scientists who are interested in the notion of deep symbolic codes but not in what they call "metaphysical" notions such as human mind or unconscious. In a sense, the question of the human mind is of secondary importance in relationship to the notion of the structuring principles of cultures and of the mathematical nature of those principles. Levi-Strauss himself has opened the way to a cybernetic, rather than a strictly intellectualist, conception of the origin of culture. "In the last analysis, if customs of neighboring people manifest relations of symmetry, we do not have to search for a cause in some mysterious law of nature or mind. This geometric perfection synthesizes at the present more or less conscious and innumerable efforts, accumulated throughout history all to the same end; to reach a threshold most profitable to human societies, where a just equilibrium among their unity and their diversity takes place" (Levi-Strauss 1971a:177). Moreover, in his 1965 Huxley lecture, Levi-Strauss stated that he "had invoked rather hastily the unconscious processes of the human mind" to explain kinship systems which "far from being the recent outcome of unconscious processes, now appear to me as true discoveries, the legacy of an age-old wisdom for which more evidence can be found elsewhere" (Levi-Strauss 1965a:15). "The question may be raised as to whether the superiority in functional yield, which most societies attribute to cross-relationships over parallel ones, far from being the outcome of unconscious processes, does not stem from a mature and well balanced reflection" (16).

In conclusion, the essential premises of structuralism are the following: (1) The isomorphic nature of mind and reality; (2) The structural nature of data and mind; (3) Mathematical properties of the deep structures of nature and mind (this later point will be discussed in the concluding chapter). These three assumptions are at the foundation of the structural approach, which has introduced the following methodological principles in social sciences: (1) The observable and conscious levels of phenomena are useful only as a starting point to inquire about their constitutive principles; (2) The task of the structuralist is to discover the logical principles of classification which organize and underlie cultural reality; (3) Structuralists should aim at formulating the mathematical laws of the organization and combination of these principles. It is precisely this cybernetic and mathematical thrust of structuralism that the empiricist detractors have often not attended to or have misunderstood (see for instance Korn 1973).

In the concluding chapter I shall prove that the notion of deep structure of nature and mind is not a gratuitous or metaphysical notion, as it finds a strong support in contemporary scientific thinking. There, I shall also clarify the mathematical nature of deep structures and its methodological implications. As of now, I hope to have cleared the reader's mind of the misapprehension that the chapters contained in this volume are nothing but futile exercises in mentalism.

Notes

[1] With the term "transformational structuralism" I refer to Levi-Strauss' and Piaget's structuralism because both of these thinkers define social structure as a system of transformations (see Rossi, forthcoming). The focus of this paper, however, is on the linguistically derived, or semiotic, structuralism of Levi-Strauss.

[2] For a detailed discussion of these issues see Rossi 1974:60-106.

[3] I do not intend to assert a basic identity in the perspective of these three thinkers but only to draw attention to an important convergence of their thoughts. For a further discussion of these points see Rossi (forthcoming).

[4] See for instance the debate between Mounin and Durbin in Rossi 1974:31-59.

[5] For a more specific discussion of semiotic elements anticipated in the latest phase of Durkheimian though see Rossi (forthcoming).

[6] In a "questions and answers" session with students of Barnard College, Columbia University.

References

Chomsky, N. and M. Halle. 1965. "Some controversial questions in phonological theory." *Journal of Linguistics* 6 (2):97-138.

Cohen, Ronald. 1977. "The emperor's clothes: Review of a review." *American Anthropologist* 79 (1):113-114.

Jakobson, R. and M. Halle. 1956. *Fundamentals of Language.* The Hague: Mouton and Co.

Josselin DeJong, J.P.B. 1952. *Levi-Strauss' Theory of Kinship and Marriage.* Leiden, Holland: Rijksmuseum Voor Volkenkunde, n. 10.

Korn, Francis. 1973. *Elementary Structures Reconsidered: Levi-Strauss on Kinship.* Berkeley: University of California Press.

Levi-Strauss, C. 1945. "French sociology." in *Twentieth Century Sociology*, G. Gurvitch and W.E. Moore (eds). N.Y.: The Philosophical Library, p. 503-537.

_____. 1963. *Structural Anthropology.* Translated from the French by Claire Jacobson and Brooke Grundest Schoepf. N.Y.:Basic Books. (French original, 1958).

_____. 1965. *Tristes Tropiques.* N.Y.: Atheneum. (French original, 1955).

_____. 1965a. "The future of kinship studies." *Proceedings of the Royal Anthropological Institute.*

_____. 1966. *The Savage Mind*. Chicago: University of Chicago Press. (French original, 1962).

_____. 1966a. "The scope of anthropology." *Current Anthropology* 7 (2): 112-123.

_____. 1969. *The Elementary Structures of Kinship*. Translated by T.H. Bell and T.R. von Sturmer under R. Needham's editorship. Boston: Beacon Press. (French original, 1949; revised French edition, 1967).

_____. 1969a. *The Raw and the Cooked*. Translated by T. and D. Weightman. N.Y.: Harper and Row. (French original, 1964).

_____. 1971. *L'Homme Nu*. Paris: Plon.

_____. 1971a. "Rapporte de symmétrie entre rites et myths de peuple voisins." in *The Translation of Culture* edited by T.O. Beidelman. London: Tavistock Publications.

_____. 1973. "Reflexions sur l'atome de parenté." *L'Homme* XIII (3):5-30.

_____. 1976. *Structural Anthropology*. Vol. II translated by M. Layton. N.Y.: Basic Books.

Natanson, M. (ed.). 1963. "Foreword." in *Philosophy of the Social Sciences*. N.Y.: Random House.

Nutini, H. 1971. "The ideological basis of Levi-Strauss' structuralism." *American Anthropologist* 73 (3):537-544.

Piaget, Jean. 1971. *Biology and Knowledge: An Essay on the Relations Between Organic Regulations and Cognitive Processes*. Chicago: University of Chicago Press. (French original, 1967).

Rossi, Ino. 1972. Reply to Nutini's "The ideological basis of Levi-Strauss' structuralism." *American Anthropologist* 74 (3):784-787.

_____. 1973. "The unconscious in the anthropology of Claude Levi-Strauss." *American Anthropologist* 75 (1):20-48.

_____. 1974. *The Unconscious in Culture: The Structuralism of Claude Levi-Strauss in Perspective*, edited. N.Y.: Dutton.

_____. 1978. "Toward the unification of scientific explanation: Evidence from biological, psychic, linguistic, cultural universals." in *Discourse and Inference in Cognitive Anthropology: An Approach to Psychic Unity and Enculturation*. edited by Marvin D. Loflin and James Silverberg. The Hague: Mouton Publishers.

_____. Forthcoming. *From the Sociology of Symbols to the Sociology of Signs*. N.Y.: Columbia University Press.

Sausurre, Ferdinand de. 1966. *Course in General Linguistics*. edited by Charles Bally and Albert Sechenhaye in collaboration with Albert Riedlinger, translated by Wade Baskin. N.Y.: McGraw Hill.

2
Anthropological Analytics

Pierre Maranda

This chapter proposes a summary of the concept of structure in social anthropology. It is also an attempt to show how that concept can lay the ground for an *analytics*—i.e., a form of calculus to model social data. My endeavour rests heavily on Levi-Strauss' work and it draws on some related domains, such as the logic of classes and Thom's Catastrophe Theory. Ethnographic examples are used as illustrations of the use of those concepts.

The chapter consists of two parts where five sets of analytic units are reviewed: reciprocity, exchange and communication, and codes in Part 1, class and structure in Part 2.

Reciprocity, Exchange and Communication, and Codes

Reciprocity. The first datum in human and animal societies is interaction: being, from birth to death, exists only through it. This follows necessarily from the juxtaposition of living organisms. In general terms, interaction is to be understood as a homeostatic process. But the organic analogy stops there. The relevance to the study of human societies of tropisms and other regulatory mechanisms at work in the animal kingdom cannot be evoked to justify biological reductionism (Levi-Strauss 1958b:Ch. 2). Mankind's cybernetic devices are too versatile to be mapped isomorphically onto organic models, as biochemistry is still far below the analytic level that would be necessary for its arguments to have adequate explanatory value. However ephemeral its epistemological value, the dichotomy between nature and culture is still needed in our endeavours.

The threshold from nature to culture is crossed once norms of exploitation are enunciated, i.e., once an at least implicit agreement has been reached and is somewhat enforced on what is permissible and what is not permissible in interacting with or preying on both human and nonhuman environments (Levi-Strauss 1949b:9ff., 29-30; 1956b:277-278; 1958:62, 389; 1960a:633; 1961:154ff.; 1962b:155, 164; 1964-1971: passim).

Reciprocity is axiomatic in mankind's exploitation strategies (Levi-Strauss 1949b:53, 64-65, 107-109; 1958:179-180). In effect, it is assumed in all societies that if A acts toward B in a given way, B will respond on the par. This rests on an at least implicit experimental recognition of the S/R arc—or of its subtler mode TOTE (Miller, Galanter, and Pribram 1960). Reciprocity, or the expectation of a predictable return, enables the member of a society to orient his behavior. The axiom governs the initiation and definition of relationships between individuals and groups. It is, in the last analysis, a probabilistic apperception on which the construction of proportions rests, as we shall see below. Hence, reciprocity is generally seen in anthropology as a distribution mechanism. More technically: it portions out fuzzy sets into types of behaviour. For example, it regulates such responses as laughter, scorn, kind words, songs of love or of war, myth telling, uses of goods and services, time budget allocations, and the like. This partitioning commands behavior according to anticipations, i.e., to the implicit knowledge of the probabilities of the interactants' types of responses in given historical contexts. Interpretation theory bears on this: the general structure is that of a quasi-deterministic automation whose flow can be at higher or lower rates of exchange or fall to zero or even become negative if the structure reaches a catastrophic threshold (Thom 1972; Petitot 1977), that is, if an interpretation that could prevail in the past must entirely be revised (for example, when love turns to hatred, trade becomes war, and so on). This catastrophic threshold is akin to the dialectic operation of reversal (Levi-Strauss' "inverted symmetry," Althusser's *"relation spéculaire"*) developed by Mao after Lenin, and can be defined as a "flip-flop" (Maranda 1971, 1978b).[1]

Exchange. The strategies of interaction open to mankind are reducible to two broad categories, war and trade (Levi-Strauss 1943)— that is, men exchange blows or goods, and both are messages. Reciprocity, or the probabilistic expectation of return, is the axiom on which exchange is founded; the latter, in turn, underlies all communications. Social life finds there its basic natural law, as established by Mauss (1923-1924) and Malinowski (Levi-Strauss 1956a:127-128; 1959:179; cf. 1944:267-278).

Forms of exchange are codified in institutions and other semantic parameters. Rules of marriage, or proper speech, of sacrifice, of tool handling, of the acquisition and use of knowledge, and the like develop along specific axes, which entails a diversification leading to the constitution and consolidation of more or less autonomous domains (fuzzy sets). The end-products of such processes are found in the observable semantic fields of kinship, mythology, ritual, management, and others, with which anthropology has been traditionally concerned. As it is impossible, in the study of most non-literate societies, to trace these back to earlier matrices, the analyst tackles the data in their actual synchronic states and seeks to build a structural model accounting for the adaptive self-perpetuation of the whole. Like the astronomer, at the pursuit of dying stars and exploding galaxies, the anthropologist races with time in his attempts to propose hypotheses which will be validated in as much as they are predictive of the eventual configurations of evolving societies.

An immediate problem in anthropological endeavors is to reduce the multidimensionality just mentioned to commeasurability. Mathematics enables physical scientists to do it in their field; in ours, Levi-Strauss has opened paths and provided tools to reach the same end by proposing the notion of an order of orders, which he later refined with the help of a hierarchy of codes.[2]

Exchange, or communication in its broad sense, is a relation established between a sender and a receiver through a medium. In human societies, senders are encoders, receivers are decoders, and the medium which links them is information (on economic or social status, military strength, moral imperatives, etc.). The encoder and the decoder in the act of communication must share the same code and be plugged into the same channel for the information to be transmitted and received. That the process is culturally conditioned and that information may be accurate or distorted (either by planned entropy—like in bluffing—or by involuntary noise) will not detain us here.

Now, the model originally adumbrated by Durkheim and Mauss (1901-1902), recently corroborated by communication engineers and often used by Levi-Strauss, presupposes three basic logical operations on the part of communicating individuals. The first operation is that of breaking up a continuum into discrete elements, to constitute the raw matter of codes, of which messages are built. The second operation is the grouping of the discrete elements obtained in the first operation into sets which reconstitute continuity but this time on a semantic level. This second operation consists in a simple rule of predication to assign set membership according to the principle of substitutability (see below, 2.1.). Finally, the third operation is the application of rules of predication to sets, that is, a form of propositional calculus (below, 2.2.). Levi-Strauss has masterfully shown the actual working out of these operations in anthropological data, first in the type of exchange prevailing in kinship (Levi-Strauss 1949b), and then on cognitive levels (1962a, 1962b, 1964, 1971a—where he uses the Saussurian terminology of paradigmatic sets and syntagmatic chains to mean sets and propositions; cf. Mandelbrot 1954; Leach 1964).[3]

The categories into which the continuous is analyzed in the first operation are of course cut according to the principles which will enable a native to group them into sets. Therefore, the two first operations cannot be dissociated. Fortunately, they can be analyzed from either end.[4]

Continuity is reconstituted operationally in the second phase . By "operational" is meant definitional processing which renders data amenable to logical treatment and manipulations. Operational definitions enable man to order things incompletely known, i.e., to define them with respect to each other despite some degree of indeterminacy (cf. Levi-Strauss 1958:358; 1949a:30-31). For example one is justified in saying that for any cardinal number, if $a + 1 = b + 1$, then $a = b$; similarly, in large areas of Melanesia, a native is justified in saying that for any being, if $a + mana = b + mana$, then $a = b$, like man = shark, shark = ancestor; or, that if $c + danger = d + danger$, then $c = d$, like in snake = woman. Such definitions lay the ground for the establishment of equivalencies, inclusions and intersections, and other operations that structure segments of the semantic universe. Classifications work on that basis, be they those of literate or illiterate people: there is no logical difference between the assignment of uranium and thorium to the class of radioactive elements and that of menstrual blood and placenta to the class of sources of danger.

In loose language, this is often called the metaphoric process; epistemologists prefer the term "analogy" (cf. Thom 1978, 1980). Operational definitions thus make it possible to map one domain into another, which is what transformations are in the language of set theory. In other words, operational definitions are prerequisite to the construction of codes (see Levi-Strauss 1962b for explicitations), whose elements are sets and which consist in the rules to pass from one set to another. And this is the crucial point where Levi-Strauss' contribution breaks through: it is the birth of anthropological analytics (1951; cf. 1958: Ch.3).

The preceding definitions lead to an operational approach to exchange and communication. To exchange is to give in order to receive by virtue of the axiom of reciprocity. A discrete encoder a_i (member of the set A and thus operationally contiguous with the other members of the same set) and a discrete decoder b_i (member of set B, etc.) are linked through the intermediary of a discrete message or concatenated units of information c_i (member of the set C, etc.) which passes from a_i to b_i. But a_i and b_i do not only the first one give and second receive. They both evaluate the message. By virtue of the axiom of reciprocity, a_i knows that what he gives is binding over b_i, a fact of which b_i is aware. b_i's operations are performed by referring c_i to a scale through statements of equivalence or non-equivalence: c_i is weighed by being mapped onto the rest of C. The evaluation always takes the form of a proportion, viz.,

$$c_i/b_i = c_j/a_j,$$

i.e., "this, which I give you, is to you what that, which you give me in return, is to me," allowing for the equivalence sign to be $+$ or $-$, with the understanding that if A gives more to B than he receives from him, B must in a second round compensate for the disequilibrium or accept "defeat." c_i is evaluated in connection with a threefold relation. a_i and b_i measure it, at least implicitly: (1) against the full C set in terms of socially determined utility functions; (2) an evaluation which they adjudge in terms of their own utility functions; and (3) with respect to each other as partners in terms of both general and specific utility functions. The operations do not vary cross-culturally but the scales do. These vary also intra-culturally from set to set, and from person to person according to their degree of structuration by the semantic domains that impregnate their trains of thoughts (stereotypes, clichés, etc.), in conformity with axioms that form probabilistic matrices describable as networks (Maranda 1976, 1978a; Maranda and Köngäs Maranda 1979).

Code. Any given society is a set of people regulated by semantic resources, rules and axioms that are managed by mass communicators, and that set is not a system. Each subset of the set "society" is a more or less autonomous end product of historical events, and these overlapping, twisted, and/or skewed subsets do not hold together in a way directly perceptible. In point of fact—to anticipate on the definition of structure (Part 2)—a society is made of "pre-stressed" elements (Levi-Strauss 1960d; 1962b:Ch.1) grouped into sets which are in turn grouped into sets of sets. But the structure of each set may be formally different, some being weakly-structured, and some only semi-structured. Furthermore, an important aspect of such structures is their threshold of defaulting. Accordingly, what is a semantic dead end in a given culture (technically, an "absorption barrier" or a "sink") may well be a productive node in another ("reflective barrier" or "carrier point"). For example, widowhood: the widow can be sacrificed on the pyre where the body of her dead husband is being consumed ("sink"), or the institution of levirate may allow her to continue to be a living member of the group ("carrier point") (for details, see Maranda, in press). And, as I said above, the task of the analyst is to map out these weaker and stronger structures on to explanatory commeasurability—including an account of how the native reduces them to behavioral commeasurability.

Now, in each communication syntagm, the encoder and the decoder may have to assume different roles when they use different channels: some roles may be more comprehensive than others, some more intensive, and so forth. Similarly, the members of the set C, "things communicated," vary according to channel and other determinants. The channels themselves are already laid out according to a communciation "topography" (Maranda 1978a), resulting on the one hand from the nature of the "terrains" where resistance is least and, on the other, from artefactual social prescriptions on the use of those easily formed channels. Thus, one-way, two-way, random access or controlled access "turnpikes" or paths are available to the members of a given social group, and new ones can be opened only through creative, revolutionary operations (Thom's "catastrophe" thresholds).

As is well known, Levi-Strauss (1953) distinguished three main communication levels, namely, that of woman, that of goods and services, and that of verbal messages (cf. Mauss 1923-24:35, 52-53, 63, 125, 129ff; Levi-Strauss 1949b:78). In his recent terminology he would say, I believe, that the communication of women is encoded sociologically, that of goods and services in economic terms, and that of verbal messages, linguistically.

The three levels are not commensurate and therefore cannot be handled isomorphically (i.e., they cannot be mapped onto each other term-to-term). In the sociological code, women, who usually cumulate economic and linguistic values, are components as well as manipulators of codes. In the economic code, goods and services, which usually include women and certain types of verbal messages (like prayer and legal advice), are subcoded in terms of money and/or barter. In the linguistic code, verbal messages, which may also be goods and services and are encoded by women as well as by men, are themselves multiplex (simultaneous transmissions of several functions over one circuit without function entropy). And all these (women, goods and services, and verbal messages) circulate either symmetrically or asymmetrically, transitively or intransitively, directly (when access is random) or through relays (when access is controlled), in one-way, two-way channels, or in channels with multiplex capacity, and so on, so that the web of relations, although not infinite, is multi-dimensional.

It is here that the notion of code as analytic device takes all its meaning, and we will have to explore it in some detail. The term "code" refers to readily understandable agglomerates of rules in such expresssions as "code of etiquette," "legal code," "the Morse code," etc. But "code of etiquette" and "code of laws" are misnomers from the point of view adopted here, while the "Morse code", a true communication device resting on a statistical model of English usage, consists of unstructured rules of transcription. Morse code has to do with the passage from one set of signals (the alphabet) to another (groups of dashes and dots), and enables its user to rewrite (recode) a message so that it becomes transmittable through a channel which could not be used otherwise. In this case, the rules are simple rules of quasi-transliteration and the operation, most elementary, is entirely mathematical. In contrast, instructions to a computer or to a drummer, although also encoded in a binary language, rest on a syntactic model and require recoding of a different order. The one-to-one mapping necessary and sufficient for transliteration must be replaced by one-to-many or many-to-one mappings (one natural word to many logical circuits in computer programming, and many natural words to one signal in drum languages).

It is clear that not a great many one-to-one mappings are given "on the ground," either from the standpoint of the society member or from that of the anthropologist. Neither finds that a kinship terminology, for example, corresponds term for term with a pantheon, or with a monetary system, or with a cosmology. Both the native and the anthropologist are faced with the same conglomerate of incommensurate sets, through which both must find their way. Now both proceed similarly, the native to reduce the data to behavioral amenability, and the anthropologist to reduce them to intelligibility: the latter tries to find out, for example, how the communication of women and that of services are related in the society *de jure* and *de facto*; the former tries to discover how he should conform to and may exploit to his advantage the prescriptions through which those two orders are connected. In both cases, the action will take place on the level of codes. The native uses them in native models, the anthropologist tries to break them and assumes that he has succeeded when his models leave out fewer residues (statistical and/or semantic) than the native models. The redundant emphasis I lay on the similarity in kind between anthropological and native models is to underscore that the only difference between them is the point at which they stop the deduction process (below, 2.2.).

Passage from one domain to another is effected, therefore, by the establishment of relations between them, and codes are the rules to do that. In the terms of Information Theory—and the definition is directly applicable to our field (Levi-Strauss 1955c)—a code is a system of rules of transformations to pass from one to another set of semantic parameters (cf. Levi-Strauss 1958:71, 364-366; 1960c:50-53). As mentioned above, such transformations are essentially the set-theoretic operations known as mappings. We will now examine them in their more specific form, that of homomorphisms.

To put it metaphorically, we can say that homomorphisms are remote control semantic devices with the help of which a native is able to reconcile incompatibilities, contradictions, and other incongruities by working on another level than that on which the incongruities are unresolvable (Levi-Strauss 1950:xix-xx; 1955a:256; 1955b; 1958: Ch.XI; 1960c:50-53). Because sets are mapped onto each other, the native has the resource of switching back and forth from one to another and can thus circumvent deadlocks and handle unknown factors. The conceptions of microcosmos—for example, anthropomorphisms—to solve the mystery of the structure of the universe represent such homomorphisms; they are also found in theologies, syncretisms, Freudian psychology, and in other uses of analogy.

Homomorphism theory will doubtless eventually contribute powerful tools of analysis to our field, but this is not the place to discuss it. I contrasted above one-to-one/many-to-one mappings, which prepared the way for a broad definition of homomorphism and isomorphism. Generally speaking, a homomorphism is a structural correspondence between two sets—and when the correspondence is term-to-term (bijection) it is called an isomorphism. The latter is a restricted, specialized form of the former. To be more precise without being technical, I add that "two systems are isomorphic if their associated sets are isomorphic *and*—in very loose language—any deduction in one of the systems can be translated in an equally correct deduction in the other. . . . The elements of the two sets may be different, *the rules of composition may be defined in entirely different ways*; but if the systems are isomorphic they are algebraically indistinguishable" (Moore 1967: 53; my italics). That is exactly the same statement, by a mathematician, as the one Levi-Strauss couched in anthropological terms (1960c:50-53).

We can now take a further step. *"By an isomorphism between two groups G and G' is meant a one-one correspondence a ⟷ a' between their elements which preserves group multiplication—i.e., which is such that if a ⟷ a' and b ⟷ b', then ab ⟷ a'b'.* . . . The notion of isomorphism is technically valuable because it gives form to the recognition that the same group-theoretic situation can arise in entirely different contexts" (Birkoff and MacLane 1965:122, 123).

Societies spend most of their mental resources on the task of consolidating available homomorphisms, and isomorphisms whenever possible, and on that of building new operators of morphisms when necessary, that will keep them from disintegrating under the impact of disturbing events threatening their laboriously established routines (cf. da Matta 1971). To use a thermodynamic metaphor this time, the construction of homomorphisms is the most efficient (and perhaps unique) negentropic device at the disposal of mankind. In other words, human societies are compelled to design different codes to cope with the multivarious randomness of the world by reducing it to an "acceptable" pattern (Maranda 1972). Likewise, anthropologists spend most of their mental resources on the task of trying to account for the homomorphisms which constitute native models, and of designing better models where higher-order homomorphisms will account for the residues native models do not deal or cannot cope with (Levi-Strauss 1958:347-348; cf. 1949b:123-124, 561; 1950:xxv, xxvii, xxxff.; 1955a:413-425; 1955d:1196ff., 1216-1217; 1958:95, 99ff.; 1960b; 1960e).

Not all codes are equally operational. Any set cannot be easily mapped onto any other set. Some transformations take long series of concatenated operations (Levi-Strauss 1966:302-307, 405). For instance, the sociological code of kinship is relatively powerless even in so-called "kinship-oriented societies" (see footnote 3). Monetary codes, on the other hand, possess greater versatility and rank higher in the hierarchy as they are eminently suitable for conversions.[5] Linguistic codes are still more powerful and capable of subsuming most sets (Levi-Strauss 1966:405; see also Maranda and Köngas Maranda (1970).

The analyst must formulate how some codes subsume, through isomorphisms, some sociological dimensions and not some others and how the same codes subsume, or are subsumed under, other codes. In conformity with the principle of operational definition, it means that he must formulate how a code as a whole is interpreted as a relation which becomes in turn the term, along with another relation (which may be either a set or a code), of a new relation of a higher order, and so on until the end of the deductive process. The native model is then mapped out (Levi-Strauss 1966:294, 302-307, a341, 407; 1971; see below, 2.2.).

Summary. Reciprocity is a universal axiom in human societies. It underlies all forms of exchange, which is essentially a proportion, that is, the construction of homomorphisms. Exchange or communication is multivalent as it prevails on all levels of social life. It is encoded in ways that depend on set formation—in the last analysis, on the principles according to which natives perceive and sort out the universe more or less fuzzily, within different defaulting and incompatibility thresholds. A whole formed of a conglomerate of relatively incongruent sets thus maintains itself in existence through series of mental operations. But the homomorphisms developed by the natives and those developed by the anthropologists are not co-extensive although they are of the same kind: the natives' codes are thought-of and lived-in, those of the anthropologist are structural (Levi-Strauss 1953).

Class and Structure

Part 2 overlaps with the three sections of Part 1, but the logic of classes will give us a slightly different perspective in order to focus (1) on the structure of classes and (2) on their constituent elements.

Encoders, decoders, and messages must be defined in two complementary ways. (1) These terms' existence is positional in that they materialize only as the summation of the values which can be assigned to them.[6] On the other hand, (2) values are not assigned freely to the members of a society as these are not empty symbols like the x's and y's to which values are assigned in mathematics. Because of the constraints inherent in predication within a given (i.e., not purely formal) semantic system—in other words, because of the dual operation to pass from the continuous to the discrete and to restore the former as mentioned above (1.2.)—the terms are ''pre-stressed' and are therefore capable of or predisposed to assuming certain values and are refractory to others. Levi-Strauss states all that clearly and in detail in his critique of Propp's formalism, and when he contrasts the *bricolage* of everyday life with scientific thought (1960d; 1962d:Ch.1; see also 1955c:526-527).

Once sets and their combinatorics are mapped out, the anthropologist still has to explicate: (1) the relations between them, which is usually done by the construction of a small-scale model (note that all models are small-scale reductions of "reality," be they in the realm of theoretical physics or in a painting); and (2) the relations between his model and the native one, a confrontation that will also show why some operations are possible while some others are beyond the scope or the borders of the cultural universe.

Now, when a hierarchy of codes has been hypothesized and tested, the anthropologist is in a position to demonstrate how sets can become operators and operators sets—or, in Levi-Strauss' terminology, how paradigmatic sets can function as syntagms and syntagms as paradigmatic sets. This is the convertibility threshold, i.e., the point where a semantic universe can be mapped out with the help of what our kind of logic calls symmetric relationships.

Then a code is broken (Levi-Strauss 1962b:101, 144; 1966:403ff.), and the logical problem of "form" vs. "content" is solved on pragmatic grounds. In effect, the analyst can define the structuring principles of his data that operate sometimes "syntactically" and sometimes "semantically." This is tantamount to the resorption of terms into their constituent relations and of relations into the terms without which they would not exist. What had been an analytic distortion at the outset is finally overcome in a dynamic structure where we define "those algebrico-geometric structures stabilizing all concepts in the space of mental activities" (Thom 1980:36).

At this point, the anthropologists not only should see the world as a member of the society he is immersed in but he should also have clear view of why the members of the society respond to events the way they do—in other words, his knowledge has acquired predictive value.

Two groups of definitions will follow. First, "class," of which three different structural types will be distinguished: second, "form," "content," and "structure" (Piaget 1949:especially 39, 41-43, 53, 69ff., 127ff.).

Class. A class is a set of terms which can be substituted for each other and still be argument to the same propositional function without altering its truth value. Thus, to take an example from the North Malaitan (Solomon Islands) monetary code, the argument to the function "is worth 1,000 taros" may be 1 x 10 strings of red shell money or 200 middle-size dolphin teeth (hereafter abbreviated respectively as rsm and dt). Rsm and dt are consequently both members of the class "monetary units" and are interchangeable. But now, the substitutability of terms must follow certain rules which, correlatively, define substitutability. These underlie the formation of sets, as pointed out above (1.2.), and the anthropologist seeks to formulate them. To continue with our example: 1 rsm = 200 dt because they have the same value in the North Malaitan money market with respect to (1) buying power and (2) reciprocal convertibility. On the other hand, 1,000 taros may also sometimes be purchased for Aust. $10. However, if it is possible, in some circumstances, to exchange 200 dt for Aust. $10, Aust. $10 cannot buy 1 rsm. In order to understand why substitutability is so restricted (1 rsm = 200 dt = 1,000 taros = Aust. $10 ≠ 1 rsm), one must reach a more comprehensive level of economic analysis, that including the bride wealth. In effect, the rules of substitutability prescribe that marital partners may exchange rights over a woman for 10 rsm, 1,000 dt, etc., but *not* for Australian currency. This, in turn, is intelligible only by taking into account the *abu-mamana* character of rsm, of which Australian currency was deprived until 1967 for Christians and of which it is still deprived for pagans (Maranda and Köngäs Maranda 1970).

Now, such rules depend on intra- and interpropositional operations. That is, the operations through which propositions are built determine their structure, on which depend in turn the way propositions are interrelated. This implies the problem of logical and extra-logical contents, which will be taken up briefly in 2.2. At this point, the focus is on the structure of classes. Three categories of structural classes are distinguished by Piaget: "weakly structured classes," "semi-structured classes," and "structured classes."

Let A, B, and C be three classes, with C including B and B including A.

(1). Weakly structured classes. The members of a paradigm B are related between themselves by the possession of common criterial attributes (see above, 1.2.). But the knowledge of these attributes does not enable one to generate the criterial attributes of the members of either C or A. Thus, let C be the Malaitan pagan economic system, B the native currency (rsm and dt), and A the Australian currency. The knowledge of the criterial attributes—here restricted to buying power for the sake of simplicity—of rsm and dt cannot be used to predicate the buying power of Australian currency (class A), nor is it sufficient to generate an adequate conception of the whole economic system (class C) as the latter includes services which can be reciprocated only by other services or by a combination of some specific goods and currencies. Weakly structured classes are the paradigms of which most domains of ethnographic reality are made.[7]

(2). Semi-structured classes. Members of A are linked to members of B, and members of B to members of C, but no given operation enables one to generate C from A. Thus, in North Malaita, since 1967, a syncretism of traditional and Christian world-views allows a local Christian to move within semi-structured classes while pagans are still coping with an economic system consisting of weakly-structured classes. In effect, the investment of Australian currency with a religious meaning was catalyzed by the Administration's switch from the duodecimal to the decimal system. I witnessed the mental process when participating in a

feast where a group of prominent and bright Christians elaborated it as follows:

> The Government now tells us that 10 should be preferred to 12 because it has decided that 12 pence = 1 shilling should be changed to 10 cents = 1 shilling. In Malaita, we knew that 10 is better because it takes 10 strings of red shell money to make one unit (*taafuli'ae*). Then, the Bible also tells about 12 and 10: there are 12 apostles and Christ but 10 commandments and God. So now we see that, as we already knew it here, 10 is better than 12.

And the talk went on, glossing on the proportions

12 pence/1 shilling = 12 apostles/Christ
10 cents/1 shilling = 10 commandments/God

and the consequence that the foreign monetary system could be invested with a religious meaning (equally foreign) somewhat similar to that of the traditional monetary system where a consecrated unit of rsm represents each lineage's *mana*.

Thus, rsm and Aust. $ now intersect Christians, as did rsm and the economic system already, but one still cannot generate the criterial attributes of C from the knowledge of those of B and A. Semi-structured classes are usually found in native models that strive at encompassing different domains of the social order, such as norms of behavior and economic activities, the division of labor and social status, and the like.

(3). Structured classes. These exist only in ethnographers' monographs. They are the condition of intelligibility of phenomena, in Leibnitz's terminology, that is, the operational constructs through which an order is built to sort out empirical data. Structured classes are defined adequately by Levi-Strauss when he states the principles of structural analysis (1958b:233): "économie d'explication; unité de solution; possibilité de restituer l'ensemble à partir d'un fragment, et de prévoir les développements ultérieurs depuis les données actuelles." Section 2.2. will also make clear how Levi-Strauss' definitions cover weakly- and semi-structured classes.

Structure. It is now time to tackle a deeper dimension of the problem. To what extent is the structural status of weakly- and semi-structured classes dependent on their contents? As mentioned earlier, the terms in sociological propositions are not mathematical symbols to which either the native or the anthropologist could assign values as fitting this or that set of coordinates. Piaget examines the question after a discussion of the viewpoints of Serrus, Wittgenstein, and Russel (1949:39). He maintains that there is no ground to assert that only inter-propositional calculus is "pure" (in Levi-Strauss' terminology, the syntagmatic level), while intrapropositional calculus would depend on the consideration of "things" (the formation of paradigmatic sets in Levi-Strauss' terminology). For Piaget, both inter- and intrapropositional structures are operations of a subject on an object, and both are equally structural-building mechanisms. The difference between the operations to build paradigmatic sets and those to relate such sets in syntagmatic chains is therefore not of kind but of degree. Levi-Strauss' "pre-stressed" elements (1960d) and his thesis on the convertibility of syntagmatic chains and paradigmatic sets once the deduction threshold is crossed (1966:302-307; 1962b:227-228,), make the same point, as I said by anticipation at the beginning of Part 2.

Piaget defines "content" as the terms mutually interchangeable, and "form" as the relation which remains constant in the course of such substitutions. Thus, if 1 rsm is worth 1,000 taros and 200 dt are also worth 1,000 taros, the terms (rsm and dt) vary but the relation—i.e., the function to which rsm and dt are arguments—remains constant. The "form," an equivalence here, is what remains constant.

Now, a "structure," for Piaget, is a logical relation which is capable of being alternately or simultaneously "form" or "content."[8] Thus, the equivalence rsm or dt = taros is a "form" with respect to class B (the native monetary system) and a "content" with respect to class C (the economic system of North Malaita), as the latter consists of a number of such and other operations to establish equivalences, proportions, and other structures of interaction.

The formation of sets is therefore to be understood as "an action of the subject on the object," and what matters is the structure of that operation. However, in all cases, it is never the properties of particular objects that are studied but the structural properties of the operations that can be carried out on the objects. In this respect, (1) forms remain constant, terms vary; and (2) a structure is a logical relation which can alternately be term and form and, consequently, logical structures may form a hierarchy—since some can be form with regard to lower-order structures and content with regard to higher-order structures, depending on where the deduction processes stop (Levi-Strauss 1971b).

Nothing is given, not even pre-stressed elements, as everything is a construct. But constructs are not all contemporary in societies. An individual or a group receives ready-made sets from prior generations, whose original constructing operations have been lost track of. But whether they are cast aside and relegated to the margins of the semantic universe or revived by being invested with new values, they bear witness to a structuring mind and thus give access to a matrix whose contents may be entirely novel without being "algebraically" different. And it is such algebraic permanences that the anthropologist wants to reveal in his attempts to describe ethnologics.

Conclusion

Many social scientists tend to overrate the explanatory power of mathematics and of quantitative methods. We may be prone to ignore, or to forget, that even in physics mathematics are a rather trivial tool, and quantification probabilistic at best. As soon as one departs from the narrow field of the Great Classical Laws (gravitation, electromagnetism), mathematics become relatively powerless—like in Quantum Mechanics, Macroscopic Physics, Thermodynamics, etc. (Thom 1980:25-26). Then, this "loss of effectiveness of the mathematical algorithm is increased on going from Physics to Chemistry" (Thom 1980:26).

Actually, our scientific quests and enquiries seem to be, like those of our colleagues in the "hard" sciences, that of mapping "soft" data onto "hard" conceptual structures. Anthropological analytics is an endeavor in qualitative methods and is more advanced, epistemologically, than, say, the physics of polymers, whose complex behavior can still be mapped only randomly even by the largest computers.

We have the privilege, denied to the "inhuman" sciences, to be able to dialogue with our object: to communicate between ourselves. Reciprocity and exchange, through coding procedures, rest on and lead to the construction of classes and are the dynamic components of structures that define mankind at least as objectively as atomic structures define non-thinking matter.

Notes

[1]On the powerlessness of linear models in semantic analysis, see Köngäs Maranda and Maranda 1970.

[2]Codes are broken when their constitutive logical operators are described; hierarchies of codes are established when the respective power of operators is measured in terms of semantic capacity and output in a network (Maranda and Köngäs Maranda 1980).

[3]Those who frown on Levi-Strauss' shift of focus from kinship to cognition and mythology (e.g., Leach 1967) seem to forget that kinship is only a constituent of the sociological code, that can be in turn a constituent of other codes. There is no *a priori* reason why kinship, as a sub-code, should be given analytic priority over other codes. The reductionist assumption still shared by many anthropologists that kinship is the "hard core" of our field has been losing ground for the last two decades.

[4]Especially today, predication rules are laid bare as societies are subject to strong extraneous pressures which their members interpret and sort out, as far as they can, in conformity with past judgments (Da Matta 1971; Köngäs Maranda 1978). Category formation and manipulation are therefore directly observable (Köngäs Maranda 1979). Then, the analysis of already formed sets reveals criterial attributes and, consequently, rules of typing. Thus, investigations of the rules and products of the two operations (the formation of discrete semantic units and their groupings) are amenable to mutual testing.

⁵'For example, four homomorphisms are represented in the following series: 1 fish = 5 dolphin teeth; 200 dolphin teeth = 1 x 10 strings of red shell money; 1 x 10 strings of red shell money = fee for sacrifice; 10 x 10 strings of red shell money + 1,000 dolphin teeth = prestation for a wife.

⁶'For an example, see the definition of some social rules in terms of Graph Theory in Maranda and Köngäs Maranda (1970) and the definition of semantic inertia in terms of networks in Maranda 1978b.

⁷'Most classes of demographic data consist of unordered sets. The operations by which they may become ordered are exemplified by the rule of consanguineal marriage. "In cases such as this, another equivalence rule must be added to the set. This must usually take priority over all other rules, so that we deal then with an ordered set" (Lounsbury 1967:380). The point was also made by Levi-Strauss (1949b) and on it actually rests the possibility of his *Les Structures élementaires de la parenté*. Only kinship sets with an extraneous closure role can display elementary structures (Maranda 1963). Ethnological and other native classifications do not form ordered sets either (Bulmer 1967; Bulmer and Tyler 1965; Levi-Strauss 1971b).

⁸'The following quotation states clearly that what matters is the structuring operation of the mind, according to Piaget. Levi-Strauss means the same thing when he says that ethno-science has no meaning in itself—i.e., that it makes sense only in the light of an "ethnologic" or a "philosophy" (Levi-Strauss 1971b).

Un fait ou un objet individualisés sont toujours relatifs au découpage exigé par l'action du sujet, et par conséquent relatifs aux structures perceptives ou intellectuelles d'ensemble qui les assimilent (et s'accomodent en retour à eux): d'un tel point de vue, il n'existe donc pas de faits isolés et les éléments individuels ne sont pas antérieurs aux systèmes qu'ils constituent entre eux, mais seulement décomposables en fonction de l'ensemble de chaque système...Le terme ultime de la décomposition logique est donc essentiellemnet relatif à l'édifice des formes assurant son individuation, c'est-à-dire que *cette individualisation elle-même est fonction de la totalité du système*. Le contenu individualisé des formes logiques n'est par conséquent extralogique que dans l'exacte mésure où il est donné et non pas construit opératoirement comme le sont les classes, les rélations et les propositions dont l'élaboration relève de structures opératoires d'ensemble. Mais les qualificatifs de donné et d'extralogique ne signifient nullement que l'on atteigne ainsi des éléments premiers en eux-mêmes, soit du point de vue physique ou psychologique, soit du point de vue logique (Piaget 1949:49, emphasis supplied).

Appendix

Hereafter are listed references where Levi-Strauss discusses the contributions of some scholars which he deemed pertinent to his work. The oversimplifications inherent in a two-entry table to sort evaluation as "positive" and "negative" are too evident to deserve comment. With all the shortcomings, the table—which does not include books and articles published after 1961—may nonetheless give an idea of the intellectual context in which Levi-Strauss' approach was defined. (References to articles are not followed by page numbers).

1. General	+		−
Rousseau, J.J.	1955a:	336f., 339, 421-425;	
	1958:	303 f.	
	1961:	41 f.	
Marx, Karl	1955a:	49 f.;	
	1955c;		
	1958:	30 f., 266, 348, 364, 368-375.	
Engels, F.	1949b:	a561;	
	1958:	364, 369, 372-374.	

2. Anthropologists			
Durkheim, E.	1949b:	381, 603;	1949b: XII, 23-29, 381;
	1955a:	62;	
	1958:	8, 16, 228, 309, 316 ff., 348, 362, 380;	1958: 179 f., 310;
	1960c.		
Mauss, M.	1945;		
	1949b:	XII f., 66 ff. 81, 382;	
	1950a;		1950;
	1958:	8, 16, 37, 115, 309, 320, 327, 362, 372, 390, 399;	1958: 179 f., 310;
	1960e.		

Radcliffe-Brown and Malinowski are also among the anthropologists most frequently referred to, although not quoted, by Levi-Strauss as his "masters"; he acknowledges his debt to Lowie, Kroeber and Boas (1955a:63), and it is probably the latter who, on this side of the Atlantic, had the greatest influence on Levi-Strauss (cf. 1958, 1962a, 1962b, 1964, 1966).

Other anthropologists occasionally evaluated are Evans-Pritchard, Fortes, Rivers and Murdock.

3. Structural Linguists

de Saussure	1945; 1955c; 1958: 1960a.	27, 230;	
Meillet	1945;		
Troubetzkoy	1945; 1955c.		
Jakobson	1945; 1949b; 1955c; 1958;	27 f., 66, 95, 102 ff.	

4. Psychologists

GESTALTTHEORIE	1949b: 1958:	Preface; 354 f.	
DEVELOPMENTAL (Piaget, Wallon, Guillaume)			1949b: 113 ff., 122 (see also 1950:XVI f.).
PSYCHOANALYSIS			
Freud	1949b: 1955a 1958:	118, 609-611; 60 f. 222 f., 363.	1949b: 113, 609-611
Jung			1949b:117, 119; 1950; 1958:230.

5. Physiologists

Goldstein	1958: ("The rule of the Struc- turalist Method")	307, 316 f.	
Others	1958:	183 f., 228.	

Others

Wiener	1958:	63-65	1958:63-65
Neumann and Morgenstren	1955a; 1958: (Ch.15)	306 ff.	
Shannon	1955c.		
Lazarsfeld, Guttman	1955c.		

References

Birkoff, G. and S. MacLane. 1965. *A survey of modern algebra*. New York.

Bulmer, R. 1967. Why is the cassowary not a bird? A problem of zoological taxonomy among the Karam of the New Guinea highlands. *Man* n.s. 2

Bulmer, R. and M.J. Tyler. 1965. The classification of frogs by the Karam of the Kaironk Valley, New Guinea. Mimeo, University of Auckland.

Da Matta, R. 1971. Myth and anti-myth among the Timbira, in P. Maranda and E. Köngäs Maranda, eds., *Structural analysis of oral tradition*. Philadelphia, pp. 271-291.

Durkheim, E. and M. Mauss. 1901-02. De quelques formes primitives de classification. *Année sociologique*.

Leach, E.R. 1964. Anthropological aspects of language: animal categories and verbal abuse, in P. Maranda, ed., *Mythology*, Penguin Books (1972)

1967. Brain twister. Review of The Savage Mind and Mythologiques 2. *New York Review of Books 9*.

Köngäs Maranda, E.K. 1978. Le monde de la mort et le monde des blancs. *Anthropologica* n.s. 20: 91-100.

1979. Folklore and culture change: Lau riddles of modernization, in R.M. Dorson, ed., *Folklore in the modern world*. Paris, The Hague, pp. 207-218.

Köngäs Maranda, E.K. and P. Maranda. 1970. *Structural models in folklore and transfor mational essays*. 2nd ed., Paris, The Hague.

Levi-Strauss, C. 1943. Guerre et commerce chez les Indiens de l'Amérique du sud. *Renaissance 1*.

1944. Reciprocity and hierarchy. *American Anthropologist 46*.

1945. L'analyse structurale en linguistique et en anthropologie. *Word 1* (1958: Ch. 2).

1949a. Histoire et ethnologie. *Revue de métaphysique et de morale 54*.

1949b. *Les structures élémentaires de la parenté*. Paris.

1950. Introduction à l'oeuvre de Marcel Mauss, in M. Mauss, *Sociologie et anthropologie*. Paris.

1953. Social structure, in A.L. Kroeber, *Anthropology Today* (1958: Ch. 15)

1955a. *Tristes tropiques*. Paris.

1955b. The structural study of myth, in T.A. Sebeok, ed., *Myth: a symposium* (1958: Ch. 11)

1955c. Les mathématiques de l'homme. *Bulletin international des sciences sociales 6*.

1955d. Diogène couché. *Les Temps modernes 110*.

1956a Les organisations dualistes existent-elles? *Bijdragen fur der lan, tot en volkenkunde* (= 1958:Ch. 8)

1956b. The family, in L.H. Shapiro, ed., *Man, culture and society*. Oxford.

1958. *Anthropologie structurale*. Paris.

1959. La geste d'Asdiwal. *Extrait de l'annuaire de l'Ecole des hautes études*, Paris (1974: Ch. 9)

1960a. *Leçon inaugurale au Collège de France*. Paris.

1960b. L'anthropologie sociale devant l'histoire. *Annales, économies, sociétés, civilisations 15*.

1960c. On manipulated sociological models. *Bijdragen fur den land, tot un volkenkunde 116*.

1960d. La structure et la forme. *Cahiers de science économique appliquée* (1974: Ch. 8)

1960e. Problème de l'invariance en anthropologie. *Diogène* 31.

1961. (with G. Charbonnier) *Entretiens avec Claude Lévi-Strauss*. Paris.

1962a. *Le totémisme aujourd'hui*. Paris.

1962b. *La pensée sauvage*. Paris.

1964. *Mythologiques I: Le cru et le cuit*. Paris.

1966. *Mythologiques II: Du miel aux cendres*. Paris.

1967. *Mythologiques III: L'origine des manières de table*. Paris.

1971a. *Mythologiques IV: L'homme nu*. Paris.

1971b. The deduction of the crane, in P. Maranda and E. Köngäs Maranda, eds., *Structural analysis of oral tradition*. Philadelphia.

1974. *Anthropologie structurale deux*. Paris.

Lounsbury, F.G. 1964. The formal analysis of Crow- and Omaha-type kinship terminologies, in W.H. Goodenough, ed., *Explorations in cultural anthropology*. New York.

Mandelbrot, B. 1954. Structure formelle des textes et communications. *Word 10*

Maranda, P. 1963. Note sur l'élément de parenté. *Anthropos 58*.

1965. Kinship semantics. *Anthropos 59*.

1967. Formal analysis and intra-cultural variations. *Social science information 9*.

1971. Cendrillon: Théorie des graphes et des ensembles, in C. Chabrol, ed., *Sémiotique narrative et textuelle*. Paris.

1972. Introduction, in Id., ed., *Mythology*. Penguin Books.

1976. Informatique, simulation et grammaires ethnologiques. *Informatique et sciences humaines* 28:15-30.

1978a. Le folklore à l'école: socio-sémantique expérimentale, in J.-C. Dupont, ed., *Mélanges en l'honneur de Luc Lacourcière*. Montréal, pp. 293-312.

1978b. Sémantographie du domaine "TRAVAIL" dans la haute-ville et la basse-ville de Québec. *Anthropologica* n.s. 20:249-292.

In press. Elementary text structures, in J.S. Petöfi, ed., *Text vs. sentence*. Hamburg.

Maranda, P. and E. Köngäs Maranda. 1970. Le crâne et l'utérus: deux théorèmes nord-malaitains, in J. Pouillon and P. Maranda, eds., *Echanges et communications*, 2 vols., Paris, The Hague, pp. 829-861.

1971. Introduction, in Id., eds., *Structural analysis of oral tradition*. Philadelphia.

1979. Myth as a cognitive map: a sketch of the Okanagan myth automaton, in W. Burghardt and K. Hölker, eds., *Textprocessing*. Hamburg, pp. 253-272.

Mauss, M. 1923-24. Essai sur le don. *Année sociologique*.

Meggitt, M.J. 1964. Male-female relationships in the Highlands of Australian New Guinea. *American anthropologist 66*.

Miller, G.A., E. Galanter, and K. Pribram. 1960. *Plans and the structure of behavior*. New York.

Moore, J.T. 1967. *Elements of abstract algebra*. New York.

Petitot, J. 1977. Topologie du carré sémiotique. *Etudes littéraires* 10:347-428.

Piaget, J. 1949. *Traité de logique—essai de logistique opératoire*. Paris.

Thom, R. 1972. *Stabilité structurelle et morphogénèse*. Paris.

1978. Espace, science et magie. *Circe* 89:605-617.

1980. Mathematics and scientific theorizing. *Scientia*, special issue:25-40.

3
Levi-Strauss' Theory of Kinship and its Empiricist Critics: An Anti-Needham Position

Ino Rossi

The Elementary Structures of Kinship (Levi-Strauss 1969) is still at the center of many on-going controversies (Barnes 1971; Brumbaugh 1978; Cohen 1977; De Ruijter 1978; Holy 1976; Muller 1973; Needham 1971, 1974, 1978; Rossi 1977 and 1978; Scheffler 1970). Levi-Strauss' book has been attacked both on theoretical grounds—for presumed Hegelian, anti-historical and functionalist biases—and on ethnographic grounds—for using inadequate data or proposing arbitrary interpretations of them.

Since the book attempts to formulate general principles capable of accounting for heterogeneous and complex data, the conceptualization of the relationship between ethnographic data and theoretical explanation is of crucial importance for structuralism. In this chapter I intend to show that many criticisms of Levi-Strauss' theory of kinship are no more than misunderstandings based on an empiricist notion of scientific explanation. Pre-eminent among the empiricist critics of Levi-Strauss is R. Needham, whose professional career has been highlighted by systematic misunderstandings of structuralism and by acrimonious attacks against many of his colleagues, myself included (Needham 1978).

I welcome the occasion of Needham's attack to reconsider the theoretical assumptions of the structural theory of kinship, an area which is more appropriate than the study of symbolic systems to show the precise nature of structural explanation and of the miscritiques proposed by anthropologists of empiricists and neopositivistic orientation. The study of kinship systems is at the core of the study of social organization which has been the traditional concern of empiricist anthropologists, in general, and of British structural functionalists, in particular.

I present, first, a brief synopsis of Levi-Strauss' theory and discuss, at some length, the theoretical premises and methodological orientation of Levi-Strauss' approach. I then examine various critiques which have been inspired by, or explicitly formulated by, Rodney Needham and are shared by other anthropologists of empiricist orientation. Finally, I conclude with a systematic formulation of the methodological principles contained in *The Elementary Structures of Kinship*.

The Core of Levi-Strauss' Kinship Theory

Levi-Strauss dedicates his book to the great American anthropologist Lewis H. Morgan, to discharge his debt to a man who believed in the compatibility of scientific observation "with a frankly theoretical mode of thought and a bold philosophical taste" (1969:xxvi). Levi-Strauss exhibits a "bold" taste of his own when he describes his anthropological work as a continuation of Kant's effort of drawing an inventory of the "constraining structures of the mind" and as an attempt to discover order behind apparently arbitrary phenomena and necessity underneath the illusions of freedom (1960a:10; 1963a:45; 1963b:630).

Levi-Strauss (1969:xxii) is concerned with elementary kinship structures, which are kinship systems prescribing marriage with certain relatives, so that it is possible to determine who one's own kin and affines are. His basic intent is to show that marriage terminology, rights and duties are inseparable aspects of the basic structure of the system.[1]

Exchange as the Fundamental Mechanism of Kinship Relationships

Levi-Strauss starts his ethnological analysis with a discussion of the incest prohibition. As a universal and elementary phenomenon, the incest prohibition can be considered as the origin of culture and therefore it is appropriately chosen to study the nature of culture. Moreover, this cultural rule seems to exhibit contradicto﹒y characteristics and, as such, it is a most appropriate starting point and justification for structural analysis. In fact, the incest prohibition possesses natural and cultural characteristics at the same time. Nature implies universality and spontaneity, while culture implies particularity and relativity of norms. Since incest is a universal cultural rule it has both a natural and cultural aspect (p.8-10).[2] Levi-Strauss goes on to say that the contradiction is only apparent, since in actuality nature imposes an empty form (an alliance undetermined in its modalities), and culture always fills this form with a specific content (the rule of incest prohibition). The intervention of the group, which puts order where there is chance, constitutes the essential characteristics of culture (p.30-32).

Levi-Strauss raises the challenging question of why human groups impose the rule of incest prohibition. His answer is that in human societies one finds (1) the mechanism of redistribution in the case of scarce goods and (2) the mechanism of reciprocal gift-giving in the case of luxury goods; both of these mechanisms impede absolute individual property and originate complex rules of social transactions (p.39-51). In the exchange of gifts, what is important are not the goods exchanged but the fact that the exchange takes place, since it is through exchange that social ties among individuals are established and maintained (p.68-83). By the same token, marriage rules are important because they are systems of exchange, in this case exchange of women. Levi-Strauss considers the exchange as the first "given" or the basic principle of human societies which cannot be explained. The mechanisms of exchange keeps the system in equilibrium because it insures that for any person lost the group receives one back; in this sense, exchange is the basic mechanism which makes possible both the existence and perpetuation of society.

According to Levi-Strauss, the prohibition of incest is the negative counterpart of the exchange system. In fact, the prohibition of incest has both a negative aspect (the renouncing to a daughter and sister for another man) and a positive counterpart (a counter claim to the daughter or sister of the other man). In this sense, the incest prohibition amounts to the establishing of an exchange (p.51)—a term by which Levi-Strauss conceptually integrates conflincting aspects of the same phenomenon. In line with Mauss' thesis that exchange in primitive societies is a reciprocal gift and "a total social fact" (p.52), Levi-Strauss considers "exchange"—in its general aspect—as a phenomenon of reciprocity (p.143).

This notion of reciprocity is a dialectic process which produces a "synthesis of two contradictory characteristics inherent in the natural order" (p.490). Levi-Strauss shows that reciprocity explains and unifies the most important kinship phenomena. He argues that incest prohibition and what he considers its positive counterpart, exogamy, are both reciprocity rules which establish exchange as a synthesis of two opposite principles. The dualistic principle itself, which implies the notions of opposition and correlation, is nothing else but one modality of the reciprocity principle (p.83). Reciprocity acts either by setting up classes of marriageable people (dual organization) or by determining relationships among individuals (incest prohibition). Both aspects of the reciprocity principle co-exist in the cross-cousin marriage (p.119). Cross-cousin marriage, then, can be seen as a system of exchange (p.48), "as the elementary formula of marriage by exchange" (p.129). Cross-cousin marriage is a preferential form of marriage because it is the most elementary product of affinal relationships between people exchanging marriage partners. Louis Dumont summarizes Levi-Strauss theory as follows: as exogamy prohibits incest among groups, so incest prohibition forbids relations among individuals: consequently, the dualist organization establishes a dichotomy valid for the whole society, and cross-cousin marriage builds a dichotomy around each subject (1971:96). In this sense, cross-cousin marriage is the connecting link between the dualist organization and the incest prohibition, and all three phenomena can be said to have the same basic structure.

The conceptual structure of Levi-Strauss' theory can be rendered in the following diagram: reciprocity→exchange →(parallel cousins)→incest prohibition→marriage →nuclear family. This diagram does not represent an historical or evolutionary sequence of phenomena, but rather logical relations among explanatory principles. Levi-Strauss reverses the traditional way of thinking which posited the nuclear family, first, and the incest prohibition, next. A great deal of conceptual clarity is produced by positing reciprocity as the first and most fundamental mechanism of social relations and by logically deriving from this mechanism social exchange, incest taboo, marriage and nuclear family in this order. Similarly, the dichotomy of cousins and the phenomenon of cross-cousin marriage are not explained in terms of the peculiarities of particular kinship systems—for instance dual organization—but are thought to derive from the nature of the exchange itself. The essential characteristic of exchange is to be found in the way it organizes social positions and relationships: marriage is to be conceived as a total relations of exchange among two groups as well as a cycle of reciprocity of the type X→Y→Z rather than a mutuality of the type X→Y (Dumont, 1971:148).

In *The Elementary Structures of Kinship* Levi-Strauss shows that these basic principles make sense of the apparent heterogeneity of the Australian, Chinese, and Indian kinship systems. A summary of Levi-Strauss' lengthy argument has been given by De Josselin De Jong (1952) and, in more critical terms, by Barnes (1971), Dan Sperber (1968), Dumont (1971) and others.

I limit myself to presenting an outline of Levi-Strauss' kinship theory according to the summary given in the last chapter of *The Elementary Structures of Kinship* (1969:493), to which I add some clarifications and insertions taken from other parts of the book: (1) all various kinship and marriage rules are as many methods of achieving integration between families composing a group; (2) the variety of these rules can be reduced to three possible elementary structures—that is, bilateral, patrilateral and matrilateral marriages (p.464); (3) these structures are constructed by means of a generalized exchange—among all social groups, in the case of the latter two structures, and by means of a restricted exchange among just two groups, in the case of the first structure (p.464); (4) an harmonic regime—that is, a system where residence and descent rules are based on the same sex line—leads (in a structural and not historical sense) to a generalized exchange, and a disharmonic regime leads to a restricted exchange. Consequently, the marriage rules can be reconstructed *a priori* from the relation between residence and descent rules (p.216); (5) the matrilateral cross-cousin marriage gives a greater integration to society than the patrilateral cross-cousin marriages (p.451-455; 1973:122) because it is a system of generalized exchange. This explains why the matrilateral cross-cousin marriage is more frequent than the patrilateral one.

The notion of elementary structure and the heuristic models of extended and restricted exchange play a crucial role in this theory. We have seen that all forms of marriage are conceptualized as systems of exchange which are thought to derive from the dialectical process of reciprocity. In attributing analytic priority to the notion of exchange as a structure of reciprocity and as a "total social fact," Levi-Strauss assigns to the principle of "descent" a secondary role in the explanation of marriage systems. As is well known, Levi-Strauss' theory of kinship is called "Alliance Theory" and it is usually contrasted with the "Descent Theory" traditionally endorsed by many British anthropologists.[3]

The Intellectual Roots of Levi-Strauss' Theory

Needham seems to reduce the controversy over the structural theory to largely a question of "technical competence" in the analysis of ethnographic data (1978). On the contrary, we must, first of all, understand that ultimately the difference between "alliance" and "descent" theories is rooted in a different way of thinking about data. Secondly, it must be unequivocally clear that empiricist critics have repeatedly shown a total incompetence in assessing "how-structuralists-explain things," to use the phrasing of my distinguished critic (Needham 1978:387).

Having discussed the theoretical premises of Levi-Strauss' orientation in the introductory chapter, we must here examine its key methodological notions, in view of Needham's claim that the real difference between him and myself boils down to one of technical competence (*op. cit.*).

Methodological Orientation Of Levi-Strauss' Kinship Theory

The Notion of Deep Structure

Methodology is a word with many meanings; what one scientist calls "methodology" may be considered by another scientist epistemology, or philosophy of science or metatheory. I certainly do admit the importance of formulating precise research procedures and techniques of analysis, but I do not accept the view that "methodology" is synonymous with "research techniques." I maintain that there is both an epistemological and an operational aspect of methodology—the first one providing the justification and the explanatory boundaries of the second one. I have explained elsewhere that by the term "epistemological methodology" I refer to the definition of the scientific object of analysis, the kind of meaning sought and the type of explanation proposed; I deal with issues of "epistemological methodology" in this section. By "operational methodology" I refer to the research techniques needed for handling the data (see in Rossi 1974:60-106); I deal with this aspect of methodology in the next section.

Levi-Strauss' originality consists in having proposed a new definition of the scientific object of analysis. He does not disregard ethnographic data, as complex as they may turn out to be; on the contrary, he claims that what we need is a "scientific" definition of the object under investigation because the empirical data appear too heterogeneous and often ambiguous when they are taken at their face value. Levi-Strauss' approach is a novel and daring one precisely because of his claim that those very facts which have been the stumbling block for many social scientists of pre-structural orientation are the starting point and justification of the structural approach.

Let us consider the case of dual organization. Lowie and Kroeber had observed that certain exogamic units vary so greatly in number and distribution in a short space and time as to elude any systematic analysis. Against this claim, Levi-Strauss suggests that if we consider dual organization primarily not as an institution but as a form of organization, we immediately realize that—together with political, religious and other forms of kinship organization—it is nothing but an application of the principle of reciprocity. The reason is that all social institutions have their logical roots in the human mind. Lowie, Kroeber, and the like considered the varieties of exogamous units as unstable and unintelligible structures. Levi-Strauss, on the contrary, considers them as contingent elements placed by history at the disposal of the mechanism of reciprocity. Systems of reciprocity are functionally permanent since they organize all fragmentary institutional elements always in reciprocity cycles (p.75-76). We can, then, say that Levi-Strauss abandons the explanation in terms of historically specific institutional functions and searches for permanent underlying systematic functions.

Levi-Strauss refutes functionalism because of its concern with empirically observable functions, since empirical data at times leads to an impasse. For instance, Malinowski states that the custom of giving gifts to one's mistress is an arbitrary and inconsequent one because it implies that the sexual relation is a service offered by women to men, while in reality one would expect it to be a reciprocal exchange of services. Levi-Strauss argues that Malinowski makes the mistake of considering merely "the visible content and empirical expression" of the custom. In reality, sexual relations are only one aspect of a global exchange of services, of which marriage is just an occasion. Marriage relations are not limited to the two people involved, but rather they produce a cycle of reciprocity among groups (p.115-116). One cannot explain the meaning of one custom if it is considered in isolation; on the contrary, a given custom has to be understood in terms of the larger system of reciprocity—in its position within the system of relationships. This is what is referred to as the *systematic notion of meaning*. Similarly, dual organization cannot be explained in terms of the function of prohibiting marriage with one's sister and, accidentally, with parallel cousins. In actuality, dual organization prohibits the marriage with half the women of the group; then, its real function must be to produce all the consequences that in fact it does produce. The *raison d'être* of this organization has to be found in a quality shared by brothers, sisters and parallel cousins—that is, in a common or group quality. Levi-Strauss finds this common quality in the fact that brothers and sisters as well as parallel cousins bear the same sign and orientation within the structure of reciprocity, while cross-cousins bear opposite and complementary signs (p.141). To explain the co-presence of apparently heterogeneous elements in terms of their oppositions and reciprocal or complementary relationships is a typical mark of the structural explanation.

It follows that the scientific object of investigation for structural anthropologists is a system of opposite (read: "distinct"), complementary, and reciprocal relationships (p.141, also p.127) which are considered to be the "profound and omnipresent cause" (p.23) or *raison d'être* of empirically observable functions, as well as of apparent disfunctions or unrelatedness of co-existing phenomena. This set of relations is like a "simple and constant form" imposed upon the multiplicity of contents (p.82 and p.143). Dual organization is like a method to solve a variety of problems and to organize a multitude of institutional arrangements. Similarly, all other kinship facts "must be fitted into the framework of such general structural laws of kinship systems" (p.352). This structural level is conceived as an "operator" of social organization and as the deepest and simplest symbolic whole which expresses itself in the different significations of kinship rules, terminologies and social structures. There is always a functional correlation between this underlying structure (signifier) and its expressions (signified), although the correlation may differ in degrees of rigidity (p.158). Similarly, the structure can assume various forms such as open, or closed, rotatory or oscillatory forms (p.444).

> This means that the reality of phenomena is not in the appearances as they are given to the observer, but at a mucher deeper level in their signification; this consists not in the objects which can remain the most obscure and difficult to describe, but in the relations between the relations which are more simple than the objects themselves. The peculiarity of the *fact* (my italics) for our science consists precisely in this *appearing* in the form of relationships between phenomena and,

therefore, in existing independently and underneath apparent phenomena (p.174-175).

Behind the varieties of phenomena there is "something which is common" that is their structure, or the "the invariant relations between terms so prodigiously diversified as the appearances, which are our raw data." This scientific contribution of structuralism consists in having introduced such a simplification among apparently heterogeneous data (p.176-177).

From this notion of structure as scientific object of analysis and the related notions of meaning, structural causality and structural law derive typically structural procedures and tools of analysis.

The Notion of Mechanical Models

Levi-Strauss is aware that his position betrays a daring attitude, and perhaps even a "bold philosophical taste," but he is far from considering such an attitude incompatible with scientific precision (p.xxvi). His methodological procedures are clearly spelled out in the preface of the volume. He proceeds by "setting up the hypothesis, guiding intuition and illustrating principles" rather than being concerned with verifying his explanation (p.xxv). In the first part of the book he considers simple and universal phenomena whose meaning is the same regardless of the context in which they occur. In the second part of the volume he considers more complex phenomena and, therefore, he has to change method; there the explanation is based on carefully selected examples or quasi-monographs on marriage systems in South East Asia, China and India (p.xxv-xxvi). This seems to echo the method of qualitative methodology and theoretical sampling, such as advocated by the proponents of "grounded theory" (Glaser and Strauss 1967). Levi-Strauss shows further awareness of such a canon of scientific rigor when he states that the cross-cousin marriage is a more significant phenomenon than exogamy and dual organization, and, therefore, it must be chosen as the crucial experiment for the study of marriage prohibition (p.123). Functional, historical and naturalist explanations approach socio-cultural phenomena at their face value and heavily rely on canons of quantitative rigor and statistical correlations. On the contrary, Levi-Strauss wants to account for concrete cultural phenomena not at their empirical and observable level, but at a deeper level of intelligibility, and, therefore, he is not bound by quantitative criteria of scientific rigor. He intends to avoid explanations based on contingent reasons and on the conscious and experimental level of social reality to reach its unconscious foundations. This is accomplished by using the notions of reciprocity, restricted and extended exchange and the like as *models* (p.57 and p.102), and not as formulae representing kinship phenomena in their observable and empirical complexity. When in the second edition of his book on kinship, Levi-Strauss replies to the criticisms of such eminent critics as

Maybury-Lewis, De Josselin De Jong, and Leach, he repeatedly emphasizes that his analysis is conducted at the level of models and not of observable reality. He is amazed that there is still a "need to emphasize that this book is concerned exclusively with models and not with empirical realities" (p.49, n.5). He also emphatically rejects the suggestion that he is confusing models with empirical data (xxxv; 254, n.2); rather, he is primarily interested in "purely formal" definitions which "involve no more...than a constant relationship between" elements (p.181, n.1).

These clarifications—which appeared in the English version of his book twenty years after the original publication in French—are explications and not innovations of his original methodological orientation. The latter has centered on the notion of structure as a constant form and a set of invariant relationships since 1949. For instance, in 1949 he explicitly maintained that exogamy and endogamy cannot be considered as independent entities but as solidary perspectives "on a system of fundamental relationships in which each term is identified by its position within the system" (p.49). He used "the system of the scarce product" as "an extremely general model" useful to explain the origin of cultural rules (p.32), and he was interested in reciprocity as a "general model" (p.57), in dual organization as a global system binding the group in its totality, in cross-cousin marriage as establishing a perfect or approximate model of relationship (p.102), in the generalized exchange as model (p.295), and in the construction of a "reduced model of patrilineal system" (p.362, 364). It is clear that since 1949 Levi-Strauss has used the models of restricted and extended exchanges as research hypotheses. For instance, he then spoke of the preferred marriage with a mother's brother's daughter as an hypothesis which would produce a restricted, unsatisfactory model (p.282). In 1949 Levi-Strauss had spelled out that the model is not a mere invention but rather formulated on the basis of the concrete distribution of data. However, unlike empiricists, he does not explain the data only in terms of geographical, historical and psychological factors, but rather in terms of the basic relational properties of the system. Therefore, he operates the transition ("transformation" in Levi-Strauss' words) from concrete data to formal models (p.397). However, the relationship between empirical data and model is not one-to-one because the system hypothesized by the model could have been distorted by contingent factors and, therefore, it might not be explicitly reflected by raw cultural data. Such underlying systems, however, are postulated to account for the presence of repeated regularities which otherwise might be unaccounted for (p.296). Consequently, the analytic distinction between empirical (and statistical) patterns and their underlying model is of crucial importance.

It is in the light of this distinction that Levi-Strauss' use of models makes sense. He notices that many cultures prohibit marriage with a parallel cousin, whereas they permit marriage with a cross-cousin. Some cultures make a distinction between father's sister's daughter and mother's brother's daughter, and others exclude the marriage with the first cousin as incestual, and encourage marriage with the second one. These rules seem arbitrary and it would be impossible to find their objective foundation if we approach them as isolated phenomena to be explained in terms of their particular history. To treat them scientifically means to apply the operation of "decoupage" and keep only few essential variables; then one contrasts these variables and determines their similarities and differences. From this point of view, empirical phenomena are as many transformations of each other and are perceived to transmit messages deriving from a common matrix.

The marriage with the mother's brother's daughter constitutes the model of extended exchange. A lineage *A* gives a daughter to a lineage *B*, which gives it to a lineage *C* and so on; the cycle is completed when a group gives a woman "to the lineage which has previously given its own women"; through this mechanism a long cycle of reciprocity is established within the total society. On the contrary, the marriage with the father's sister's daughter implies a short cycle of reciprocity because in this case a group restitutes in the next generation a daughter to a group from which it had received one in the previous generation; since the cycle of reciprocity is immediately closed, the restricted exchange cannot serve the function of integrating the whole society as the extended exchange does. In Levi-Strauss' opinion, this is the reason why the extended exchange is practised by human societies more frequently than the restricted exchange.

This kind of reasoning offers a typical example of structural thinking, which is diametrically opposed to the empiricist way of thinking of some critics of Levi-Strauss. Francis Korn, for instance, argues after her mentor Rodney Needham that we must search for the "reasons for the existence of the prohibition of incest in each particular case" (Korn 1973:16) because "the -meaning- of each rule prohibiting incest could vary according to the sort of social categories it involves and the kind of society where it is expressed" (*loc.cit.*). Certainly, a good ethnologist has to take into account the specificity of particular cultural and historical contexts, but such a specificity does not necessarily exclude the presence of underlying systemic tendencies common to different social systems. Korn claims that Levi-Strauss' conceptions of social structure and model are rather idiosyncratic and, worst, they cannot be empirically tested. Given Korn's empiricist conception of verification it is not surprising that she finds incomprehensible Levi-Strauss' concern with models rather than with empirical reality (*Ibid.*:143). If one equates "models" with "statistical models" (which are based on the frequencies of occurrences of empirical events), he cannot find intelligible the distinction between models and empirical reality. This point is of crucial importance, and leads us to consider the difference between statistical and mechanical models.

An explanation in terms of statistical models is based on empirical regularities and functional relationships. On the contrary, an explanation in terms of mechanical models is based on relational constants among the basic constituents of empirical systems. Van der Leeden characterizes the differences between the French and British anthropological styles as respectively a concern with "whole systems" and "partial systems," formal structures and empirical structures, constant relationships and variables, synchronic and diachronic relations, structure and function, systemic and individual points of view (1971). These dichotomies of Van der Leeden are well taken as long as they are not understood to indicate mutually exclusive concerns. It would be a gross—although not infrequent—misinterpretation to believe that Levi-Strauss wants to formulate the grammatical and constitutive rules of experimential phenomena, or partial systems, or empirical structures. As a methodological corollary, Levi-Strauss' notion of elementary structure, cross-cousin marriage, preferential marriage, and extended and restricted exchange have to be interpreted as heuristic models and research hypotheses about the structural properties underlying empirical social phenomenon. It is a fundamental misinterpretation of many critics of Levi-Strauss to interpret these notions as descriptions of the external manifestations of empirical phenomena and, consequently, to find them hopelessly misleading and useless for ethnographic inquiry. This is what Buchler and Selby (1968:120ff) and Banaji (1970:80) have called interpretative error—that is, the error of substituting observable ethnographic data for the terms of mechanical models. Mechanical models are not abstract conceptualizations of empirical phenomena but representations of their underlying relational constants. Such a misconception, and Levi-Strauss' repeated rejection of it, have transformed early admirers into opponents of Levi-Strauss' approach (see the case of Needham and Leach).

Empiricist Misunderstanding of Levi-Strauss By Rodney Needham and His Followers

The Issue of Prescriptive versus Preferential Marriage

The notions of prescriptive and preferential marriage have filled many volumes of controversies. In the first edition of his book, Levi-Strauss stated that he was concerned with elementary structures or what are usually called preferential marriages as a function of the structure of the system. In the first section of this paper we have seen that, for Levi-Strauss, cross-cousin marriage is a preferential form of marriage because it is the most elementary product of the relationship between men who exchange women, and because it provides a link between the incest prohibition and dualistic systems. On the contrary, Needham interpreted the notion of preferential marriage as referring to the statistical patterns of actual marriage choices. Moreover, he complains against Schneider and Homans for their failure to distinguish between preferential and prescriptive systems. For Needham a preferential marriage system implies a choice among categories of marriageable persons, while prescriptive marriage is characterized by the lack of choice among categories of persons which can be married (1962:8-9). It is Needham's view that Levi-Strauss is concerned only with prescriptive systems, or at least he so intended, if he had not confused the two forms of marriage (see in Levi-Strauss 1969:xxxi).

Needham's error consists in conceptualizing the "preferential" and "prescriptive" character of marriage in terms of personal or subjective reasons for marrying. Such a conceptualization directly contradicts Levi-Strauss' definition, explicitly contained in the first edition of his book. There he stated he was concerned with preferential marriage as an elementary structure, that is, as a function of "the structure of the system under consideration" (p.xxii).

In his 1965 Huxley lecture Levi-Strauss expresses embarrassment at the results obtained by both Needham and Leach with their distinction between preferential and prescriptive marriages—a distinction Levi-Strauss doesn't consider significant. Levi-Strauss argues that Needham deals with marriage systems as operating between types of relatives rather than between social groups. In that lecture Levi-Strauss states again that he is concerned with the selection of a marriage partner in terms of his/her belonging to a given group or category, and he defines the relationship between intermarrying people "in terms pertaining to the social structure" (Levi-Strauss 1965:18). Structural principles like the "matrilateral operators," or the prescriptive marriage to a mother's brother's daughter, are real principles at work within the system as structural tendencies, even though very few people seem to practice it (*Ibid.*:17). The reason is that at the level of practice there are "demographic conditions," situational, psychological, and other contingent factors which interfere with the structural tendencies of the system. Whereas statistical models describe marriage systems as they occur in practice—that is, as a byproduct of the interaction between structural and contingent factors—mechanical models are tentative formulations of underlying "structural operators."

Such a distinction between these two types of models, and the two related levels of analysis, renders perfectly clear and legitimate a famous sentence of Levi-Strauss, which has angered many of his critics: at the level of the model there is no difference between prescriptive systems and preferred systems. Here Levi-Strauss refers to mechanical models which are concerned not with the actual frequencies of marriage practices but with the structural reasons of these practices. Levi-Strauss' passage is the following: "even a preferential system is prescriptive at the level of model, while even a prescriptive system cannot but be preferential at the level of the reality" (*loc. cit.*). Such a reasoning has remained unintelligible to Levi-Strauss' empiricist critics, so that Levi-Strauss had to insist on it again in the second edition of *The Elementary Structures of Kinship*. "An elementary structure can be equally preferential and prescriptive" as long as the "imperative relationship is a function of the social structure" and not of a "subjective inclination" (1969:xxxiv). By "subjective inclination" Levi-Strauss means the marrying of a woman because she is rich or blond or intelligent. These reasons for marrying are not dictated by the social structure and, in this sense, they are "subjective" or "contingent." The reason for choosing a marriage partner is structural when "the spouse is the spouse solely because she belongs to an alliance category or stands in a certain kinship relationship to Ego" (*loc. cit.*).

To Levi-Strauss the statistical meaning of prescriptive and preferential sytems—that is, a marriage rule determined on the basis of actual marriage choice—is of secondary importance, because the actual choices may be often determined by contingent reasons. On the contrary, Needham understands the meaning of "preferential" only on the basis of actual marriage choices. The statistical frequencies of actual marriage choices are of interest to Levi-Strauss only in so far as they can help to detect the systemic tendencies of the system. This is equal to saying that Levi-Strauss is interested in preferential marriage systems only in the structural and not in the statistical sense. "In the case of elementary structures as well as in that of complex ones, the use of the term 'preferential' does not suggest a subjective inclination toward a certain degree of kinship, but states an objective fact. I call 'preferential' a system in which notwithstanding the lack of any—prescriptive—constraints ('at the subjective psychological conscious level'), the rate of marriage with a given type of kin is higher than would be the case if all marriages were made at random" (1965:18). This statement has to be understood with the following clause: "all possible contingent factors controlled." Under this condition a statistical tendency greater than a random choice is an "objective rate (which) express certain structural properties of the system," even if the members of the group may be unaware of them (*Ibid.*).

Once we have clearly understood the difference between the contingent and the structural level of analysis, we can make sense of another apparently questionable statement of Levi-Strauss—namely, that the difference between preferential and prescriptive systems is not a property of the system themselves (read: "in their empirical observable reality") but it depends on whether the systems are conceptualized at the level of "mechanical" (read: "at the level of structural explanation") or at the level of "statistical" models (read: "at the empiricist's level of explanation").

This interpretation should clear up many of the presumed inconsistencies in Levi-Strauss' writings. For Levi-Strauss the mechanical model is the one which express the structural rules of the system.[4]

Moreover, he is interested in prescriptive and preferential marriage systems only as mechanical models. On the contrary, Needham and other British critics of Levi-Strauss are interested (and are capable of understanding) only the "statistical" meaning of these two concepts, which they interpret in a purely empiricist sense.

We can, then, see why empricist anthropologists like J.A. Barnes (1971) are puzzled by the following sentence of Levi-Strauss: "For even a preferential system is prescriptive at the level of the model, while even a prescriptive system cannot but be preferential at the level of the reality" (Levi-Strauss 1965:17). The puzzle is easily resolved if we interpret the sentence "prescriptive at the level of model" to mean "mechanical model," and the sentence "prescriptive at the level of reality" to mean "at the level of statistical model or observable reality."

J.A. Barnes states that *The Elementary Structures of Kinship* deals with prescriptive rules rather than statistical preferences (Levi-Strauss 1969:150). In reality, Levi-Strauss deals with both types of rules, but at the level of mechanical models—that is, insofar as they reveal the tendencies of the system as a system. Barnes' failure to see the distinction between the empirical and structural level of analysis prevents him from seeing why Levi-Strauss argues against Leach and Needham that the distinction between "preference' and "prescription" is an unimportant one (Barnes 1971:150-151).

Francis Korn, a pupil of Needham[5], offers a more recent example of self-perpetuating misunderstandings of structuralism operated by anthropologists of empiricist orientation. Chapter three of Korn's book on the meaning of the terms "prescriptive" and "preferential" offers a perfect example of empiricist shortsightedness. She starts by establishing the equivalence of the following concepts:

incest prohibition = elementary structure = mechanical model
marriage choice = complex structure = statistical model
(Korn 1973:37)

Then she goes on to equate "prescriptive" with "mechanical," based on the misinterpretation of the passage where Levi-Strauss asserts that the difference between prescriptive and preferential systems depends not on the systems themselves but from their conceptualization at the level of the mechanical or statistical model. Whereas we have seen that Levi-Strauss is interested in mechanical models and corresponding preferential systems understood in the structural sense, Korn reiterates Barnes' mistake of identifying prescriptive and preferential systems respectively with mechanical and statistical models. From an empiricist point of view this identification is logical. In fact a prescriptive rule—understood in terms of actual marriage choices—implies that all people follow that particular rule, whereas a preferential rule simply means that the particular rule is the most frequently followed by people.

Korn combines the first misinterpretation with a second one. When she equates preferential marriage to a prescriptive marriage (*Ibid.*:38), she speaks of statistically preferential and statistically prescriptive marriage. On the contrary, Levi-Strauss equates prescriptive and preferential systems only at the structural level of analysis—that is, on the basis of whether preferential or prescriptive statistical patterns are a function of the system or not. On the basis of her twofold misinterpretation F. Korn establishes the following sequence of equations:

prohibition = elementary = mechanical = prescriptive = preferential

choice   = complex   = statistical = preferential = elementary

(*Ibid.*)

Korn offers such a sequence as a brilliant demonstration of contradictions (elementary = complex) and inconsistencies (prescriptive = preferential) which are present in Levi-Strauss' theory. However, once we correct her two errors, the sequence of equations should read as follows:

choice subject = elementary = mechanical = preferential (in = prescriptive
to a rule   structural
                                             sense)

choice oriented = elementary = statistical = prescriptive (in = preferential
                                             statistical sense)

In view of these considerations I fully subscribe to De Ruijter's statement that Korn "makes no real attempt to understand Levi-Strauss' typology in the context of his own intentions" (19787:168).[6]

Structural versus Historical Explanations

Another kind of interpretative error consists in attributing to structural explanations an historical or evolutionary meaning. For instance, J.P.B. de Josselin de Jong interprets Levi-Strauss' explanation of the asymmetric eight-section system of the Murngin society as an historical reconstruction, whereby the inital four intermarrying groups based on two patrilineal moieties are supposed to be later intersected by matrilineal moieties (de Josselin de Jong, 1952:17, 39-40). Levi-Strauss rejects this interpretation because he was not dealing with the actual Murngin system and the stages of its evolutionary development, but rather with a "hypothetical model of generalized exchange" and its relative rules of conversion from one stage to another. He was concerned not with a portrait of a society and its historical developments, but with structural operational procedures (Levi-Strauss, 1969:181). The issue is analogous to the one I have discussed in the previous section: structural analysis is concerned with structural models and related procedures of transformational analysis, rather than with the description of actual historical process at their empirical level.

Leach's historical interpretation of Levi-Strauss' explanation of the Kachin society has met a similar rebuke by Levi-Strauss. Levi-Strauss did not intend to say that the Kachin system came into being as the result of borrowing from an archaic Chinese system (Leach 1961:249). Levi-Strauss merely intended to say that the Kachin system attests to the existence of a type of social structure or structural operator which must have spread over a large part of Asia (Levi-Strauss 1969:241). Leach repeatedly asserts that Levi-Strauss' theory is concerned with "the general laws of development governing all Asian societies," "evolutionary history of half of Asia and European kinship system," and "general process of social evolution" (Leach 1961:77, 90, 101, 103). From our previous analysis it is clear that the processes explaining the actual cultural evolution include both structural and contingent explaining factors. Levi-Strauss then is concerned with the diffusion of structural operators which are often only partially and distortedly reflected in actual cultural systems. In Levi-Strauss' words, historical reconstructions provide only incomplete and approximate transfigurations of a dialectical process (Levi-Strauss 1969:454).

The same kind of misinterpretation is made by Korn, who attributes to Levi-Strauss an "hypothetical reconstruction of the evolution" of the Dieri system (Korn 1973:40) or a "genetic connection between four-section and eight-section system" (*Ibid.:*79). Korn asserts also that Levi-Strauss proposes "another possible evolutionary sequence in the formation of alternating systems" (*Ibid.*:111) and that the Mara system as explained by Levi-Strauss illustrated the "passage from a patrilineal system to a formula of restricted exchange" (*Ibid.*:112).

This interpretative mistake runs throughout Korn's book and the other empiricist critics I have already mentioned.

Generalized Exchange and Descent as Structural Models

Levi Strauss uses in a structural sense many other concepts. For instance, when he has been criticized for equating "the notion of marriage class as a system of generalized exhange to that of lineage," Levi-Strauss has replied that this equation is true only at the level of the most "abstract model" (Levi-Strauss 1969:269, n.3). This is certainly not Leach's level, when he states that the Kachin conceives of the lineage as a localized group identified with a particular place where it has a special ranking status in respect to that status (Leach 1954:167).

Even the notion of unilineal descent is used by Levi-Strauss in a purely formal way—that is, as a set of constant relationships between the personal status of the ego and the status of his parents (Levi-Strauss 1969:181, footnote). Levi-Strauss rejects Leach's suggestion (1961) that he has confused clan models with the empirical situation, and insists that he conceptualizes the Kachin marriage as a mechanical model. The statistical model is necessary only when one wants to consider the number of exchange units and permanence of ties among them (Levi-Strauss 1969:254, n.2).

Similarly, in his comments to Goody's article, Levi-Strauss makes the point that Goody is interested in "descent," "filiation" and "local group" per se, "while I am trying to get at their meaning in a given context, namely the kind of reciprocal systems which they allow or hinder" (Levi-Strauss 1961:17). Once again, the structuralist is concerned with the systemic principles operating in empirical cultural data.

Against Maybury-Lewis' complaint that Levi-Strauss does not take into account the difference between "descent" and "filiation" (Maybury-Lewis 1960:196), Levi-Strauss replies that his book is "concerned exclusively with models and not with empirical realities" (Levi-Strauss 1969:49, n.5).

Conclusion: The Methodological Lesson of the Controversy about *The Elementary Structures of Kinship*

My intent in this chapter was to show that the confrontation between the empiricist and structural orientations is so divisive and fundamental primarily because it is a confrontation between two radically different ways of looking at the data. The three issues I have discussed in this chapter do not exhaust all the major theoretic-methodological differences between the two orientations, but they abundantly document the following conclusion. Points of controversy about the structural theory of kinship—which, according to R. Needham (1978), are purely "technical" in nature—in reality are rooted in fundamental differences in the ways structuralists and empiricists look at data. This conclusion is in direct antithesis to the empiricist's contention that "data" should and can be studied "objectively"—that is, independently of one's theoretical orientation. The merit of structuralism consists, first and most of all, in proposing a theoretical orientation based on anti-empiricist epistemological views. In turn, structural epistemology is based on, or paralleled by, a particular view of the nature of socio-cultural phenomena (ontological views), which has been amply discussed in the conclusion of the last volume of *Mythologiques* (Levi-Strauss 1971).

Structuralism has introduced a fundamental break into contemporary social sciences at the ontological, epistemological and methodological levels, but not many anthropologists have perceived the direct bearing of the epistemological and theoretical assumptions of structuralism on the structural theory of kinship. The notable exceptions are Büchler and Selby (1968), L. Dumont (1971), D.M. Schneider (1965), and Van der Leeden (1971). To this list we must add J. Banaji, who explicitly makes the point that the structural method is based on two key axioms, the homology of linguistics and social phenomena and their common foundation on the unconscious mechanism of the human mind.[7] Banaji clearly sees the direct relevance of these two axioms for the structural theory of kinship when he states that, by translating mechanical models into conscious models, Leach washes away the peculiarity of structural analysis and demonstrates his allegiance to the functionalist approach. Leach is not the only Englishman who "naturalizes structuralism" (Banaji 1970:78), but he is joined in such an enterprise by R. Needham, who apparently has felt the compelling mission of spreading all over the corners of the world his misinterpretations of structuralism, and blindly insists on doing so. Banaji is absolutely correct in his claim that both Leach and Needham fall into the interpretative error of substituting ethnographic objects for the terms of the model (*Ibid.*:80).[8]

I am certainly not affected by such acute naïveté as to nourish the illusion that empiricist critics might one day see the "structuralist light." It is, however, certain that they would save much of their time (and my distinguished and angry critic, R. Needham, would spare himself further embarassment), were they at least to grasp the precise meaning and the coherence of the methodological principles of structuralism.

On the basis of my critique of the empiricist miscriticisms, I systematize the methodological principles of structuralism in the following propositions:

(a) Levi-Strauss' theory of kinship "is concerned exclusively with models and not with empirical realities" (Levi-Strauss 1969:49, n.3). Korn outrightly objects to the incomprehensibility of such a statement: "Models of what," she argues, "if they are not models of empirical reality?" (Korn 1973:143). As I have already stated, Levi-Strauss is concerned with models as heuristic devices or hypotheses about the structural principles of cultural phenomena. We need such models because the structural principles are usually visible in the observable dimensions of data only partially, due to the interferences of economic, demographic, and psychological factors with systemic tendencies (Levi-Strauss 1965:107). Since Levi-Strauss' ultimate concern is not with "empirical" reality but with the underlying systemic principles of reality, he can assert that the model ("mechanical" model that is) is more true than reality, or it has "a logical priority over its empirical applications" (*Ibid.*:16).

(b) Models are "hypotheses about the empirical structure of the system" (185). This statement should make one cautious against giving ontological status to models—as if they were sorts of mental structures encapsulated within cultural data, with the function of giving ultimate meaning and justification to their epiphenomenal appearances. Far from being a mentalist, Levi-Strauss keeps in close touch with empirical data. Structural models are research hypotheses which have the functions of orienting the attention of the anthropologists to scientifically relevant properties of empirical structures, and helping him to isolate contingent from structural properties.

(c) A structural model must be distinguished from a diagram (Levi-Strauss 1969:xxxiv, n.2)—the latter being a conceptual tool used to simplify the study of ethnographic reality (*Ibid.*:269, n.3). The aim of structural analysis is not to produce a simplified description of empirical data, but to use such simplifications to discover the systemic properties underlying the data.

(d) The mechanical model is not a capricious invention but it is isolated from ethnographic reality, "although not necessarily from an objective part of this reality" (*loc. cit.*). As I said above, the model is not a partial or simplified portrait of the observable aspects of the data, but an hypothesis about their underlying relational properties. Consequently, the formulation of models implies a "transition from a concrete distribution (of data), explicable in terms of geography and history" to a formal model, and vice versa. (*Ibid.*:397).

(e) Because of its formal nature, the model is rigid and not flexible like empirical reality, and it remains valid if what it loses in one direction is equaled by what it gains in another direction (*Ibid.*:193). The interaction between contingent factors gives a fluidity to the empirical occurrence of data—a fluidity which is by definition absent from the notion of constant relational properties.

(f) The correspondence of a mechanical model to empirical reality can be only partial and precarious (*Ibid.*:248). This is so because empirical data are the resultants of the interaction between contingent and structural factors, and mechanical models are hypotheses about structural factors.

Interaction Between Mechanical and Statistical Models

The crucial process in structural analysis is not the matching of models with raw empirical data—as the empiricist critics of Levi-Strauss argue—but the ability to distinguish the contingent from the structural dimensions of empirical systems. If structural hypotheses are not borne out in a repeated number of cases and there are no contingent reasons to account for such a failure, then we have to formulate new models. One could object that we can always invent contingent explanations or new types of models, so that structural models become irrefutable by definition. However, this objection loses much of its apparent cogency if we remember that the anthropologist must continuously justify his constructs in terms of empirical data, and he can propose more abstract conceptualizations only if they permit a better account of a given set of data or account for a larger set of data than is possible with already available concepts. Levi-Strauss explicitly recognizes that at times anthropological analysis is of a somewhat limited interest because of deficiencies in ethnographic documentations (1969:271). However, the lack of information on the empirical modalities of marriage systems is for Levi-Strauss an occasion to formulate hypotheses on their empirical structure (*Ibid.*:185). Levi-Strauss also states that new analytic procedures enable him to offer reinterpretations of data, and even to show the unreliability of previous documentary material (Levi-Strauss 1965:13).

I have previously stated that often the disagreement between Levi-Strauss and his critics is not about the adequacy of data but about their interpretation (see for instance, Levi-Strauss' account of his differences with R. Needham and Radcliffe-Brown in Levi-Strauss 1969:201, no.4; 219, n.3). In Korn's books one can find numerous examples of interpretations of data different from those proposed by Levi-Strauss. The position that disagreements in interpretation are often a function of the different theoretical perspectives brought to bear upon the data is well-documented by a recent essay of Levi-Strauss. In polemics with De Heusch, Levi-Strauss shows that the alleged exceptions to the notion of the atom of kinship mentioned by De Heusch do not have a foundation in the data but in De Heusch's forgetting that the structuralist is concerned with the relationships among the terms and not with the terms themselves (Levi-Strauss 1973).

Levi-Strauss admits the importance of empirical ethnography, but he rightly claims that we can make real progress in the study of kinship only through the combined study of mechanical models of marriage prohibitions, statistical models of marriage choices and terminological systems (1965:20). But can statistical and mathematical tools make a real contribution to structural analysis? Korn maintains that the various mathematical translations of marriage rules proposed by Weil, Kimen, Snell and Thompson, Bush, White, Courrège do not add anything to the ethnographic facts already known (1973:131), so she cannot find justification for Levi-Strauss' claim (1960:53) that they can "bring out properties not immediately apparent at the empirical level" (Korn:139). Actually, the French text of Levi-Strauss states that the aim is to make appear properties which are not immediately accessible to observation (Levi-Strauss 1958:99), and not to create or add facts. Rigorous statistical studies can help to formulate precise statistical models, which may show the presence of structural tendencies either in the manifest patterns of marriage choices or in significant exceptions to those patterns. However, the discovery of hidden properties is achieved through the formulation of mechanical models on the basis of observation and intuition. Since mechanical models are formulations of constant relational properties, they are similar to mathematical statements, and mathematical formulations are helpful to rigorously define relational properties, establish transformational rules and elaborate logical consequences or models which are relatable to empirical data.

These considerations lead us to conclude that there must be a continuous interaction between mechanical and statistical models. An example of such interaction is illustrated by Guiart in an article which has attracted Levi-Strauss' comments. Guiart reminds us that the cross-cousin marriage is a "model" and he quotes the following passage of Levi-Strauss: "Marriage classes are much less conceived of in extension, as groups of objectively designated individuals, than as a system of positions whose structure alone remains constant, and in which individuals may change position...provided that the relationships between them are maintained" (Levi-Strauss 1969:113). This is, of course, the structure that the mechanical model hypothesizes. Guiart indicates that structural models can be tested by deriving logical consequences from the model. If we find few cases of cross-cousin marriages in a society which has a terminological system built around these logical consequences, the model keeps the value of a provisional tool of demonstration (Guiart and Levi-Strauss 1969:81, 87). Both logical deductions from the model and statistical data are needed to test the model. The author goes on to say that it may well be that some of the concrete expressions of these logical consequences have not yet been discovered (*Ibid.*:87). This position is a reversal of the empiricist way of thinking. Statistical exceptions are not necessarily interpreted to mean a refutation of the hypothesis, but rather they can suggest new directions of research and refinement of the hypothesis. In this sense structural models have a great heuristic power.

Empirical, Formal and Structural Concepts

I conclude this chapter by locating Levi-Strauss' approach within the context of contemporary anthropological theory, since such a contextualization helps clarify the pioneer character of Levi-Strauss' approach. Manners and Kaplan criticize the empiricist inductive mode of theorizing because it goes against the practice of most anthropologists; in fact, theory plays a crucial role in the selection and formulation of the issues studied and in the determination of the kind of data one needs to collect (Manners and Kaplan 1969:6). These two authors make the important point that theories are never subject to direct confirmation or disconfirmation by direct and simple observation. In fact, theories are not empirical generalizations but abstract constructions which refer to the underlying similarities of observable properties. The connections between theory and generalizations is only conceptual so that we can subject to the test of observation only some consequences of a theory but not the theory itself (*Ibid.*:7). We have seen Guiart and Levi-Strauss concur with this methodological principle.

Many empiricist anthropologists seem to suffer from the error of misplaced concreteness which D. Willer and M. Webster lament in sociology. These two authors argue that sociologists are concerned with "empirical" rather than with "conceptual" explanations. Empirical explanations are based on "observables," i.e., concepts which are directly connected with sensory observations. Since they are based on observed empirical regularities, "observables" are concepts with a minimum degree of abstraction. And they lead to explanations in terms of previously occurred observables empirical relationships. On the contrary, conceptual explanations are propositions or laws relating theoretical constructs to each other. Such constructs—like status, structure, form—refer to abstract properties of the phenomena observed and apply to all possible cases and groups which fall under their scope. In other words, theoretical constructs are not constrained by any set of empirical instances since they are formulated on the basis of utility and simplicity. The connection of theoretical constructs to empirical data is not immediate and direct but it is determined through the formulation of logically derived observable consequences. It is the judgement of D. Willer and M. Webster that while the most exact sciences—like physics and chemistry—have developed conceptual explanations, sociology has suffered from a great opposition to theoretical constructs. In his opinion, such an opposition is responsible for the lack of cumulative sociological knowledge (1970:756). By and large, this criticism against sociological knowledge holds true for much of the theorizing which has prevailed in anthropology before the advent of structuralism.

I agree with Willer and Willer that there exists a qualitative difference between facts—which are by definition particular and contingent—and theories—which are by definition abstract and general. Consequently, it is inappropriate to maintain that theoretical propositions can be established by induction on the basis of empirical observations or that we can deductively explain empirical observations or that we can deductively explain empirical observations on the basis of theoretical propositions (1972:483-486). I agree with Manners and Kaplan that we explain facts if we subsume them under a set of theoretical statements, but this cannot always be rigorously done by deductive procedures or probabilistic statements, as Manners and Kaplan contend ought to be done (1969:8). To begin with, social phenomena are open and complex systems, and this is especially true of symbolic systems—where the free play of man's symbolic function is particularly important. Secondly, Kaplan and Manners are correct in stating that a theory should go beyond the observed facts and should direct the attention to new observations (*Ibid.*) This statement seems antithetical to Korn's epistemological attitude, and it is useful to characterize the heuristic power of Levi-Strauss' structural models. However, since mechanical models can predict empirical phenomena insofar as they are functions of structural properties, they cannot be used to make rigorous predictions about the occurrences of particular empirical events; in fact, we saw that empirical events are the resultants of the interaction between structural and contingent variables. Structural concepts can bring a great insight into the data we are already sensitized to, and they can also sensitize us to the possible existence of additional sets of data or to latent relationships existing among already known data. Appropriately, then, Levi-Strauss has substituted probabilistic and deductive statements with transformational predictions and permutational analysis.

Ultimately,there are two major criteria for determining the strength of a scientific approach: a careful definition of the phenomena investigated, and the formulation of effective criteria of prediction and validation. The novelty of structuralism consists in having selected as objects of investigation the symbolic codes of underlying cultural phenomena, rather than approaching cultural data as observable entities with quasi-physical properties. These symbolic codes can be understood only through a logical and semantic interpretation of their empirical manifestations. Barnes shows an inadequate understanding of these notions when he insists that Levi-Strauss' work suffers from a dichotomy or a presumably ambiguous conceptualization of the relationship between the world of thought and the world of action (Barnes 1971:153).

From a structural point of view it is preposterous to state that there is a dichotomy between a concern with thought (alliance theorists) and a concern with behaviour or social action (descent theorists). In reality, Levi-Strauss looks for cognitive designs underlying both thought and behavior, symbolism and action, since the human mind is the combinatory operator which mediates both.

The subject matter of anthropological analysis is to discover the combinatory logics underlying cultural phenomena, but combinatory logics cannot be directly observed. Consequently, structural explanations can be verified not through direct and immediate reference to empirical data but only by comparing alternative models of the logical structure of symbolic system. Willer and Willer propose a conception of scientific theorizing which is consistent with this notion of verification. If a theory is formulated by rational-mathematical extensions or the embracement of new concepts, it can be displaced or invalidated with the formulation of a more inclusive theory — that is, a theory applicable to a larger number of phenomena. A theory is related to data not in the sense that it is derived from or confirmed by data but in the sense that a theory orders and explains facts by comparing them to isomorphic theorectical models (Willer and Willer 1972:484-485). This conceptualization is particularly appropriate for structural explanations because they are based on the assumption that the natural, psychological, and socio-cultural levels of reality are isomorphically organized. This isomorphic view of reality provides the ontological foundation to the structural notion of verification (see Rossi 1973).

Ardener has proposed a notion of verification which is consistent with the views propounded here. According to Ardener, for structuralists "data" are "all symbolic systems" and the "objectivity" of a system is tested by contrasting it against "all other systems." A given system (or model of a system) is disproven when it is subsumed under another system. In Ardener's view, this procedure is analogous to the falsification procedure of the positivists (Ardener 1971:462) I, rather, consider such a view to be a more appropriate form of validation of symbolic explanations than the neopositivistic notion of falsification.

The epistemological and methodological views proposed in this chapter seem totally alien to Needham's way of thinking. Worse, Needham and other empiricist critics, including some of his pupils, do not understand the structural way of thinking — much less are they aware that the structural way of thinking has strong parallels in pioneer contemporary research trends in natural and physical sciences (see Levi-Strauss 1971, Rossi 1978). Gunter S. Stent, a microbiologist from Berkeley, has argued that recent neurological research gives a strong support to the structuralist rather than to the empiricist way of thinking and, in particular, it gives unequivocal credence to the notion of deep mental structures (Stent 1972, 1975); yet, my critic R. Cohen relegates this notion into the category of "mumbo jumbo" ideas (Cohen 1978).

Shortsightedness is the only valid — although hardly justifying — account for the repetitious miscritiques of Levi-Strauss' theory, of which Rodney Needham has been offering such a vociferous and indefatigable example. (See Levi-Strauss 1969: Passim in the footnotes; Ackerman 1976; de Ruijter 1978; Schneider 1965; Rossi 1978).

Notes

[1] In 1969 Levi-Strauss deemphasized the opposition "nature-culture" and stated that culture is better understood as a "synthetic duplication" of nature (1969:xxx).

[2] References with only page numbers are from *The Elementary Structure of Kinship,* (Levi-Strauss 1969).

[3] For an excellent discussion and comparison of the two theories see Schneider 1965.

[4] I came to this conclusion on the basis of a contextual reading of *The Elementary Structures of Kinship* the 1965 Huxley lecture. this interpretation has been supported and clarified by a Levi-Strauss letter to me, the gist of which I have published in *The American Anthropologist* (Rossi 1977).

[5] Korn was a pupil of Needham at Oxford, but she acknowledges also the helpful comments of E.R. Leach and P.G. Rivière.

[6] However, De Ruijter himself does not seem to fully appreciate the value of structural insights, as he expresses puzzlement (1978:468) at the equations I have published in *The American Anthropologist* (Rossi 1977).

[7] For a succinct and clear illustration of these two axioms see respectively chapter 2 and 7 of Levi-Strauss 1963.

[8] On the misinterpretation of Levi-Strauss' thought by "la Pensée Leacheènne," see the perceptive review of Leach's paperback on Levi-Strauss by Scholte and Simonis (1972).

References

Ackerman, Charles. 1976. "Omaha and -OMAHA-," *American Ethnologist* 3 (4):555-572.

Ardener, Edwin. 1971. "The New Anthropology and its Critics," *Man* 6 (3):449-467.

Banaji, Jairus. 1970. "The Crisis of British Anthropology," *New Left Review* 64:71-84.

Barnes, John Arundel. 1971. *Three Styles in the Study of Kinship.* (Berkeley: University of California Press).

Brumbaugh, Robert C. 1978. "Kinship Analysis: Methods, Results and the Siriono Demonstration Case," *Bijdragen Tot De Taal – Land – en Volkenkunde* 134 (1):1-29.

Buchler, Ira R. and Henry A. Selby. 1968. *Kinship and Social Organization.* (New York: Macmillan).

Cohen, Ronald. 1977. "The Emperor's Clothes: Review of a Review," *American Anthropologist* 79 (1):113-114.

Dan, Sperber. 1968. *"Le Structuralisme en Anthropologie"* in *Qu'est ce Que le Structuralisme?* ed. by O. Ducrot et al. (Paris: Du Seuil).

DeJosselin, De Jong, J.P.B. 1952. *Levi-Strauss' Theory of Kinship and Marriage.* (Leiden, Holland: Rejkemuseum Voor Volkendunen).

De Ruijter, A. 1978. "A Reconsideration Reconsidered," *Bijdragen Tot de Taal – Land – en Volkenkrunde* 134 (1):165-169.

Dumont, Louis. 1971. *Introduction a Deux Theories D'Anthropologie Sociale.* (Paris: Mouton).

Glaser, Barney G. and Anselm L. Strauss. 1971. *The Discovery of Grounded Theory.* (Chicago: Aldine).

Guiart, Jean and Claude Levi-Strauss. 1968. "Evenement et Scheme-Discussion," *L'Homme* 8 (1):80-87.

Holy, Ladislav. 1976. "Kin Groups: Structural Analysis and the Study of Behavior," *Annual review of Anthropology* 5:107-131.

Korn, Francis. 1973. *Elementary Structures Reconsidered: Levi-Strauss on Kinship.* (Berkeley: University of California Press).

Leach, Edmund R. 1954a. *Political systems of Highland Burma.* (Cambridge, Mass: Harvard University Press).

1954b. *Rethinking Anthropology.* (London: The Athlone Press).

Levi-Strauss, Claude. 1958. *Anthropologie Structurale.* (Paris: Plon).

1961. "Comment" to the "Classification of Double Descent Systems" by J. Goody, *Current Anthropology* 2 (1):3-25.

1963. *Structural Anthropology,* translated from the French by Claire Jacobson and Brooks Grundfest Schoepf. (New York: Basic Books).

1963a. "Intervista a Claude Levi-Strauss," *Aut Aut* 77:27-45.

1963b. "Responses à Quelque Questions," *Esprit* 322:628-653.

1965. "The Future of Kinship Studies," *Proceeding of the Royal Anthropological Institute.*

1969. *The Elementary Structures of Kinship.* Translated by J.H. Bell, J.R. von Sturmer under the editorship of Rodney Needham. (Boston: Beacon Press). (French original 1949).

1969a. *The Raw and the Cooked.* New York: Harper and Row). (French original 1964).

1971. L'Homme Nu. (Paris: Plon).

1973. "Reflexions sur L'atome de Parenté," *L'Homme* XIII (3):5-30.

Manners, Robert A. and David Kaplan (Eds.). 1969. *Theory in Anthropology: A Sourcebook.* (Chicago: Aldine).

Maybury-Lewis, D.H.P. 1960. "Parallel Descent and the Apinayé Anomaly," *Southwestern Journal of Anthropology* XVI:191-216.

Muller, Jean-Claude. 1973. "On Preferential Prescriptive Marriage and the Function of Kinship Systems: The Rukuba case (Benue-Plateau State, Nigeria)," *American Anthropologist* 75 (5):1563-1576.

Needham, Rodney. 1962. *Structure and Sentiment: A Test Case in Social Anthropology.* (Chicago: University of Chicago Press).

1971. "Introduction," in *Rethinking Kinship and Marriage,* ed. Rodney Needham. (London: Tavistock).

1974. *Remarks and Inventions: Skeptical Essays about Kinship.* (London: Tavistock).

1978. "Pronouncement vs. Competence," *American Anthropologist* 80 (2):386-387.

Rossi, Ino. 1973. "Verification in Anthropology: The Case of Structural Analysis," *Journal of Symbolic Anthropology* n.2 (September), 27-56.

1973a. "The Unconscious in the Anthropology of Levi-Strauss," *American Anthropologist* 75 (1):20-48.

1974. *The Unconscious in Culture: The Structuralism of Claude Levi-Strauss in Perspective,* ed. Ino Rossi. (New York: Dutton).

1977. "Reply to Cohen," *American Anthropologist* 79 (1):114-115.

1978. "On Theoretical and Technical Incompetence: The Case of Needham," *American Anthropologist* 80 (3): 675-676.

1978. "Toward the Unification of Scientific Explanation: Evidence from Biological, Linguistic and Cultural Universals," in *Discourse and Inference in Cognitive Anthropology: an Approach to Psychic Unity and Enculturation,* edited by M.D. Loflin and J. Silverberg (The Hague:Mouton Publishers), pp 199-280.

Forthcoming. *From the Sociology of Symbols to the Sociology of Signs.* N.Y.: Columbia University Press.

Scheffler, Harold W. 1970. "The Elementary Structures of Kinship by Levi-Strauss," *American Anthropologist* 72 (2):251-268.

Schneider, David M. 1965. "Some Muddles in the Models: Or, How the System Really Works," in *The Relevance of Models for Social Anthropology,* Bantom Michael, (ed.) (New York:Praeger).

Scholte, Bob and Yvan Simonis. 1972. "Levi-Strauss and La Pensee Leacheenne," *Semiotica* 6:289:293.

Stent, Gunther G. 1972. "Cellular Communication," in *Communication,* (Chicago:Freeman).

1975. "Limits to the Scientific Understanding of Man," *Science* 187 (21 March):1052-1057.

Van Der Leeden, A.C. 1971. "Empiricism and Logical Order in Anthropological Structuralism," *Bijdragen Tot De Taal—Land-en Volkenkunde* 127 (1):15-38.

Willer, David and Murray Webster, Jr. 1970. "Theoretical Concepts and Observables." *American Sociological Review* 35 (4):748-757.

Willer, David and Judith Willer. 1972. "Why Sociological Knowledge is not Cumulative: A Reply to Professor Freese," *American Sociological Review* 37 (4):483-487.

4
Transformational Processes and Models: with Special Reference to Mayo Indian Myth and Ritual

N. Ross Crumrine

Continued growth of structural analysis in anthropology presently is hampered by the problem of verification or evaluation of structural models. For our purposes, verification demonstrates that a model reveals predictive or explanatory powers when external data, either historic or ethnographic, are presented. By opening structural analysis to diachronic testing, a means of verification is generated. Based upon a recent version of "Goldilocks and the Three Bears," Eugene Hammel's (1972) synchronic analysis is verified through an examination of the transformations in earlier variant tales, which he shows led towards the modern balanced model. Developing his point, I refer to transformation in a broad sense as a modification from one state to another, rather than in the narrow linguistic meaning of the term. Structural transformational methods whose promise in the analysis of a broad range of subject matters, from the work of Jean Piaget (see 1968) in psychology and of Pierre and Elli Maranda (see 1971) in the analysis of oral narratives to the numerous transformational linguistic analyses by Chomsky, Bach, Katz, Harris, Rosenbaum, and many others. In order to restrict this discussion, I shall focus upon a specific body of data and upon a restricted set of three structural models as developed by Claude Levi-Strauss.

The data are based upon research in Northwest Mexico on Mayo myths and rituals. One Mayo myth refers to the transformation from death to life in a pot, and the structural analysis predicts that Mayos actually buried their dead in pots in the prehistoric past. Mayo cosmology and ritual is organized in terms of a folk model, the "Holy Family." A more general structural model shows predictive and explanatory powers by revealing the broad parameters of the "Holy Family" model throughout Mayo ritual and myth, and by clarifying changes in the Mayo kinship system. The analysis of stability and change in cultural systems, and the development of transformational structural models which explain or predict the dynamic behaviour of groups of individuals participating in such systems, provide the theme of this chapter. In examining three structural models of interrelated transformations, the argument commences with the origin of the most simple formulations of logical relations, metaphorical and oppositional thought processes which characterize the transition to humanity. The analysis proceeds to a geometric model of logical relations and to a final semi-mathematical statement of the relations. In these transformations to the more analytical model, the logical power revealed in each model provides a symbolic means of describing more complex cultural transformations. Thus our verification procedures become both deductive and empirical; deductive in regard to the logical transformations integrating the three models, and empirical and inductive in regard to the ethnographic data.

The Transformation To Culture

Following suggestions by Levi-Strauss (1936b) and others, how may we analyse and verify the first and most general set of transformations—transformations from pre-human to human mind and to symbolic systems? First Levi-Strauss presents the mechanisms of this transformation from pre-human culture to human social and conceptual systems (Levi-Strauss 1963b, 1969). Then he develops and analyses the structure of this conceptual mechanism in the achievement of thinking, of humanity (Levi-Strauss 1966a). Finally he demonstrates relations between specific types of social segmentation and the coding of this transformation (Levi-Strauss 1969). First, primordial or autochthonous unity is broken into a segmented system. Then this segmented conceptual system finds an application in the classification of social units or segments. To test Levi-Strauss's structural model we turn to a Mayo myth in which many of the logical processes and relations presented by Levi-Strauss are replicated.

Mayo beliefs and practices regarding death and the cult of the dead play a crucial and important role in the Mayo view of the world, and in family and pueblo integration (see Crumrine 1968a, 1974b, 1977a). Mayo rituals in the home patio and the church-cemetery area, the church patio, establish Mayo ethnic identity as well as provide explanations of human existence. At death, Mayos rest in their home patio for a night's wake, are carried to the local church for a religious service, and are buried in the cemetery near the church. Eight days and one year after death, the family gives a ceremony in its home in honour of the deceased. Although modern burial takes place in a cemetery, Mayos still place a wooden cross in their house patio, especially at the time of a wake or during Lent, the time of Christ's death and funeral. Also, Mayos still use a large red or green pot (*tina*) for household water storage. "Yes, we have dead here." This Mayo response when questioned about the *tina* indicates a relationship between the household water pot and their ancestors. The following myth, collected from two different individuals, unifies these details.

> ...God made all the world... He is the creator of humanity just like the father is the creator of His Son. But there is also death ... God, El Señor, formed it to teach man ... Then El Señor said, "Good, but man shall not die but be reformed. The reforming shall be in a *tina*." El Señor made it in order to produce reformation. The woman who was watching El Señor opened the *tina*. She wanted to see inside. There was an old man, an ancient one. He was inside for the renewal of his body. From this old man the power of God was producing a child. This was the renovation through the power of El Señor. But because the woman looked, because she saw the meat of his body, the ancient one died forever. No human had the power to look into the pot ... The old one said, "kill me." They killed him and cut up the bones and the flesh and put it in the pot in order to produce a little boy. If the old person was a woman the child would be a female. But the daughter-in-law of El Señor saw the bones, the meat in the pot. This pained El Señor because humanity did not respect the *tina*. Thus man dies forever.

With a few exceptions, the other version parallels the above, and the time period required for rebirth is fixed at nine months.

By transforming old people into infants, the synchronic transformational structure of the myth provides a means of resolving the life/death opposition, which according to Mayos was established by God to educate man. In achieving this transformation the myth utilizes a powerful metaphor, the transformational pot, coupled with the powers of structural liminality. A unity, the old man, is literally torn apart, passes nine months in liminality inside the pot, and is reconstituted as a new unit, a little child, due to the powers of God. The pot, a bipolar symbol (Turner 1967:28), provides a metaphor for the human uterus at the orectic pole and for liminality of "inbetweenness" at the ideological pole. Contrasting with the role of the pot as metaphoral operator, the myth represents a means of opening up the opposition and creating a productive structural liminality between the two terms of the opposition. The transformation is achieved by spreading the opposition over nine months of liminality and accomplishing it within a liminal secret metaphorical uterus or a pre-uterus. Even though the regeneration pot is lost, the myth still provides a possible but not actual solution to the life/death dilemma. Hinting that if man respects God, other solutions to the problem of death could be found, the myth structure suggests that these solutions will involve the creative application of liminality. In summary, metaphor, opposition, and structural liminality provide the myth with its transformational power and suggest to the analyst the logical operators and relations which form the structure of myth. Beyond the synchronic transformation within the myth, a diachronic transformation is also involved, as the pot today is lost. This result establishes modern death as opposed to regeneration and will be discussed later.

For the original problem of the transformation to humanity, the Mayo pot myth proves extremely enlightening. The same logical operators—metaphors and opposition—which characterize the relations between terms in the Mayo myth, also characterise these relations in "totemic" systems, as discussed by Levi-Strauss (1963b). He argues that the origin of thought is rooted in the transformation from nature to culture and in the co-occurrence of the nature/culture opposition. The first structural model, dealing with transformation to humanity represents one term or series of terms as related to a second term or series. The relationship is oppositional or metaphorical and the terms are drawn from nature and from culture—for example, death (nature) and life (culture) in the pot myth. In the Mayo All Saints ritual, a series of known ancestors are related to a series of Mayo families through the gifts of food, candles, flowers, water, fire-crackers, and prayers. On the night of 1st November, in front of the family and beside the graves, the Mayo lay minister prays for the dead, calling each by name. In the Mayo pot myth, the chopping up of the old man created the original diminished totality, or discontinuity, while the loss of the pot produced the original ancestors. Structured like a "totemic" system, groups of Mayo ancestors are opposed as families are opposed. The two series which were mediated in the past by the resurrection pot are mediated today by food, flowers, water, candles, and prayers (see Fig. 1).

At this point it is worth comparing and contrasting the transformation from nature to culture and the nature/culture opposition in terms of the roles played by "totemism" (Levi-Strauss 1963b, 1967) and the pot as metaphorical and oppositional operators (see Figure 2).

The pot, a metaphor for the uterus and natural birth, is opposed to the natural process which results in permanent death. Also, the pot—a metaphor for the cultural process of regeneration—is opposed to life in the killing and cutting up of the old man. "Totemic" compassion, according to Levi-Strauss, plays a similar type of mediating role between unity and multiplicity. But the pot, an original unity, has been lost and today has been broken into the multiplicity of ancestors (see Section 3).

The pot myth itself also suggests another interesting transformation.

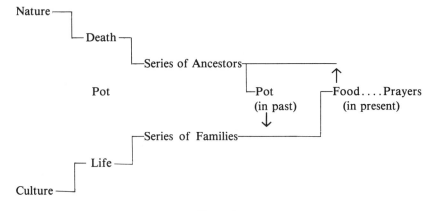

Figure 1

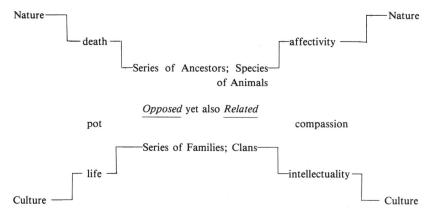

Figure 2

Today it operates as a metaphor for a hypothesized ancient custom and belief. Acting as a metonym, the pot, a cultural item, actually had replaced the natural uterus in Mayo thought, and ancient Mayos believed that deceased old people should be placed in a pot in order to be reborn as children. The myth explains the shift from metonymical to metaphorical function of the pot symbol. Thus we may generate the following hypothesis. The diachronic transformational structure of the pot myth suggests a shift from an ancient metonymical to a modern metaphorical funtion of the pot symbol. If this is true, then Mayos—or at least, some Mayos—must have actually buried their dead, or at least some of their dead, in pots, believing that they would be reborn as little children. Also, as if symbolizing this diachronic transformation, an invented relationship exists between the present belief that an old person resurrects in a child of the opposite sex (see Beals 1945:67, 73) and the myth in which an old man resurrects in a male child. Simply, we predict, archaeological research will show that Mayos buried their dead in burial pots. Unfortunately, there is little good archaeological material for the Mayo River valley; however, supporting evidence does exist (see Crumrine 1974:280, Edkolm 1942, Kelly 1938, Meighan 1971, 1974, Pailes 1972 and Robertson 1964:220).

An additional aspect of the diachronic transformational structure of the pot myth proves extremely interesting. The problem of the opposition of life and death was resolved in the past through metonym and belief in a resurrection pot. Natural death was transformed into a cultural cyclical process. Today the pot has been lost, replaced by a natural organ, the uterus, and the metonymical relation transformed into a metaphorical one. The original myth, now lost, must have explained the reason for pot burial and thus established the metonymical relation. A second, perhaps later, myth explained why the pots of time did not resurrect individuals, thus initiating the metaphorical relation. Finally, the present myth provides a metaphor on a second metaphor, and explains why the original metonymical relation was transformed into a metaphorical one. The crucial point here involves the shift away from the cultural pot to a natural process as the metaphorical and oppositional operators gain power and ability to exist separately from the myth. Losing the mediation between the life/death and the nature/culture opposition, death becomes permanent and birth natural. On the positive side the results of this mythical process prove useful and a series of ancestors are opposed and related to existing Mayo families. These results characterized by oppositional and metaphorical operators are homologous to the results of "totemic" systems, with the exception that families are replaced by clans, and groups of ancestors by animal species. On the negative side, the dynamic transformation throws the Mayo structure into imbalance. With the past loss of metonymical relations and the present loss of the regeneration pot, Mayo religious and logico-mythical systems are placed in jeopardy. Since both these Mayo systems are still dynamic aspects of the modern Mayo way of life, we may predict that a new mediator and a means of re-establishing metonymical and thus religious relations will be found as we examine additional Mayo ritual and mythology. Regarding this impasse and with the tools it had available, Mayo thought must have sought a solution in the form of new mediators or "saviours," who could open up liminality, incorporate and symbolize metaphorical relations, and mediate and transcend the life/death and culture/nature oppositions.

In summary, the "totemic" model, which generates and utilizes oppositional and metaphorical logical operations, proves useful in the analysis of the transformation to culture and to logical systems, however it will be incorporated into the following geometric and analytical models. Opposition and metaphor provide the basic relations which the triangle of double oppositions and the permutational equation are constructed.

Explanation and Restricted Prediction: A Triangle of Double Oppositions

How may oppositional and metaphorical relations be utilized to construct a more comprehensive model, to open up the model? The simplest method involves the culture/nature opposition and the mediating resurrection pot. Instead of placing the pot on the line directly between culture and nature, which symbolizes its metaphorical and mediational relations to these two terms (N.——————mediator pot——————C.), it is shifted away from the opposition N./C., forming a triangle. This logical transformation symbolizes the pot's oppositional as well as its metaphorical relations with nature and with culture and produces a model in the form of a geometric figure, the triangle with the lines N.P., C.P., and N.C. of equal lengths. Although this geometric model proves to be too specific to be generally useful, nevertheless it indicates how oppositional and metaphorical relations may be utilized in the construction of a more general geometric model. The *nature/culture* opposition provides the horizontal axis, while the *unity (unelaborated)/multiplicity (elaborated)* opposition provides the vertical axis. The latter is dropped from the center of the former, with the upper end *multiplicity (elaborate)*—because of the *nature/culture* opposition—and the lower end *unity (unelaborated)*—due to the *lack* of opposition (see Fig. 3a).

In the model (Fig. 3a), two sets of oppositions are metaphorically related like the two series of oppositions which were metaphorically related in the regeneration pot and "totemic" systems discussed in the preceding section. The similarity exists in like processes of opposition, and the triangle model represents a simple logical transformation of the "totemic" model. Using this dual set of oppositions as the general model, a full range of relations between specific terms may be represented. For example, in the pot myth the relations between mother, father, and child are mediated by the resurrection pot, which may be added on a third dimension above the model of dual oppositions (see Fig. 3(b)). In the mythical past the pot replaced the Mother-Father-Child, the dual oppositions, and in this sense represents the resolution or mediation point of the geometric triangle. Thus, the third axis would be the diachronic one, with past time constructed as a tetrahedron on the present family triangle. On a more symbolic level, the pot's position proves to be a sacred one because its movement or opening violates its sacred and mediating powers. In summary, the pot myth provides an empirical basis drawn from the Mayo materials for the utilization of oppositional and metaphorical relations in the construction of a more general geometric model.

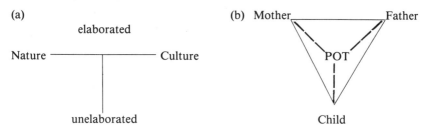

Figure 3

In his article "The Culinary Triangle," Levi-Strauss (1966b) generates this model in an abstract and generalized fashion by considering the early and crucial development of a dual oppositional logical structure within the realms of language and cooking. Rejecting any assumption of biogenic or ontogenetic development, we prefer a theory of the inheritance of broad learning abilities and of a universal "developed human nature" (see C. Geertz 1964 and R. Redfield 1957). Certain types of learning programs and kinds of logical relations seem more efficiently acquired by the unprogrammed yet genetically structured maturing infant's brain. Likely metaphorical parallels between sets of oppositions fit this pattern. On the other end of the spectrum, all societies face some similar kinds of problems and offer some similar kinds of solutions and satisfactions to members. Often the triangle of oppositional and metaphorical relations proves applicable at this level as well. In summary, we do not wish to imply that there is a direct necessary relation between transformatons which take place in the life of the individual and those which characterized man's becoming human or describe societal change. Yet contingent relations exist between these processes. Here the triangle of dual opposition appears as a basic structure in human learning, language, and culture, as well as a developmental transformation from the "totemic" model.

Using the double opposition *unelaborated vs. elaborated* and *culture vs. nature,* Levi-Strauss (1966b:93) generates a culinary triangle of raw, cooked and rotten. In terms of the Mayo materials, we have already demonstrated the powers of this general semantic field, the triangle of double oppositions, in its specific application to the analysis of the pot myth. Also, this structural model has a specific application in the Mayo folk model, "The Holy Family," the triangle of Father (God), Mother (Mary), and Child (Jesus Christ). This model outlines the typical Mayo family organization as well as the structure of Mayo myth and ritual (see Crumrine 1973, 1977a, 1980).

In order to verify this analysis based upon the dual opposition model, we shall examine a Mayo myth which deals with the origin of the "Holy Family" (see Appendix A). In summary, the myth or set of myths discuss the creation both of the world and of the "Holy Family." The dynamic role of Kaifas—which shifts from a friend, trickster, and imitator of God to that of an enemy—causes death and, by his opposition, assists in the appearance of the Holy Family, of fertility, and of language. In opposition to Kaifas' role, the role of Christ mediates life and death and sets in motion the cyclical aspect of the Holy Family metaphor: marriage, fertilization, birth, maturation, curing, death, and return or regeneration. The role of speech also proves crucial, because

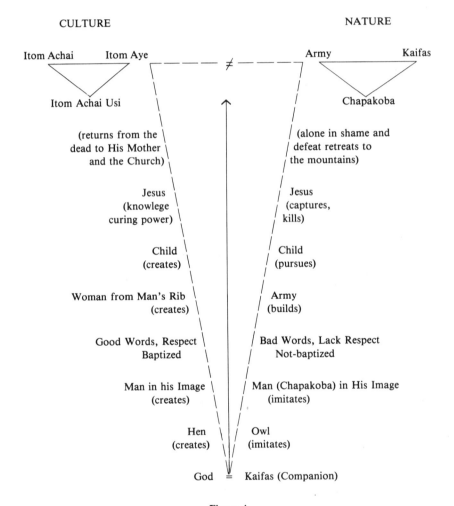

Figure 4

the Chapakobam do not speak. As speech separates human from animal, from Chapakobam, speech also separates small children from adults. Thus the development of opposition and of two enclaved opposed triangles provides the structure of the myth (see Fig. 4). The "Holy Family" is a productive mediation of *culture vs. nature,* whereas Kaifas' mediation is much too far on the *nature* side and only reproduces Kaifas. Kaifas attempts to destroy the "Holy Family" only to provide the ultimate and cyclical solution to the question of death, as Jesus returns triumphant from the dead on Easter Sunday and the Chapakobam are burned up by the power of God on Easter Saturday.

Before turning to its more general application, we should re-emphasize that the family triangle model has been derived in two ways. On one hand a semantic field may be constructed based upon two sets of oppositions: *nature-culture,* and *unelaborated-elaborated.* Then the relations between objects or actors are examined in terms of the model (see Levi-Strauss 1963b:16). Or, on the other hand, the raconteur may narrate the Mayo myth concerning the creation and development of the Holy Family. Actually we have combined both methods, permitting each to qualify and verify the other. The phenomenon has been defined in terms of two sets of oppositions, a table has been constructed in the form of the triangle of Figure 4, and the formation of the folk model has been analysed in terms of the table. The verification of the power of the model involves the testing for homologues in relations when different terms are placed at focal points in the table or model.

We predict that the types of relations between entities are the loci for homologues or at least closely parallel convergences. Suggesting that Mayo culture and society is being groomed in the direction of a dual oppositional model which can be seen as manifest at both folk and analytical levels, absorbs a great deal of the apparently contingent data which we do not have time to present in this chapter (see Crumrine 1977a and 1980). At certain levels this folk model symbolizes Mayo ethnic identity, and thus opposes the Mayo way of life against that of mestizo Mexico. At other levels it permits Mayos, enclaved in modern Mexico, to adapt ideologically to sociocultural changes and losses completely beyond their own control. Homologues in terms and especially relations exist between the structural model and the family organization. The homologues in relations also are extended to natural and supernatural realms: the sun (Itom Achai, Our Father), the moon (Itom Aye, Our Mother), the stars (Ili Usim, Little Children); the forest old man (huya o ola, old man of the forest), the forest old woman, and the animals (their children); the old man of the sea, the old woman of the sea, and the fish (their children). The term Itom Achai (Our Father) refers to God the Father, the Sun, the Cross, all male Images, and the Holy Trinity. Itom Aye (Our Mother) includes all the female Images, the several Images of the Virgin Mary, the Church, the Holy Spirit, the Moon, and some aspects of the Earth. Itom Achai Usi (The Son) refers to Jesus Christ and, as Children of God, all the Saints' Images. In summary, this model of the "Holy Family" (Sagrada Familia, Utes Yo oriwa) provides (1) the structure for a series of ceremonials which integrate Mayos, as well as (2) the structure for the individual Mayo family and for the Mayo concept of the organization of the natural and supernatural worlds. Also the model proves useful in understanding and predicting changes taking place in the Mayo kinship, social, and ceremonial systems (for full evidence and discussion of these points see Crumrine 1968a, 1969, 1977a and 1980).

Thus both logical and empirical arguments present dual oppositional relations as contributing variables in the transition from nature to culture, from animal to man, and from Mayo tribal society to a modern enclaved group. The power of the analytical model as well as its concrete manifestation in Mayo thought is verified by its predictive and explanatory success. Constructed upon metaphorical and oppositional relations, this double opposition which generates the triangular model provides the basis for the third and most general and complex formulation, a semi-mathematical model of the transformation from prehumanity to humanity.

General Prediction: Reduction of Unity

Beyond two or three dimensions the triangle of oppositions becomes difficult to manage. Concerning the use of geometric models, Levi-Strauss (1963a:219) warns "that multi-dimensional frames of reference are often ignored or are naively replaced by two- or three-dimensional ones." In his analysis of myth, Levi-Strauss (1963a:228) generates a third model:

$$F_x(a) : F_y(b) :: F_x(b) : F_{a-1}(y)$$

In this transformational and permutational model, the actor (a) is transformed into a^{-1} and becomes the functon of (y), and (b) acts as mediator. Thus this model represents a logical transformation of the triangle of dual oppositions with "a" opposed to "a^{-1}" as the base of the triangle and "b" as the peak, because the opposition of "b" to "a" is a metaphor of its opposition to "a^{-1}". However the two functions "x" and "y" and the transformation from "a" to "F_{a-1}" have been added, yielding a model with multi-dimensional relations and transformational permutational powers. The transformational theme in the Mayo pot myth presents an opportunity to test the predictive powers and to exemplify the meaning of the model. In terms of the model, the following relationship is produced:

$$F_{death}(\text{old man}) : F_{line}(\text{pot}) :: F_{death}(\text{pot}) : F_{child}(\text{life})$$

The old age and death of the old man is to the regeneration or life-giving powers of the pot as the chopped up bones and flesh, the death, of the old man is to the regenerated, reborn child carrying the implication of eternal life. Thus the structure of the myth mediates the life/death opposition by replacing it with a transformation process driven by the pot metaphor and the liminal state which it symbolizes. The Marandas (1962 and 1971:36-37) also clearly present this transformational power embodied in the model.

In Section 1 of this paper, we suggested that the pot myth is in structural imbalance and hypothesized that Mayo thought must have sought another mediator, or kind of "saviour," and a new means of re-establishing structural balance, the "gain" or "victory" as expressed by the Marandas. If we substitute Jesus Christ for the pot this prediction is verified. Jesus, part-man part-God, in his resurrection from the dead, mediates the life/death opposition. Thus he represents a very powerful mediating symbol and actor.

$$F_{death}(\text{old man}) : F_{live}(\text{Jesus}) :: F_{death}(\text{Jesus}) : F_{child \text{ or humanity}}(\text{life})$$

Like the resurrection pot, the life, death, and resurrection of Jesus Christ yields eternal life for mankind. Also in both cases the same restriction holds: humans must respect God. Lent, the crucial liminal period in Jesus's assumption of mediating powers, is the most intense period of ritual activities for Mayos. Besides church center ceremonies, all-night home ceremonies take place most nights of Lent and several run concurrently during the week just preceding Holy Week, when Jesus is portrayed as an old man (see Crumrine 1968a, 1974b and 1977b). Thus Mayos re-enact the process of solving the life/death opposition each Easter season. The possibility of equating Jesus and the resurrection pot, as suggested in the model presented above, in part suggests why the Jesuit missionaries appeared to have had little trouble converting Mayos and why the figure of Jesus Christ remains focal in modern Mayo ritual—in spite of the fact that the Jesuit missionaries were removed from Mayo country in the 1770s and the area has not been missionized since (see Crumrine 1977a). Thus history, culture-change and structure converge.

The high explanatory and predictive power of this transformational model is embodied in its processual nature. In applying the model to our original problem, the structure of the transformation to man reveals a permutational form in which (b), the mediating term represents *compassion*.

$$f_{affective}(\text{Nature})(\text{animal}) : f_{intellectual}(b) :: f_{human \text{ culture}}(\text{intellect})$$

Also, a process of reduction, in which a whole is reduced to parts and one or more parts removed, is involved in the transformation to humanity. As models Levi-Strauss (1969a:52-55) discusses in Ojibwa,

Tikopia, and Bororo myth, while we add a Mayo example. In the Ojibwa case, a unity of six masked Ojibwa Gods is broken, reduced. In the Tikopia myth, a unity, or an indeterminate number of foodstuffs is diminished when a strange Tikopia God, Tikarau, steals all but four foodstuffs. In two Bororo myths a hero of the Cera moiety kills a population of "ghosts" bringing gifts which were shared out unequally among the clans. Thus an original continuity was broken by radical elimination, and a hierarchy in clan organization established. In the Mayo myth, quoted in Appendix A, a unity—the first man—is broken and a part of his rib is used to create the first woman. Although this myth is not indicative of a totemic system, we are concerned at this point with mediation and the mythical transition from continuous to discrete quantity. The Mayo myth solves the logical problem in a somewhat different manner than the other myths. A non-productive unity (Adam) is put into a sleep-like, death-like state and cut open by God. The original unity is broken and a part removed. From this part a fertile duality, and ultimately a multiplicity, is formed. Like the other myths, the Mayo one solves the logical problem and at the same time provides useful categories to distinguish several dual social groupings: male-female, old-young, and Mayo-mestizo. Interestingly, the units created in the myth are not equal in the sense that Adam represented the original unity, yet on the other hand, after the creation, he lacks a rib. Nor are the Mayo social categories equal, with males and the old being more powerful than females and the young. In terms of the structure, Mayos should be more powerful than mestizos, which Mayos in part believe and certainly would like to believe completely, while in fact mestizos control the economic and political systems.

The permutational model draws out and clarifies the oppositional and transformational processes embodied in this set of myths. In terms of this model, we now understand how these myths conceptualize the logico-symbolic transformations involved in the origin of human society (Fig. #5.2 represents the Ojibwa myth, 5.3 the Tikopia one, 5.4 the Boroto ones, 5.5 the Mayo one, 5.6 a general statement of the preceding four, and 5.7 a geometric illustration of the unfolding permutational transformational power, showing the two fixed end terms and the expanding mediating terms of the center).

In summary, our analysis suggests that the process of reduction is a specific type of permutational structure. The myths presented contain the structure as predicted by Levi-Strauss's original equation. In this set of equations the "x" function is negative and is either specifically death or symbolic of death; masked and unmasked (causing death), stranger and falling (symbolic of death), ghosts and killed, and Adam without fertility or the ability to live and produce life and asleep (a death-like state). The "y" element is either life or symbolic of life, such as running, bringing, or living (awake). The "b" element provides the mediator: the

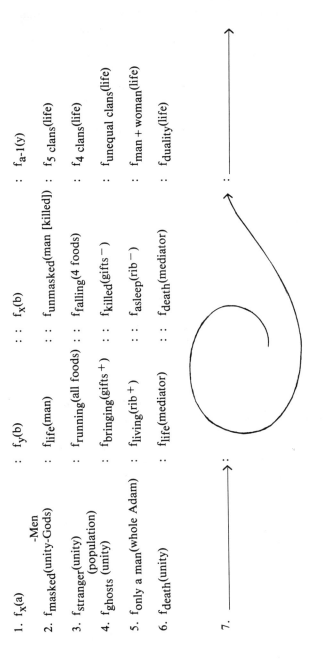

1. $f_x(a)$: $f_y(b)$: : $f_x(b)$: $f_{a-1}(y)$

2. f_{masked}(unity-Gods) -Men : f_{life}(man) : : $f_{unmasked}$(man [killed]) : f_5 clans(life)

3. $f_{stranger}$(unity) (population) : $f_{running}$(all foods) : : $f_{falling}$(4 foods) : f_4 clans(life)

4. f_{ghosts} (unity) : $f_{bringing}$(gifts$^+$) : : f_{killed}(gifts$^-$) : $f_{unequal\ clans}$(life)

5. $f_{only\ a\ man}$(whole Adam) : f_{living}(rib$^+$) : : f_{asleep}(rib$^-$) : $f_{man\ +\ woman}$(life)

6. f_{death}(unity) : f_{life}(mediator) : : f_{death}(mediator) : $f_{duality}$(life)

7. ⟶ : : ⟶ : :

Figure 5

man who is killed by the glance of the unmasked god, all foods which are reduced to four, gifts and the rib which are both given and taken depending upon the positive or negative nature of the defining function. The center terms of this processual model reveal the positive and then negative role of the mediator and the resulting permutational transformation, while the last term shows the completed transformation.

On the basis of this model and as a conclusion to a monograph on the Mayo Indians (Crumrine 1977a) written previous to the Fall of 1972, I hypothesized a pattern of future revitalization movements in the Mayo River Valley. Indeed, the prediction proved accurate and the latest movement appeared in November, 1972. At the cult center a new Mayo church was constructed of adobe brick completely by volunteer labour and small donations. By a stroke of good fortune, I was in the Mayo Valley and was able to observe the development of this new Mayo religious cult (see Crumrine 1975). Thus the permutational transformational model reveals predictive value at the socio-ritual level.

Conclusions

We have briefly examined transformation as a general symbolization process. The original transformation from animal to man, from nature to culture, would seem to have involved a capacity for compassion resulting in the appearance of metaphorical and binary oppositional logical tools or forms of discursive thought. Building upon the original transformation, double sets of oppositions metaphorically related generate a triangular semantic space which proves useful at a second more general level of analysis. At the most general level of permutational paradigmatic structure, the transformation to humanity is shown to characterize other transformations both at the levels of myth, society, and the individual. Inverted symmetry (mirror images), generation, and reduction processes also play an important part in these transformations. Running through all these transformations at one or several levels is the drive to mediate and make useful and meaningful the problem of *unity* vs. *diversity* and of *death* vs. *life*.

Finally, in regard to verification, how may we satisfy ourselves that we are discussing general ritual symbolic processes and not a set of idiosyncratic thoughts? What is to count as evidence of verification? Having recently returned from field research, I am again impressed by the complexity of the field situation. At this point one seeks any heuristic or model which reveals new relationships, patterns, and means of ordering the field data which in themselves represent organized observation or relevant parts of a way of life. Structural analysis should generate insights concerning the relations and patterns within a way of life and perhaps also across ways of life. On the other hand, when research serves the model, then at this point we must deny the reality of a connection between the model and social reality and return to the way of life as the basic anthropological fact (see Crumrine, 1968b). as previously argued (see Crumrine, 1968b:45, and Leach 1973:81), form and meaning must be treated as a unit. The criticism of formalism or form without content is, as Erik Schwimmer (1974:260) notes, "always a danger." The rather complex discussions of the Mayo materials have been presented in part as a response to his suggestion (Schwimmer 1974:360) that, "it would be helpful if the authors (Crumrine and Macklin 1974) reported more fully on concrete details and specific symbols occurring in rituals and myths as it is here that we find the raw materials of symbolic thought." In this chapter, it has not been our aim to concentrate "on generalities and ignore particulars" (Leach, 1973:82), but to discuss a pattern which appears rather broadspread and can be stated and examined in terms of a general model which incorporates two other somewhat simpler models. Only through continued dialogue focusing upon the application of models and new revelations achieved through their use may we show the value of one or another structural analysis. This is the importance of a dialogue such as the incipient one between the Marandas (1962, 1971) and Leach (1973), and further examination of Marandas' structures and methods in terms of the Mayo materials.

With these suggestions in mind, let us return to the theme of this inquiry, the verification of the structural analysis of human transformations. First, we have pointed toward similar transformational structures which emphasize the key roles played by metaphor, opposition, reduction, mediation, and mediator. Additional study of these functions in specific transformational processes should prove very interesting.

Second, we must broaden our sampling, bringing additional mythical and ritual systems to bear upon the general models discussed in this chapter. This additional empirical material would either (l) pattern in terms of the transformational models already developed, (2) suggest modifications in the formulations, or (3) provide the basis for a re-evaluation or total rejection of the paradigmatic approach to ritual symbolic transformation.

Third, study of the transformational mechanisms involved as the individual learns the meaning of a myth, a ritual, or takes part in a revitalization movement provides another method of evaluating the paradigmatic permutational model (see Anthony Wallace, 1966:289-342, in regard to the "ritual learning process" and Jonathan Cowan, 1975, in regard to "state/context dependent retrieval").

Fourth, the transformational models suggested here may be evaluated by their success or failure in the prediction of the future behaviour of transformations in cultural systems. Thus the value of a model depends upon this ability to organize wholistic data which reflect differing ways of life, so that new relationships with predictive powers are discovered. Through continued analysis of stability and change in cultural systems and the development of transformational models which predict the dynamic behaviour of such systems, we have a means of evaluating the models and formulations developed in this chapter.

Appendix A:
Myth of Origin
Of "Holy Family"

(Where did the Chapakobam live? Aren't there stories about them?) It is a custom, they imitate what happened with Itom Achai (Our Father, God). They imitate the time when Jesus appeared and the Pilatos killed him. (But what do the Chapakobam signify and why the masks? Why do they have this form?) They require it because they have paint. They paint themselves on their body with red paint which symbolized the blood of Christ. (But I still do not understand why they need the masks?)

A long time ago in that time they were like Kaifas. And Kaifas was truly very hairy. Kaifas, when Our Lord was taken prisoner, when they took him prisoner in order to kill him, Kaifas was truly very bearded, very hairy. The masks are like this, are an imitation of this beardedness. (I do not know anything about Kaifas?) Kaifas is God's opposite, contrary. He is God's enemy. (He isn't the Devil?) Exactly, he is the Devil. Kaifas is not baptized, not a Christian, he is the Devil, Lucifer. (And does he have soldiers?) Certainly, he has soldiers. (Are the Pariseros and the Chapakobam in his army?) Certainly. (Today where is Kaifas?) Today Kaifas is ashamed because Our Lord arose from the dead at Gloria in such a manner giving life to sinners. Kaifas has retreated to the forest. His soldiers have been killed, are dead, but Kaifas still lives. (Is it possible to see Kaifas in the forest?) Of course... Kaifas is the Devil, he is dangerous, bad. He does bad things. He tries to gain, to win, good men. It's diabolical... The Chapakobam (Pariserom) imitate the story of Itom Achai (God, of his death, burial, and resurrection. In the end they ask the pardon of Itom Achai. They make the ceremony of Itom Achai. They do the passion of Itom Achai.

[One year later.] (When I was here last year you told me about an enemy of God. His name was Kaifas. But I still do not know who Kaifas was?) There are two roads, a good one and a bad one. God takes the good road, and Kaifas takes the bad one. (A long time ago, were Itom Achai and Kaifas friends?)

In that time when this world commenced, Itom Achai began to make hens and all the other things which exist. God made things correctly. The very close, very intimate, friend of Itom Achai, Kaifas began to imitate God. Kaifas began to imitate God. When El Señor (God) made the hen, the hen saw the world and liked the world. The hen was happy, gay, because El Señor gave the hen breath. And Lucifer, this Kaifas, also began to make a hen. This hen he made of clay (*barro*). In clay Kaifas began to make a hen. Instead of a good hen coming out a *tecolote* (owl) came out. Kaifas made an (mu⁷u, Mayo). Kaifas imitated El Señor. But this was not yet the sin which Kaifas was going to commit against El Señor. This wasn't much. Nothing much because Kaifas had equal power with El Señor. He controlled equal power to that of God. Kaifas was able to use the power, but he used it for bad purposes, for evil. And El Señor made the light of day and saw everything was good. In the light of day everything was good. People, men, he made. Because He foresaw them, saw that they were going to live in the world. Kaifas also made men, people. But the people Kaifas created were just like, were similar to him. They were equal to Kaifas. (That is to say they were the Chapakobam, the Pariserom). When Kaifas made men, they came out equal to him, that is bad. To turn to the understanding of the Good and the Bad. The Bad is to act in excess. Many, many of the men, especially those of Kaifas, wouldn't do because a man needs to have respect, value for all other people. One can sin with on- ly a few words when they are about another. This danger converges in the tongue, the mouth, when a person talks of another. This is very bad, dangerous. Because to speak much about people who are not at fault, that is to say, to speak badly of a person is a sin which God will not pardon...

[A second Mayo man continues.] But we are all of the same family. Along with Christ, we are all descendents of God. We speak dif- ferent languages but He understands them all and hears everyone everywhere, even though many may be speaking at the same time. Yet we are all brothers. This according to the holy scriptures.

But also when Itom Achai formed man, He used clay. But He created only a man. Then the man fell into a sleep-like state and God removed a rib. He used the rib to form the first woman. Thus we lack a rib. The rib which Itom Achai used to form the woman.

The material in parenthesis are questions which I put to the Mayo man with whom I was talking. At least two separate discussions are included, which I have placed together.

References

Beals, Ralph, L. 1945. *The contemporary culture of the Cahita Indians.* Bureau of American Ethnology, Bulletin 142.

Cowan, Jonathan. 1975. "A Lesson from Don Juan About State Dependent Learning?" *Medical Anthropology Newsletter* 6(3):10-12.

Crumrine, N. Ross. 1968a. The Easter Ceremonial in the Socio-cultural Identity of Mayos, Sonora, Mexico. University of Arizona: Ph.D. dissertation. Translated and published as *El Ceremonial de Pascua y la Identidad de los Mayos de Sonora,* 1974. Instituto Nacional Indigenista, Mexico.

1968b. "Anthropological antinomy: The importance of an empirical basis for a concept of anthropological fact." *Anthropological Quarterly* 41(1):34-46.

1969. "Capakoba, the Mayo Easter ceremonial impersonator: Explanation of ritual clowning." *Journal for the Scientific Study of Religion* 8(1):1-22.

1973. "La tierra te devorará": un analisis estructural de los mitos de los indigenas mayo. *Américan Indígena* 33(4):1119-1150.

1974a. "God's Daughter-in-Law, the Old Man, and the Olla: an Archaeological Challenge." *Kiva* 39(3-4):277-281.

1974b. "Anomalous Figures and Liminal Roles: A Reconsideration of the Mayo Indian Capakobam, Northwest Mexico." *Anthropos* 69:858-873.

1975. "A New Mayo Indian Religious Movement in Northwest Mexico," *Journal of Latin American Lore* 1(2):127-145.

1977a. *The Mayo Indians of Sonora, Mexico: A People who Refuse to Die.* Tucson: University of Arizona Press.

1977b. "El Ceremonial Pascual Mayo de Banari, Un Drama Ritual Sagrado," *Folklore Americano* 24:111-139.

1980. *The Mayo of southern Sonora, Mexico: Socio-economic assimilation and ritual-symbolic syncretism, split acculturation.* Anthropological Papers of the University of Arizona.

Crumrine, N. Ross and B. June Macklin. 1974. "Sacred Ritual vs. the Unconscious: The Efficacy of Symbols and Structure in North Mexican Folk Saints' Cults and General Ceremonialism. In: *The Unconscious in Culture: The Structuralism of Claude Levi-Strauss in Perspective,* edited by Ino Rossi, pp.179-197. New York: E.P. Dutton & Co., Inc.

Eckholm, Gordon F. 1942. *"Excavations at Guasave, Sinaloa, Mexico." Anthropological Papers of the American Museum of Natural History* 38(2).

Geertz, Clifford. 1964. "The transition to humanity," In *Horizons of Anthropology,* Sol Tax (ed.). Chicago: Aldine.

Hammel, Eugene A. 1972. "The Myth of Structural Analysis: Levi-Strauss and the Three Bears," Module 25, an Addison-Wesley Module On Anthropology. Reading, Mass.: Addison-Wesley Pub. Co.

Kelly, Isabel T. 1938. "Excavations at Chametla, Sinaloa," *Ibero-Americana 14.*

Leach, Edmund. 1973. "Plus royaliste que le roi," *Semiotica* 7(1):77-90.

Levi-Strauss, Claude. 1963a. "The structural study of myth," In *Structural Anthropology.* New York: Basic Books.

1963b. *Totemism.* Boston: Beacon Press.

1966a. *The savage mind. Chicago: University of Chicago Press.*

1966b. "The culinary triangle," New Society, December 22:937-940.

1967. "The story of Asdiwal," In E. Leach (ed.) *The Structural Study of Myth and Totemism.* Edinburgh: Tavistock Publications Ltd.

1969a. *The raw and the cooked.* New York: Harper and Row.

1969b. *The Elementary Structures of Kinship.* London: Eyre & Spottiswoode.

Maranda, Elli Kongas and Pierre Maranda. 1962. "Structural models in folklore," *Midwest Folklore* 12:133-192.

1971. *Structural models in folklore and transformational essays.* The Hague: Mouton.

Meighan, Clement W. 1971. Archaeology of Sinaloa. In *Archaeology of Northern Mesoamerica,* Part Two, edited by G. F. Elkholm and I. Bernal, pp.754-767. Handbook of Middle American Indians II. Austin: University of Texas Press.

1974. "Prehistory of West Mexico," *Science* 184:1254-1261.

Pailes, Richard A. 1972. An Archaeological Reconnaissance of Southern Sonora and Reconsideration of the Rio Sonora Culture. Ph.D. dissertation, Southern Illinois University, Carbondale, Illinois.

Piaget, Jean. 1968. *Structuralism.* Translated from the French, *Le structuralisme.* New York: Basic Books.

Redfield, Robert. 1957. "The universally human and the culturally variable," *Journal of General Education* 10:150-160.

Robertson, Thomas A. 1964. *A Southwestern Utopia: An American Colony in Mexico.* Los Angeles: The Ward Richie Press.

Schwimmer, Erik G. 1974. "Comments on the Essays of Part Two: The Practice of Structural Analysis," In *The Unconscious in Culture: The Structurism of Claude Levi-Strauss in Perspective,* edited by Ino Rossi, pp.179-197. New York: E. P. Dutton and Co. Inc.

Wallace, Anthrony F.C. 1966. *Religion: An anthropological view.* New York: Random House.

5
Verification in Structural Theory: A Linguist's Point of View

Harvey Rosenbaum

> We dance around in a ring and suppose
> While the Secret sits in the middle and knows.
>
> Robert Frost, "The Secret Sits"

By its very definition, basic theoretical research is practiced within a resource framework which makes the actual nature of the Secret indeterminable. That is, we can only determine if a proposed model or theory for some aspect of the universe is inadequate or incorrect; it is not presently in our power to 'know' that it is ultimately correct. This state of affairs renders the attempt to understand the universe through the utilization of scientifically constructed frameworks to being fundamentally a 'suppose' or 'if' activity. The crucial question which derives from the basic nature of this activity is, how can we determine if some proposed model or theory is one which we should currently hold to?

In the attempt to answer this question, a number of techniques and criteria have been created as part of the development of scientific inquiry. However, it is quite clear that there is no single technique or set of techniques which one can mechanically resort to in order to obtain an answer to this basic question. I take this state of affairs to be natural and expected given the above suggested relation between models or theories and 'secrets'. The intent of this chapter is to bring to bear on structural research in anthropology the specific orientation developed toward theory evaluation in the transformational-generative approach to language investigation. The close historical affinity between structural linguistics and structural anthropology is itself sufficient justification for such an attempt (e.g., Levi-Strauss 1963a, Jokobson 1957, Troubetzkoy 1969). Moreover, recent efforts by Piaget (1970) to place current research in anthropology, linguistics, and psychology in a common structuralist framework of the social sciences provides an intrinsic justification for this type of interdisciplinary effort.

The first part of this chapter presents a general discussion of theory evaluation centering around the notion of verification. Following this, there is a detailed illustration of how one would go about constructing a theoretical analysis of a small part of English grammar within the transformational-generative approach. This presentation is related to the earlier section on verification. The final section attempts to assess the potential for verification in the structural models of Levi-Strauss and El Guindi within the framework outlined in the earlier sections.

Theory Evaluation

This discussion of evaluation criteria is not intended to be comprehensive nor exhaustive. It should be understood as representing a general orientation toward a problem whose inherent properties are non-systematic for reasons suggested in the introductory paragraphs.

One of the more powerful organizing concepts in theory evaluation is that of verification. I take "verification" to be a loose cover term that refers to the various ways by which one can provide support for the "correctness" of some set of hypotheses which are claimed to explain or account for some set of real world data. I make a possibly arbitrary (but not new) distinction between two types of support or verification: internal and external. Internal support is in part a general quality of the set of hypotheses or theory. It should all hang together; or as de Saussure put it "tout se tient." The absence of internal contradiction is in principle the minimally acceptable requirement for any viable set of hypotheses. Thus it could be argued that internal consistency should not be considered as providing support. In reality, however, researchers will often work within a framework containing internal inconsistencies because there exists no viable alternative. The classic case is that of the wave-particle contradiction in physics which was resolved by quantum mechanics. There is also an important distinction to be made between the stage of theory development and a mature or final theory. During development, finding that an initial set of hypotheses productively integrate with new hypotheses proposed on the basis of previously unconsidered data can be considered to be support for both the initial and new set of hypotheses.

External support is a function of various discoverable modes by which our set of hypotheses can be shown to map (or not map) to existing, possible, or non-existing facts in the real world. Thus we provide external support for our set of hypotheses when we can show: (a) the hypotheses do indeed account for the set of data that they are intended to account for in an interesting and revealing way; (b) the hypotheses predict that certain data which can be shown to be relevant will not occur and these data do not in fact occur; (c) the hypotheses correctly predict the occurrence of all relevant data that do occur but were not part of the original set of data from which the hypotheses were originally formulated; (d) the hypotheses are able to satisfactorily resolve apparent contradictions whose existence was created by some previous set of hypotheses; (e) the hypotheses are able to bring into sufficient focus a set of problems to allow productive and insightful investigation. This list is intended to be illustrative, not exhaustive. External support appears to be a non-systematic phenomenon, largely determined by the type of hypotheses and the kind of data involved.

A general factor determining the ability to evaluate a set of hypotheses is their degree of explicitness and systematicity. Obviously, hypotheses so inarticulate as to be indeterminate in regards to inconsistency or vague about prediction can not be evaluated. I will not go into the other side of the coin, that of falsification or discrediting a set of hypotheses, except to note that (1) falsification can be both internal and external; (2) most of the modes of support can be stated negatively and used for falsification.

Linguistic Analysis and Argumentation

The purpose of this section is to illustrate in detail the approach by which the transformational linguist argues for the existence of specific categories, rules, and structures at various levels of abstraction. While the following discussion presupposes no specific knowledge of transformational theory, I will assume that the reader has at least a passing familiarity with the the transformational concepts of phrase structure or base rule, transformational rule, components of the grammar (i.e., phonology, syntax, and semantics), and the notions of deep and surface structure, as well as the notion of generative in the sense of explicitly define.[1]

Surface descriptions of the reflexive construction

For the most part, this investigation will be limited to a very small segment of the English grammar—that of the reflexive construction as illustrated by:

(1)   a. Mary shot herself.

b. They pinched themselves.
c. He saw himself in the mirror.
d. I know that he saw himself in the mirror.

There are a number of other ways that the reflexive can be used, such as emphatically, as in:

He, himself, told me.

or topically, as in:

As for myself, I will leave immediately.

This investigation will focus on the major use which is illustrated by the sentences in (1).[2]

The specific problem is to provide a precise characterization of the conditions under which we can and must use the reflexive construction in English. On comparing the sentences in (2) with their nearly identical counterparts in (1), we see by the sentences in (2) that the reflexive form is required if the noun or pronoun corresponding to the reflexive pronoun in (1) is meant to be interpreted as referring to the earlier noun or pronoun.[3]

(2)   a. *Mary$_i$shot Mary$_i$
      b. *They$_i$pinched them$_i$
      c. *John$_i$saw him$_i$in the mirror.
      d. *I knew that he$_i$saw him$_i$in the mirror.

On the other hand the ungrammatical sentences in (3) indicate that there are many environments in which the reflexive pronoun cannot occur.

(3)   a. *Herself shot Mary.
      b. *They pinched myself.
      c . (Mary saw John in the lobby.) *Himself was looking in the mirror.

These three sets of sentences suggest the following hypothesis, which I will call Hypothesis A:

Hypothesis A: reflexives occur if and only if: (1) they refer to an earlier noun or noun phrase, (2) both the reflexive and the earlier noun (phrase) are in the same sentence.

However, sentences like those in (4)

(4)   a. *I knew that he saw myself in the mirror.
      b. *Dick saw that himself was looking worse every day.

show that Hypothesis A is not correct, even though it does account for the grammaticality of the sentences in (1) and the unacceptability of the sentences in (2) and (3). We might attempt to account for the ungrammaticality of the sentences of (4) through the following revision of Hypothesis A:

Hypothesis A': reflexives occur if and only if: (1) they refer to an earlier noun (phrase), (2) both the reflexive and the earlier noun (phrase) immediately flank the same verb.

But sentences like (5)

(5) Mary gave the money to herself.

make Hypothesis A' questionable. Sentences like (6)

(6) John wanted to hit himself.

show Hypothesis A' to be completely incorrect. For those of you who find sentences like (7) completely acceptable, it will be clear that the presence of intervening verbs is irrelevant:

(7) The king gave the slave girl to herself.

A comparison of sentence (1d) with (4a) suggests a different approach to this problem:

(1)   d. I knew that he saw himself in the mirror.

(4)   a. *I knew that he saw myself in the mirror.

Both sentences are similar in that they are complex sentences and the reflexive word is in the subordinate clause. This suggests that the proper restriction on the occurrence of reflexives is:

Hypothesis A'': reflexives occur if and only if: (1) they refer to an earlier noun (phrase), (2) both the reflexive and the earlier noun (phrase) are in the same clause.

Notice that the sentences of (8) support this hypothesis:

(8)   a. I told myself that I would finish the paper.
      b. *I told myself that myself would finish the paper.

However, Hypothesis A'' incorrectly claims that sentences like (6) are ungrammatical since the reflexive word is in the subordinate clause "to hit himself" and the earlier noun is in the main clause. The situation so far is that Hypothesis A—with its unit of occurrence being the 'sentence'—can handle all sentences except ungrammatical ones like those of (4a), and Hypothesis A''—with its unit of occurrence being the 'clause'—can handle all sentences except the grammatical ones like those of (6). In point of fact there is no unitary way to describe the conditions under which reflexivization can and must occur if we limit ourselves to only considering sequences of words and the traditionally acknowledged properties of sentences.

Abstract structure

An adequate description of the process of reflexivization requires that we attribute a set of abstract structural properties to complex sentences. The first claim to be made is that the internal structure of complex sentences is organized in terms of a basic unit which will be referred to as an S. The S can be thought of as being equivalent to a simple sentence since it contains most of the properties of the simple sentence. Thus, a simple sentence like (1c) can be represented by the structure in (9):

(9)

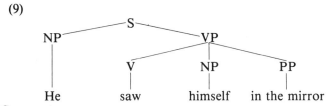

S   = sentence
NP = noun phrase
VP = verb phrase
V   = verb
PP = prepositional phrase

The structure of a complex sentence like (1d) can be represented by the structure in (10):

(10)

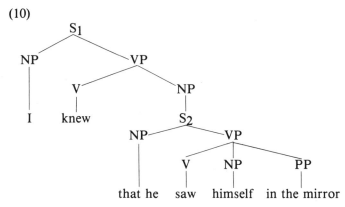

The subordinate relation of the clause 'he saw himself in the mirror' (S_2) is represented by its being a constituent within the main clause (S_1). One form of support for the claim that subordinate clauses like the one in (10) are structurally an S comes from the fact that many (but not all) of the processes that can occur in simple sentences can also occur within such subordinate clauses. For example, the transformation of There Insertion (Bach 1974), which derives (11b) from (11a)

(11)   a. A unicorn is in the garden.
        b. There is a unicorn in the garden.

can also apply in the subordinate clause of complex sentences.

(12)   a. Bill knows that a unicorn is in the garden.
        b. Bill knows that there is a unicorn in the garden.

Other processes which occur in both main and subordinate clauses are Passivization, Particle Movement, Dative Movement, Negation, etc.

The repeated occurrence of the category S in the structure of complex sentences allows us to consider the hypothesis that the unit of occurrence for the reflexive pronoun may be this fundamental abstract unit. Thus we can formulate the following hypothesis:

Hypothesis B: reflexives occur if and only if: (1) they refer to an earlier noun phrase, (2) both the reflexive and the earlier noun phrases are contained within the same set of Ss.

This hypothesis can formally be stated as the transformational rule given in (13):

(13)   Reflexive Transformation

X	NP	Y	NP	Z	
1	2	3	4	5	$\longrightarrow$
1	2	3	4 + self	5	

Conditions: (1)   2 is coreferential with 4,
               (2)   any node labled S which dominates 4 must also dominate 2.[4]

For the moment, however, Hypothesis B is no better than Hypothesis A''. Both erroneously predict that sentence (6) is unacceptable. That this is true for Hypothesis B can be demonstrated with the following argument. The unacceptability of (14):

(14)   *John$_i$wanted Mary to hit himself$_i$

is accounted for under Hypothesis B if its structure is something like (15):[5]

(15)

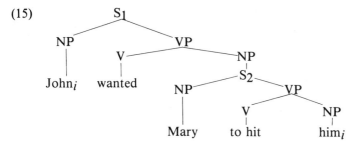

According to Hypothesis B, the object of *hit* in S2 can not be reflexivized even though it is coreferencial with *John* because S2 does not also dominate *John* in S1. Now assuming that the general structure of sentence (6) is similar to that of (15):

(16)

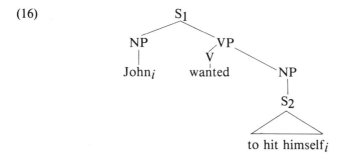

The object of *hit* in the S2 of (16) should not be reflexivized for the same reasons that the object of *hit* in the S2 of (15) can not be reflexivized.

This impasse can be resolved if we hypothesize that the deep structure of sentence (6) contains in S2 the noun phrase *John* which is eventually deleted. Accordingly, sentences like (6) and (17)

(6) John wanted to hit himself.
(17) Mary wanted John to hit himself.

share identical deep structure in regard to their subordinate clauses:

(18)

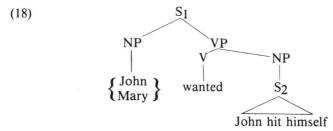

There are a number of arguments, independent of the reflexive construction, that can be given to support the deleted noun phrase hypothesis. For example, notice that in the following sentence pairs John is understood to be the subject of the subordinate verbs (i.e., *pass, paint*) even when there is no subject immediately preceding these verbs as in the (b) sentences:

(19)   a. Mary expects John to pass the test.
        b. John expects to pass the test.
(20)   a. Mary would like John to paint the house.
        b. John would like to paint the house.

We can account for this consistent interpretation of the (b) sentences if *John* is indeed present as subject of the subordinate clauses in their deep structure.

A different type of argument is provided by the unacceptability of sentences like those in (21) where identical subscripts indicate coreferential noun phrases:

(21)   a. *John$_i$ would prefer for him$_i$ to paint the barn.
        b. *Mary$_x$ wants her$_x$ to pass the test.

Comparing sentence (21a) with those in (22), we see that the subject of the subordinate clause (S$_2$) can only be overtly present when it is not coreferential with the subject of the main clause:

(22)   a.   John$_i$ would prefer for him $_x$ to paint the barn,
        b.   John would prefer for her to paint the barn.
        c.   John would prefer for Bill to paint the barn.

When the subject of S$_1$ and S$_2$ are coreferential, the subject of S$_2$ must not be present in the sentence:

(23)   John would prefer to paint the barn.

We can account for this by a transformational rule (often called Equi-NP Deletion) which obligatorily deletes the subject of this type of subordinate clause when it is coreferential with a noun phrase in a higher clause.[6] Thus the requirements of the reflexive rule, the desirability of assigning a structure which provides an adequate basis for semantic interpretation, and the need to explain why sentences like (21) are ungrammatical, converge to support a process which deletes coreferential subject noun phrases in subordinate clauses. Furthermore, through their mutual reinforcement, each specific analysis provides a measure of support for the others.

Before summarizing this section, it would be useful to briefly consider the problems posed by the following reflexive sentence:

(24) John saw himself hit himself.

This could be quite appropriately uttered if John was watching a movie of himself. In order to derive the second reflexive noun phrase the structure underlying (24) must be:

(25)

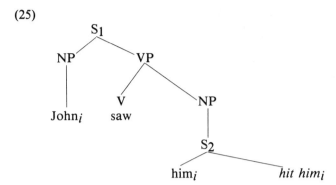

Both coreferential reflexive pronouns must be dominated by S₂ in order to account for the reflexive form of the first pronoun, sentence (24) must have a structure like:

(26)

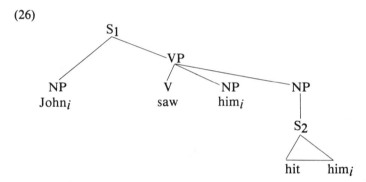

where the first prounoun is in the main clause (S₁) with the subject.

The problem in this case does not concern a missing noun phrase as with sentence (6). This difficulty can be resolved if we allow (24) to be assigned more than one structural description. Its deep structure representation would be (25). A transformational rule would take the subject noun phrase of S₂ in (25) and raise it to object position in S₁, resulting in the surface structure (26). This rule, referred to as Raising, can be justified on other grounds.

Consider the sentences in (27):

(27) a. John knew that Mary hit herself.
      b. John saw Mary hit herself.
      c. John wanted Mary to hit herself.

Presumably in their structural descriptions, the various forms of the subordinate clauses "(that) Mary (to) hit herself" constitute an S constituent. However, when the noun *Mary* is replaced by a pronoun, it must be in the objective case in Sentences (27b) and (27c):

(28) a. John knew that she hit herself.
b. John saw her hit herself.
c. John wanted her to hit herself.

This means that the pronouns in (28b) and (28c) must be the object of their main verbs (i.e., *saw, wanted*) and must also be constituents in S₁.

This means that the pronouns in (28b) and (28c) must be the object of their main verbs (i.e., *saw, wanted*) and must also be constituents in S_1.
This contradiction can be accounted for by assuming that the rule of raising has applied in (27b) and (27c) to place *Mary* in object position in S_1. The effect of this rule, however, does not show up unless the raised constituent is a pronoun.

In this analysis I have tried to show that in order to formulate a general statement that accounts for a set of acceptable and non-acceptable English sentences involving the reflexive construction, we must posit (1) the category S as an abstract unit of structure; (2) the existence of structural representations at more than one degree of abstraction—note that even surface structure is an abstract representation; and (3) rules that create structure, rearrange structure, and delete structure. Let us briefly review some of the arguments given in support of these claims. We introduced the abstract category S in order to describe the general structure of complex sentences. Support for the category S was provided by the fact that it enables us to formulate an adequate description of a number of unrelated transformational rules, such as Raising, Equi-NP Deletion, and Reflexivization. The general hypothesis that a sentence has associated with it structural representations of various degrees of abstraction was proposed in order to resolve a number of contradictions. One of the arguments in support of this hypothesis concerned sentence (6) with its underlying structure represented in (18). The subordinate clause of sentence (6) was claimed to have a subject in S_2 of its deep structure that is not present in the actual sentence. Support for this claim was essentially of the internal type and was based on the fact that several independent phenomena converge to require the same type of claim. However, the basis of support for the reflexive transformation itself was even more complex. Its credibility is a function of the fact that (1) it systematically accounts for an extensive set of relevant data, (2) it requires a number of additional hypotheses which are also required in order to account for completely unrelated sets of data. In retrospect, we see that theory building of this type is more analogous to building an arch than to building a multi-layered structure like a pyramid.

Structural Analysis in Anthropology

Levi-Strauss' utilization of linguistic concepts has engendered a number of controversies among linguists and anthropologists (e.g., Mounin 1969, 1974, Durbin 1974, Leach 1971, Chomsky 1972). This section, however, is not intended to address the questions raised by this controversy. Instead, we will examine, from a transformational orientation, some examples of structural research (i.e., the work of Levi-Strauss and El Guindi) in terms of their potential for verification. It must be pointed out that Levi-Strauss made no attempt to utilize the transformational-generative machinery. Accordingly, the following comments on Levi-Strauss frequently do not fall within the parameters of Levi-Strauss' own stated objectives.[7] In part, the discussion in this section reflects the degree to which these anthropological studies can be matched up against the linguistic framework of the transformationalists. To the extent, however, that this linguistic framework is in accordance with the practices of scientific research, these comments also constitute suggestions toward the clarification and extension of the methodology utilized in structural studies in anthropology.

Levi-Strauss

In *The Raw and the Cooked* (1969), Levi-Strauss states that his goal is to search for the constraining structures of the mind. As I understand it, this search is pursued in the following manner. First, find the pattern of dominant and recurring elements in the myth or myth series. Second, organize these in terms of oppositional relations and, where possible, mediating categories. Underlying this step is the assumption that mythical thought always progresses from the awareness of oppositions toward their resolution. This assumption is borne out in many of Levi-Strauss' analyses. Third, draw on the general knowledge of the people and the culture to find the meaning or purpose of the myth as it is presented in the content of the oppositonal and mediating categories. The meaning is nearly always the resolution or attempted resolution of some basic dilemma or contradiction in the human condition. This is consistent with Levi-Strauss' assumption about the goal of mythical thought. Fourth, reinforce the validity of the structural patterns by finding the same structural-content patterns or their transformational variants in other myths or rituals of the same or related peoples. This fourth activity constitutes both an enlargement of the application of the analysis and a form of verification.

The question is, why haven't other more compelling modes of verification evolved in the course of this research? I suggest that the answer to this question involves four partially integrated factors. First, the structural patterns which Levi-Strauss discovers through his analysis are surface patterns. Clearly they are abstractions, but for the most part they reflect the less abstract properties of the system which underlies the structure of myth and ritual. Second, the system proposed by Levi-Strauss does not have sufficient potential to adequately engage the facts and events of the real world, (i.e., external verification) nor to integrate with itself (i.e., internal verification) because it is not rich nor detailed enough in its total apparatus.

I will try to illustrate these two points by some examples from linguistics. We observe the sentences:

(29)   a. John looked up the phone number.
         b. Richard gave the tapes to Margery.
(30)   a. John looked the phone number up.
         b. Richard gave Margery the tapes.

We can go on to notice that sentences (29a) and (30a) are related to each other, just as sentences (29b) and (30b). Observing that in a general sense the identical relation seems to hold between the two pairs, we can state these two relations as a correspondence:

'John looked up the phone number.' is to 'John looked the phone number up.' as

'Richard gave the tapes to Margery.' is to 'Richard gave Margery the tapes.'

The common relation between these two pairs is some type of movement transform. We can thus go on to find many more sentence pairs of the two types just considered, as well as new types such as:

(31)   a. John quickly left the room.
         b. John left the room quickly.

The resulting claim that there is a movement transform in the English language by which different sentence structures can be said to be related is clearly supported on the basis of this data, and is significant. But neither this analysis nor the claim it makes takes us very far into the systems underlying English specifically or language in general. In fact, because of the limited scope of the claim and its associated machinery the only support available for this claim is the extensiveness of the general pattern.

For example, without a more detailed analysis, containing specified abstract properties, it is impossible to even describe the basis on which this transform applies and doesn't apply in the following sentences:

(32)   a. John looked the phone number up.
         b. *John ran the hill up.
         c. John picked her up.
(33)   a. John looked up the phone number.
         b. John ran up the hill.
         c. *John picked up her.

Even more important is the fact that a more precise description will suggest that the transformation relating (29a) and (30a) is only found in the Germanic languages; while the one relating (31a) and (31b) is found in many languages and may be universal. The ability to distinguish between the occasional and universal is of obvious significance to anyone interested in the properties of the human mind.

Returning to the reflexive analysis in the previous section, Levi-Strauss' use of the principle of opposition is somewhat analogous to the use of the category S for the subordinate sentence in (10). Both examples are instances of the type of abstraction in which the overt occurrence of the phenomena is clearly observable and suggested by the surface data. But in order to have the capablility to explore larger aspects of the underlying system, it may also be necessary to go a step further, as was the case for sentence (6) in diagram (18), and posit entities which are not directly reflected in the surface data (e.g., an underlying S with a deleted subject.[8]

The third factor affecting the potential for verification seems to me to be the over importance given to the role of meaning or purpose in the myth analysis, where meaning relates to some profound aspect of the human condition. If the goal of the research is to discover the underlying structural properties of a system, meaning is an important methodological aid, not an end. For example, identity of meaning was used to set up the correspondences between "John looked up the phone number," and "John looked the phone number up." And meaning played a crucial role in supporting the relation between "John wanted to hit himself," and "Mary wanted John to hit himself." But here meaning was used to arrive at more abstract structure, not to serve as an explanation in itself. I do not mean to imply that Levi-Strauss' myths may not have within their culture the meaning which he claims for them. My point is that the emphasis on the role of meaning impedes progress in two ways: (1) it deters him from finding the more abstract structures and processes at work in the system, and (2) it creates the possibly misleading feeling that the structural system must incorporate and revolve around profound human issues. It is equally as likely that the totality of the system is devoted to the organization and structuring of relatively mundane human events.

This leads me to the fourth and final factor. Myth treated by itself has not shown itself to provde a sufficient context for the external verification of abstract structures. The reasons for this are not clear, but the frequent rejoinder that structural analysis "explains nothing" and the criticism that its methods and results are "too subjective" clearly attests to the existence of this problem.

New Trends

Despite the above comments, Levi-Strauss' work does not need a defender. It has provided a crucial point of departure and a partial methodology for structural analysis in anthropology. What is now required is an extension of its data base and a justified expansion of its theoretical machinery. Fortunately, one can point to a certain amount of work along these lines. There is, for example, Levi-Strauss' limited analysis of ritual (1936b) and the work of Crumrine and Macklin (Crumrine and Macklin 1974, Crumrine-this volume).

However, the line of research being developed by El Guindi (e.g., this volume) is of particular interest in that it addresses a number of the problems discussed earlier. On the basis of her research in a Zapotec village in Oaxaca, Mexico, El Guindi has developed a framework which characterizes the structure underlying various aspects of the Zapotec belief system and is empirically realized in their myths, rituals, etc.[9] Briefly, her claim is that fundamental to all areas of Zapotec belief is a basic structure consisting of a pair of closed concepts in opposition which are mediated by an open concept. In ritual, the opposition pair serves as the determining model for relating the sociological categories of people within the structural opposition of power and nonpower. In fact, ritual structure is the specific outcome of the structuring of people into sociological categories which takes place in ritual activities and events. This structuring process can be stated as a ritual-specific set of rules which serve to categorize and recategorize peope.

Within the context of this chapter two important characteristics of El Guindi's work stand out. First, her analysis involves a rich set of clearly specified hypotheses. Second, for the purpose of structural analysis, she makes no distinction between the traditionally separate areas of myth, ritual, belief, and sociological knowledge, maintaining that a single structuring system underlies all of them. The interaction of these two factors represents a major expansion in the set of opportunites for evaluative contact points between hypotheses and between hypotheses and data. The remainder of this chapter will be devoted to discussing three such contact points. However, this discussion is not a substantive evaluation of El Guindi's work. It is an exploration into the kinds of hypotheses, method of argumentation, and data which could lead to the development of a sounder basis for theory evaluation in structural anthropology.

Arguments for an Abstract Category

Consider the claim that a finite set of sociological categories function as the crucial or structuring units in ritual.[10] As an example of the kinds of evidence that can be adduced for this claim, let us examine the category Casero which is claimed to play a crucial role in the structuring of many rituals and myths. The empirical content of the category Casero varies from ritual to ritual. For example, the set of people that make up the category Casero in the ritual Fandango are not determined on the basis of the same principles that determine the set of people who are *caseros* in the ritual Defunto (El Guindi 1973)[11] The *caseros* in Fandango are parents of the groom, in Defunto they are the surviving spouse and/or the adult children living in the same house. Regardless of the empirical content however, all *caseros* share certain properties. It is they who command or *manda* in the ritual. They see to it that jobs and errands are done, obligations are met, etc.

What are the specific claims being made relevant to Casero and what kinds of support is available for these claims? The two relevant claims are:

(1)   In each ritual there is a ritual-specific set of people who are in command;

(2)   These ritual-specific sets are members of a more general sociological category which serves as a structuring unit in a number of rituals.

Evidence for the first claim is easily obtainable. Completely independent of the events observed by El Guindi, any anthropologist can attend a large number of Fandangos and observe that at each occurrence of this ritual there is a limited set of individuals who are in commmand. On inquiring, she will find out that the members of this set are always the parents of the groom. If she attends other rituals like Defunto or Anjeleto she will find that in each of these rituals there is a limited set of individuals in command and that the compostion of the set is ritual-specific.

Observable evidence provides strong support for the first claim, which is essentially an empirical one. The second claim, however, involves a generalization with reference to a completely abstract category and cannot be supported as directly. Native statements will refer to the individuals in command, regardless of the specific ritual, as *caseros*. This does not necessarily mean that the various, ritual-specific sets of *caseros* reflect, in a structural sense, one category.

If Casero in a non-ritual-specific sense is to be taken as more than a convenient descriptive device, there must be some empirical evidence in support of this claim. For example, the category Casero could place a common set of imperatives and restrictions on those so categorized regardless of the ritual. El Guindi does not provide detailed data on this point, but it might be found that across rituals *caseros* perform certain clearly definable activities and are prohibited from others.

A specific example of this type of restriction involves the category Godmother (El Guindi, this volume). Based on her analysis of the two delivery dances, it should be the marriage godmother who provides the saint for the bride. As marriage godmother to the groom she would be groom's fictive and an affine to the bride's side. Since only affines give wedding gifts of household items (based on anthropologists' observations and native statements), she should be able to also. But in fact she doesn't. She has been transformed by the wedding ritual to a fictive of the bride's side also and cannot perform an affinal activity. In the same vein, if it could be found that *caseros* in Fandango must do X and cannot do Y and that the same pattern holds true for *caseros* in Defunto and Angelito, this would be evidence that these various ritual specific *caseros* share more than a general similarity of being in authority.

These questions about the status of the categoryhood of Casero and Affine are parallel to the situation in linguistics where one attempts to establish that a number of superficially different constituent types are members of the same general syntactic category. Consider the following sequences:

(34)   Bill
        I
        a boy
        the big truck
        the idea that he might be rich
        flying glass
        the man with a red tie

At one level these sequences are clearly quite different: (34) would be described as including a proper noun, a pronoun, an adjectival phrase, a relative clause, etc. However, one might also claim that they have some property in common since they can all occur before a sequence such as 'hit Sam':

(35)   a. Bill hit Sam.
        b. I hit Sam.
        c. A boy hit Sam.
        d. The big truck hit Sam.
        e. The idea that he might be rich hit Sam.
        f. Flying glass hit Sam.
        g. The man with the red tie hit Sam.

One way of supporting the hypothesis that the words and phrases of (34) share a common property is to show that they are all subject to the same transformations, for example, the Passive transformation. This transformation would derive sentence (36b) from (36a):

(36)   a. [The cat] scratched [the girl.]
               NP_1 NP_2
        b. [The girl] was scratched by [the cat.]
               NP_2 NP_1

Roughly, what this transformation does is replace the first noun phrase (NP_1) with the second noun phrase (NP_2), move the first noun phrase to the end of the sentence with the addition of *by*, and change the form of the verb. If we apply the Passive transformation to the sentences in (35) we get:

(37)   a. Sam was hit by Bill.
        b. Sam was hit by me.
        c. Sam was hit by a boy.
        d. Sam was hit by the big truck.
        e. Sam was hit by the idea that he might be rich.
        f. Sam was hit by flying glass.
        g. Sam was hit by the man with the red tie.

This demonstrates that proper nouns, pronouns, adjectival phrases, relative clauses, etc., are all members of the category NP.

The Passive transformation can also be used to show that certain sequences of words do not constitute an NP. For example, the following sequences

(38)   presumably John
         with obvious enthusiasm he
         in the middle of the argument the police

can occur before "hit Sam":

(39)   a. Presumably John hit Sam.
         b. With obvious enthusiasm he hit Sam.
         c. In the middle of the argument the police hit Sam.

But the fact that the Passive transformation cannot apply to them indicates that they are not noun phrases:

(40)   *a. Sam was hit by presumably John.
         *b. Sam was hit by with obvious enthusiasm him.
         *c. Sam was hit by in the middle of the argument the police.

The additional fact that there are passive forms of (39)

(41)   a. Presumably, Sam was hit by John.
         b. With obvious enthusiasm, Sam was hit by John.
         c. In the middle of the argument, Sam was hit by the police.

shows that the ungrammaticality of (40) is due to the incorrect application of the passive transformation.

This general parallelism between the structure of categories in ritual and structure of syntactic categories in human language is interesting. But one would not want to make any theoretical claims at this point. However, drawing comparisons of this type can be helpful in suggesting new perspectives. The syntactic category noun phrase includes many less abstract categories like proper noun, pronoun, relative clause, etc. Analogously, the Zapotec may have a general category Casero which in context-specific situations includes the less abstract categories of parents of the groom, parents of the deceased, surviving spouse, etc. The particular people who are parents of the groom, for example, are of no importance to the structural analysis. They could be Juan and Maria or Enrique and Juana. Similarly, in the analysis of the structure of sentence (35a), it does not matter if it was Bill, Bob, or Betty who hit Sam. The specific lexical items are irrelevant. One of the tests for the category NP is the acceptable application of the Passive transformation to appropriately structured active sentences. Through a detailed analysis of the behavioral parameters that define *manda*, it may be possible to formulate criteria tests for Casero.

A Metaconstraint for Categoryhood

The claim that there are specific types of structural relations that hold between categories provides the possibility of developing metatheoretical arguments for the categoryhood of a particular element. El Guindi seems to have implicitly assumed that the only elements that can enter into the structural relations of opposition and mediation are categories. This is a very powerful principle—though quite plausible. However, it is only an hypothesis, and does require independent support.

As an example of how this principle might be used, consider the ritual Fandango with its opposition between the parents of the groom *(caseros)* and parents of the bride *(consuegros)*. If there is strong independent support for the existence of the category Casero, this principle supports the claim for the existence of a category Consuegro which includes 'parents of the bride.'

In transformational theory there is a similar type of working hypothesis, to the effect that transformational operations only apply to constituent units. There seems to be general support for this hypothesis with regard to movement rules. But its validity for deletion transformations is being questioned.

An incident of the type that could provide support for the 'category hypothesis' is mentioned in a footnote in El Guindi (1973). El Guindi's informant was standing in the street in the village watching a funeral (Defunto) go by. He was called by the *casero* and asked to do a ritual-related errand. Even though he had not at all participated in the ritual, he was obligated to comply, as he later explained, because he was a blood relative of the deceased. On the basis of the ritual itself, El Guindi (1973) has analyzed Consanguine as being one of the categories in opposition to Casero. The important point is that the man had to comply not because of who he was (John or Joe), or for personal reasons, or because he had or had not attended the ritual, but because he is included in a category which in this ritual is in opposition to the category Casero. Part of the claim being made here is that in this type of incident the Casero would never have called upon a person who was, for example, a personal friend but not a member of a category in opposition to Casero.

Empirical Data for a General Property

The final example of verification involves the claim by El Guindi (this volume, 1973) that it is only the class of open categories that can allow for novel input and change. El Guindi posits a formal distinction between closed and open concepts or categories. Closed categories are "well defined, highly coded and rigidly marked by invariant syntactic properties." Open categories are loosely defined, often ambiguous, and flexible. This claim, which limits the possible occurrence of change and novel input, would appear to be difficult to support without a precise description of what constitutes the class of such events. However, El Guindi relates a number of events which provide some support for this claim and suggest that stronger support may not be difficult to obtain.

One such incident involves the category fictive. Based on her analysis of a number of rituals (El Guindi 1974) she has argued that Fictive is an open category. The following incident (El Guindi 1973) which took place during a Difunto is strikingly consistent with this hypothesis.

> While attending a Difunto, I was asked to raise the cross, which is the central event in that ritual. Surprised, I asked the reason. I was told that the only female relatives present in the ritual at the moment are *cunadas* (affines). Only a *comadre* (godmother) can raise the cross to a female deceased. In other words, it is category fictive that should raise the cross. Only the category affines was present. But why me? I was already in the house where the ritual was taking place. In order to be in a ritual I have to be categorized. Could I have been categorized affine or consanguine in case it was either of these categories that needed personnel? My hypothesis would be no. Affine and consanguine are closed categories.

In conjunction with this data, we would want more tangible evidence that the anthropologist (or non-relative) could not have been classified as an Affine or Consanguine. One encouraging aspect in regard to finding such support is that it could come from any ritual that involves the categories affine and/or consanguine.

Another category for which there is interesting data consistent with the property of openness is that of ritual official. During a ritual which includes a meal, food is served by category group. For example, *invitados* (invited kin) eat together and ritual officials eat together. Members of one category do not eat with the other. According to her analysis of Difunto and Angelito (El Guindi 1973) ritual officials are an open category. At the rituals attended by El Guindi, she was always asked to eat with the ritual officials.

A more dramatic incident consistent with ritual officials being an open category involves the *musica* (band) which are members of the category ritual officials at an Angelito or Difunto. The commonly held belief among Middle American Anthropologists and the Zapotec themselves is that an Angelito is the death of a child and a Difunto is the death of an adult. El Guindi, however, has data from a number of Angelitos that clearly demonstrate that the real difference is between the death of a person who has never married (Angelito) as opposed to one who has married (Difunto). The most interesting fo these Angelitos is the death of an 87-year-old spinster.

At an Angelito the *musica* or band, play fast, happy music. At a Difunto they play a dreary or sad type music. During the Angelito of this woman the *musica* played fast, happy music except while they were accompanying the procession to the cemetery. At this time they played

Difunto music. According to native statements, many of them were quite surprised that, considering her advanced age, she was still buried as an Angelito. The fact that it was one of the subcategories of ritual officials that modified what seemed to be a very usual instance of an Angelito supports the claim that open categories allow for change and novel situations. According to El Guindi's hypothesis, one would never find members of a closed category attempting such actions.

Before concluding, I have a few comments on the status of native judgements as relevant evidence for a hypothesis. In regard to the general distinction between Angelito and Difunto—especially the death of the old woman—native statements are not consistent with the demonstrable facts. Thus their account of a child-adult distinction was taken as being incorrect. But in the ritual in which the anthropologist was asked to participate as a fictive because all others present were of the wrong category, I accepted the natives' explanation as partial support for the claim that Affines are a closed category and Fictives are an open category. Does this represent an inconsistency? I don't think so.

Native statements should be treated no differently than any other type of evidence. When a proposed piece of data (native statements, native accounts, etc.) is consistent with a number of other kinds of evidence, it provides further support for an hypothesis. But when a piece of data (native statements, native actions, etc.) is in conflict with a number of other well-founded data in support of some hypothesis, the contradicting item can be judiciously set aside—hopefully to be subsequently explained.

Structural analysis in anthropology has often been regarded as merely an interesting way of describing phenomena. But there now seems to be developing a theoretical framework within which theoretical claims can be shown to have empirical content and/or specifiable consequences within the theory. I have indicated some of the ways that linguists think about these problems that might be useful to the anthropologist.

Notes

An earlier version of this paper was presented at a Symposium on Verification in Structural Anthropology at the 1972 AAA Meeting under the title "Verification from a Linguist's View." I would like to thank Fadwa El Guindi for extensive discussion of various aspects of her work. However, this should not be taken as meaning that she is in complete agreement with my comments. I would also like to thank Robert Berdan for discussion of a number of linguistic points. The work upon which this article is based was in part performed pursuant to Contract NE-C-00-3-0064 with the National Institute of Education, Department of Health, Education, and Welfare.

[1]See Back (1974) for an excellent description of transformational research, methodology, and problems. Bierwesch (1971) is written from a structuralist orientation and contains a simple introduction to transformational linguistics.

[2]The form of this presentation of the reflexive has been influenced by Peters (1971).

Further discussion of the reflexive can be found in Lees and Klima (1963) and Postal (1971). Jackendoff (1972) and Helke (1973) present a different analytic approach.

³The asterisk (*) is used to indicate that a sentence is ungrammatical. Identical subscripts (e.g., Mary$_i$. . . .Mary$_i$) indicate that the two constituents refer to the same person—i.e., are coreferential.

⁴The second condition is included in a general condition called the Insertion Prohibition which applies to any transformation (Chomsky 1965). It is necessary in order to prevent strings like (4a) which would have the structure:

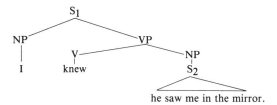

he saw me in the mirror.

The subject of S_1 and the object of S_2 are within S_1. But the Reflexive transformation cannot apply since these two constituents are not both within S_2.

⁵It will be subsequently shown that (15) is only one of the structures necessary for describing (14) or its acceptable version. This point, however, does not effect this argument.

⁶Equi-NP Deletion does not apply in all types of subordinate clauses as for example, those introduced by that:

(a) John$_i$would prefer that he$_i$paint the barn.

(b) *John would prefer that paint the barn.

⁷In fact Levi-Strauss has argued that much of the methodology of experimental research is not applicable to his work. Thus he has recently rejected the relevance of concepts such as empirical refutation and verification and emphasized notions such as understanding, extensiveness, economy of analysis, etc.

⁸Chomsky's (1972, p.74-75) comments are also along these lines. He suggests that Levi-Strauss conclusions turn out to be limited in scope because he utilized the concept of opposition from structuralist phonology without its rule systems and substantive universals.

⁹Her analysis in this volume represents an extended structural analysis of the wedding ritual, *Fandango*.

¹⁰The following discussion assumes a minimal familiarity with El Guindi's work to the extent of her article in this volume.

¹¹In order to avoid confusion *caseros* will be used to refer to the ritual-specific level and Casero to refer to the general category.

References

Bach, E. 1974. *Syntactic Theory*. Holt, Rinehart, and Winston.

Bierwisch, M. 1971. *Modern Linguistics*. The Hague: Mouton.

Chomsky, Noam. 1965. *Aspects of the Theory of Syntax*. MIT Press: Cambridge, Mass.

    1972. *Language and Mind*. N.Y.: Harcourt Brace Jovanovich.

Crumrine, N.R. and B.J. Mackin. 1974. Sacred Ritual vs the Unconscious: The Efficacy of Symbols and Structure in North Mexican Folk Saints' Cults and General Ceremonialism. In *The Unconscious in Culture*. I. Rossi ed. N.Y.: E.P. Dutton. pp.179-197.

Crumrine, N.R. (this volume). Transformational Processes and Models: With Special References to Mayo Indian Myth and Ritual.

Durbin, M. 1974. Comments. In *The Unconscious in Culture*: I. Rossi, ed. E.P. Dutton, pp. 53-59.

El Guindi, F. 1973. The Internal Structure of the Zapotec Conceptual System. *Journal of Symbolic Anthropology*. 1, 15-34. The Hague: Mouton.

1974. Structure and Natives Knowledge of Culture. Paper presented in Symposium: Symbolism and Behavior at Annual AAA Meeting, Mexico City.

1976. *Religion in Culture*. W.C. Brown Co.

(this volume). Internal and External Constraints on Structure.

Helke, M. 1973. On Reflexives in English. *Linguistics*. 106, 5-23.

Jackendoff, R.S. 1972. *Semantic Interpretation in Generative Grammar*. Cambridge: MIT Press.

Jacobson, R. and M. Halle. 1956. *Fundamentals of Language*. The Hague: Mouton.

Leach, E. 1970. *Levi-Strauss*. London: Fontana.

Levi-Strauss, C. 1963a. *Structural Anthropology*. Basic Books, Inc.

1963b. Structure and Dialectics. In *Structural Anthropology*. pp. 232-241.

1969. *The Raw and the Cooked*. N.Y.: Harper and Row

Mounin, G. 1969. Levi-Strauss et la Linguistique. In *Introduction á la Semiologie*. Paris: Editions de Minuit

1974. Levi-Strauss' Use of Linguistics. In *The Unconscious in Culture*. I. Rossi ed. E.P. Dutton. pp. 31-52.

Peters, P.S. 1969. On the Complexity of the Brain as a Language Processor. In *Information Processing in the Nervous System*. K.N. Leibovic Ed., N.Y.: Springer-Verlag.

Piaget, J. 1970. *Structuralism*. N.Y.: Basic Books, Inc.

Troubetzkoy, N. 1969. *Principles of Phonology*. Berkeley: University of California Press.

Postal, P. 1971. *Cross-Over Phenomena*. N.Y.: Holt, Rinehart, Winston.

PART TWO

STRENGTHENING THE ETHNOGRAPHIC APPLICATION OF THE STRUCTURAL PARADIGM

6
A Small Problem
Of Fish Bones[1]

Charles Ackerman

Introduction

Franz Boas published three versions of the myth of Asdiwal. In the first (1895) the protagonist is called Asiwa, and he dies a strange death:

> Asiwa yearned to be back again among the sea lions. His son asked him, "Why do you want to return to them?" Asiwa did not want to answer. His son insisted; and Asiwa said, "They gave me a rock-cod and olachen oil to eat and that is very good." As soon as he said this he fell dead; and fish-bones grew out of his stomach. This happened because he had said what happened among the sea lions. (1895:289).

In Boas' second translation of the myth (1902) the protagonist is called Asi-hwil; his death is not described. In the third version (1912) the protagonist is Asdiwal, and he dies a strange death:

> When it was fall again he arose and went up to the lake of Ginadas to hunt mountain goats. . . . . After a short while, he remembered that he had forgotten his snowshoes in his house; then he could not move on the great slippery mountain, for he had forgotten his snowshoes . . . . . Where might he go now? He could not go up, he could not go down, he could not go to either side. After a little while his father came. It was he who went away with him to his own home, but his body stayed behind and became stone. . . . . (1912:143-5).

In his interpretation, "The Story of Asdiwal" (1967), Claude Lévi-Strauss does not consider Boas' 1895 version of the myth. He notes it, however, in 1973 and comments:

> On se souvient que la version 1912 explique la mort d'Asdiwal par un oubli.....Or, la version 1895 remplace l'oubli par une autre faute: l'indiscrétion dont Asiwa se rend coupable en révélant à son fils le menu du repas qu'il a partagé chez les phoques. Dans l'état actuel de nos connaissances sur l'ethnographie des Tsimshian, nous ignorons pourquoi cette révélation constitue une faute.....La solution de ce petit problème n'est heureusement pas nécessaire pour établir le point qui nous importe.....(1973:229-30).

Lévi-Strauss' *point que lui importe* is that since

> l'indiscrétion...consiste à révéler à quelqu'un ce qu'on n'aurait pas dû lui dire

and

> oublier, c'est manquer de dire à soi-même ce qu'on aurait dû pouvoir se dire,

the two versions of the myth present us with an interesting inversion: as an indiscretion is an *excess* of communication to *someone else*, so forgetting is a *lack* of communication to oneself.

In this chapter I shall: (1) demonstrate that in the present state of our knowledge of Tsimshian ethnography we *can* know why Asiwa's statement is an offense; (2) demonstrate that a solution of the "small problem" *is* necessary—for without it, Lévi-Strauss was led originally to a wrong interpretation of the myth of Asdiwal and subsequently to a wrong interpretation of "la position sémantique de *l'oubli* dans les mythes" (1973:230).

Asdiwal as Father

Asdiwal's son, Waux, also dies a strange death:

> Waux himself was transformed into stone, with his hunting hat and his mat blanket and his pole, and his dog also was transformed into stone.....The reason is that he forgot to take his spear. He has used the spear often before when some mountains were shaking. He just put the spear across the chasms between rocks after they had shaken, and a way opened for him; but this time he had no way.....(Boas 1916:246).

In Figure 6:1 I have represented schematically the relevant aspects of the three deaths. The food remembered by Asiwa was food given to him by a *father*, the chief of the sea lions saying of Asiwa (at the end of Asiwa's sojourn to the home of the sea lions):

> "Take my own canoe to the fire. I will lend it to my son, and also my ballast" (Boas 1912:135).

The snowshoes forgotten by Asdiwal were given to him by his *father*:

> When the boy was able to walk, his father made snowshoes for him...and said to him, "With these snowshoes you can climb mountains, however steep they may be" (Boas 1902:226).

The spear forgotten by Waux was given to him by his *father*:

> When he went up the mountains with his father, his father would give him a spear and his dogs, and also his large hunting hat, his little basket, and mat blanket, and his pole.....and the young man took care of all the weapons which his father had given him (Boas 1916:244).

Indeed, *everything* which petrified along with Waux had been given to him by his father.

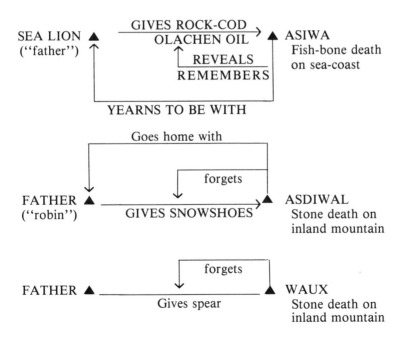

Figure 1

As there is a *sea* "father"—the sea lion, so there is a *land* "father"—a robin: at the beginning of the myth Asdiwal's mother

> heard the one sing whose name is Hatsenas, it is like a robin (Boas 1912:73).

and this bird "like a robin" becomes human and Asdiwal's father. The metaphorical identity of sea lion and robin (they are both "father" of Asdiwal) is an identity well-grounded in Tsimshian reality: they are both "totem" animals of the same Tsimshian matriclan—the Ganhada (Boas 1916:504; Sapir 1915:19); and Asdiwal is, we may deduce, the son of a Ganhada.

The *land/sea* opposition of the two totemic "fathers"—evident also, to some degree, in (1) the several gifts given by the father and (2) the circumstances of each death—is recurrent throughout the myth, appearing earliest in conflicts between Asdiwal and his wife's (or wives') brothers (WBs):

1. **Land** (Bear Hunting)

   After marrying his first wife, Asdiwal travels with her and her brothers into hunting territory. He travels in the canoe of the eldest WB. More successful in the hunt than WB, Asdiwal is deserted by WB.

2. **Sea** (Sea-lion Hunting)

   After marrying his second wife, Asdiwal travels with her brothers into hunting territory. He travels in the canoe of the eldest WB. After killing many sea lions (WB kills none), Asdiwal is deserted by WB.

Three things seem obvious to me:

First, the myth emphasizes a fault in the relationship of the protagonist to what his father has given to him. Asiwa remembers the food; he dies. Asdiwal forgets the snowshoes; he dies. So also Waux: he forgets the spear, and he dies, his father's gifts petrified as he is petrified.

Second, the protagonist's fault—whatever it may be (and this we must discover or we fail to understand the myth)—involves the protagonist's relationship also to his father's home. Asiwa yearns to return to the sea lion's rock, his "father's" place. Asdiwal goes away with his father to his own place.

Third, the myth emphasizes a fault in the relationship of Asdiwal to WB in the context of hunting. In each case (1) Asdiwal's greater success is followed by WB's desertion of him, (2) so long as Asdiwal is subordinate (e.g., travelling in WB's canoe), there is equanimity.

I hypothesize, therefore: Asdiwal asserts a wrong relationship to both his father and his wife's brother, and this wrong relationship has to do primarily with (1) receiving and longing for the sustenance received in his father's home, and (2) being dominant in WB's hunting territory.

At this point another consideration becomes relevant. We may construct a plausible gloss on Asiwa's name by noting:

1. *asi*—"foot" in Tsimshian (Boas 1916:967); and
2. *-wa*—"without" in Tsimshian (Boas 1916:968).

The name *Asiwa* may, then, evoke the image of *footless person*; and the theme I have suggested—a wrong relationship *to the ground*—may be adumbrated for the Tsimshian who listens to the singing of the myth by the name of the protagonist.

Inheritance

What among the Tsimshian is a proper relationship of a man to (1) his father's place, to (2) his wife's brother's place—*to the ground*? As Boas describes the Tsimshian law of inheritance:

> Property—embracing a man's hunting ground, fishing ground, canoes, slaves, etc., as well as his name, the dancing privileges, traditions, songs that belong to the same—is inherited first by the nephews; if there are none, than by the deceased's mother or aunt (1916:499).

The nephew to whom Boas refers is the sister's son: Tsimshian society is matrilineally organized and property is held in the matrilineage by inheritance of it by sister's son from mother's brother. As Sapir puts it:

> ...the Tsimshian are divided into four exogamous phratries...with maternal descent, i.e., the crests and other privileges descend from a man to his sister's son; one's predecessor in the holding of any title or right is thus not his father but his maternal uncle (1915:3-4).

Appropriately, therefore,

> a child is born in a house belonging not to his own phratry, but to that of his father; when still young, however, he was sent away to be brought up at the house of his maternal uncle, where he would live with his family kinsmen (Sapir 1915:27).

Knowing this, we may ask:

> *By what right does Asdiwal assert dominance on the sea lion rock, the rock of his "father?" By what right does Asiwa yearn to return to that place, the place of his father? Are not these "criminal" assertions and yearnings in this matrilineal society? Is Asdiwal's fault "patrifiliation?"*

The myth's emphasis upon WB as (1) the man with whom Asdiwal *may* travel into the hunting/fishing territory, so long as he travels as guest, subordinate, and as (2) the man who deserts Asdiwal after he asserts dominance in the hunting/fishing territory, indicates to me that WB is *the rightful tenant of the territory*, justifiably offended by Asdiwal's behaviour.

If WB is the rightful tenant of the territory, WB is the sister's son of the previous rightful tenant, having inherited from his mother's brother. Asdiwal's "father," the sea lion chief, is tenant of the sea lion's rock. Asdiwal's father is, therefore, his WB's mother's brother; that is, WB is a member of Asdiwal's father's matriclan—and the rightful inheritor of Asdiwal's "patri-territory." As a result of these considerations, I argue:

1. The wrong relationship asserted by Asdiwal to his father and his father's place is *patrifiliation*, a "crime" in a matrilineal society.

2. The wrong relationship asserted by Asdiwal to his wife's brother is *usurpation*, a "crime" in any society, and a necessary consequence of patrifiliation in a matrilineal one.

If Asdiwal's WB is a member of Asdiwal's father's matriclan, Asdiwal's wife must be also. A particular marriage must, therefore, have taken place: Asdiwal must have married a woman of his father's matriclan—a "father's sister's daughter."

Patrifiliation

Given the metaphorical identity of the deaths of both Asdiwal and Waux, we should find in Waux's career also *patrifiliation* and a *patrilineal* marriage. We do: the myth states both without equivocation:

First, the myth describes Waux's patrifiliative violation of Tsimshian custom in Waux's childhood:

> When his uncles left his father...he did not want to go with them, but they compelled him to do so. Therefore he wept bitterly (Boas 1916:244).

These uncles were his mother's brothers, men of his own matriclan, *men with whom he should have lived, according to Tsimshian law.* Of course, a boy may weep—and yet come to learn and obey; but Waux became

> a very skillful hunter. He knew his father's hunting ground, and he knew also how to use his father's weapons (Boas 1916:244),

and

> he went always alone to hunt on his father's hunting ground (Boas 1916:244).

Indeed, Waux dies still asserting his dominance in his father's hunting grounds. The home in which he was living and from which he sallied forth to his death is described in the myth:

> There was a great mountain on which his father used to hunt mountain goats in the fall, when they were very fat. He went there, and camped in the hut that his father had built at the foot of the high mountain.....He enlarged the old hut which his late father had built, and filled it with dried meat and fat (Boas 1916:244-5).

Second, the patrilaterality of Waux's marriage is also demonstrable. Boas' translation of the circumstances of his marriage states:

> Before his mother died she wanted her son to marry one of her cousins, and he did what his mother wanted him to do (1916:244).

The Tsimshian text of the first clause of this statement is

> *na gauga dem dzake na'°t da hasa'x a dem naksde lgu⁰lget a k!âlda lgu-txaât* (Durlach 1928:124).

in which text the term translated as "her cousin" is *lgu-txaât, lgu-* being a diminutive (or, more generally, "slippery salmon"), *txaâ* being a cousin (whether male or female), and *-t* being a third-person possessive (whether the possessor be male or female). The Tsimshian text is, obviously, somewhat ambiguous: (1) the laterality of the cousin is

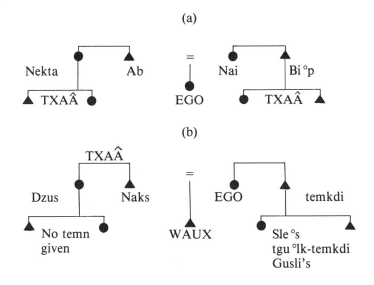

Figure 2

unspecified; and (2) the cousin may as well be Waux's as his mother's. We may, however, understand what Waux's mother has requested, and what Waux has done, by noting certain aspects of Tsimshian female-speaking kinship terminology. In Figure 6:2 I present the relevant terminology—in (a) before the marriage of a woman to her *txâa*, in (b) after her marriage. (The terms are taken from Boas 1916:490-1 and Durlach 1928:145-51).

Although Boas gives *sle°s* for "brother's child," Durlach argues that the term is rather the descriptive *lgu°lk lemkdi* (literally "child" "brother") or the vocative *gusli's*. Whether the proper term be Boas' or Durlach's, *it does not appear in the myth*—Waux's mother does *not* request that he marry her "brother's child," his "mother's brother's daughter." Which cousin, then, *does* she ask him to marry?—her "small" *txâa*. In Figure 6:2 (b) which can this be? It seems to me it can be but one person—her husband's sister's daughter, Waux's father's sister's daughter. In this context it should be noted that in a geneology Durlach gives *kwutxa'aw* as a patrilateral cross-cousin (1928:150), and Barbeau gives *gwutrha'aw* as "cousin on the father's side" (1929:150): over a simple transformation (Barbeau transcribing as *rh* the phoneme Durlach transcribes as *x*), Barbeau's *gwutrha'aw* is Durlach's *kwutxa'aw*. Is this not Boas' *lgu-txâa?*—Waux's father's sister's daughter?[2]

"Messages"

The *land/sea* opposition of the two hunting episodes—and of the two totemic "fathers," and the several gifts, and the deaths—is a vehicle for two "messages" of the myth: the two episodes lead the protagonist into two different outcomes.

First, at the end of the *land* (bear-hunting) episode, Asdiwal finds himself deserted and alone, his wife and small son (Waux) having accompanied, however reluctantly, WB. As the myth puts it:

> Then he was heavy at heart. Therefore he was sitting up at the foot of
> a tree and was crying. He felt cold and was hungry, and his beloved
> wife was gone (Boas 1912:121).

His misery is rapidly assuaged: travellers approach, a young woman and her four brothers; and Asdiwal marries the young woman, travelling onward with her and the WB.

Second, deserted by WB and left stranded on the sea lion rock where he had hunted so successfully, Asdiwal escapes from the rock, returns to the shore *and murders his WB*. Why? On the sea lion rock, Asdiwal is assailed by a storm:

> At midnight a wind arose; and as the morning came a strong gale

> arose and blew against the great rock.....Then his father, the bird,
> came and gave him his blanket (Boas 1912:127).

With this nice juxtaposition of the two relevant totemic references, the
sea lion and the *robin*, the myth emphasizes the (violative) father-son
bond and identifies the "rock": it is the ground of the Ganhada
matriclan. Next:

> Behold! a little mouse came towards the place where he was lying. It
> poked him and said, "My grandfather invites you in".....Behold!
> the top of the ladder stretched down in the ground.....He went
> down into the house on the ladder (Boas 1912:129).

Asdiwal enters the rock of the sea lion/father/Ganhada-matriclan.
Received with kindness and generosity by the sea lion chief ("They gave
me rock-cod and olachen oil to eat and that is very good"), Asdiwal remains

> for some time in the house of the sea lions.....The love of the
> master of the sea lions and of his whole tribe increased very much.
> One day...homesick for his wife and child...he told the master of
> the sea lions. Therefore the chief said to his attendants, "Go and say
> that I want to borrow the canoe of Self-Stomach (All Stomach)."
> Thus said the chief to his attendants. Then they left. When they came
> (back), they said to the chief, "He says the canoe that you want is
> cracked." Then he said again, "Go and tell Self-like-Sea-lion that I
> want to borrow his canoe." They went again; and when they came
> again, they said, "O Chief! the canoe that you want to borrow is also
> cracked." Therefore the chief said to his attendants, "Take my own
> canoe to the fire. I will lend it to my son, and also my ballast." Then
> the attendants of the chief did so. His attendants took down a great
> sea lion's stomach.....Then Asdiwal entered the great stomach,
> and he himself tied it up (Boas 1912:133-5).

Tying himself into the sea lion's stomach, Asdiwal floats in it across the
water from the sea lion rock to the mainland, climbs out of the
stomach—and murders his WB. Why?

An incremental sequence has been stated by the myth—from Self-
Stomach (All Stomach) to Self-like-Stomach to sea-lion-stomach; that is,
from an unspecific "generalized" stomach, the myth brings Asdiwal to
enter a specific stomach, the stomach of the sea lion—*and this is the
totemic stomach of the Ganhada matriclan,* the stomach of Asdiwal's
father's matriclan. Having already entered the patrilocus, the sea-lion
rock, Asdiwal now enters the matriclan, the sea-lion stomach. His
"crime," previously "local" only (assertion of dominance in the patri-
territory), is now "lineal": emerging from this stomach, *Asdiwal is
reborn a member of his father's matriclan.* Thus, Asdiwal's "fault," his
patrifiliative violation of Tsimshian custom, is total.

Why, therefore, must he murder WB? He can usurp WB's local

rights by hunting triumphantly in his territory, but how can he successfully usurp WB's lineal rights? How can he occupy WB's place *in the matrilineage?* Only by causing that place to be vacated, only by killing WB. Asdiwal's murderous act is the logically (and, therefore, mythically) appropriate consequence of his "father-fixation."

A *footless person,* Asdiwal murders his matriclan "brother." (Asdiwal is reborn a Ganhada before he murders *the* Ganhada.) A *footless person,* Asdiwal's crime is a result of "father-fixation." Elsewhere and in another myth a *club-footed man,* "mother-fixation," kills his father; and Oedipus also marries his mother. Does Asdiwal marry his sister? Of course: reborn a Ganhada, he has married a Ganhada, his father's sister's daughter, now a matriclan "sister."

Patrifiliative Violations

Augmenting his patrifiliative violations in the *sea* episodes, Asdiwal *diminishes* them in the *land* episodes:

> One day he wished to return to those whom he had left behind on the Skeena River. Therefore he started and left his wife and child (Boas 1912:143).

This wife and child is his second (incestuous) *sea* family; and "those whom he had left behind" are his mother's wulwulaisk at the inland village of Gitsalas (Boas 1912:82). This Tsimshian word is a kinship term:

> The members of the exogamic group...term one another *wulaisk*...plural *wulwulaisk* (Boas 1916:488).

Asdiwal, travelling toward his *wulwulaisk,* moves (sociologically) toward the Tsimshian norm, toward a final acceptance of a *proper relationship to the ground.* This diminution of violative behavior is echoed in the circumstances of his *land*/death: Asdiwal *forgets* the snowshoes his father gave him—and in this forgetting (*pace* Lévi-Strauss) Asdiwal in fact *says to himself what should be said,* i.e., a statement of non-patrifiliation. This is no "manquer de dire á soi-même ce qu'on dû pouvoir se dire": it is precisely—and exquisitely—the opposite.

Diminishing his patrifiliative violations in the *land*-episodes, Asdiwal further *augments* them in the *sea* episodes. Rather than leaving his sister-wife and son to return to his *wulwulaisk,* Asdiwal (Asiwa) remains with them: he dies speaking to his son. Rather than "wishing to return" to his own matriclan, he "yearns to be back again among the sea-lions"—back, that is, among his father's people. More: rather than *forgetting* what he has received from his father (the rock-cod, the olachen oil), he *remembers* and (herein I agree with Lévi-Strauss) *he says* to someone what should not be said *("révéler á quelqu'un ce quón nàurait pas dû lui dire")*—a statement of patrifiliation.

Both the *land*-Asdiwal and the *sea*-Asiwa must be punished. Both have violated Tsimshian custom. On both land and sea Asdiwal and Asiwa have asserted patrifiliation. Nevertheless, the violative behavior of the *land* episodes is less than that of the *sea* episodes; and in the *land* episodes Asdiwal moves in the direction of the Tsimshian norm. Should there not be some reward in the *land* death? There is:

> After a little while his father came. It was he who went away with him to his own home (Boas 1912:145).

Finally helpless in his "relationship to the ground"—

> Where might he go now? He could not go up, he could not go down, he could not go to either side (Boas 1912:145)—

Asdiwal is taken to his father's home. This can only be after his death: in life on earth one's place is with one's mother's brother. And should there not be *no* reward for the defiantly criminal Asiwa? There is none:

> ...he fell down dead and fish bones grew out of his stomach (Boas 1895:289).

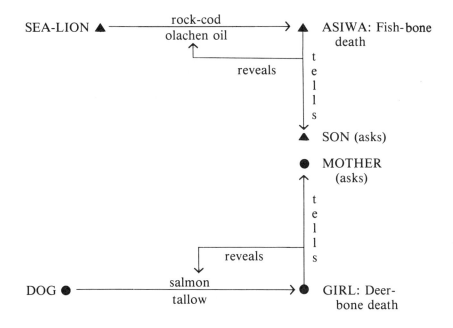

Figure 3

Identity and Inversion

Among the Bella Bella (neighbours of the Tsimshian), a tale is told:

> Starving and weeping a little girl goes to sleep by the campfire. During the night a dog lies down beside her, takes off its skin and becomes a beautiful woman. She gives the starving little girl food—salmon and tallow. She warns the little girl to say nothing. In the morning, the girl's mother asks her why she is so happy; and the girl tells her mother what happened. Immediately the girl screams and falls dead, deer bones piercing her stomach (paraphrased from Boas 1932:165-6).

In Figure 6:3 I compare this death among the Bella Bella to the death of Asiwa. The deaths are, it will be noted, in all respects *identical*—over transformations by (1) opposition and (2) inversion.

I have argued that the mythemes of the Tsimshian tale bear quite specific relationships to the reality of Tsimshian social organization. The Bella Bella tale allows me, it seems to me, to *test* the validity of my argument and my interpretation of the Tsimshian myth. I need argue only that

$$M_T \; : \; O_T \; : \; : \; M_B \; : \; O_B;$$

that is, as the Tsimshian myth is to Tsimshian organization, so the Bella Bella myth is to Bella Bella organization. It seems to me that the *identity* of the two deaths requires I so argue. But

$$M_B \; = \; M_T^{-1};$$

that is, the deaths are identical *over an inversion*. Therefore, logically,

$$O_B \; = \; O_T^{-1};$$

with respect to those aspects of social organization to which the myth is addressed, Bella Bella organization is the *inversion* of Tsimshian organization. If I am right in my argument that the "faults" of Asiwa are, initially, patrifiliation and, ultimately, incest, *these are not "faults" among the Bella Bella.* If in these aspects of organization

$$O_B \; = \; O_T^{-1};$$

my analysis of the Tsimsian myth is incorrect: I cannot "have it both ways."

I present Boas' relevant statements about these aspects of Bella Bella social organization:

1. The primary position of an individual is definitely with his

mother's division. However, position is not by any means permanent, but in the same way as among the Kwakiutl a person
may take his father's or his grandfather's position(1940:373).

2 . ...maternal descent prevails, although it is not rigidly adhered
to in so far as there is great freedom in assigning an individual in
later life a position in any one of the clans to which his ancestors
belonged (1940:374).

3 . ...the Bella Bella have the same clans that are found among the
Tsimshian, but they lack entirely the function of regulating marriage, and the idea that intermarriage between two members of
the same clan is incestuous is entirely foreign to the thoughts of
the people (1940:374).

4 . There is no rule of exogamy connected with the four-fold division of the tribe....Some elderly Bella Bella expressed
themselves very clearly in regard to their concept. They said:
"The northern tribes make a great mistake. Who has ever seen
a wolf mating with an eagle? It is right that an eagle should mate
with an eagle." Although they are perfectly familiar with the
customs of the northern tribes, the idea of exogamy is
entirely foreign to them (1940:372-3).

Notes

[1] An abridged version of this paper was read at the XLI Congress of Americanists
(Mexico 1974). I wish to acknowledge the many contributions to this research by my assis-
tant, Brad Campbell, now of the University of British Columbia. His own analysis of certain of the myth's symbols, "Semen and Fish-bones," will appear in *Tsimshian Dialogues
with Reality* (editors, John Cove and Charles Ackerman), in preparation.

[2] I do not herein address myself to the question of whether or not these patrilateral
marriages are proper ones. I present a discussion of this aspect of Tsimshian social
organization in my contribution to *Tsimshian Dialogues with Reality* (op. cit.) and in my
Death in the High Mountains (forthcoming, Oxford University Press).

References

Barbeau, Marius. 1929. *Totem Poles of the Gitksan, Upper Skeena River, British Columbia*. National Museum of Canada Bulletin 61, Anthropological Series No. 12.
Ottawa.

Boas, Franz. 1895. *Indianische Sagen von der Nord-Pacifischen Kuste Amerikas*. Berlin.

_____. 1902. *Tsimshian Texts*. Bulletin 27, Bureau of American Ethnology. Washington.

_____.1912. *Tsimshian Texts, New Series.* American Ethnological Society Publications, Vol. III. Leiden and New York.

_____. 1916. *Tsimshian Mythology.* United States Government Printing Office. (Reprinted by Johnson Reprint Corp. New York).

_____.1932. *Bella Bella Tales.* Memoirs of the American Folklore Society XXV. G.E. Steichert and Co. New York.

_____.1940. *Race, Language and Culture.* Free Press. Glencoe.

Durlach, Theresa. 1928. "The Relationship Systems of the Tlingit, Haida and Tsimshian." In *American Ethnological Society Publications,* XI.

Lévi-Strauss, Claude. 1967. "The Story of Asdiwal." In *The Structural Study of Myth and Totemism.* (Ed., E.R. Leach). Tavistock. London.

_____.1973. *Anthropologie Structurale Deux.* Librairie Plon. Paris.

Sapir, Edward. 1915. "Social Organization of the Nass River Indians." National Museum of Canada, Bulletin 19. Ottawa.

7
Shamanic Symbolism
In Salish Indian Rituals

Wolfgang G. Jilek and Louise Jilek-Aall

This is an attempt to analyse therapeutic ceremonials practised today among the Coast Salish Indians of the Pacific Northwest. Our analysis will be conducted on two levels, the level of symbolic content and the level of formal structure. We use original materials collected while working as psychiatrists and anthropologists in the Coast Salish area from 1967 to 1978, together with relevant data of ethnographic literature.

Symbolic Processes in *Indian Doctoring*

The Salish shaman or "Indian Doctor" is the one who travels to search and find the patient's lost soul or guardian spirit, and restores it to the rightful owner. Consequently, his name, $\check{s}x^w l\hat{\hat{e}}.m$, derives from $\check{s}x^w \partial li\text{-}\hat{e}.m$, "searcher of souls" and $\check{s}x^w \hat{\partial} l.\partial m$, "on one's course of travel."

Two basic disease concepts appear to have been brought from Central and Northern Asia to North America with consecutive waves of palaeolithic immigrants: (1) soul or spirit-power loss; and (2) intrusion of a pathogenic object or spirit-power into the patient. Attending to these conditions has exclusively been the shamanic healer's business in Asia as well as in America. In contemporary Salish *Indian Doctoring* the concepts of soul and spirit-power are closely associated, and it is believed that spirit power, as traditionally the soul, may leave a person due to a sudden fright experience. The loss of soul and loss of spirit power have the same cause—capture by shaman or ghosts—and call for the same therapeutic procedure: shamanic travel beyond this world and recapture of soul or spirit power; without this the patient would ultimately die.

We have observed *Indian Doctoring* of patients suffering from psychogenic symptoms which were diagnosed as due to spirit intrusion and soul loss. On one of the occasions when we shared a patient with an "Indian Doctor" and were invited to witness the curing rites, the shaman announced that the patient was suffering from "soul-loss sickness." He said that his special spirit power had let him see and find the lost soul "on the other side of the river," i.e., in the land of the dead (note the archetypal river Styx symbolism). He was going to return the lost soul to her rightful owner; however, he also stated that his spirit power had advised that the patient should become a spirit dancer for her own future protection, or else ancestral spirits would take hold of her soul and cause her serious ills. While the patient appeared to re-enter the trance state in which she had been put initially under the effect of continuous rhythmic chanting and drumming, the shaman made gestures as if capturing the lost soul from the air, holding it in his closed hands. He then transferred the soul back to its owner by rubbing it on the patient's chest and sides.

The Symbolic Process of the Power Board and Pole Ceremonial

We have observed the *sk^{w}əníləc* procedure on several occasions in the "smokehouses" of the Coast Salish, performed by *Indian Doctors* for diagnostic and therapeutic purposes during the winter ceremonial. The paraphernalia used in this ceremony consisted of either a pair of cedar boards or a pair of loop-shaped cedar branches or bark, bandaged with scarlet cloth. The "power boards" were rectangular cedar boards approximately 30 × 45 cm, with slots by which they were held. They were painted black and white, either showing the bare outline of a mask-like face, or a skeletonized figure. The following characteristics are attributed to the *sk^{w}əníləč* paraphernalia: they (1) have innate power; (2) move by themselves; (3) seek out their objects and (4) have the capacity to cure.

In the rituals we saw that the *sk^{w}əníləč* ran wild, and the strong workers, in spite of desperate attempts to tame them, were pulled around the hall. Again and again the power-charged instruments would pull together and had to be separated and pacified by the *Indian Doctor* who occasionally "blew power" into his hands before touching them. From time to time, he held them close to his ears, listened attentively and nodded his head. The instruments would then move around slowly, "smelling" and "searching" while the people watched on in suspense. The *sk^{w}əníləč,* just like the spirit dancer, is "blind" and yet seeing. The eyes painted on the power boards appear blind and the twisted power sticks are "blindfolded" by red cloth wrapped around them, and yet these paraphernalia point at and single out persons in the audience for recognition, reprimand, or treatment. In the *skʷənílə̌c* curing rite, a sick person singled out by the paraphernalia would be quickly surrounded by relatives and friends. The power-laden tools would move up and down on all sides of the trembling patient, emanating their healing power while the *Indian Doctor* chanted his song. At the end, with all drums being beaten, the *skʷənílə̌c* in a final display of power would chase its keepers four times around the "smokehouse" hall with such speed that the excited audience perceived them all as flying.

We have to turn to older ethnographic sources on Coast Salish culture, and to the etymology of Salish terms, in order to reconstruct the derivation of this ceremonial and comprehend its symbolic significance. All over the Northwest Coast area the ritual journey to the land of the dead, in order to recover a lost or abducted soul or guardian spirit, was performed by individual shamans with the help of their special spirit powers. In the form of a pantomime rite uniting the powers of a group of shamans in the effort to retrieve a patient's soul or guardian spirit, this shamanic voyage has been noted among Coast Salish and Interior Salish populations. The prototype of this shamanistic performance was the famous Coast Salish spirit canoe ceremony, a curing rite of great antiquity, photographed in 1920 by Dr. Leechman of Victoria but never witnessed by any of the area's ethnographers who described it under various related names; e.g. *smitinák,* Klallam (Curtis 1913); *sbEtEtda'q,* Snohomish (Haeberlin 1918); *sptda'qʷ,* Dwamish (Waterman 1930); smatnatc, Lummi (Stern 1934); *spadák,* Puyallup-Nisqually (Smith 1940); *bəsbətəda'q,* Twana (Elmendorf 1960); *bə́ttadak,* Skagit (Collins 1974).

Dr. Leechman's unpublished photographs picture boards with hand-holds painted on the cedar planks of the spirit canoe, quite similar in shape to the power boards used today. "Power entered these things during certain ceremonies and they dragged people about causing them to quiver and shake. The particular term for this object is *skudi'litc''*, wrote Waterman (1930 : 302). According to the original informants, the painted designs on the spirit-boat planks represent the shamans' spirit helpers travelling to the other world. They are surrounded by dots which stand for the "songs" revealed to the shaman by his particular spirit helper. On one of the planks (Wingert 1949), Plate 16) the painting represents a spirit power which can twist a victim into a knot. This twisting power is called *sxuda'tc* in Dwamish dialect. In his classical report on the Salish spirit canoe, Haeberlin (1918) relates that there was a painted cedar board beside each man in the ceremony, owned by the shaman and depicting his vision experiences; the Snohomish term for these "magical boards" is rendered as *swan'c.* It will be noted that by inserting into Dwamish *sxuda'tc* and Snohomish *swan'c* the mystical suffix *îl*, which is used in Coast Salish languages to denote special supernatural relationships, terms equivalent to Halkomelem *skʷənîləč* can be derived. Images with skeletal details found on shamanic boards and spirit-canoe figures were recorded in the drawings of Coast Salish planks by members of Wilke's United States Exploring Expedition 1838-1842 (Wingert 1949, plates 6,7,14, 21). To the old Coast Salish shamans, deer-hoof pendants attached to ceremonial objects signified "rattling bones" (Willoughby 1889 : 278). Today, the spirit dance candidate is still symbolically "clubbed to death" and "rattled' with a deer-hoof stick. In the now ob- solete Salish spirit-canoe rite, each of the participating shamans carried a long staff or "magical pole" which was handled in the manner of canoe poles or paddles to propel the magic vessel to the land of the dead (Dorsey 1902 : 234; Waterman 1930 : 540; Haeberlin 1918 : 253). Among the Lummi who are the southern neighbors of the Fraser River Salish, each of the medicine men enacting the spirit-canoe ceremony took his position in the symbolic boat armed with a pole "just as he would were he to go out into the water" (Stern 1934 : 80). These poles were referred to as *qakwa,* which term takes us to the *qʷaxʷəqs,* spirits who travelled in canoes, held long poles, and were associated with the Sea *skʷənîləč* by the Fraser River Salish. In conclusion : the contemporary Salish *skʷənîləč* rite is vestigial of the ancient psychodramatic enactment of a collective shamantic boat journey to the land of the dead. The Salish spirit-canoe of old retraced the voyage of the deceased person's soul, as it were, for in the past the dead were commonly buried in the southern Coast Salish area in a canoe which journeyed to the other world with them. The grave canoe was placed on a support frame which held a special power for the recovery of abducted souls. This power was known by the term *sbətəda'q* (Elmendorf 1960 :452) which also labels the spirit- canoe ceremony.

The Symbolic Process of the *sxwaixwe* Ceremonial

A few families in the Fraser Valley region and the Gulf of Georgia have hereditary rights to a most elaborately carved wooden mask, the *sxwaixwe.*. Comparison of earlier descriptions and pictorial representa- tions of the *sxwaixwe* mask and costume (Boas 1897; Curtis 1913; Stern 1934; Codere 1948; Barnett 1955) with recent specimens shows that over many decades its strange appearance has changed very little. It is obvious from the myths of origin that the mask is thought of as having super- natural properties, and that it bestowed shamanic curing power upon its first owner. The young man who received the mask is presented as being at the age of, or in the process of, training for his spirit quest (Boas 1894; Stern 1934; Codere 1948). He falls ill and in order to get cured he has to go through the initiation experience of death and rebirth : he drowns, i.e. he journeys to a beyond which is under water, encounters water spirits and is reborn, coming out of the water and returning home with the *sxwaixwe* mask, the representation of the spirit power he has acquired. Most versions of the origin myth relate that he got cured after having healed the underwater people and that he knew medicines and could cure certain diseases upon his return (Codere 1948). The hero thus has become an *Indian Doctor*—he can make people sick and also cure them (Hill-Tout 1902). The boy who is to receive the *sxwaixwe* has been singled out in his family, which is often the case with shamans-to-be. He is afflicted with a skin disease, a condition often attributed in North American Indian myths to a hero who is at first rejected but then acquires supernatural powers stronger than anybody else's. In the version related to us by a prominent local owner of the mask, the hero's previously unsocialized attitude is epitomized in the traditional text of the *sxwaixwe* song, which states that he had a "stomach of stone." Through the *sxwaixwe* experience he undergoes a personality change, a social cure such as is also effected by the spirit-dance initiation (cf. Jilek 1974). In the spirit quest, the initiate sees his ceremonial attire and face painting in a dream or in a vision.

It appears that the shamanistic properties of the *sxwaixwe* mask have been lost, and that it has been taken out of the spirit ceremonial complex where it undoubtedly once belonged. However, the power inherent in the mask is still believed to be so strong that the vulnerable new spirit dancers present at the *sxwaixwe* ceremonial must be shielded and protected from its influence. This power may be seen as deriving from the stark combination of binary oppositions symbolized in the mask itself, in the ceremonial costume, and in the choreographic drama of the *sxwaixwe* rite. The bird-fish nature of the mask, combining the aerial and aquatic realms, is repeated in the costume. The dancer is adorned with feathers while holding a sea-shell rattle. Most conspicuous in the *sxwaixwe* rite is the antagonism of the sexes : the wild power of the male dancers—only strong young men can perform the *sxwaixwe* dance—is tamed by the women's peaceful soothing song, which imposes order and rhythm on chaotic energy. In agreement with Lévi-Strauss' interpretation of the *sxwaixwe* (1975) we can perceive that, on the level of cosmos and nature, the *sxwaixwe* is a mediator of distant elements, joining heaven and earth, sky and water, bird and fish. On the level of human society, *sxwaixwe* is a mediator between distant kin groups, joining man and woman in exogamous marriage and also joining distant tribes in ceremonial functions at which the *sxwaixwe* mask is displayed. However, beyond these important mediator functions of the *sxwaixwe* mask, the myth attests to its shamanic origin and power, which is still manifested in the contemporary *sxwaixwe* rituals we observed.

The Symbolic Process of Spirit-Dance Initiation

In contemporary Coast Salish society, *spirit illness* is often fused with reactive depressive and psychophysiologic symptom-formation in the context of socio-cultural deprivation (cf. Jilek 1974). However, its traditional meaning has been preserved. The afflicted is said to be suffering from *syíwils tǝq'á.q'ey, "the spirit song's sickness."* He is conceived of as being possessed by a wild, untamed power, which could destroy him unless it is tamed and utilized as guardian spirit power for the benefit of the patient, who can only be cured through initiation into spirit dancing. This power is ambivalently perceived as beneficial to those who follow the traditionally prescribed "Indian ways" of dealing with it, but as destructive to the resisting deviant. It is called *syǝ́wǝn* in Western Halkomelem dialects, a word usually translated as "spirit song" and derived from the root *yǝw*, "having contact with the supernatural." In contemporary usage *syǝ́wǝn* denotes the essence of the whole guardian spirit ceremonial performed annually during the winter season. The sufferer from spirit illness is *q'a.q'ǝy*, "dying sick." His utter destruction is inescapable unless he submits to a vicarious ritualized "death" in the ordeal of spirit-dance initiation, in which he is "grabbed" and symbolically "clubbed to death," only to be resurrected ("stood up again") and born again to a new life as a "baby," after a quasi-fetal period of regression while secluded under the nursing care of "baby-sitters." Once he has "found his song," i.e. expressed his power publicly, the initiate is invested with his regalia, with the new dancer's "hat" and "pole." This is expected to occur on the fourth day of initiation. The "hat" or headdress, made of thick, long, woolen strands, is called *sáyiws,* which derives from *sæy*, "wool," and *-yiw*, "having contact with the supernatural." The Musqueam have another term for the initiate's hat, *sxa'yus* (Kew 1970 : 163) which is reminiscent of Puget Sound *skayu,* "inhabitant of the land of the dead" (Haeberlin 1918 : 254), and again evokes the death-rebirth theme. After four years of faithful adherence to the spirit-dance ceremonial, the human-hair-headdress(*m æqǝl tǝ sáyiws* from *mǽqǝl*, "human hair") is bestowed on the mature spirit dancer as insignia of his responsibility. We may interpret this ascent from animal to human hair as graduation from an animal-like level of untamed wild power to a human-like level of controlled and socialized power.

The Structure of Salish Healing

(1) *Basic Symbolism :* Shamanic Journey to the Land of the Dead. Very aptly the Halkomelem Salish term for shaman *šxʷ lǽ.m,* is derived from the verb *lǽm,* "to go," he is "the one on his course of travel." In his therapeutic pursuits, the shaman travels to the other world, to the Land of the Dead, whence only he returns who has acquired shamanic powers. As we have shown with our data, this shamanic voyage is most conspicuous in the *skʷǝní'lǝč* rite, which derives from the now-obsolete spirit-canoe ceremony, and in *Indian Doctoring,* when a lost soul or guardian spirit is fetched from the Land of the Dead "across the river." the *sxwaixwe* myth combines the shamanic travel to another world under water with the hero's cure and shamanic initiation. It thus repeats a

general theme of North American Indian mythology (cf. Eliade 1964 : 312). Salish spirit-dance initiation, with its leit-motif of death and rebirth, implies the novice's travel to the Land of the Dead. His journey starts when he is "clubbed to death," and he does not return fully to the land of the living before he has found his spirit song and re-emerges to a healthier and socially more-rewarding existence. Like the shamans in the spirit canoe the initiate is highly vulnerable, and while on his trip has to be protected by "babysitters" and by his uniform and staff. With the staff he "poles upstream, toward life" in the same manner as the spirit-canoe voyageurs. The initiate has to fast and must resist the temptation of accepting food with which he is "teased," for the myths tells him that he who accepts food in the Land of the Dead will remain there forever. The mature spirit dancer relives this archetypal journey at every winter ceremonial when, in trance, he dances around the hall of the "smokehouse," which always extends in East-West direction, "looking to the Land of the Dead." Although blindfolded, he finds his way past obstacles just as the shaman on his voyage to the other world. The spirit dancer has to beware of stumbling or slipping, which augurs ill, as did the shaman's misstep or fall during the spirit-canoe ceremony. When returning to his seat, the dancer feels rejuvenated "like a new-born baby."

(2) *Structural Pattern:* Our data on the therapeutic ceremonials of the Coast Salish can be summarized in a schema representing the dialectic process of supernatural power in the four types of ritual activity:

	Power Acquisition	Power Manifestation	Power Taming	Power Utilization
Indian — Doctoring	Shaman's quest for healing power	Shaman's initiatory sickness	Shamanic initiation ordeal; Intervention by senior shamans	Treatment of soul and guardian spirit loss; Treatment of spirit intrusion
Power — Board and Pole Ceremonial	Shaman's quest for $sk^w\partial\ ni'l\partial\ \check{c}$ power; ritual preparation of paraphernalia	Display of "wild" power of paraphernalia	Manipulation of paraphernalia by shaman in $sk^w\partial\ ni'l\partial\ \check{c}$ ceremony	Diagnosis: "smelling out" and "searching" power; Therapy: transfer of healing power from paraphernalia to patient

	Power Acquisition	Power Manifestation	Power Taming	Power Utilization
Spirit Dance — Initiation	Spirit quest; Power appears in dream-vision; finding of song	Spirit Illness; Display of "wild" power of new spirit dancer	Spirit dance initiation ordeal; Intervention by ritualist workers, babysitters, drummers.	Therapeutic social econo-mic benefits of guardian spirit power
sxwaixwe — Ceremonial	Mythical quest, hero's acquisition of mask; later by inheritance	Display of "wild' power of *sxwaixwe* dancers (male)	Intervention by chorus (female) in *sxwaixwe* ceremony	In myth: ther-apeutic social and economic benefits; In ceremonial so-cial and eco-nomic benefits of *sxwaixwe* power

Supernatural Realm   *Human Realm*

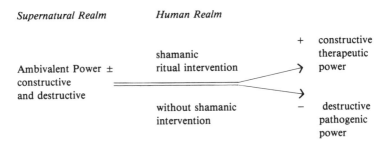

The Salish concept of power implies an inherent ambivalence due to the combination of binary-opposed destructive and constructive forces. Resolution is achieved through shamanic ritual intervention, which tames the potentially dangerous power, transforming it into construc-tive, therapeutic power for beneficial utilization. Without such interven-tion the destructive, pathogenic potential of supernatural power is real-ized to the detriment of the individual.

References

Adamson, Thelma (Ed.). 1934. "Folk-Tales of the Coast Salish," *Memoirs of the American Folklore Society* Vol. XXVII. New York: Stechert.

Amoss, Pamela T. 1972. The Persistence of Aboriginal Beliefs and Practices Among the Nooksack Coast Salish. Doctoral Thesis, Dept. of Anthropology University of Washington, Seattle.

Barnett, Homer G. 1939. "Culture Element Distributions IX: Gulf of Georgia Salish," *Anthropological Records* vol. 1, no. 5. Berkeley: University of California Press.

_____. 1955. *The Coast Salish of British Columbia.* Eugene: University of Oregon Press.

Benedict, Ruth F. 1923. "The Concept of the Guardian Spirit in North America," *Memoirs of the American Anthropological Association,* No. 29.

Boas, Franz. 1894. "The Indian Tribes of the Lower Fraser River," *Report of the 64th Meeting of the British Association for the Advancement of Science,* 1894: 454-463.

_____. 1895. *Indianische Sagen von der Nord-Pacifischen Küste Amerikas.* Berlin: A. Ascher.

_____. 1897. "The Social Organization and the Secret Societies of the Kwakiutl Indians," *Report of the U.S. National Museum for the Year Ending June 30, 1895* (Annual Report of the Board of Regents of the Smithsonian Institution) pp. 311-738. Washington: Government Printing Office.

_____. 1898. "The Mythology of the Bella Coola Indians," Publications of the Jesup North Pacific Expedition 2. *Memoirs of the American Museum of Natural History,* Vol. II - Anthropology, i. New York: Knickerbocker Press.

Codere, Helen. 1948. "The *Swai'xwe* Myth of the Middle Fraser River: The Integration of Two Northwest Coast Cultural Ideas," *Journal of American Folklore 61* : 1-18.

Collins, June McCormick. 1974. "Valley of the Spirits: The Upper Skagit Indians of Western Washington," *The American Ethnological Society Monograph 56.* Seattle: University of Washington Press.

Curtis, Edward S. 1913. *Salishan Tribes of the Coast, The Chimakum and the Quilliute, the Willapa. The North American Indian, IX.* Norwood, Mass. (Edition cited: New York: Johnson Reprint Corporation 1970).

Dorsey, George A. 1902. "The Dwamish Indian Spirit Boat and its Use," *Bulletin of the Free Museum of Science and Art of the University of Pennsylvania 3* : 227-238.

Drucker, Philip. 1950. Culture Element Distributions XXVI: Northwest Coast. *Anthropological Records* vol. 9, no. 3. Berkeley: University of California Press.

_____. 1951. The Northern and Central Nootkan Tribes. *Smithsonian Intitution Bureau of American Ethnology Bulletin 144.* Washington: Government Printing Office.

Duff, Wilson. 1952. The Upper Stalo Indians of the Fraser Valley, British Columbia. *Anthropology in British Columbia Memoir 1.* Victoria: Provincial Museum of British Columbia.

Eells, Reverend Myron. 1889. The Twana, Chemakum, and Klallam Indians, of Washington Territory. *Annual Report of the Board of Regents of the Smithsonian Institution for the Year Ending June 30, 1887* - Part II, pp. 605-681. Washington: Government Printing Office.

Eliade, Mircea. 1964. *Shamanism, Archaic Techniques of Ecstasy.* London: Routledge and Kegan Paul.

Elmendorf, William W. 1960. "The Structure of Twana Culture," *Washington State University Research Series Monograph Supplement 2.* Pullman: Washington State University Press.

Furst, Peter T. 1973. "The Roots and Continuities of Shamanism," *Arts Canada 30* : 33-60.

Gunther, Erna. 1927. "Klallam Ethnography," *University of Washington Publications in Anthropology 1/5.* Seattle: University of Washington Press.

Haeberlin, Hermann K. 1918. *"sbEtEtda'q*, A Shamanistic Performance of the Coast Salish," *American Anthropologist 20* : 249-257.

Haeberlin, Hermann K. and Erna Gunther. 1924. Ethnographische Notizen über die Indianerstämme des Puget-Sundes. *Zeitschrift für Ethnologie*, Jahrgang 1924: 1-74.

Hill-Tout, Charles. 1902. Ethnological Studies of the Mainland Halkomelem, A Division of the Salish of British Columbia. *Report of the 72nd Meeting of the British Association for the Advancement of Science* 1902 : 355-449.

Hultkrantz, Åke. 1953. Conceptions of the Soul Among North American Indians: A Study in Religious Ethnology. *The Ethnographical Museum of Sweden Monograph Series Publication No. 1*. Stockholm: Caslon Press.

Jenness, Diamond. 1955. The Faith of a Coast Salish Indian. *Anthropology in British Columbia Memoir 3*. Victoria: Provincial Museum of British Columbia.

Jilek, Wolfgang G. 1974. *Salish Indian Mental Health and Culture Change: Psychohygienic and Therapeutic Aspects of The Guardian Spirit Ceremonial*. Toronto: Holt, Rinehart and Winston.

Jung, Carl G. 1952. *Symbole der Wandlung*. Zurich: Rascher.

Kew, John E.M. 1970. Coast Salish Ceremonial Life; Status and Identity in a Modern Village. Doctoral Thesis, Dept. of Anthropology, University of Washington, Seattle.

Lévi-Strauss, Claude. 1963. *Structural Anthropology*. New York: Basic Books.

_____. 1975. *La Voie des Masques*. Genève: Éditions Albert Skira.

Margetts, Edward L. 1975. Canada: Indian and Eskimo Medicine, with Notes on the Early History of Psychiatry Among French and British Colonists. In *World History of Psychiatry*, John G. Howells, Ed. New York: Brunner/Mazel. pp. 400-431.

Ray, Verne F. 1942. Culture Elements Distributions XXII: Plateau. *Anthropological Records* vol. 8, no. 2. Berkeley: University of California Press.

Robinson, Sarah A. 1963. Spirit Dancing Among the Salish Indians, Vancouver Island, British Columbia. Doctoral Thesis, Dept. of Anthropology, University of Chicago, Chicago.

Smith, Marian W. 1938. MS Notes from 1938 Field Trip. cit. Codere (1948), pp. 2-4.

_____. 1940. *The Puyallup-Nisqually*. New York: Columbia University Press. Columbia University Contributions to Anthropology Vol. XXXII.

Stern, Bernhard J. 1934. *The Lummi Indians of Northwest Washington*. New York: Columbia University Press.

Waterman, T.T. 1930. The Paraphernalia of the Duwamish "Spirit-Canoe" Ceremony. Indian Notes, Museum of the American Indian, Heye Foundation, New York: 7 : 129-148; 295-312; 535-561.

Wickersham, James. 1898. Nusqually Mythology: Studies of the Washington Indians. *Overland Monthly 32* : 345-351.

Wike, Joyce A. 1941. Modern Spirit Dancing of Northern Puget Sound. Master of Arts Thesis, Dept. of Anthropology, University of Washington, Seattle.

Willoughby, C. 1889. Indians of the Quinaielt Agency, Washington Territory. *Annual Report of the Board of Regents of the Smithsonian Institution for the Year Ending June 30, 1886* - Part II, pp. 267-282.

Wilson, Capt. E.E. 1866. "Report on the Indian Tribes Inhabiting the Country in the Vicinity of the 49th Parallel of North Latitude," *Transactions of the Ethnological Society of London 4* : 275-332.

Wingert, Paul S. 1949. *American Indian Sculpture: A Study of the Northwest Coast*. New York: J.J. Augustin.

8
The Lizard's Tail:
An Ambiguity Analyzed

Kenneth Maddock

Over the past twenty years the study of myth and rite has been renewed by a radical reconsideration of their relation to each other. Some of the results are surprising. Stanner (1961a; 1961b) has shows that Murinbata religion includes, first, a rite-less myth; secondly, a myth-less rite; and thirdly, myths which are structurally parallel to rites, even though the Aborigines may not connect them with each other. These findings would not be expected on what Lévi-Strauss (1968) has called "the current approach" to myth and rite, according to which they correspond to each other: either rite enacts myth or myth explicates rite.

Lévi-Strauss does not reject "the current approach" out of hand, but he insists that the correspondence it postulates is no more than a special case, in which one of the two terms is strictly superfluous, since it conveys nothing not already expressed by the other. He shows how complicated matters can become by giving Pawnee myths, which invert Pawnee ritual while directly expressing the rites of neighbouring Indians (the example had been more fully described in Lévi-Strauss 1956).

Finally it may be mentioned that P.E. de Josselin de Jong (1965), by developing the methodological suggestions of his paternal uncle, J.P.B. de Josselin de Jong (1935), has been able to make sense of some puzzling features of Mnong Gar agricultural ritual by considering them in relation to Javanese and Malayan myths and rites. The assumption is that if two or more societies belong to the same "ethnological field"—a part of the world the peoples of which are so culturally similar as to form a single object of study, yet are varied enough locally to make internal comparison worthwhile—then a model formulated for one of them may be used to explain what is obscure in another. There is obviously an affinity between this approach and the method used by Lévi-Strauss in his *Mythologiques,* as P.E. de Josselin de Jong (1973: 99) has pointed out.

My aim here is not to compare and evaluate these new approaches to an old problem but to exploit the wide prospects which Stanner, Lévi-Strauss, and de Josselin de Jong have opened up, in the hope that I may be able to explain an enigmatic Northern Territory ritual.

On what Lévi-Strauss calls "the current approach," one would expect the rite to be duplicated by an accompanying myth. A reading of Stanner, however, would prepare us for the possibility that no such myth exists, or that the myth-rite relation consists in structural parallels which the tellers and actors do not recognize. Following Lévi-Strauss, we would be ready for a dialectical relation between myth and rite, and we should not feel constrained to stay within the boundaries of the society to which the ritual belongs. Following de Josselin de Jong, we might hope to elucidate the rite by referring it to patterns of belief and conduct in other parts of the same ethnological field.

There is no need to commit oneself to one of these approaches. It is best to bear in mind Johansen's sensible observation that myth and rite can stand in variable association "and therefore must preferably be elucidated in each separate case" (1958: 3). Each approach has developed as a solution to an ethnographic problem; the affinities between the different approaches show that fairly similar puzzles come up in Australia, American and Southeast Asia; but the value of the approaches is less mechanical than therapeutic: by being attentive to them, we are put on guard against a narrow conception of our task and we are made aware of the strange paths by which apparently independent phenomena can be joined.

In the first part of what follows, I shall describe the rite; in the second part, I shall look for its relationship to myth; and, in the third part, I shall suggest some conclusions about the nature of Aboriginal culture.

The Rite of the Lizard's Tail

This ritual occurs by night between the penultimate and final days of the Jabuduruwa, a cult practised by Aborigines in some northern areas of the Northern Territory. The whole cult consists in a series of rites performed in the space of a few months, and it cannot be described as having one aim or purpose. A Jabuduruwa is a ballet-like display of totemic imagery through which mythical allusions are made, juvenile males brought nearer to full manhood, spirits of the dead transformed into a state for which they may be reincarnated, relations between the sexes defined, and relations between some of the main segments of the social structure set forth in successive permutation.[1]

Most of a Jabuduruwa is carried out within a precinct access to which is restricted (see Maddock 1974, for the principles governing this). The peculiarity of the lizard's tail rite is that it requires women—who at all other times are kept out of the secret precinct—to penetrate to the middle of the ceremonial grounds, where objects and activities of which they must remain ignorant are displayed.

The night chosen for this rite should be one on which the moon, being on the wane, will not appear until the early hours. The women are led about midnight into the secret precinct, where they are shown to a sleeping place at a short distance from where the men dance. The fires between which they lie down are kept low lest the scene be too widely lit up, and the women are expected to fall asleep, not to look about or gossip among themselves. It is thought desirable for some married men to lie down there, too, so that the women will behave properly.

The men are busy before the women arrive. If a man has an actual or prospective mother-in-law taking part, he will make a roll of bark—called 'goanna tail' in English—which he will bury a few inches deep at her sleeping place. She will know to find it when the time comes. Those men who belong to the patrilineal moiety named *Dua* start their honeybee rite, which will not end until after the women have left, while those who belong to *Jiridja*, the other patrilineal moiety, begin to adorn their bodies for the clan-associated rites they will dance around sunrise when the women are gone. But let us consider the lizard tails more closely.

Because a woman needs one if she is to take part, and because men make them for their mothers-in-law, a woman is able to join in the rite—i.e., to enter the secret precinct—only if she has an actual or prospective son-in-law present. One dimension of this rite is accordingly that it gives symbolic expression to a critical social relationship.

That these rolls of bark should be known as goanna tails in English, which has become Aboriginal lingua franca, is explicable from the Jabuduruwa's mythical association with the goanna. But the Aboriginal name for them has a pleasing ambiguity to it. They are called *molo*, which means "tail," but also "penis." In the days before the Aborigines learned English, which is now the only tongue spoken by them all, the rolls of bark must have lent themselves to a play on the double meaning of their name. But when English was adopted, a decision must have been taken to render *molo*, in a Jabuduruwa context, as "tail," though it may be expressed as "penis" in other contexts.

Because I shall be arguing that "penis" would have made an apt translation of *molo* in the Jabuduruwa, I should point out that the same Aborigines use penis symbolism in some other ritual situations, so that their choice of "tail" cannot just be put down to prudery. Moreover, another word they have for "penis" is not used for the Jabuduruwa rolls of bark. It follows that if Jabuduruwa *molo* is (or used to be) evocative of penes, it is (or was) only equivocally so. Perhaps the ambiguity was important, thus explaining why, when English (which, unlike German, cannot make a double entendre of tail and penis) was adopted, the more "innocent" translation was made. But these suggestions are bound to remain speculative, for the Aborigines must have made their choice at a time when the present-day Jabuduruwa performers would have been too immature, even assuming them to have been alive, to take part in such decisions: we know from Elkin (1961: 192, 194) that the rolls of bark were tails in 1949, when he saw a Jabuduruwa. But back to the ritual.

The women are roused from their sleeping place soon after the moon rises. Having dug up their rolls of bark, they are led to a fire a little to the side of the dancing ground on which *Dua* men are busy with their rite and *Jiridja* men with their preparations. As the women approach, they are admonished to keep their eyes down, and a body of men forms up across the line of vision from fire to dancing ground so as to conceal the secret things there. Once at the fire, the women go in circles around it, beating into it with their goanna tails until these catch alight. The fire springs up under this treatment. The combined light of fire and moon makes everything clearly visible, yet the women see nothing—or so the men say—for they continue to keep their eyes turned down. Probably they are dazzled by the firelight.

Now that the tails are burning torches it is time for the women to go. They are led away from the fire and out of the secret precinct to a public meeting place, where they arrange the blazing tails like the spokes of a wheel.

What are we to make of the lizard's tail rite? Evidently it belongs to the class of "rites of exclusion" (Maddock 1972: 146-51), the dramatic function of which is to mark the differentiation of men and women in access to arcane lore: in spite of having been brought *near* the secret things and activities, the women are *far* from knowing what they are, though they must be able to sense that the men are up to something momentous; by an artful paradox, then, spatial proximity is made to serve the purposes of logical distance. But this leaves unexplained the specific symbolism of the rite.

We have seen that *molo*, the original name for the rolls of bark, is intrinsically equivocal and evocative. So far as one can judge, there is nothing about it—considered as a material object—to favour one meaning against the other. The English name, by contrast, is univocal and trite. The case for the (original) ambiguity of the rolls of bark does not depend, however, on lexical considerations alone, for an inconclusive argument can be put forward in favour of each meaning.

Suppose that *molo* symbolizes tail, as the present-day Aborigines say. This makes sense in the ritual context: because a man's *molo* (penis) is properly for this wife; his mother-in-law—who is not a licit sexual partner for him—should get a *molo* of the other sort (a tail), if she is to

get one from him at all. This interpretation of the rite makes it express
the formula that

molo (tail):*molo* (penis):: mother-in-law : wife

But suppose that *molo* symbolizes penis. A man's *molo* (penis) being properly for his wife, his mother-in-law does well to get rid of it by
setting fire to it after he makes it for her. Yet in what sense does she
destroy it? Is there not more ambiguity here? Before and after burning,
the *molo* might be taken to signify the tumescent and the detumescent
penis, with fire symbolizing coitus. That the women do not look about
and that the men do not want them to look, might be taken to symbolize
the shame which is attached to sexual relations between women and their
sons-in-law.

These and other understandings might have been concurrent while
the name for the rolls of bark was equivocal, especially if we assume—as
seems justified in ritual matters—that conflicts of motive, inchoate feelings and unconscious or only partly-conscious wishes and fears were involved. The adoption, at some time before 1949, of a univocal English
word must have helped to dispel this rich semantic atmosphere.

The position at which we have arrived is, then, that although *molo* is
rendered in a Jabuduruwa context as tail, a case can be made for
understanding it as penis. The former, being sexually neutral, might be
thought to have been the circumspect and inoffensive choice to make
when an English translation was decided upon, especially given the
nature of the relationship in which the gift is made and the fate of the
molo at the hands of she who receives it. But because the considerations
which have occupied us so far are bound to be inconclusive, the question
comes up of using myths to unlock the secret of the lizard's tail rite.

The Moon's Tale and the Lizard's

The Jabuduruwa performers have no myth to explain the lizard's tail
rite. Their myth to explain the whole cult says that Goanna founded it
after quarreling broke up a community of animals. But, following Stanner, Lévi-Strauss, and de Josselin de Jong, we need not limit our search
to myths which the performers tell in connection with their ritual. Our
task is to find myths which throw light on the specific symbolism of the
lizard's tail rite: e.g., mothers-in-law are given *molo,* they set alight to
them, goanna are alluded to, the moon is relied upon to coordinate the
movements of the actors, and sexuality is evoked by the *molo* transaction's significance for marriage.

Now a myth which varies the imagery of the rite is told by these
Jabuduruwa performers to explain the permanence of death in the flesh
(it will be recalled that Jabuduruwa performances put spirits of the dead
in a state from which they may be reincarnated). According to M_1, as I

shall call it, Wallaby was married to Blacknosed Python and Moon to Redbellied Water Snake. The two men argued about whose urine the women should drink. Moon wanted them to drink his, but finally they chose Wallaby's urine. Moon told the other three that had the women drunk his urine people's bodies would have been renewed after death. Then he rose into the sky as the moon, which regularly comes back after its wane and disappearance.

Obviously the myth is not an oral version of the rite or the rite an enactment of the myth, but each makes an allusive variation upon the interwoven images of the other. Thus wives in the myth/mothers-in-law in the rite; fleshly return/spiritual return; men's urine, a *molo* product/symbolic molo (equivocally tail or penis); men's conflicting advice to women about the drinking of urine/men's common admonitions to women not to look about; moon rises after women take the *molo* product/moon rises before women take the symbolic *molo*; women, by wrongly ignoring Moon, cause the possibility of resurrection to be lost/women, by correctly observing men's admonitions, enable the Jabuduruwa to be properly performed and hence maintain the possibility of reincarnation.

M_1 alludes to the *molo* (penis), because that is the source of men's urine, but the *molo* of the rite is separate from the body of which it is the tail or penis: it is a severed organ. Now the Lunga of northeast Western Australia, about 450 miles west of the known distribution of the Jabuduruwa, tell a story of a severed penis (Kaberry 1939: 199).

M_2 relates that moon tried to seduce Snake, his mother-in-law. She and her women companions were enraged by his attempt. They cut off his organs, which turned to stone. He angrily announced that he should return five days after death, but that when the women died it would be for ever.

Here, too, the possibility of resurrection is lost by the actions of women, but M_2 is generally closer to the lizard's tail rite than is M_1. In particular, this new myth associates a severed *molo* (as the Jabuduruwa performers would call it) with the relation between a man and his mother-in-law. It is apparent, however, that M_2 is a variation of M_1, which we have seen to be a variation on the rite:

M_1	M_2	Rite
Moon offers the product of his *molo* to his wife;	Moon tries to copulate with his mother-in-law;	Man gives a symbolic *molo* to his mother-in-law;
She refuses the offer;	She resists the attempt;	She accepts the gift;
Moon keeps his *molo* intact;	Moon loses his *molo* - it is cut off and petrifies;	The *molo*, already severed, is burnt;
Moon acts;	Moon acts;	Moon watches;
Human resurrection is lost.	Human resurrection is lost.	Human reincarnation remains possible.

The relation between these myths and the rite cannot be coincidental, even though the actors of the rite do not seem to associate it with M_1 and could not associate it with M_2. But the net in which they are caught would be drawn closer if myth parallels could be found for the ritual burning and if a lizard's *molo* could take the place of the moon's *molo*. The wanted features are given by two myths from the Karadjeri (Piddington 1932: 58, 59-61), about 300 miles southwest of the Lunga.

M_3 tells that Moon would invite people to visit him for a dance. The visitors would then be pushed into a fire which Moon and his two wives had lit. When the bodies had cooked, Moon and his wives ate them. One day, however, the intended victims, seeing what Moon was about to do, managed throw him into the flames, where he perished and subsequently became the moon.

This tale has Moon (and therefore his *molo*) suffering the fate of the rite's symbolic *molo*, i.e., burning. Together with his wives, he is set against people whom he wishes to absorb into himself by eating their flesh. In the first two myths, Moon was set against women whom he wished to take his urine or semen into themselves.

M_4 tells of a goanna man, Kamida, who travelled with his uncircumcised sons. They killed many goannas. Kamida told the boys that they were to be circumcised, but when they asked him what he had said he angrily answered that he had told them to eviscerate the lizards. As they approached the camp which was their destination, Kamida lit fires as in the Kuramidi ceremony. Once in the camp, he saw with head bowed, because he had a mother-in-law present. After dancing at sunset, Kamida wriggled about so that his penis became buried. Then it travelled beneath the ground to penetrate the mother-in-law's vagina. Kamida's sons, noticing that she was sick, told their father, who withdrew his penis, whereupon the woman recovered. Next day Kamida told the people that they might circumcise his sons, but he took offense when the operation was carried out while he was away searching for food. He avenged the slight by starting a fire in which all the people died; as for Kamida and his sons, they escaped the heat by taking refuge in a pool where they may still be seen as a group of stones.

The pattern of images in these four myths and the rite (with + and − to signify presence or absence) may be shown thus:

	M_1	M_2	M_3	M_4	Rite
Molo offering to wife:	+	−	−	−	−
Molo offering to Mother-in-law:	−	+	−	+	+
Cut *molo*:	−	+	−	+	+
Burned *molo*:	−	−	+	+	+
Petrified *molo*:	ı	s	ı	s	ı
Buried *molo*:	−	+	−	+	−
Moon:	+	+	+	−	+
Lizard (goanna):	−	−	−	+	+

This tabulation suggests that M_4 is the closest myth to the rite. The other resemblances are the more striking because of this myth's stress on ceremony, which is missing from the first three tales.

No myth has so far brought together moon and lizard. If, however, we move even farther afield—to the southeast of Western Australia—we can find a myth (Elkin 1940 : 327) which resembles the rite not only in having both moon and lizard but in evoking correct marriage.

M_5 relates that Moon chased the Pleiades, who were women, and bothered them until the two Wati Kutjara, who were iguanas—i.e., goannas—cut off his penis and admonished him to marry according to law instead of behaving promiscuously. As in M_2, the severed organ turned to stone.

It is not made clear what Moon's relation was to the Pleiades or whether his offense consisted in seeking sexual partners outside marriage or sexual partners having the wrong relation to him. Perhaps it was both. Here it is interesting that M_2 accounts for wrong marriages as well as for death (Kaberry 1939: 12, 128). M_5 may accordingly be put in close connexion with both M_2 and the rite:

M_2	M_5	Rite
Moon wants to copulate with his mother-in-law;	Moon wants to copulate with women;	Man puts symbolic lizard *molo* for his mother-in-law to find;
Women cut off Moon's *molo*;	Lizards cut off Moon's *molo*;	The symbolic lizard *molo* is already a severed organ;
The *molo* petrifies; Sanction for marriage.	The *molo* petrifies; Sanction for marriage.	The *molo* burns; Sanction for marriage.

M_5 is not on its own in the southern regions of Australia. According to M_6 (Roheim 1945: 41-3), from near Ooldea in South Australia, Moon wished to copulate with some women, but he died soon after being wounded by the magical boomerang of the Wati Kutjara heroes. According to M_7 (Tindale 1936: 171-6), Kulu (the name of Moon in M_6) chased the women of the Wati Kutjara. He died after being wounded by their boomerang.

Tindale does not mention the species with which the Wati Kutjara are identified, but in Roheim's version, as in Elkin's, it is goanna lizard. The women of M_7, like those of M_5, are the Pleiades. Moon dies in each tale from a wound inflicted on him because of his improper sexual behavior. It is obvious that M_{5-7} are extremely close variants of each other.

The last myth to which I shall refer substitutes a lizard for the moon. Roheim (1945: 45-6) gives it to explain a Pidjandjara rite, in which a man, who represents a lizard, dances with a phallus held erect towards a retreating body of women, who represent the Pleiades. M_8 tells that a lizard, whose penis was permanently erect, chased the Pleiades, with whom he wished to copulate. His penis kept breaking off and petrifying, but he continued in pursuit with penis erect (Roheim remarks on the contradiction). This myth, incidentally, is a good example of an oral version of a rite.

We may now return to the lizard's tail rite in the Jabuduruwa. Although the actors in this rite do not explain it by a myth, variant combinations of its imagery occur in a number of myths scattered about the huge Australian continent. With their aid the rite can be interpreted. Admittedly $M_{2\text{-}8}$ are not directly related to the rite, in the sense of being known to the ritual actors, but they belong to the same chain of connexion as M_1, which is known to the actors, even though they do not treat it as an oral version or explanation of the rite. Oddly enough, however, M_1 is semantically more removed from the rite than are some of the other myths in the chain.

Two myth-rite equations may be suggested:

Rite		**Myth**
symbolic *molo*	=	severed penis
burning of *molo*	=	burning or petrifaction of penis (either severed—$M_{2,5,8}$ —or unsevered—$M_{3,4}$)

The Jabuduruwa *molo* is thus interpreted otherwise than by actors. If this seems high-handed, it may be explained that I am not really correcting or contradicting the ritual performers. I am looking at their lizard's tail rite from a standpoint which is not theirs, and from which I can see a significance hidden from them. That is to say, the meaning of *molo* is relative to the point from which it is viewed.

In ordinary language, *molo* means tail or penis. According to the Jabuduruwa performers, the *molo* of their lizard's tail rite is a tail, not a penis. On an anthropological interpretation of the rite, the *molo* is equivocal. But seen in the light of the myths we have examined, the ritual *molo* looks to be a penis, not a tail. These are not rival views. Rather they add to each other, so that we understand the rite to have many aspects. But, recalling what was earlier suggested about the loss of equivocality in translation, it is reasonable to think that the myths enable something of the ritual's pre-English meaning to be grasped.

Let us next consider the roles of moon and lizard. Two formulas can be given for their relation in the myths:

$$\text{moon} = \text{lizard}$$
$$\text{moon} \neq \text{lizard}$$

The first formula is abstracted from $M_{1,2,4,8}$, each of which has the moon thrusting his penis (or a product of it) on a woman in a myth which has no lizard characters, or a lizard doing so in a myth which does not have the moon among its characters. Moon and lizard may accordingly be accepted as substitute terms. The second formula is abstracted from M_{5-7}, each of which has a lascivious moon punished by lizards.

Now it is the second formula which belongs to the rite, for while the mothers-in-law are on earth burning the symbolic lizard's tails given to them by their sons-in-law, the moon is in the sky looking down upon the actions which have been organized to take place according to his movements. Is it possible, then, that the second-formula myths throw a special light of their own upon the rite?

If we thought of the rite as a symbolic enactment of the myths, then we should have to identify the ritual *molo* as the moon's penis, which would also fit well with M_2. The mothers-in-law of the ritual would be the women of the myths, for whom the moon hungers. But then the castrating—the *molo*-severing—role could be ascribed either to the men of the ritual, who would thus take the part of the lizards of M_5, or to the women, who would thus take the part of the women of M_2. Such a doubling of role for the female characters would be true to the latter myth.

No great ingenuity is required, then, to find among the body of Australian myths some which are fairly literal oral versions of the rite, provided only that lizard's tail is transformed to moon's penis. So literal a version cannot be obtained if we keep to the native view that the Jabuduruwa *molo* is a lizard's *molo*. M_4 does bring lizard *molo* into conjunction with mother-in-law, but the severed-penis theme is missing (the closest to it being the circumcision of the boys), as is the moon. M_8 fits its associated rite well, but is not strikingly close to the Jabuduruwa rite.

Ethnographic information comes patchily to us in both time and space, so perhaps there is or was a myth version of the lizard's tail rite. But to insist on this would betray an unreasonable adherence to the theory that rites and myths come in matching pairs. All that the evidence enables us to say is that Aboriginal minds are apt to associate such themes or images as sexuality and death, severed penes and mothers-in-law, lizards and the moon. Variant combinations of these are recognizable in widely scattered myths and rites, the complexity of which is added to by transformation of basic images, e.g., mother-in-law to wife, semen to urine, penis to tail.

This analysis of myth and rite can usefully be brought to an end by considering the significance of those pages of *L'homme nu* (1971: 596-603) in which Lévi-Strauss defends his approach to myth, and argues against critics who have doubted its applicability to rite. There is here, he says, a powerful source of confusion, consisting in failure to see that myth may be explicit—i.e., take the form of tales—or implicit—i.e., take the form of notes, sketches or fragments tied to particular phases of ritual performance. Implicit myth is a gloss on rite, and it should be treated together with explicit myth *as mythology,* instead of being confused with rite and treated together with it in opposition to explicit myth.

The tales which I have presented as M_{1-8} are explicit myths on this view. That a roll of bark in the Jabuduruwa is a *molo,* that *molo* means tail in this context, that the tail is of a lizard and that the making and use of the tails is significant for a man's relation to his mother-in-law, are implicit myths, for they amount to so many glosses on the standardized actions required at that stage of a Jabuduruwa performance.

There seems to be no difficulty in treating explicit and implicit myths together, but the question is what sort of study could be made of rite in abstraction from implicit myth, i.e., apart from the standard meanings which the actors ascribe to their performance. A purely behavioural study of rite would dissolve the myth-rite problem altogether, unless we were able to recognize descriptions of ritual in some of the explicit myths. If we accept that people are prone to give standard meanings to their actions, then it is more productive to treat implicit myth as intermediary between rite and explicit myth than to identify it with either.

The Nature of Aboriginal Culture

A Jabuduruwa rite belongs to the same complicated network of affinities as a number of moon and lizard myths. Only one of the myths is from the Jabuduruwa area. Some of the others are more than a thousand miles away from the place where the lizard's tail rite is performed. How to explain this?

It might be that myth is primary, as well as more widespread, and that the rite is a dramatiç variant upon a body of themes and images the distribution of which is much greater than its own. Or the rite is primary, despite its narrow distribution, and the myths from the west and south result from the disturbing effects of rite on Aboriginal minds: rite provokes the formation of myth in an outwardly spreading series. This possibility would assume that myths are worked out in response to other myths, as well as to rite. Again, it might be that myth and rite have a common basis in, say, masculine ambiguity to women generally or to mothers-in-law particularly, so that men appear now as womanizers, indifferent to sexual propriety, and now as moralists, insistent upon lawful marriage. These conflicting attitudes are respectively embodied in the moon and lizards of M_{5-7}, and perhaps in the lizard and his sons of M_4, but in other myths propriety is upheld either by women (M_2) or by a sort of permanent "self-destruct" process characterizing the lascivious male (M_8). Such a common basis would not explain the specific symbolism of the rite or the variant combinations to be found in the myths.

Clearly, then, there are two main reasons. One is why certain themes and images should be associated in Aboriginal thought. The answer to this, assuming it to be discoverable, lies outside the myth-rite problem. The other is how to account for patterns of resemblance which cannot be coincidence, but which, because of the huge areas involved, are hard to reduce to conscious design. The answer to this is relevant to the myth-rite problem as posed here.

It seems inescapable that myths and rites are worked out in relation to other myths and rites (see Maddock 1970; 1976; 1979). Very possibly the lines of influence run in all conceivable directions: myth to myth, myth to rite, rite to rite, rite to myth. Evidently there are countervailing pressures at work in this process: on the one hand, to keep part of the original (hence the recurrence of severed penes, of mothers-in-law, of moons and lizards); on the other hand, not to follow the original so closely as to duplicate it. The result is that variant combinations can easily be recognized over great distances, but imitations are hard to find. Thus a puzzling feature of a rite or myth in one place can be interpreted in the light of myths or rites from other places, with a fair confidence that the interpretation is more than caprice.

We know that dreams are important to Aborigines, and it would not be surprising if they played a part in the process of diffusion-in-variation which has here been suggested as a solution to the myth-rite problem. Men, who learn while awake of the stories and rituals of other Aboriginal groups (whether directly or by hearsay, whether fully or in fragmentary fashion), rework these materials while asleep. They would also have in mind the stories and rituals of their own group. The mind, both when dreaming and when awake, subjects the material to controls which affect its content and organization, e.g., a wish to solve problems, an inability to drift too far from compelling themes and images, a structuring principle of opposition, a need not to plagiarize what belongs to another group. The result is that distinctive combinations are produced, which yet are recognizable as recombinations. And, because little that was new would have entered Aboriginal thought in pre-European times, the chain of variant combinations can sometimes look more alike at its extremes than it does over shorter lengths.

Notes

[1] My studies of the Jabuduruwa were carried out mostly on the Beswick Reserve, and the lizard's tail rite discussed in this chapter is in the form it takes among the Beswick people.

References

Elkin, A.P. 1940. "Kinship in South Australia," *Oceania* 10: 295-349.

_____. 1961. "The Yabuduruwa," *Oceania* 31: 166-209.

Johansen, J.P. 1958. *Studies in Maori rites and myths.* Copenhagen: Munksgaard.

Josselin de Jong, J.P.B. de. 1935. *De Maleische Archipel als ethnologisch studieveld.* Leiden: Ginsberg.

Josselin de Jong, P.E. de. 1965. "An Interpretation of Agricultural Rites in Southeast Asia, with a Demonstration of Use of Data from Both Continental and Insular Areas," *The Journal of Asian Studies* 24: 283-91.

_____. 1973. "Voltooide symphonie: de *Mythologiques* van Claude Lévi-Strauss," *Forum der Letteren* 14: 95-120.

Kaberry, P.M. 1939. *Aboriginal Woman: Sacred and Profane.* London: Routledge.

Lévi-Strauss, C. 1956. "Structure et dialectique," In *For Roman Jakobson: Essays on the Occasion of His Sixtieth Birthday* (pp. 289-94). The Hague: Mouton.

_____. 1968. "Religions comparées des peuples sans écriture," In *Problèmes et méthodes d'histoire des religions: mélanges publiés par la section des sciences religieuses à l'occasion du centenaire de l'École Pratique des Hautes Études* (pp. 1-7). Paris: Presses Universitaires de France.

_____. 1971. *L'homme Nu.* Paris: Plon.

Maddock, K. 1970. "Myths of the acquisition of fire in northern and eastern Australia," In *Australian Aboriginal anthropology: modern studies in the social anthropology of the Australian Aborigines* (pp. 174-99), edited R.M. Berndt. Nedlands: University of Western Australia Press.

_____. 1972. *The Australian Aborigines: a Portrait of Their Society.* London: Allen Lane, The Penguin Press.

_____. 1974. "Dangerous Proximities and Their Analogues," *Mankind* 9: 206-17.

_____. 1976. "Communication and change in mythology," In *Tribes and boundaries in Australia* (pp. 162-79), edited N. Peterson. Canberra: Australian Institute of Aboriginal Studies.

_____. 1979. "A Structural Analysis of Paired Ceremonies in a Dual Social Organization," *Bijdragen tot de Taal-, Land- en Volkenkunde* 135: 84-117.

Piddington, R. 1932. "Karadjeri Initiation," *Oceania* 3: 46-87.

Roheim, G. 1945. *The Eternal Ones of the Dream.* New York: International Universities Press.

Stanner, W.E.H. 1961a. "On Aboriginal Religion: IV. The Design-Plan of a Riteless Myth," *Oceania* 31: 233-58.

_____. 1961b. "On Aboriginal Religion: V. The Design-Plan of Mythless Rites," *Oceania* 32: 79-108.

Tindale, N.B. 1936. "Legend of the Wati Kutjara, Warburton Range, Western Australia," *Oceania* 7: 169-85.

9
Myth and History
in Ancient Peru

R.T. Zuidema

Introduction

During the last 20 to 30 years our ethnographic knowledge of Ancient Peru has expanded enormously, through the discovery and analysis of Spanish administrative documents on indigenous religion and social organization in early colonial times, and through a renewed study of the Spanish chroniclers. A handicap will always be that we do not have accounts of Peruvian culture written before the Spanish conquest in 1530, from before the time of the complete disruption of the Inca empire. One way of circumventing this handicap is an analysis of Andean mythology—placed in a pre-Spanish setting, with the assumption that this information recorded by the chroniclers reflects the most authentic ethnographic material of the indigenous culture.[1]

The two most important written sources on pre-Spanish Peru are, on the one hand, the chronicles dealing with the history of the Inca royal dynasty and the conquest of their empire from Cuzco, their capital, in Southern Peru; and, on the other hand, the apparently complete mythology of a village, *San Damian de Checa,* in the upper valley of the coastal river of *Lurin* or *Pachacamac* in Central Peru. Although we must recognize the uniqueness of such a full mythological description of an insignificant village, there are circumstances that do account for this accident. Spanish missionary activity in the 16th and early 17th centuries was particularly strong in the diocese of Lima, the Spanish colonial capital, and so we can consider as part of this endeavour the fact that the priest Francisco de Avila, a mestizo, had recorded around 1608, in Quechua, all the religious information available from this village. San Damian was, however, also situated near two important religious centers. At the mouth of the Lurin valley was the most important pyramid and religious center of coastal Peru in Incaic and pre-Incaic times. This center was dedicated to Pachacamac, the "Creator of the World," the chthonic god of earthquakes. Above San Damián, to the East, is the snow-capped mountain range of *Pariacaca,* one of the most sacred mountains in the Andes. In Central Peru Pariacaca is identified with *Yaro*, the local name for the god of Lightning, Thunder and all atmospheric events (Davila Brizeno 1881: p. 71; Mariscotti 1970: p. 161).

In another analysis, based on a document from 1622 (Zuidema 1973a), I showed how the complex organization of the ancestral mummies and their attendant priests in a small village from Central Peru could be compared in detail to the socio-religious organization of Cuzco. I hope to demonstrate that the mythology of San Damián and imperial Incaic concepts of their past are built upon the same complex structures, and that we are dealing in both cases with a similar way of conceptualizing space and time.

The best introduction to an understanding of this structural model and its transformation is, in my opinion, by way of an analysis of certain terms used by the Incas in Cuzco, and similarly by all Quechua- and Aymara-speaking peoples in Central and Southern Peru.

The Binary and Triadic Classifications

The first classification found in Inca culture is the distinction between the denominators *saya,* "upright," and *suyu.* Saya refers to hierarchical divisions within political units and to the cultivated lands within a town or village; suyu refers to the divisions of land outside town and to the cyclical service—suyu also means "turn"—of subject groups to the political center. In their opposition, saya has a male and phallic connotation, suyu, a female one (Zuidema 1973b).

The second binary classification uses the terms *Hanan,* "upper," and *Hurin*, "lower," to distinguish any two social or other categories which are considered to be related to each other as, respectively, "higher" or "major" and "lower" or "minor." As far as I am aware, only the denominator saya can be attached to these words: *hanansaya* and *hurinsaya.* When the saya-suyu opposition is expressed by hanan and hurin, the suyu category becomes hurinsaya. In the case of proper names of local and/or social groups, hanan and hurin can be placed before the name, as in Hanan-Cuzco and Hurin-Cuzco—that is, they replace the term saya. Suyu is placed after the proper name, as in the names of the four local subdivisions outside Cuzco and of the whole empire: *Chinchaysuyu* (N.W.), *Collasuyu* (S.E.), *Antisuyu* (N.E.) and *Cuntisuyu* (S.W.).

In conclusion, the denominator saya only allows a binary, hierarchical and vertical distinction; the denominator suyu only allows horizontal and spatial distinctions, but not necessarily defined by a specific number: the terms saya-suyu define the binary distinction of hierarchy to non-hierarchy in terms of an inside-outside opposition.

Triadic classifications are obtained by different series of terms that can be used synonymously. The most important series in Cuzco is:

Collana, "first, principal, chief-"
Payan, "second"
Cayao, from *calla* "origin, base"

Other series are:

Allauca,	"to the right"	*Capac,*	"rich" or "royal"
Chauin or *Chaupi,*	"in the center"	*Hatun,*	"big" or "numerous"
Ichoc,	"to the left"	*Huchuy,*	"small"

The binary and triadic classifications are irreducible to each other in Incaic thought. The most significant context, in which they are used over and over again, is in their combination in a six-fold model. The *first* reason for this is that the terms Hanan and Hurin, besides their primary use as indicated above, can also be used for the oppositions of Collana (=Hanan) to Payan + Cayao (=Hurin), and of Collana + Payan (=Hanan) to Cayao (=Hurin). The *second* reason is due to the fact that the process of subdividing a binary and a triadic relationship can be repeated, producing sequences of 2, 4, 8, 16 and of 3, 9, 27, 81 subdivisions. Applying next the terms Collana, Payan and Cayao to a fourfold division, a fourth category is distinguished, indicated by the term *caru*, "far away." Combining the original Hanan-Hurin division in the sixfold model with the second Hanan-Hurin division, one four-fold model is created; combining it with the third Hanan-Hurin division, another, wider four-fold division is created. In the context of the first four-fold division, Cayao (= 5 + 6) is considered as the unbounded outside to (1 + 2 + 3 + 4), whereas in the second four-fold division 5 and 6 are brought within these limits.

The numbers of the six-fold model indicate, moreover, that within the context of

the first four-fold model:
1 = Hanan-Hanan = Collana
2 = Hanan-Hurin = Payan
3 = Hurin-Hanan = Cayao
4 = Hurin-Hurin = Caru

the second four-fold model:
(1 + 2) = Hanan-Hanan = Collana
(3 + 4) = Hanan-Hurin = Payan
5   = Hurin-Hanan = Cayao
6   = Hurin-Hurin = Caru

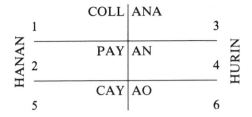

These principles of classification allowed an almost unlimited expansion. Only in the organization of Cuzco do we become fully aware of the potential of these classificatory principles. Three hundred twenty-eight sacred places *(huacas)* in and around Cuzco were organized according to 41 lines *(ceques)* going out from the central temple of the Sun. There were three groups of three ceques in each-of the four suyus of Cuzco—the individual ceques being called Collana (a), Payan (b), and Cayao (c)—with the exception of one suyu, which had 14 ceques. A comparison of this system to the social system of other Inca political units shows that the categories Collana, Payan and Cayao could also be applied to, respectively, the groups of ceques (1, 2 and 3) in each suyu and to the suyus Chinchaysuyu (I), Collasuyu (II), and Antisuyu (III). In this four-fold context, Cuntisuyu (IV) fulfilled the role of Caru. We are able to analyze structurally the symbolic implications of these systems (Zuidema 1964) because of the multiple ritual roles of huacas, groups of huacas, ceques, groups of ceques and suyus in the social, religious and calendrical systems of the Incas in Cuzco, as expressed by way of their ideas about their past.

The Use of Kin Terms

Kin terms were used to indicate relationships between categories of the six-fold division, and they were also used for groups associated either to huacas, ceques, groups of ceques or suyus in the ceque system. In some cases, these relationships may have been of a real kinship character, but probably more often they were of a symbolic kind. It will be necessary, therefore, to review some of the properties of this system and of its wider, symbolic implications (Zuidema 1977b).

(1)

The terms *yaya,* "father," and *churi,* "child," both have a strong genealogical conotation. In a stricter sense *churi* is "son" in opposition to *ususi,* "daughter." The latter term derives from the root *usu,* "being lost" (Gonzalez Holguin: *ucuni;* B.J. Isbell 1977). The *mama-huahua* relationship stresses the fact of biological procreation. The mother is not included in the genealogical unit of the father and his children. Like the wife (*huarmi*) and the mother (*mama*), their brothers are also considered as outsiders to the genealogical unit of a father and his children. A man, therefore, uses the same term, *caca,* for his wife's brother or mother's brother. Caca also means "person living outside a town or village" and "contributor."

(2) A group of four generations in either a patriline or a matriline which descend from a male ancestor can be represented as a group of four brothers or four sisters when opposed as such a group to relatives that are further removed. The inverse of this rule is also possible.

(3) A man's sister's children are equated to his own children in secondary wives.

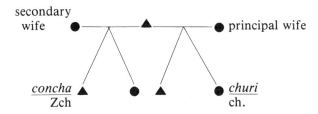

Each man has only one principal wife, who is theoretically given to him by the Inca king or by one of his representatives. In the case of the king himself, his principal wife is his full sister, the daughter of his father and mother, who were also the former king and queen.

(4) Primary cross-cousins are prohibited from marriage to each other. Allowance for secondary cross-cousins to marry is combined with a preference for sister- or daughter- exchange. This preference can be expressed in terms of a patriline-matriline opposition as follows (FF-FZddd = MMBdd = MFZdd, etc.):

(5) The matriline symbolically represents the line of secondary descendants, as opposed to the patriline, which represents the principal line of descendants. We can therefore transform the given model also into the next one:

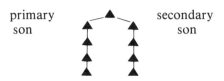

(6) Kin terms are associated in two different ways to the terms Hanan and Hurin and to the terms Collana, Payan, Cayao and Caru. We define the first way as the absolute use of kin terms, since they are applied in a fixed way to established social groups and animal categories. The following associations of kin terms of Collana, Payan and Cayao are registered:

Collana:	ego	ego	ego	ego	ego	ego
Payan:	son	son	father	prim. son	son	son
Cayao:	father	grandson	grandfather	sec. son	daughter	wife

(7) The terms Collana, Payan, Cayao and Caru can also be used to indicate genealogical distance from ego. The principal difference with the first use (see 6) is that ego now becomes a category by himself, excluded from the position of Collana, Payan, Cayao and Caru.

Collana:	relatives of the first degree
Payan:	relatives of the second degree
Cayao:	relatives of the third degree
Caru:	relatives of the fourth degree

The degree of relationship counts equally to the common ancestors as to each of his co-descendants. In the contexts of the ancestral system and the administrative system where ranks are indicated by kin terms for, respectively, ascendants or descendants, the first four generations can be considered as brothers and sisters; that is, respectively, as four "fathers" and four "mothers" or as four "sons" and four "daughters." The FFFFF then becomes an "F" and a similar inward projection is applied to other ancestors and descendants. In the context of the six-fold division, we encounter the following examples:

(1) F	(3) FFF		(1) 1st brother	(3) 3rd brother
(2) FF	(4) FFFF		(2) 2nd brother	(4) 4th brother
(5) FFFFF	(6) FFFFFF		(5) father	(6) grandfather

The same principles of organization are applied also to the female or secondary line of descendants or ancestors, thereby producing a Hanan-Hurin opposition of two six-fold divisions (the primary and the secondary lines), both integrated into a twelve-fold division.

(8) The role of ego with respect to all these models can be discussed in the context of the following model:

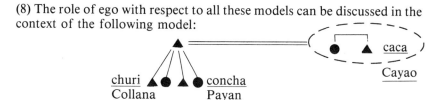

churi

Collana

concha

Payan

caca

Cayao

I mentioned before that in the context of kinship only a father could make distinctions between son and daughter and between primary and secondary son. On a more symbolic level, however, ego enters into a symmetric, binary relationship either with his primary children, his secondary children, or his wife and wife's brother. In turn he thereby assumes characteristics in common with each of these classes. In the context of the six-fold division, ego's role occupies a central, "zero" position. The saya (vertical)—suyu (horizontal) relationship clearly expresses the opposition of ego as saya on different planes in the vertical context, against the four-fold, six-fold or twelve-fold divisions, as suyu, in a horizontal context. I will not analyze the saya-role of ego in the following examples of Andean history and mythology. In the Inca context, a concrete example of a symbolic role representing the position of ego is the king marrying either his full sister or mother, thereby creating a dynasty that is patrilineal and matrilineal at the same time. A modern example, from the indigenous *cargo* or *envarado* organization, is the fact that the *alcalde*, the "mayor," is considered as the *tayta-mama*, the "father-mother" of the other functionaries, who are his "major children," his "minor children" and his "children-in-law."

(9) In the foregoing paragraphs I have analyzed Incaic classificatory thought by way of binary and triadic structures. Morissette and Racine (1973), inspired by the work of Piaget (1949), have applied a similar but more mathematical analysis to modern Quechua classificatory thought in terms of the hierarchy of the sacred mountains. They only used the Quechua terms for binary distinctions, although they envisioned the possibility of triadic structures and their combination with binary ones. My analysis of Inca (Quechua) kinship was completely possible within this framework. I should emphasize, therefore, that Inca terminological equations do not impose any kind of marriage rules or social system, but only classify the given reality.

San Damián Mythology and Inca History

Generally speaking, we can detect in each story—be it Inca history as a whole, or San Damián mythology, or individual myths—a developmental pattern of four phases. The first, introductory, phase sets the stage in terms of argument and location. The second phase, the central part of the argument, discusses a six-fold classification. The third phase has a "vertical" argument, in distinction of the "horizontal" one of phase two. Finally, the fourth phase mentions a real event, of which the existence is explained by relation to the former phases.

Inca history and San Damián mythology relate these phases to respectively the actions of the three major Gods: first *Viracocha,* the Creatorgod; second the Thundergod; third the Sungod and finally,

Chaos as an expression of primordial times and of the present. Viracocha is generally characterized as an old man who travels through the country either creating—that is, bringing forth the different peoples out of caves, etc.—or destroying—by a flood. He belongs to a time before socio-political organization, the organizations of men, existed. In terms of calendrical time, he is related to the rainy season when the seeds are under the ground and the plants are growing. Moreover he is related to the night; in terms of space he belongs to the outside and to uninhabited areas. The Thundergod, as the god of atmospheric events, is the god of war and conquest and of the defense at the borders of urban and in-habited areas. In terms of calendrical time, this means the beginning (sowing) and end (harvesting) of the agricultural season; thus, the tem-poral boundaries of the wet and the dry seasons. He belongs to dawn and dusk, when Venus is the most important celestial body and when the Sun is rising and setting. In terms of space, then, he defines the borders of the political units. The Sungod is the god of dry season when political ad-ministration can best be carried out. Besides being the God of the dry season, he also governs the day. In terms of space he belongs to the center. In conclusion, Andean peoples also defined the three gods in the triadic classificatory scheme of Collana (the Sun), Payan (the thunder) and Cayao (Viracocha) (Zuidema 1977a)

In Cuzco, the first phase of Inca history deals with the creation of the world and of the Inca ancestors down to the conquest of Cuzco by *Manco Capac,* the ancestor of two Inca dynasties. The second phase deals with the history of ten kings and their conquests. The third phase is concerned with the ritual founding of a new capital, *Tumibamba,* near the border of Peru and Ecuador by the eleventh king, *Huayna Capac.* Finally, the last phase concerns the death of Huayna Capac in Tumibam-ba when he already knew about the coming of the Spaniards; his division of the empire between his two sons; their civil war, and finally, the destruction of the Inca empire by the Spaniards.

I have dealt with the formal, ritual, and mythological aspects of the first and third phases of Inca history elsewhere (Zuidema 1972 M.S. and 1973b). I will concentrate here on certain data of the second phase. The ten Inca kings were divided into two dynasties of five kings each, one belonging to Hanan-Cuzco and one to Hurin-Cuzco. According to some of our earlier chroniclers both dynasties were contemporaneous, one king of Hanan corresponding to one of Hurin, about whom similar details are mentioned. To other chroniclers, the Hurin-dynasty came before the Hanan-dynasty, with the kings described by the same characteristics. I will be interested here principally in the Hanan dynasty. Each king was attached to the worship of one deity, thereby assuming characteristics similar to the latter. We are especially well-informed on the last three kings. In this way, we get the following double relationship of Gods to the two Inca dynasties:

	God	kings of Hanan	kings of Hurin
Viracocha		......Manco Capac	
		Inca Roca............	Sinchi Roca
		Yahuar Huacac.........	(Tarco Huaman)
Thundergod...	Viracocha..	Viracocha Inca........	Lloque Yupanqui
	Thundergod	Pachacuti Inca........	Mayta Capac
	Sungod....	Tupa Yupanqui........	Capac Yupanqui
Sungod		.....Huayna Capac	
Chaos (civil war, coming of Spanish)...	Huascar		Atahuallpa

In San Damián, the first myth deals with the travels of *Coniraya Viracocha* and his classifications of wild animals as an expression of a relationship to non-human habitats. Then come the myths of Pariacaca, the Thundergod, who was composed of five brothers, and *Chaupiñamca*, their five sisters. These myths describe the establishment of human society, both on a cosmic level, and on a "historical" level, by the expulsion of the coastal peoples from the San Damián area where they had lived previously. The most detailed, and most confused, part of San Damián mythology concerns the actions of the sons of Pariacaca. This is also the time that *Tupa Yupanqui* is mentioned as king (ch. 23). Most mythological descriptions discuss political organization on a local and a more state-wide level; the worship of the Sun as a state cult; and the origin and religious organization of huacas and calendrical rituals. Another myth (ch. 14) deals with Coniraya Viracocha, now in the role of priest-king, and Huayna, Capac, the Inca king. Their division of the country into coastal and mountain kingdoms is similar to the division made by Huayna Capac with the establishment of a capital in Tumibamba (Zuidema 1964, 1973b). Although the divisions mentioned in each case are different, and although one story uses far more mythical details than the other, their apocalyptic function is the same. In both cases the quarrels and fights between men and the ambiguous role of priests bring about the coming of the Spaniards. Together, Huayna Capac and Coniraya Viracocha, by the travels of the latter and his messengers from the coast up to lake Titicaca (where Huayna Capac was at that time), define the saya position in relation to the suyu position of the six-fold divisions which we will discuss for both Inca history and San Damián mythology.

In order to correlate San Damián mythology to Inca history, we discover that we must make use of the associations of the history to the actions of the three major Gods in order to understand the correspondence. We discussed the correlation of certain San Damián myths to the kings Tupa Yupanqui (ch. 23) and Huayna Capac (ch. 14). The problem starts with the actions of the Thundergod and the Creatorgod. The indigenous chronicler *Guaman Poma* (f. 109, 286) correlates the occurrence of a great drought in the time of Pachacuti Inca to a similar event in the mountains of Pariacaca. He ascribes the latter event to the actions of Viracocha, while the mythology of San Damián imputes it to

Pariacaca. In the next pages I will analyze in some detail two myths about Pariacaca, one on a human and one on a cosmic level. I will argue that the actions of the five brothers Pariacaca correspond, first, to the deeds of the Inca line of five kings in Hanan-Cuzco and, second, to the deeds of Pachacuti Inca in particular. In the same way, we can correlate the actions of Coniraya Viracocha, both to the Inca origin myth and to the deeds of Viracocha Inca in particular. This correlation problem is in fact a good example of the genealogical shortening or lengthening, as we discussed this in the paragraph on kinship, points 2, 4, 5 and 7.

```
Coniraya Viracocha ⟵ . . . . . . . . . . . . . Manco Capac
                                              Inca Roca
                                              Yahuar Huacac
                                            ⟶ Viracocha Inca
Five brothers Pariacaca ⟵ . . . . . . . . . . Pachacuti Inca
Sons of Pariacaca . . . . . . . . . . . . . . . Tupa Yupanqui
Coniraya Viracocha + H.C. . . . . . . . . . Huayna Capac
```

The San Damián Myths

The two myths (Avila ch. 5 and 7) take place in the primordial time of the *Purunruna*, "the wild men, like those who now live outside the villages and towns." The first myth is about the adventures of a man who saw the birth of Pariacaca, the Thundergod, and who became the first person to worship him. The second myth replicates the first one, but is now removed to the cosmic plane with the battle of Pariacaca against *Huallallo Caruincho* as the first god who reigned after or during the "primordial black night," *Yanañamca Tutañamca.* The four phases of the development in the first myth are abbreviated as follows:

(1) Once a poor man, called *Huatyacuri,* who only ate potatoes cooked in an earth oven, slept at a place halfway along the valley from San Damián to the coast. There he overheard two foxes, one coming from the coast and the other from the mountains, who told each other what they had experienced recently. The fox from the mountains said that a rich man was sick because of the adultery of his wife, a fact that the man did not know. Huatyacuri went to the rich man, Tamtañamca, and cured him in exchange for getting his youngest daughter, Chaupiñamca, in marriage.

(2) However, the husband of Chaupiñamca's older sister could not consent in having a poor man as a brother-in-law. He challenged Huatyacuri to six competitions. First they would compete in drinking and dancing. Huatyacuri asked his "father" Pariacaca, what to do in order to win and the latter advised him to go to the top of a mountain and lie down as a dead *huanaco* (wild llama). Then, a fox and his wife, a

skunk, would come with a small vessel, a small drum and a flute. When the animals laid down the instruments in order to drink, Huatyacuri should get up and take the instruments away. He did as was told and with these instruments he was able to defeat his brother-in-law. The latter danced with 200 women, but when Huatyacuri started to dance with his wife alone, the whole earth trembled. In the drinking bout he won by inviting all the people to drink cornbeer from his small vessel. As the vessel could never be completely emptied they all got drunk, except Huatyacuri.

In the next two competitions Huatyacuri won by dancing first in a dress called *casacancho*, white as snow, and then with a red puma skin that came out of a well at the same time that a rainbow appeared in the sky.

The fifth competition was won by building in one night a big house with the help of wild animals: birds, serpents, huanacos and vicuñas.

In the sixth competition, a dance, Huatyacuri wanted to start first. He then danced in a blue skirt and a white loin cloth.

(3) Huatyacuri's brother-in-law became so frightened of this dance that he changed into a deer and fled to the mountains. His wife fled to the coast. Huatyacuri, however, turned her into an upside down stone. She was still worshipped in the time of Avila by people who placed coca leaves on her upturned vagina.

(4) Also, in that time deer were eating men. Once, however, a young deer, instead of saying "how shall we eat men?" said "how shall men eat us?"; from that time on men pursued deer. At the time that Huatyacuri accomplished all this, Pariacaca was born in the form of five falcons *huaman* from five eggs. Pariacaca then started a rain which sent deep waters down the river, dragging along with them to the coast houses and llamas. At that time, two huge trees grew up on the mountaintops on both sides of the river just below San Damián. Their branches grew into each other forming an arch and in the arch lived monkeys, toucans and other birds. They were all brought down to the coast by the waters.

The second myth describes how

(1) People and animals from the coast originally lived high up in the mountains of Pariacaca. When the five falcons (i.e., Pariacaca) changed into five brothers and went up the mountain Pariacaca, and there played together the game of the bolas (rivi), it became very cold and hail began to fall. Also at that time, a man went up the mountain to sacrifice his son to Huallallo Caruincho. Pariacaca detained the man from doing so, saying "when I have defeated Huallallo Caruincho you will worship me and you will not have to sacrifice your son."

(2) Pariacaca then fought in the form of five brothers as a red rain. He fought against Huallallo Caruincho who used a yellow fire

coming from below. So much red rain came down that a lake, *Mullucocha*, "lake of red *mullu* shells from the coast," was created. Huallallo was not defeated yet, however. He escaped higher into the mountains and started to fight again, now as a double-headed serpent. But Pariacaca nailed him down with a golden staff and turned him into stone (ch.16). (The serpent can still be seen in the rock at the pass where one crosses the Pariacaca mountain range. From colonial times it has been known as the *Escaleras* (Albornoz p. 23, 24).) In a third and final battle, still further away from San Damián, Huallallo Caruincho fought as a parrot in a mountain gorge and was defeated. He fled into the Eastern Lowlands, and there one of the five brothers Pariacaca now defends the entrance to the mountains.

(3) Pariacaca then fought Huallallo Caruincho's wife who lived in the lower part of the valley of Lima. In the battle she broke the foot of one of Pariacaca's sons, called *Chuquihuampu*. He was sent against her as a guardian when she fled towards the coast.

(4) In that place people, especially those from near the coast, now make offerings of coca and sterile llamas to Chuquihuampu.

Analysis of the myths

The two myths of Huatyacuri and Pariacaca present similar events on two different levels: the human and the cosmic. Huatyacuri discovers Pariacaca. He is the first human to worship the God, and by his actions triggers the latter to start a flood which carries the original inhabitants of San Damián down to the coast. Pariacaca's actions in the second myth are initiated by another man who wanted to sacrifice his child to Huallallo Caruincho. The result of Pariacaca's actions is mentioned in terms of the sacrifice of coca and sterile llamas that people on the coast now make to him.

The myth of Huatyacuri especially deserves a detailed, formal, and internal analysis. I will indicate two possible analytical approaches: First I will deal with the six competitions between Huatyacuri and his brother-in-law.

The material details mentioned in the competitions each describe a function of an Incaic temple as we know it: (1) through the general description of Guaman Poma (262, 263)—who calls it a temple of the Sun; (2) through actual examples of such temples; and (3) through pictures of these temples on lacquered wooden beakers, called keros, which were used in Central and Southern Peru. The actual temple I am thinking of, called *Sunturhuasi*, was a round structure with a high conical roof. Near to it was a round basin, called *Ushnu*, that was used for libations given to the ancestors in the underworld.[2] In the walls of the Sunturhuasi were a number of windows which were used for observing the rising and setting Sun. Therefore, Sunturhuasi had the function of an observatory. At the foot of the building, Guaman Poma describes, and the *keros* show, two pumas who hold a standard with a flag which bear the motive called *Casana*. The heads of the two pumas may be shown also with the two ends of a rainbow coming out of their mouths. In addition, Guaman Poma and the keros give the detail of two men standing at the sides of the building blowing a conch-shell trumpet. The Sunturhuasi and the Ushnu of Cuzco stood on the central plaza—called *Haucaypata*, "plaza of rejoicing"—because here much drinking and dancing went on after important state rituals in the cult to the Sun.

If we now place the details of the six competitions in the following hierarchical scheme, they form three groups, each with two functions expressing one of the binary oppositions or relationships described also for the Sunturhuasi.

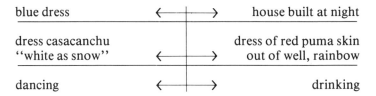

The dancing and the drinking were two activities going on at the foot of the building, in a Cayao position. Drinking was part of the ritual activity of drinking with the ancestors, pouring cornbeer into the Ushnu. Dancing and drinking express the opposition of an external to an internal activity (drinks within the stomach, within the earth).

The words casacanchu and casana have the term casa in common and probably refer to the same concept. The two competitions which make use of the two dresses casacanchu, "white as snow" (that is the snow of the high mountains) and the puma skin, (which comes out of a well) express a high-low opposition, as hanansaya-hurinsaya, and accentuate the vertical function of the Sunturhuasi.

The blue dress and the house built at night refer to day and night in relation to the roof of the Sunturhuasi. The blue dress, especially, may refer to the central position of a chief. In the case of the Inca king the blue dress, *Tarco huallca*, symbolized his "celestial" royal position.

The six-fold classification is constructed by way of three different binary oppositions which each say something of the system as a whole. For instance, the outside-inside opposition of the Cayao position (dancing, drinking) carries through in the casacanchu–puma, well opposition of the Payan position. Here, the first element refers to the mountains on the horizon and the second element to the well connecting with the underworld. A similar argument can be given for an above-the-roof–under-the-roof opposition in the Collana position. On the other hand, the primary light-no-light opposition becomes an opposition in the

Payan position of white (the snow) to red (the Puma) and perhaps to black as the puma coming out of a well (the underworld). The same light–no–light opposition was also, of course, involved in the dancing (outside)–drinking (to the ancestors, inside) opposition.

Rather than continuing this discussion of the possible binary oppositions in a six-fold context, I should stress here one peculiarity of the sixfold division as used in the six competitions and in the Sunturhuasi. In both examples Hanan, Upperworld, is related to light and outside, while Hurin, Underworld, is related to dark and inside. In other words, this seems to be an inversion of Hanan (inside)–Hurin (outside) opposition as we initially postulated. However, we must be aware that the myth of Huatyacuri or the Sunturhuasi themselves are in a Payan position: both express the values of the rising and setting Sun, connecting Under- and Upperworld. The myth of Pariacaca, the companion myth to the one of Huatyacuri, stresses another aspect of the Payan position: the defeat of Huallallo Caruincho. Pariacaca fights with red rain from above and Huallallo Caruincho with yellow fire from below. But the latter is first changed into a lake (water below), and is thrown out of the country which will now worship Pariacaca. The two myths and the Sunturhuasi all stress, in similar ways, the role of mediation and change which belong to Payan.

The second approach to the myth of Huatyacuri deals with a progression of six binary oppositions, each opposition concerning the relationship to one or more animals.

First there are the two foxes, from above and from below, who discuss events of the past and the future. They are especially concerned with the fate of Tamtañamca. Second, there is the male fox and the female skunk from whom Huatyacuri steals the instruments for the first two competitions by lying down like a dead huanaco.

Third, there is the relationship between Huatyacuri and his future father-in-law, Tamtañamca. In his list of most important huacas in the Inca empire, Albornoz (p. 34) mentions Tamtañamca as a dead fox at the entrance of the temple of Pachacamac. The Earth god himself was represented here in the form of a golden fox. In a genealogical context, "fox" is used to refer to caca (WB, WF, MB). Moreover, our first Quechua dictionary, written by Domingo de Santo Tomas (1560) describing the coastal dialect, mentions *cacay* as a kin term and a term for "contributions." In this light, the myth of Huatyacuri now reveals itself as a description of the ambiguous relationship between a wife-taker (Huatyacuri) and a wife-giver (Tamtañamca). On the one hand, the father-in-law receives respect from his son-in-law; however, the respect paid by a rich son-in-law may be so condescending that it is insulting (personal observation; but also Guaman Poma f. 857), whereas a poor son-in-law can be in a completely subservient position. On the other hand, from the point-of-view of kin terminology, the woman who is married to the founder of an ayllu and who is the mother to his descendants is considered an outsider to his ayllu. This outside-role is extended to her family through her brother, the caca to the ayllu. The myth describes this father-in-law to son-in-law opposition not as a static relationship but as a processual one developing through the six binary oppositions. First Huatyacuri, the potato-eater, is the poor outsider, a contributor (of a daughter); meanings implied in the concept of caca.

The fourth binary opposition transforms this two-generational relationship between Huatyacuri and Tamtañamca into a one-generational relationship between Huatyacuri and the husband of Tamtañamca's other daughter. The relationship of Chaupiñamca and her sister is now like that of respectively, primary child (churi) to secondary child (concha) in the Incaic context.

Then we come to the fifth and sixth oppositions. The brother-in-law of Huatyacuri becomes a deer and flees to the puna; his wife flees to the coast where she turns into stone, upside down.[3]

In San Damián (Avila, appendices to Quechua text) and elsewhere (Bertonio, see: sucullu) deer, together with vicuñas and huanacos, were the primary representatives of hunted animals, in opposition to llamas as the domesticated ones.

The six binary oppositions describe a process of transformations. It may be possible, then, to describe them within the context of a six-fold model, and to correlate this to the model of the six competitions between Huatyacuri and his brother-in-law. In the first two oppositions no distinction between men and animals is made, even though one opposition involves two male animals and the other a male and a female one. After the kin relationships described in the next two oppositions, the last two oppositions show the separation of men from animals. Here, a male-female distinction also occurs: the brother-in-law is a deer and his wife, apparently (Avila ch. 10, 13), was a skunk. The model then would be:

$$\text{DEER } (\male) \leftrightarrow \underset{\text{HUA}}{} \leftrightarrow \text{ skunk } (\female)$$
$$\text{father-in-law} \leftarrow \underset{\text{TYA}}{} \rightarrow\text{brother-in-law}$$
$$\text{2 foxes } (\male, \male) \leftrightarrow \underset{\text{CURI}}{} \leftrightarrow\text{fox } (\male), \text{ skunk } (\male)$$

The model is only tentative, and further research probably will force us to revise it. In a general sense, however, it is comparable to the model of the six competitions. Huatyacuri's involvements with the foxes and with the fox and the skunk correspond to a Cayao position. Challenging his future father-in-law and competing with his brother-in-law express a Payan-value, as does war. In fact, we found Tamtañamca mentioned as a guardian at the foot of the temple of Pachacamac in the same way as the puma with the standard and flag, casacanchu, stood at the foot of the temple Sunturhuasi. When Tamtañamca still was a rich man, his own house had been called casacanchu. After having conquered Tamtañamca and his brother-in-law, Huatyacuri and his wife come into the Collana position. Something of the day/night opposition that we except here is expressed in their separation from the deer and the skunk, since the latter was considered as an animal of the night (Avila ch. 2). In conclusion, we could suggest that the progression of the six binary oppositions expresses, through time, the same structure as found in the six competitions. The latter accomplishes this in a more compact form with explicit references to the structure of the Sunturhuasi.

The War of Pachacuti Inca against the Chancas

In the foregoing paragraphs I have already compared Inca history to San Damián mythology, while in the case of the myth of Huatyacuri, I made a more specific comparison to one architectonical and ritual element of Inca culture. As mentioned above, Guaman Poma suggested a correlation between a drought during the reign of Pachacuti Inca and the creation of a lake in the myth of Pariacaca. I will now discuss some of the more salient facts of Pachacuti Inca's reign in order to suggest the structural correspondence to the myths of Huatyacuri and Pariacaca.

When Pachacuti Inca was still a young man, Cuzco was attacked by a people, the Chancas, who came from the West across the great river Apurimac. Viracocha Inca, the king, fled to a valley in the north. The valley was either that of nearby Chita, or a valley leading into the other great river near Cuzco, the Urubamba. Pachacuti defended the city and not only defeated the Chancas near Cuzco, but also pursued them over the Apurimac and defeated them in their homeland. Whatever may be historical of such a war, in Inca epic history it grew to cosmic proportions and the Incas considered it as the starting point of their own empire-building. Moreover, they included in their accounts of this war and its aftermath events that do not seem to be related to the Chanca war. Many of the events also occur in the myths of Huatyacuri and Pariacaca.

(1) The first such myth that interests us in this regard is the rebuilding of Cuzco by Pachacuti Inca. Sarmiento (ch. 30, 31) gives a detailed account of this which I will use here. Pachacuti first went to visit the cave Tambotoco, from where the ancestor of the Inca dynasty, Manco Capac, had originated. He then disinterred the mummies of the first seven kings, down to Yahuar Huacac, adorning them with ritual paraphernalia. He had two golden statues made, one of the Creator god, *Viracocha Pachayachachi*, which he placed to the right of the image of the Sun, and one of the Thunder and Lightning god, *Chuquiilla*, which he placed to the left. Since Chuquiilla once appeared to Pachacuti Inca as a double-headed serpent, he took the latter as his personal huaca.

Let me first comment on this partial account of the rebuilding of Cuzco. No mummies are mentioned for Viracocha Inca, Pachacuti Inca and Tupa Yupanqui (they were still alive); in the case of Pachacuti Inca, his mummy is replaced by the statue of the Thundergod. We may suppose, therefore, that the statue of Viracocha Inca is related in the same way to Viracocha the Creatorgod as the statue of Tupa Yupanqui to the Sungod. These personal statues, or huacas, were also known as *huauque*, "brother." The one of Viracocha Inca was called Inca Amaru, "Inca Dragon-serpent" (Sarmiento ch. 25). I will have occasion to mention this one later.

(2) Next, I want to consider together different mythical fragments that all seem to be comments on the same huacas, those located on ceques directed to the north. These ceques are directionally related to the nearby valley of Chita and to the Urubamba river.

(a) As a boy Viracocha was expelled by his father from Cuzco to Chita (Cobo XII, ch. 10). There he had a vision of Viracocha the Creatorgod. From then on he adopted the name of the latter. When, as a king, he fled from the Chancas, he went to Chita, according to some accounts, but to others he went further away, towards the Urubamba river.

(b) Part of the rebuilding program of Pachacuti Inca (Sarmiento ch. 32, 33) was the resettlement of Cuzco's old inhabitants outside a perimeter of some 20 kilometers. Viracocha Inca, apparently as their most important representative, was banished towards the river Urubamba. Another son of Viracocha Inca, who had followed his father, Inca Urco, tried to reconquer Cuzco. He was defeated by Pachacuti Inca, who was assisted by his brother *Inca Roca*, "a great necromantic." During the triumphal march back into Cuzco, the captives were dressed "in long shirts with many tassels." Pachacuti Inca then (Sarmiento ch. 34) battled against *Tocay Capac*, king of the *Ayarmaca*, who lived to the North of Cuzco along the Urubamba. Tocay Capac's kingdom had originally included Cuzco, but he had been defeated already once before by Manco Capac, the ancestor of the Inca royal dynasty.

(c) The antagonism between Pachacuti Inca and a man whom we can identify with Viracocha, the God, is told by one chronicler (Murua I ch. 86) on a cosmic scale. In this case Pachacuti Inca is considered to be the son of Manco Capac (who himself had been created by and in the time of Viracocha, the Creatorgod (Molina p. 11, 12).) The myth says that during a whole month heavy rains caused so much damage that the earth was threatened with destruction. (A "flood" or *"huno pachacuti,"* in the words of Sarmiento (ch. 7) .) In that time, a huge man in a long red dress, with a trumpet and a staff, appeared on a mountain pass to the north of Cuzco, called *Chitacaca* ("the pass to Chita"). The man had come down on the waters of the river Urubamba. Pachacuti asked him not to play the trumpet, as, if he did, the world would be destroyed. Pachacuti Inca received his name because of this event. He later turned into stone.

(d) An event of just the opposite effect is told by Guaman Poma (f. 109, 286) about Pachacuti Inca, the ninth king. During his reign there was a great drought. It made the stones crack, the food freeze; it hailed and there was a plague of birds, like partridges and parrots, and of wild animals, like deer, foxes and skunks. Guaman Poma compares this event, caused by the actions of the Thundergod, to the creation of Mullucocha and of the Escaleras in the mountains of Pariacaca by the god Viracocha.

(e) Santacruz Pachacuti, another indigenous chronicler, tells the same story, but combines the effects of (c) and (d). He places it in the time of Tupa Yupanqui, the tenth king, but the story is told about *Amaru Tupa*, the oldest son of Pachacuti Inca. At the birth of Amaru Tupa (Santacruz Pachacuti, p. 242), there were volcanic eruptions and a dragon, Amaru, entered the Cuzco area from the north. At the feast celebrating his birth in honor of the god Viracocha, during the December solstice (that is, in the raining season), all wild animals were thrown out of the Cuzco area. Amaru Tupa was associated with tigers, hermaphrodites, dwarfs and hunchbacks, and he is said to have dedicated himself to weaving. Weaving, symbolizing the supreme act of creation, is also associated with his grandfater, Viracocha Inca (Sarmiento ch. 25); with the Creatorgod (Molina p. 9) and, in San Damián, with Coniraya Viracocha (ch. 2). Therefore, it may be that we can identify Amaru Tupa, the person, with Inca Amaru, the statue or huauque of Viracocha Inca. The detail concerning Amaru Tupa in which I am interested here (Santacruz Pachacuti p. 246, 247) tells how during the great drought mentioned above, only the land of Amaru Tupa—including *Amarumarcahuasi*, "the house where the special (corn) for the Amaru was guarded"—had sufficient clouds over it to guard it from the frost. The result of this was that only these lands received a good crop and thus Amaru Tupa became the inventor of the agricultural storehouses. Amarumarcahuasi was situated on the road to Chita, and is mentioned in the ceque system as a huaca on the first ceque of Antisuyu. The cult and the care of this ceque was in the hands of Viracocha Inca's descendant, and its first huaca was said to be the huauque, "brother," of the god Viracocha.

The last three fragments all discuss an athmospheric event which today is referred to by the Spanish term *sequía*, "drought." In indigenous parlance, sequía refers to excessive rain and to the lack of it. The effect in both cases is the same: a bad harvest. In these myths, however, Pachacuti Inca is indentified with frost and hail (not rain) and Viracocha, the god or the king, with excessive rains. Both persons correspond, respectively, to Pariacaca and Coniraya Viracocha in the myths of San Damián (ch. 8 and ch. 2), and in the context of the myth of Pariacaca alone, to the

Pariacaca who goes up the mountain causing frost and hail and to the Pariacaca who fights against Huallallo Caruincho with a red rain.

In the myths of (b) and (c) we find references, respectively, to a "long dress with tassels," worn by prisoners, and to a "long red dress," worn by the god from the waters of the Urubamba river who came over Chita into Cuzco. Both descriptions probably refer to a long dress with tassels that was actually worn by celebrants, together with a puma-skin and puma-head, during the rituals of the December solstitial feast. All three myths have a symbolic reference to the red turbulent water of the rainy season, waters that may be either contained, "emprisoned," or not.[4]

With the help of these data we can now come to our final conclusions about the mythical significance of the Chanca war and its aftermath: this involves the reconstruction of Cuzco by Pachacuti Inca and his antagonism to Viracocha Inca. All the ten kings of Cuzco were mentioned in the reconstruction of Cuzco, either by way of their mummy or of their statue. In the battle between Pachacuti Inca and Inca Urco, names of the kings of Hanan-Cuzco—with the exception of Tupa Yupanqui—are mentioned again. Tupa Yupanqui, however, is not absent from the reconstruction of Cuzco. In fact, he is the crowning part. It was for his initiation and coronation that Pachacuti Inca rebuilt the temple of the Sun in Cuzco and four other temples of the Sun around it (Sarmiento ch. 41, 42).

The descendants of these five kings of Cuzco were each related to a group of three ceques belonging to Hanan-Cuzco. From this distribution in the ceque system it is apparent that the model is parallel to that of the Sunturhuasi in Cuzco and of the six competitions in the myth of Huatyacuri in San Damián:

six competitions		Sunturhuasi		Dynasty of Hanan-Cuzco	
blue dress	house built at night	no roof (light)	roof (no light)	I 1 (10th king) Tupa Yapanqui	III 1 (8th king) Viracocha Inca
dress casacanchu	dress of red puma	flag Casana	puma	I 2 (9th king) Pachacuti Inca	III 2 (7th king) Yahuar Huacac
dancing	drinking	music, dancing	drinking	I 3 (6th king) Inca Roca	III 3. King of Ayarmaca. Tocay Capac

(The roman cipher + the arabic cipher in the last diagram refer to the position in the ceque system.)

Tupa Yupanqui and *Viracocha Inca*: When Guaman Poma in general describes the temple of the Sun he mentions it specifically in relation to Tupa Yupanqui. However, in the same paragraph he says (f. 262) that this king calls himself Viracocha Inca when he asks the huacas of Cuzco about the past and the future. When Tupa Yupanqui was initiated in the temple of the Sun, he wore all the royal paraphernalia, including the blue dress, *Tarco huallca*. On the other hand, the high priest in Cuzco was considered to be a descendant of Viracocha Inca. When carrying out bloody sacrifices the high priest was not allowed to the central and sacred part of Cuzco. (In fact, Tupa Yupanqui as Viracocha Inca also talked to the huacas outside town!) The temple of the god Viracocha was dark, in opposition to that of the Sun (Las Casas ch. 131; Santacruz Pachacuti p. 229, 230). Tupa Yupanqui and Viracocha Inca, then, represent the highest social position (Collana) with its internal oppositions of saya (inside) and suyu (outside) and of Hanan (upper) and Hurin (lower).

Pachacuti Inca and *Yahuar Huacac*: In a later study I will argue that the shirt called Casana, as related to the shirt casacanchu, had a special relationship to Pachacuti Inca. My earlier discussion of this theme centered on the relationship of this king to frost, hail and snow (casacanchu, "White as snow"). I argued that Yahuar Huacac, "he who weeps (red) blood," was related to the long red shirt with tassels worn by men with a (red) pumaskin. Both kings are related to the aspect of war (Payan): the first as the conqueror, the second as the conquered. But both also express the opposition of sterility, sequia (frost, floods) and fertility (the plowing and harvesting; the fertility of the irrigation-water and the fertility of the women brought from the outside as contributions (cacay)).

Inca Roca, Tocay Capac and the Ayarmaca: The Ayarmaca, defeated by both Manco Capac and by Pachacuti Inca, are related to the sixth group of three ceques in Hanan-Cuzco. The mythological data on Inca Roca relate him, as well as the Ayarmaca, to shamanism. For instance, when this king fought against the peoples of the Eastern lowlands, either in his role as king (Guaman Poma f. 103, 154) or as a general for Tupa Yupanqui (Santacruz Pachacuti p. 252), he changed into a jaguar, *otorongo*, and was addressed by the Aymara term for grandfather, *achachi*. For the moment I will only make use of the data on dancing and drinking. Inca Roca and an ayllu called *Huacaytaqui*, "the dancers and singers of the huacas" belonged to the same group of three ceques. We find a similar symbolic reference in the name of Ayarmaca.

Maca (ayarmaca, ancestor maca), a tuber used to make a hallucinogenic drug (Albornoz p. 36), together with the *villca* seed, is mixed in corn beer (Guaman Poma p. 71). With their attributions of shamanism and witchcraft, both Inca Roca and the Ayarmaca of Tocay Capac represent the Cayao aspect of the Underworld and of the non-Inca outside. Inca Roca represents its Hanan-aspect—the conqueror who identifies himself with the non-Inca as a jaguar—and the Ayarmaca its Hurin-aspect.

I want to finish this section with two observations. First, we notice how much the color red is stressed in relation to the Hurin side (III, Antisuyu) of this six-fold division: red blood; red dress; red muddy waters; probably the red corn beer used for the villca and maca drug. White (snow, hail) and blue (the sky) are associated to the Hanan side (I, Chinchaysuyu).

Secondly, I want to refer to one aspect of the peculiar, but regular, association of kings to groups of ceques: Pachacuti Inca associated to a group 2, but in I; Viracocha Inca to a group 1, but in III; Inca Roca to group 3, but in I. The Ayarmaca, associated to 3 and III, belong on both accounts to the non-Inca outside, not represented by an Inca king. Especially important in this context is the double role of kinship, which is represented by Tupa Yupanqui and Viracocha Inca together. It demonstrates, for one thing, how much the *spatial* dimensions (the reconstruction of Cuzco; the six competitions; the Sunturhuasi) and the *sequential* dimensions (the six episodes in the myth of Huatyacuri involving animals; the different fights between Pariacaca and Huallallo Caruincho; the Ayarmaca and the dynasty of five kings in Hanan-Cuzco) are but two aspects of the same structure.

Conclusions

In this chapter I have not intended to make an exhaustive analysis of the mythology of San Damián or of Inca history. My purpose has been to present an analytical methodology which is called for by the Peruvian data themselves. Moreover, I do not feel that an exhaustive analysis of every mythological and historical detail is necessary to prove the validity of the method. The boundaries of my units of analysis can be defined in an empirical way since these units are stories which always include a six-fold division. The existence of such a model and its logical properties are given by the content and structure of the stories themselves.

In these concluding remarks I will deal with two subjects: (1) the relevance for my analysis of Lévi Strauss' *Mythologiques*; and (2) the historicity of Inca history.

(1) The correlation that we were able to establish between the hierarchical progression in San Damián mythology and in Inca mythical history introduces the problem of structure in relation to myth on the one hand and to kinship on the other. Our analysis led us to the conclusion of the basic similarity between structure in the myth of Huatyacuri and the structure both of Inca kinship and systems built on categories like saya-suyu, hanan-hurin, and collana-payan-cayao. These categories and the ones of kinship are not dependent upon the existence of any kind of a social system implying special rules of descent and marriage. Our explanation of the equation Wife's Brothers = Wife's Fathers = Mother's

Brothers, as *not* indicating a marriage rule, *but* as the equation of a man to his children in their common designation of their WB or WF and MB, is important in our understanding of Andean structural principles. With Boon and Schneider (1974, p. 807) we can conclude that there is a kinship of myth and a myth of kinship in the sense that the Andean idiom of kinship or of social organization and of myth or history are conditioned by the same structural principles. Lévi Strauss made his structural analysis of kinship dependent on its social use-function (Lévi Strauss 1949, Boon and Schneider p. 815); that is, kin-terminological equations in relation to postulated marriage rules, especially those of unilineal groups. This led him in the case of Brazilian social systems (Lévi Strauss 1958, ch. 7, 8), to oppose binary relationships—never completely expressed by the people themselves—to triadic social relationships, expressing the more real and basic values of the societies in question. These considerations probably led him to the, in our view unwarranted, practice of separating so radically the study of structure in myth from that in kinship and social organization.

A case in point is the Bororo myth (M 1) with which Lévi Strauss starts his whole analysis, and of which a rapid comparison to the myth of Huatyacuri shows the same elements, development, structure and, possibly, the same function (Lévi Strauss 1964, p. 43-45).

myth of Huatyacuri	**Bororo myth (M 1)**
(1) Wife of Tamtañamca commits adultery	(1) A boy violates his mother
(2) Huatyacuri is advised by Pariacaca to steal two musical instruments and a vessel in order to win in two contests	(2) the boy is advised by his grandmother to steal three musical instruments and a staff in order to fulfill four tasks
(3) to obtain these objects, he has to play dead on top of a mountain to a fox and a skunk; that is, one animal with a "rotten" (black) tail and one that stinks.	(3) the boy competes with his father
(4) Huatyacuri first cures his future father-in-law, then competes with his brother-in-law	(4) in the fourth task, the boy hunts on top of a mountain lizards that stink; he is first attacked and then helped by vultures who eat rotten meat
(5) Huatyacuri appears in 6 different roles or dresses	(5) the boy appears in the form of 6 different animals

(6) the brother-in-law changes into a deer. First deer attacked men, but now men hunt deer. wife of brother-in-law turns into stone (upside down) near the coast, and is offered coca.

(6) a violent thunderstorm extinguishes all the fires in the village except that of the boy's grandmother

(7) a flood brings all the original people and animals of San Damián down to the coast.

(7) the boy makes himself antlers and hunts and kills his father as if the latter were a game animal. Body of father falls in lake and from it grow aquatic plants.

The similarities between both myths are so striking that the myth of Huatyacuri would have been a prime candidate for inclusion in the *Mythologiques*. However, following Lévi Strauss' guidelines it would have been difficult to make a comparison of the two myths, not only due to the geographic distance, but also due to the social distance. Lévi Strauss repeatedly refrains from making comparisons to mythologies from the Central Amazon (Myth. II, p. 232), the Andes (Myth. II, p. 295) and Mexico (Myth. I, p. 184) on the grounds that they are consciously elaborated by well-established classes of priests. Obviously, I will not deny that San Damián mythology is related to a conscious ideology. But neither do I see any useful purpose in opposing conscious and unconscious thought or structure since, as we found, they do not make contradictory claims in the Andean case. Equally, I do not see any reason to make such a claim for the Bororo. The socio-political organization of a Bororo village is very similar to the ceque system as it existed in Cuzco and in many Andean villages (Polo 1917, p. 56-58), probably including San Damián. Each Bororo moiety, clan and section had specific rights to totems and myths. M 1 belonged to the clan Paiwoe and was built around a classificatory list of six animals. The second myth (M 2) that Lévi Strauss analyzes has the explicit purpose of explaining the dual chieftainship in a Bororo village and how it was initially inherited. Excluding these facts impoverishes the myths by stripping them of their social organizational foundation. Analyzing the Bororo myth as a comment on the structure of Bororo kinship, social organization and cosmology would open far more possibilities of comparison to other mythological systems.

We may conclude that the myth of Huatyacuri and the Bororo myth (M 1) not only were very similar, but also that they had the same explicit reference and relationship to the Thunder. The Incas fragmented the corresponding "mythemes" of which both other myths had been built up and distributed them over their epic pseudo-history of ten kings, but with a concentration on the ninth king, Pachacuti Inca. At least one detail of the Inca version of the Thundermyth is closer to the Bororo version than is the San Damián one. During the great drought in Cuzco, the house and lands of Amaru Tupac were saved because of overhanging clouds. This is similar to the Bororo myth in which the house of the grandmother was saved from thunderstorms. The two details are the same in relation to the whole myth, but they are an inversion of the type of "sequía" chosen: in one case the lack of rain, in the other case abundant rain.

(2) In my earlier work (Zuidema 1964) I made a critical assessment of the historicity of the Inca history, mostly on the basis of Inca data alone. In a later article (Zuidema 1973), I compared the Inca royal dynasty as an ancestral system of mummies to a colonial system on which we have complete data. In this chapter I have compared Inca history from Cuzco to the mythology of a village in Central Peru. The similar structure and content of the latter two examples make it probable that they also had a similar function in their respective societies. Inca history has always been considered to be just that, perhaps with some mythological details added. The great structural similarity of Inca history and San Damián mythology obliges us now, however, to consider the problem differently.

Both Inca "history" and San Damián "mythology" are based on a common intensive interest in a complicated social model applied to kinship, socio-political organization, ritual, theology and the calendar. Both use as their building blocks references to huacas, ayllus, place-names and, especially in the case of the Incas, remembered events. These events were considered within a hierarchical order that did not conform to a chronological (linear) one. For instance, almost all accounts relate the Inca war against the Chancas to Viracocha Inca's fleeing to the north. However, each is also overlaid with an independent and cosmological aspect which is similar to the mythological actions of Huatyacuri and Pariacaca for the first event and of Coniraya Viracocha for the second. We must assume therefore that the Chanca war was *chosen* not because, chronologically and historically, Pachacuti Inca had fought such an enemy, but because as a mythical figure he had to reflect the actions of the Thundergod. Any real battle could have served as a basis for adding details of local color to the mythical battle. However, the battle and its details had to meet certain conditions necessitated by the ideological system; conditions, it should be stressed again, that were not necessarily historical.

Given this situation, I would consider the whole of Inca history up to the time of the Spanish conquest, and even to a certain extent beyond, as mythological. Inca "history," then, integrated religious, calendrical, ritual and remembered facts into one ideological system, which was hierarchical in terms of space and time. This Incaic hierarchical ideology should not be confused with the Western linear conception of history imposed by the Spanish. Only comparative research can help us here determine which facts are of a local and remembered nature and which are borrowed from outside and therefore not historical. An historical chronology, up to the Spanish conquest, will have to be established independently by archaeology.

Notes

[1] I wish to thank here Mr. Gary D. Urton for his critical comments and for reviewing the English of the text.

[2] The identification of the Sunturhuasi, as a temple of the Sun to which applied the description of Guaman Poma, will be dealt with in a separate article (Zuidema M S.). An analysis of the data on the Ushnu is given in a paper published in Spain (Zuidema 1979).

[3] The literal meaning of this last statement was probably well understood by the people who told the myth and who listened to it. Bertonio, at least, mentions that in Aymara the phrase *Phekena cayuni saattatha*, that is "to put the head on the ground and the feet in the air," methphorically means: "to contend in that one does not do what people advise him."

[4] I have dealt with the references to turbulent waters in the myth of Inca Urco in a paper presented at the Congress of Americanists, Vancouver, B.C., 1979.

References

Albornoz, Cristobal de. See: Duviols.

Arguedas, J.M. 1966. *Dioses y hombres de Huarochiri* (1608). Translated by J.M. Arguedas. Lima.

Avila, Francisco de. See: Arguedas, and Trimborn.

Bertonio, Ludovico. 1956. *Vocabulario de la lengua Aymara* (1612).

Boon, James A. and David M. Schneider. 1974. "Kinship vis-a-vis Myth: Contrasts in Levi-Strauss' Approaches to Cross-Cultural Comparison," *American Anthropologist, vol. 76, no. 4, (December 1974), pp. 799-817.*

Cobo, Bernabé. 1956. Historia del Nuevo Mundo (1653). *Biblioteca de Autores Españoles 91-92.* Madrid.

Dávila Brizeño, Diego. 1881. Descripción y relación de la provincia de los Yauyos toda, Anan Yaugos y Lorin Yauyos, hecha por....(1586). in: Jimenez de la Espada, M. *Relaciones Geograficas.* Madrid.

Duviols, P. 1967. "Un inédit de Cristobal de Albornoz: la instruccion para descubrir todas las guacas del Piru y sus camayos y haziendas," *Journal de la Société des Américanistes* vol. 56. Paris.

Emboden, William. 1972. *Narcotic Plants.* New York.

Gonzalez Holguin, Diego. 1952. *Vocabulario de la lengua... Qquichua, o del Inca* (1608). Lima.

Guaman Poma de Ayala, Felipe. 1936. *El primer nueva coronica y buen gobierno* (1584-1614). Paris.

Hernandez Principe, Rodrigo. 1923. *Mitología Andina. Inca.* vol. 1. Lima.

Isbell, B.J. 1977. Kuyoq: Those who love me. In: R. Bolton and E. Mayer, Editors, *Andean kinship and marriage.* Washington, D.C. 1977.

Kelm, Antje. See: Trimborn.

Las Casas, Fray Bartolomé de. 1958. Apologetica Historia (1564) Vol. III *Biblioteca de Autores Espanoles,* 105. Madrid.

Lévi-Strauss, C. 1949. *Les structures élémentaires de la parenté.* Paris.

————. 1958. *Anthropologie Structurale.* Paris.

————. 1964. *Mythologiques I. Le crut et le cuit.* Paris.

————. 1966. *Mythologiques II. Du miel aux cendres.* Paris.

Mariscotti, Ana Maria. 1970. *Die Stellung des Gewittergottes in den regionalen Pantheen der Zentralanden.* Baessler Archiv, vol. 18.

Millones, Luis, 1964. Un movimiento nativista del siglo XVI. el Taki Onqoy. *Revista Peruana de Cultura.* No. 3. Lima.

————. 1965. "Nuevos aspectos del Taki Onqoy," *Historia y Cultura,* Vol. 2. Lima.

————. 1971. "Las informaciones de Cristobal de Albornoz," *Sondeos,* vol. 79. Cuernavaca.

Molina, Cristobal de (El Cuzqueño). 1943. *Fabulas y ritos de los Incas* (1573). Lima.

Morissette, J. et Luc Racine. 1973. "La hiérarchie des Wamani: essai sur la pensée classificatoire Quechua," *Signes et Langages des Amériques. Recherches amérindiennes au Québec,* vol. III, Nos. 1-2. Montréal.

Murúa, Martín de. 1962. *Historia general del Peru* (1613). Madrid.

Piaget, J. 1949. *Traité de Logique.* Paris.

Pizarro, Pedro. 1944. *Relación del descubrimiento y conquista de los reinos del Peru.* (1571). Buenos Aires.

Polo de Ondegardo, Juan. 1916. *Los errores y supersticiones de los indios, sacados del tratado y averiguación que hizo el Licenciado Polo.* Ed. Urteaga y Romero. Col. Libr. Doc. Ref. Hist. Peru. la serie, vol. 3, pp. 1-143. Lima.

Racine, L. See: Morissette.

Santacruz Pachacuti Yamqui Salcamaygua, Joan de. 1950. "Relación de antiguedades de este reyno del Peru (1613)," *Tres relaciones de antiguedades del Peru.* Asuncion del Paraguay.

Santo Tomás, Domingo de. 1951. *Lexicon, o vocabulario de la lengua general del Peru* (1560). Lima.

Sarmiento de Gamboa, Pedro. 1947. *Historia de los Incas.* Buenos Aires.

Schneider, D.M. See: Boon, J.M.

Schultes, R.E. 1972, "An overview of hallucinogens in the Western hemisphere," in Furst, P.T., *Flesh of the Gods; the ritual use of hallucinogens.* New York.

Trimborn, H. und Antje Kelm. 1967. *Francisco de Avila.* Berlin.

Zuidema, R. T. 1964[a]. "The relationship between mountains and coast in ancient Peru," in *Mededelingen Rijksmuseum voor Volkenkunde,* Vol. 15. Leiden.

————. 1964[b]. *The ceque system of Cuzco; the social organization of the capital of the Inca.* Leiden.

————. 1965. "Apuntes sobre el taqui Onqoy," in *Historia y Cultura,* No. 2, Lima.

————. 1973[a]. "La Parenté et le culte des ancétres dans trois communautés péruviennes; un compte-rendu de 1622 par Hernandez Principe," *Signes et Languages des Amériques. Recherches amérindiennes au Québec,* Vol. III, nos. 1-2. Montréal.

————. 1973[b]. "La quadrature du cercle dans l'ancien Pérou," *Signes et Languages des Amériques. Recherches amérindiennes au Québec,* Vol. III, nos. 1-2. Montréal.

————. 1977[a]. "The Inca calendar," In A.F. Aveni, Ed, *Native American Astronomy,* Austin.

————. 1977[b]. "The Inca kinship system: a new theoretical view," in F.R. Bolton and E. Mayer, editors, *Andean Kinship and Marriage,* Washington, D.C. 1977.

————. 1979."The Ushnu," in I.A. Franch, ed., *Economía y Sociedad en los Andes y Mesoamerica Revista de la Universidad Complutense* XXVIII, 117, Madrid.

————. MS. The Sunturhuasi.

10
Internal and External Constraints on Structure

Fadwa El Guindi

"It simply does not make sense to believe that all the properties of
the elements are contained in one number: the atomic weight. The
weight of an atom might be a measure of its complexity. If so, it
must hide some internal structure which generates those properties. But, of course, as an idea, that was inconceivable so long as
it was believed that the atom is indivisible."

(J. Bronowski 1973: 330)

The utility and necessity of conceptualizing certain phenomena as divi-
sible and structure as invisible has been convincingly demonstrated in the
physical sciences. In the social sciences, this notion developed by way of
structural theory (cf. de Saussure 1959 and R. Jakobson 1956 in
linguistics, and Lévi-Strauss 1963, *Mythologiques* 1964, 1966, 1968a
1968b in anthropology). I will assume the postulation of phenomena and
structure in this fashion to be paradigmatically acceptable as a possible
explanation for phenomena of human experience in order to move to a
more productive level of issues.

One such issue is the topic upon which this volume is partially based:
Verification in Structural Anthropology. This issue involves questions
like: Can we verify structural claims? Will two analysts arrive at the same
conclusions if they follow the same analytic procedures? And what
verificatory procedures or levels are there?

This chapter will not directly deal with those questions. However, it will sketch a structural/analytic framework within which some of these questions can be more precisely stated and addressed, and in addition probably raise a few more issues.

Specifically, a detailed analysis of the Zapotec Fandango (wedding) will reveal a structure containing three components: conceptual, syntactic, and semantic. In this analysis, I propose that meaning can be derived only if we consider the systemic way in which the three components are interrelated. This property of interdependence functions as an internal constraint on the system. Furthermore, the system is externally constrained by the limitation of empirical possibilities. These two kinds of constraints will be demonstrated through the examination of specific wedding events and related processes of kinship organization.

Brief Background to the Zapotec

The analysis presented here is based on twenty-two months of intensive research in a small, predominantly farming, community in the Oaxaca Valley.[1] The community consists of approximately 900 nominally Catholic Zapotec, mostly bilingual (Spanish and Zapotec). Introductory and background aspects of Zapotec culture will not be reviewed here. Instead the reader is referred to general references such as Nader (1969), Parsons (1936), and Whitecotton (1977) for general Zapotec ethnology; Nader (1964) for Zapotec social organization; Pickett (1960, 1967) and Briggs (1961) for the Zapotec language; Kearney (1972) for their world view; Paddock (1970) for their history; Selby (1974) for witchcraft; Chiñas (1973) on women; and El Guindi (n.d.) on ethnography of ritual.

Structure in Zapotec Ritual

My analysis of a number of Zapotec rituals: *Todos Santos* (All Saints), *Angelito* (Death of Unmarried), *Difunto* (Death of Married), *Cambio de Comite del Templo* (Change of Church Committee), and *Fandango* (Wedding), provides support for my claim that ritual is formally structured (El Guindi 1973, 1976a, 1976b).

In these analyses I demonstrated that there is a "syntax" of ritual which serves to map the conceptual plane onto the empirical by means of a series of operations. These operations generate the categories of people admissible in ritual. The constraints imposed by these syntactic operations (rules) and also by the conceptual structure specify the formal relationship between these categories, specifically as oppositions and mediations. I will subsequently consider a number of such operations in the analysis of Fandango.

One significant property of ritual is that it sets up the behavioral framework (or environment) which allows for the categorizing and recategorizing of people in a pattern that corresponds to significant divisions within the natives' own conceptualization of their sociological world.

Ritual structure is the outcome of the structuring of people into categories which take place in ritual activities and events. The outcome is intended in a logical, not chronological sense, since ritual structure is reflected in that structuring itself which leads to it. Structuring is a process of combination and recombination of elements (people) into categories. The relationship between categories is fixed: it is in the form of opposition and mediation. The content of the categories shifts and varies, however, not only within the same society across rituals but within the same ritual, as we shall subsequently see in the analysis of wedding.

Fandango Setting

Rituals have to take place somewhere: house, church, village plaza, or the like. When the spatial locus of a ritual is the house, the people of that house become categorized *Caseros* (literally, "people of the house") and are called "caseros." They are distinguished from other people attending the ritual by the fact that they are *"los que mandan"* ("those in command"). Caseros are in a position of power. They have the authority to control throughout the ritual. They see to it that jobs and errands are done, obligations are met, and conflict is avoided or resolved.

The empirical content of the category Caseros is not fixed, however. By that I mean that the individuals belonging to the category Caseros vary. This variation depends on the point of the domestic cycle at which the ritual occurs and on the residence rule. For example, the caseros in angelitos would typically be the parents of the deceased, since they are usually the adult persons of the house when an unmarried child dies. Similarly, in difuntos the caseros would typically be the surviving spouse and/or adult children living in the same house.

Likewise in weddings. The people of the house become caseros. But whereas in a death "the house" is that of the deceased, in a wedding it is less obvious since two persons are equally getting married: the groom and the bride. Hence the house of the bride's parents seems equally important, and either house might "qualify" as the wedding house.[2]

The Zapotec "choose" the house of groom's parents to be "casa del fandango" (wedding house). This "choice" is consistent with the prevalent male-oriented ideology and the patrilocal residence rule. Thus in weddings the groom's parents become the caseros and their house serves as the physical base for the wedding activities.[3] But looking at "house" simply at the level of physical boundary can obscure the enormously significant dimension that unfolds in ritual; a dimension that leads us to the natives' conceptual world and the way their spatial domain is mapped onto their kinship and moral domains.

There seems to be in the Zapotec culture various significations of "house" associated with different levels. At a concrete level, there is the label *casa* ("house") which is used to refer to: (1) a room built with concrete material, as opposed to a hut; or (2) the whole house, including the *solar* ("courtyard") and physically bounded by a fence, a wall, a bush, or the like.

At an abstract level the Zapotec conceive of casa as a conceptual category House, in opposition to Field. The importance of House and Field as a contrast pair of categories in their conceptual system is made evident through analysis of their myths, rituals, and statements. The contrast pair House/Field is characterized by a positive/negative relationship. Both House and Field are well-defined by a set of features that are in the form of binary oppositions. These features are given in another of my studies (1973: 25). For my purposes here, it suffices to discuss only the concept House, without Field, and specifically in terms of two basic features: (a) that House has boundary; and (b) that House is associated with ritual. Both are related. Ritual space is bounded.

The nature of its boundary is what concerns us here. Wedding-related events and sociological participation are not confined to the physical boundary of wedding. Wedding house is not concretely defined by fence, wall, bush, or bamboo.

Rather we find Wedding House defined and redefined throughout the wedding day in terms of the conceptualized sociological boundary: the people who are categorized and recategorized as participants in the wedding ritual. The processes of categorization and recategorization lead to the structure of sociological (kinship) relationships permanently associated with the marital union.

Through these processes wedding activities become the means by which the Zapotec extend wedding beyond the physical boundary of the wedding house to the conceptual boundary of the sociological universe. This conceptual boundary defines the wedding world in terms of kinship categories and the relationships between them.

In this chapter I will demonstrate how a structural analysis of wedding activities (1) reveals the dynamics of kinship categorization in ritual; (2) shows the utility of structural theory for adequacy and precision in ethnographic description; and (3) delineates the systemic property of interrelatedness of components.

Fandango Structure

Groom, Bride, and Godmother

The notion of marriage among the Zapotec, as among all peoples, minimally involves a union between two individuals: a man and a woman. In ritual, they become Groom and Bride. Represented formally we can say that in a wedding ritual, a man getting married is rewritten Groom and a woman, Bride as in (1a) and (1b):

(1a) A man ⎯⎯⎯⟩ Groom

(1b) A woman ⎯⎯⎯⟩ Bride

But Groom and Bride are not merely two individuals getting married. They represent wedding as a dual conceptual structure. Various ritual activities taking place on that wedding Sunday clearly express and reinforce the division of wedding people into those associated with the groom's side and the opposing people on the bride's side. The wedding explicitly provides the behavioral environment for this differentiation.

Mediating the opposition Groom/Bride is the Marriage Godmother (*madrina de casamiento*). She is the one who actually arranges for the religious consummation of the marriage in church. It is the marriage godmother who provides the wedding clothes for both the groom and the bride, and it is in her house that both are prepared and dressed up for the church ceremony. The godmother then takes them both to church where the priest performs the appropriate religious rites. The godmother arranges for the priest to be available that day and pays the necessary fee and other costs involved. In one sense, then, marriage godmother brings together the groom and bride.

As a category, Marriage Godmother functions in linking the two oppositional categories Groom and Bride. In that sense the three categories: Groom, Bride and Godmother, are related to each other in the form of an opposition and a mediation,[4] represented diagrammatically in (2).

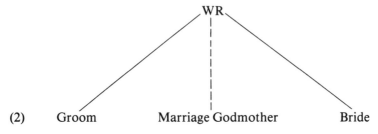

(2)   Groom   Marriage Godmother   Bride

where WR stands for wedding ritual and the broken line for mediation.

Caseros, Consuegros and Compadres

As a set, the Groom-Bride opposition mediated by Marriage Godmother, provides a model for the sociological differentiation in wedding. This differentiation occurs in the context of specific ritual activities. For example, at an early hour in the morning of the wedding day (Sunday) the *Caseros del Fandango* (people of the house of the wedding, or the Groom's parents) send three messengers, who are relatives on the groom's side of kin. One messenger carries a burner with incense, a second carries necklaces of bougainvillea, and a third carries candles. They go in a musical procession, first to the house of the marriage godmother, then the house of the bride's parents.

Upon arrival at the house of the marriage godmother, the musical band enters into the courtyard and remains there while the messengers enter the altar room. There, the incense man burns *copal* and blows the incense smoke at the saints on the altar. The candle man lights a candle and places it in the candle holder on the altar, and the necklace man puts a bougainvillea necklace around a saint's picture on the altar.

They face the altar, kneel, and cross themselves, and then they turn around and face the godparents (godmother and godfather) and their invited guests. At this point the messengers deliver the message: that they came as messengers of the *caseros* (the groom's side) and the *caseros* are inviting the *compadres* (the godparents) along with their guests over to caseros' house to have the morning meal (*almuerzo*). The *compadres* acknowledge the delivery of the message and formally accept the invitation to their *compadres'* house (who are also the *caseros* of the wedding).

The procession proceeds next to the house of the bride's parents. The ritual of entry and delivery of items (incense, candle, bougainvillea necklace) are repeated in the house of the bride's parents exactly as in the house of the *compadres*. Receiving them in this case are the bride's parents, the bride's consanguines, and their invited guests. The message is formally delivered: the caseros are inviting the (and their) *consuegros* (co-in-laws) over for the morning meal. The *consuegros* formally accept the invitation.

The messengers, accompanied by the musical band, return to the Fandango House and inform the *caseros* that the messages have been delivered and the invitations accepted. The *caseros* at this point serve and have their morning meal.

After the meal two messengers are sent to bring the *compadres* and the *consuegros* to the Fandango House to have their morning meal. When the *compadres* and the *consuegros* arrive they are seated facing each other at a long table with two benches. The *compadres* sit on one side and the *consuegros* on the other. The groom and the bride sit between the marriage godparents, with the groom sitting by the godmother and the bride by the godfather. The *caseros* serve and supervise the whole meal. When the non-*caseros* (*Compadres* and *Consuegros*) are formally asked to begin eating, the *"el palomo"* ritual takes place: the godmother and the groom feed each other simultaneously while the godfather and the bride do the same. At the same time, the musical band plays the musical piece known as *"el palomo."* Following the meal the *compadres* and the *consuegros* return to their houses.

It is evident that during these ritual activities several relationships unfold between a finite set of categories of people. Above I discussed the importance of the category *Caseros* in various rituals. In the wedding activities and right at the onset of the wedding ritual *Caseros* are clearly distinguishable as a group opposed to all the other invited participants in the wedding, the non-caseros. The two categories of noncaseros, consuegros and compadres, become revealed during the messengers' delivery ritual. That this set of categories comprises the wedding sociological world, is confirmed in the ritual activities and, though not discussed here, in the ritual statements. Statements from natives not involved in the wedding ritual also agree with this sociological categorization. In other words, these kinship categories are not seen in relative terms. They are *the* categories of people in wedding and they have unambiguous labels confirmed both in the native's statement and in the ritual: *caseros, consuegros, campadres.*

Clearly, uncovering the set of relevant categories is an important step but it is not sufficient if we wish to reveal the structure of wedding. In order to delineate the structure of its sociological universe we have to determine how the categories are related to each other as well as understand their nature and properties.

We already know that *Caseros* is the people of the Groom's Side, and it becomes clear later that *Consuegros* is the people of the Bride's Side. The *Consuegros* are co-in-laws. Two relationships can be delineated here: on the one hand, we have two opposing categories (*Caseros* and *Consuegros*) that are clearly defined in contrast to each other and stem from the simple opposition Groom-Bride. In that abstract context these two categories in opposition are closed.

I have demonstrated elsewhere (El Guindi 1973, 1975, 1976) that conceptual systems contain categories which are well-defined, highly coded and rigidly marked by invariant syntactical properties, and thus "closed." Conversely, there are categories which are loosely defined, highly flexible and hence "open." Closed categories are mediated by open categories.

In other words "closed" and "open" are properties of categories that make up the conceptual structure. The syntactical operation of mediation specifies the formal relationship between these categories (oppositions) (cf. El Guindi 1977a). This basic structure is represented in (3) below:

(3)

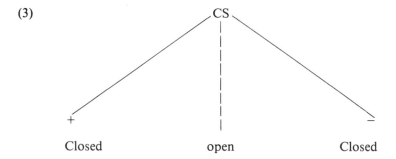

Associated with the two closed categories, *caseros* and *consuegros* are the universally significant kinship relationships of consanguinity and affinity. Though perhaps obvious I wish to emphasize the point that it is only when we have a category in-laws that we have a relationship of affinity versus that of consanguinity. Wedding recreates sets of categories that reflect a basic conceptual differentiation within the kinship universe.

On the other hand we have the more empirical relationship which is created in wedding between the two sets of parents: the relationship of consuegro-ship. The parents of the bride and the parents of the groom are in-laws to each other. It is a reciprocal horizontal relationship. Not quite symmetrical however. We find that in terms of obligations, respect and authority there is an asymmetry. The parents of the groom are superior in the relationship. They are the caseros, the people of the wedding house, and it is in this house that a union between all categories takes place. And they are the ones to invite and receive.

But caseros as a category comprises not only the groom's parents, but also their relatives and guests. That is, in wedding Groom's Parents, Consanguines, and Guests are, in formal terms, syntactically rewritten Caseros as in (4): 4) Groom's Parents, Groom's Consanguines, Groom's Guests ⎯⎯⎯→ Caseros and similarly, on the bride's side, the following rewrite rule operates in (5): 5) Bride's Parents, Bride's Consanguines, Bride's Guests ⎯⎯⎯→ Consuegros. Therefore, the basic opposition is between Caseros represented in bracketing (6):

(6)   Groom's Parents + Groom's Consanguines + Groom's Guests
              CASEROS   CASEROS
and Consuegros in bracketing (7):

(7)   Bride's Parents + Bride's Consanguines + Bride's Guests
              CONSUEGROS   CONSUEGROS

But there is a third wedding category, Compadres. This means co-parents. A fictive relationship. But whose fictives are they? Surely in a Zapotec (nominally Catholic) community there are fictive kin on both sides, the bride's and the groom's. The bride has godmothers and the groom has godmothers. And godfathers of course. But, among the Zapotec, "godfather" is almost always the male version of "godmother." Godfathers are the husbands of Godmothers and the various labels and associated roles applied to Godmother extend to Godfather.

Should all the godmothers on both sides, the groom's and the bride's, be subsumed under the fictive category of Compadres? Or should each side constitute a separate category? Is it possible that fictive kin on each side are subsumed under the category of each side: those on the groom's side as Caseros and those on the bride's side as Consuegros? Does that mean that fictives can simultaneously be consanguines and affines? We know so far from the ritual events described earlier that Marriage Godmother and Godfather comprise Compadres. But who is the marriage godmother?

Perhaps some background information is necessary at this point for clarification. I will present a somewhat detailed analysis of the category "Godmother" and then demonstrate how specific ritual activities allow movement and transformation within it.

Godmother

In a person's life, there are two important godmothers: the baptismal *(madrina de bautizo)* and the confirmation *(madrina de confirmacion)*. If a child dies, the baptismal godmother is obligated to provide the *mortaja* (basket of clothes and decorative items necessary for the corpse and coffin preparation) and she becomes the *mortaja* godmother *(madrina de mortaja)*. The confirmation godmother provides the coffin and becomes the coffin godmother *(madrina de caja)*.

On the other hand, if the child does not die but lives and gets married, then both godmothers, baptismal and confirmation, again have important positions and functions in the wedding, although then a sex distinction of the person getting married becomes significant.

In the case of a female, the baptismal godmother becomes the chest godmother *(madrina de baul)*, the person who provides the storage chest for the bride. Put formally, a rewrite rule operates on baptismal godmother of a female as in (8):

(8)   Females's Baptismal Godmother ⟶ Bride's Chest Godmother.

In the case of a male child, she becomes marriage godmother *(madrina de casamiento)* for both the bride and the groom. This rule operates as in (9):

(9)   Male's Baptismal Godmother ⟶ Marriage Godmother

It is the groom's baptismal godmother, then, who becomes the marriage godmother. I have shown how marriage godmother mediates between groom and bride, in the sense of linking the two, as represented in (2).

Correspondingly, the confirmation godmother provides the grindstone and becomes the grindstone godmother *(madrina de metate)* to a female (bride). In the language of rules, Confirmation godmother is rewritten Grindstone godmother as represented in (10):

10) Female's Confirmation Godmother ⟶ Bride's Grindstone Godmother.

The male's confirmation godmother, interestingly enough, becomes unlabelled. As a category she ceases to exist. As a person she does not have any recognized functions in the wedding. She is both delabelled as well as decategorized. Again a rewrite rule operates here:

11) Male's Confirmation Godmother ⟶ Groom's Unlabelled
   Godmother.

In other words we see how both godmothers have important positions in the death as well as in the life of a person. But since we are concerned here with wedding, I will confine the discussion to the structural function of godmother in the life of an individual.

To recapitulatè in structural terms: there are two godmothers, baptismal and confirmation. The godmother is baptismal if the person is not married and either chest godmother to a married female (bride) or marriage godmother to a married male (groom).

Similarly, godmother is confirmation to an unmarried person. She is grindstone godmother to a married female (bride), and is "unlabelled" to a married male (groom). This can be diagrammed as in (12):

12)   GODMOTHER

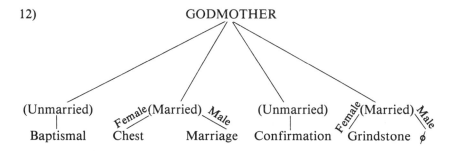

Reading across the bottom of diagram (12) we detect a homologous relationship between one Godmother, Baptismal, and its transformations, Chest and Marriage, and the other Godmother, Confirmation, and its transformations, Grindstone and Unlabelled. Utilizing the criteria of marital status, M/M, and sex, M/F, we find that: Baptismal (unmarried) is to Confirmation (unmarried) as Chest (baptismal, married, female) is to Grindstone (confirmation, married, female) as Marriage (baptismal, married, male) is to Unlabelled (confrontation, married, male). Accordingly, we can set up the logical equation (13a, b, c):

13a) Baptismal Godmother : Confirmation Godmother ::
13b) Chest Godmother   : Grindstone Godmother   ::
13c) Marriage Godmother   : Unlabelled Godmother   ::

In terms of the wedding we find that the groom's fictive kin comprise Marriage godmother and Unlabelled godmother represented in bracketing (14):

14) Marriage godmother + Unlabelled godmother
Groom's Fictives   Groom's Fictives

The bride's fictive kin comprise Chest godmother and Grindstone godmother as in bracketing (15):

15) Chest godmother + Grindstone godmother
Bride's Fictives   Bride's Fictives

But we have already seen how empirically the ritual of invitation to
the meal functioned as the behavioral environment which allowed for the
formal operation on the Marriage Godmother, the marriage godfather,
and their invited guests to be syntactically rewritten Compadres (co-
parents).

16) Marriage Godmother, marriage godfather, their guests ──────→
                                                        Compadres

They become the Compadres of the wedding:

17) Marriage Godmother + marriage godfather + guests
COMPADRES   COMPADRES

Essentially then Groom's Fictives, in wedding, becomes Compadres.

18) Groom's Fictives ───────→ Compadres

If we go back to (14) we find that logically, Groom's Fictives include
both godmothers, Marriage and Unlabelled. Empirically, the unlabelled
godmother, "disappears from the scene," as it were. She does not have
any categorical existence in the sociological world of the ritual. The
system "took care of her" and left us only with marriage godmother.

A word about Compadres. "Compadrinazgo," says Robert Ravicz,
"forms an essential part of many Middle American social organizations..." (1967: 238). In response to sacraments and other ritual,
"kinlike ties *(padrinazgo)* are established between a child *(ahijado/a)*
and a man and woman *(padrino* and *madrina)* who serve as its *padrinos*
(godparents). In turn, a relationship—*compadrazgo*—is ritually formed,
binding the padrinos and the parents as *compadres* (co-parents: the term
of address and of reference is *compadre,* male; *comadre*, female). With
the child as basis for both relationships, relations within each are marked
by mutual rights and responsibilities" *(ibid:*239). This web of relationships is characterized by *"respeto"* (respect), which is highly formalized
and ritualized in their behaviors.

With respect to wedding, we find a similar differentiation of relationships being created in various ritual events. On the one hand, we
have the vertical "padrinazgo" relationship between madrina/padrino
and bride/groom. This is activated in the ritual *"el polomo"* described

above where food is exchanged cross-sex between godparents and god-children. Later in the wedding this relationship is again activated in the dance *"el jarabe"*: here godfather dances with the bride and the god-mother dances with the groom to the music of el jarabe. On the other hand, we have the horizontal "compadrazgo" relationship established during the delivery ritual and reinforced throughout the various activities of the wedding.

The horizontal relationship involves two sets: the bride's mother/father and comadre/compadre, and correspondingly the groom's mother/father and comadre/compadre. The Compadres are co-parents to both sides, by virtue of being godparents to both bride and groom. We can see in that sense Compadres is in fact a structural link between two sides:

19)

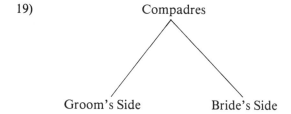

As one of the three main categories of the wedding ritual, (Caseros, Consuegros, Compadres), Compadres serves as mediator, linking the two:

20)

This leads us to a more abstract level where the properties of the mediating category Compadres needs to be clarified. It is another good example of an "open" category which is flexibly defined. Compadres as a category is created in wedding. Empirically, in terms of the warm bodies within the category, the groom's baptismal godmother is the ma-jor individual in the Compadre category. Yet we are told she is also mar-riage godmother for both bride and groom. And even though she is the same "body" that is a fictive relative on the groom's side, she ends up being the fictive relative to both the groom's parents and the bride's parents.

Another feature of the category fictive is that it is not a rigidly bounded, clearly defined set of kin. It includes sets of relationships that are modelled after consanguineal ties, yet one clearly very different from them. That is they are related but are not relatives. It is ambiguously defined and combines opposite features. Moreover, empirically fictive relatives are constantly mediating in situations of conflict. Category Fictives is open; and because of that property, it is *the* kin category that admits novel output, such as the anthropologist. It is absolutely impossible for an outsider to be randomly categorized Consanguine (closed category) or Affine (closed category). If the outsider is to be admitted into the kinship universe at all it will be by means of open categories as conceptualized by the people. Fictives serves that way.

The Dance of the Turkey

So far I have examined Groom's Fictives. What happens to Bride's Fictives? In the wedding ritual two specific wedding events demonstrate further formal operations on the category Bride's Fictives. These two events are "the dance of the turkey," which takes place during the day of the wedding, and its reciprocal "the dance of the gifts," which occurs in the evening of the same day.

In the "dance of the turkey," two men with two live turkeys which have cigarette packages hanging around their necks, and two women with two baskets containing ingredients for *mole* (a typical Oaxaca dish of chili and chocolate) are sent in a musical procession by the groom's parents to the houses of the bride's fictives. All along the road the musical band plays the tune of the "dance of the turkey," and at each intersection each man holds the wings of his turkey and dances with it. Each woman dances, holding the basket on her head. This goes on until the procession arrives first at the house of the bride's baptismal godmother (now chest godmother). One of the two men delivers his turkey and one of the two women delivers her basket of *mole* ingredients. The baptismal godmother joins the procession, while the second turkey is danced with until the house of the bride's parents is reached. There the second turkey and basket of *mole* are delivered to the bride's parents. This ends "the dance of the turkey."

The Dance of the Gifts

In the evening of the same day a reciprocal ritual of "the dance of the turkey" takes place in the house of the bride's parents (which is now house of the affines, *Consuegros*). In "the dance of the gifts," gifts are offered by the bride's kin (now Consuegros) and received by the groom's kin (now Caseros).

Man$_1$, who delivered the turkey to the baptismal godmother during the "dance of the turkey," carries the chest which is delivered by the chest (baptismal) godmother, and dances with the Woman$_1$ who delivered the mole to the baptismal (now chest) godmother. This woman dances holding a *santo* (the saint's picture for the altar of the newly married couple).

Correspondingly, the Man₂, who delivered the turkey to the bride's parents, carries the grindstone which is delivered by the grindstone (confirmation) godmother, and dances with Woman₂, who delivered the mole to the bride's parents. The latter woman would be carrying a basket of something unlabelled.[5]

The sequence of activities is summarized in (21):

21)   Man$_1$ delivers turkey$_1$ and receives Chest
                Woman$_1$ delivers mole$_1$ and receives Saint
                Man$_1$ dances with Woman$_1$
                Chest dances with Saint

                Man$_2$ delivers turkey$_2$ and receives Grindstone
                Woman$_2$ delivers mole$_2$ and receives ∅
                Man$_2$ dances with Woman$_2$
                Grindstone dances with ∅

From this sequence we can derive equation (22a):

22a) Chest :Grindstone :: Saint : Unlabelled Gift

In other words, the baptismal godmother in "the dance of the turkey" receives a turkey and a basket of mole, and later in "the dance of gifts" delivers a chest and becomes chest godmother, as represented in (8):

8) Female's Baptismal Godmother ⟶ Bride's Chest Godmother

Similarly, this logic should extend to the Confirmation Godmother. If we look at what in fact happens, we find that she does deliver a grindstone in "the dance of the gifts" and becomes Grindstone Godmother as represented earlier in (10):

10) Female's Confirmation Godmother ⟶ Bride's Grindstone
                                                      Godmother

Something is missing, though. Based on that logic, the Confirmation Godmother should have received the second turkey and basket of mole which was instead delivered during the "dance of the turkey" to the house of the bride's parents. The description of that dance is based on my own observation of the events and my own participation accompanying the messengers from one house to the other. But according to my analysis, the empirical activities do not follow ethno-logic (logic derived from and based on the natives' own activities and statements. The logic that the natives themselves should follow for their system to be consistent).

So I checked with my informants. I asked the people. "There is something wrong with your system," to which they smiled. I continued, "based on my analysis, the second turkey and basket of mole ingredients should have gone to the *'madrina de confirmacion de la novia'* and not her parents.''

Of course they were right and I was wrong. But there was no way for me to know this ethnographic detail. Yes, the second turkey and basket of *mole* ingredients are delivered to the house of the bride's parents. Later the parents send those items to the house of the Confirmation Godmother. So turkey$_2$ and mole$_2$ are in fact eventually delivered to the "appropriate" (in the sense of logical) Godmother. Except by sheer accident there was no way for any ethnographer to have found out that detail. I was led to it through the logico-structural analysis. The natives would have never volunteered it and the ethnographer would only by accident know that the items had been privately delivered. I missed it despite the fact that I followed every event in the wedding ritual.

I suggest a reason for delivering the items to the parents' house instead of moving with the procession to the house of the Confirmation Godmother. It may be less easily verbalizable by the people but is definitely in their conscious conceptualization. This is the simple fact that between the two important godmothers, baptismal and confirmation, there is hierarchy. In agreement with all the ethnographic literature on Middle America, the baptismal godmother is more important. Ritual activities function to activate such implicit orderings in the natives' sociological world. The procession actually went to the house of the baptismal godmother and delivery took place there. Delivery to the secondary godmother was done indirectly and with less ritual. A functional statement certainly!

Eventually the two godmothers (bride's fictives) end up in the house of the bride's parents and remain there during "the dance of the gifts." This allows for further operation on bride's fictives by means of which they join the bride's side and become affines:

23) Bride's Fictives (Baptismal and Confirmation) $\longrightarrow$ Consuegros

If we readjust the bracketing to include this addition, (7) can be represented as follows:

24) Bride's Parents + Bride's Consanguines + Bride's Guest +
    Bride's Fictives
    CONSUEGROS   CONSUEGROS

Internal Constraints

Let us now reexamine equation (22a, 22b) in relation to (13a) and (13b), given here as (22c, 22d):

22a) Chest : Grindstone :: 22b) Saint : Unlabelled Gift
22c) Chest Gm : Grindstone Gm :: 22d) Marriage Gm : Unlabelled Gm

We immediately detect a partial correspondence between the two sets of relationships: the chest godmother delivers the chest and the grindstone godmother delivers the grindstone. If this correspondence in (22a) and (22c) is carried over to (22b) and (22d), then "logically" the marriage godmother would deliver the saint. Empirically, she does not. Rather, it is an aunt of the bride who provides that gift. This is in accordnace with ethno-logic.

If we go back to the categories of people involved in the wedding ritual according to the operation represented in (16), Marriage God-mother becomes Compadres (fictives), whereas according to bracketing (7), Bride's Consanguines are Consuegros (affines). On the conscious conceptual plane, affines give gifts, and not fictives, and once the mar-riage godmother has been syntactically rewritten Fictives (see equation (16), she cannot, by definition, perform an affinal role. That is why an aunt can give the saint, and the marriage godmother cannot.

How, then, do we account for the lack of correspondence between the terms in (22b) and the terms in (22d)? The answer lies in the fact that the gift used in the dance by Woman$_2$ is unlabelled, i.e., is decategorized and so represented by the null category $\emptyset$. Similarly, the Male's Confir-mation Godmother has been unlabelled and decategorized and so is also represented by the null category. Thus the two equations are of the form represented in (25):

$$25) \qquad \text{term} : \text{term} :: \text{term} : \emptyset$$

The relationship represented as (22b) and (22d) is undefined, formally speaking, just as the relationship x/0 is undefined in mathematics. Con-sequently, the two equations (22a, b) and (22c, d) are not admissible.

This fact could not be known until the nature and properties of the categories had been empirically determined. Thus the "logically" ex-pected relationship that the marriage godmother delivers the picture of the saint is due only to an incomplete analysis which does not recognize the special character of the two null categories in (22b) and (22d).

The argument is even more powerful. Previously, it was observed that the male's confirmation godmother was unlabelled and decatego-rized as an empirical fact. Similarly for the gift with which Woman$_2$ dances. Suppose, though, that these two entities were labelled categories. That is, suppose the rewrite rule represented in (11) above had relabelled and recategorized Male's Confirmation Godmother instead of unlabel-ling and decategorizing it. Suppose also that the gift were labelled. Then we would have equations (22 a'/b') and (22 c'/d'):

22a'/b') Chest: Grindstone :: Saint : Labelled Gift
22c'/d') Chest : Grindstone Gm :: Marriage Gm : Labelled Gm

But now we would have equations of the form (26):

$$26) \qquad \text{term} : \text{term} :: \text{term} : \text{term}$$

In that case (22a'b') and (22c'd') would be admissible equations, and the fact that marriage godmother does not deliver the picture of the saint (as she cannot) would be a contradiction of ethno-logic.

But the fact that the godmother and the gift are both unlabelled prevents this contradiction in ethno-logic. In essence, godmother *must* be delabelled and uncategorized, and similarly the gift danced with by Woman₂ to make (22a, b) and (22c, d) inadmissible equations. That the godmother and the gift are unlabelled, an ethnographic fact, is a necessary part of ethno-logic and is made understandable only by examining the structure of ritual and its logic.

A more abstract reason for the inadmissibility of a gift-giving fictive in the wedding ritual lies in the formal nature and properties of conceptual categories. I have proposed earlier that a conceptual system contains two kinds of categories: closed categories in opposition related by open categories. "Fictive" is an example of an open mediator. Mediators perform operations which create specific structures. Mediations are temporary; once they create permanent structures and relationships they are formally deleted. They can then be utilized in other combinations within the system.

As mediators they cannot be terms in a relationship or an exchange. At the risk of oversimplification I would say they are more equivalent to operations in logical and mathematical expressions. Were marriage godmother to have given the saint (as she "should" have), the equation would be of the form (27):

27) $\text{term} : \text{term} :: \text{operator} : \emptyset$

which would be as inadmissible as the mathematical expression (28):

28)   2   +   2   =   + $\emptyset$

         (term) (operator) (term)   (operator) (term)

The exchange in the wedding is in fact between two closed categories: consanguines (Caseros) and affines (Consuegros). Fictive relatives of the bride had to be transformed to affines. Only then can they give the gifts. Consanguines receive the gifts. Part of this exchange is represented in equations (22a) and (22c) above. Marriage godmother, being a fictive, hence mediator, cannot be part of that exchange.

Summary

To recapitulate: First, this analysis of the Zapotec wedding shows the dynamics of categorization and recategorization of people in ritual. Categories, which are created in specific wedding events, make up the ritual structure.

Second, the kinship category Godmother and two reciprocally related wedding events, namely, the "dance of the turkey" and the "dance of the gifts," have been reduced to their structural elements and related in a set of equations that show a "potential" homologous (corresponding) relationship between them through terms representing categories of gifts in equation (22a, b) and terms representing categories of godmother in equation (22c, d).

Going over the two equations we find an apparent contradiction between the "logical" model and the empirical model. In order to explain the contradiction we had to go to:

1) the syntactic level of rewriting and transformation between categories of people. That is, Marriage Godmother, which "logically" corresponds with the Saint, in empirical reality does not offer the gift (saint) because according to the syntactic rules she is a Fictive,

and 2) the more abstract level of the nature and properties of conceptual and logical categories: null categories, closed categories, mediators. These fundamental distinctions in the conceptual (logical) system cannot be ignored. Mediators cannot be terms in a relationship. Null categories do not have empirical existence.

By considering the property of systemic interdependence of levels, I am able to reach a better understanding of what otherwise appears ambiguous or contradictory in phenomena of human experience.

Notes

[1] The research on which this paper is based was conducted for a total period of 21 months: summer 1967, summer 1968, one year 1970-1971, and summer 1974, in a community in the Oaxaca Valley, Mexico. This research was supported by NIMH Fellowship and Research Grant MH 48273-01. I wish to thank the UCLA Academic Senate for supplying a grant that made analysis for this paper possible, and the UCLA Latin American Center for a grant that enabled me to present an earlier version of this paper in a symposium.

This analysis has benefitted from long discussions with generative linguist and mathematician–anthropologist Dwight Read.

[2] The house of the godmother is also important. It is deleted, though, on the basis of its position in the structure, namely, mediation.

[3] Although Zapotec weddings are preceded by much organized preparation and activities which take place over a period of days and weeks prior to the ritual, Fandango itself is a one day (Sunday) set of activities.

[4] Opposition is a specific form of relationship. Mediation is both a relationship and a formal operation. A mediating category performs the operations of linking, or transforming, or defining/differentiating.

[5] I did not arrive at that through interviewing nor observation. I missed it. The gift carried and danced by Woman[2] was not volunteered by the natives. During the analysis of the data and when the logic of the activities began to unfold I checked with my informant about what Woman[2] carried in the Dance of the Gifts. He said: "something, anything." There was no specific category nor label for that gift. This was consistent with my findings and confirms ethno-logic.

References

Briggs, E. 1961. *Mitla Zaptoec Grammar*. Mexico: Institute Linguistic Verano and Centro Inv. Antr. Mexico.

Bronowski, J. 1973. *The Ascent of Man*. Boston: Little, Brown and Co.

Chiñas, B. 1973. *The Isthmus Zapotecs*. New York: Holt, Rinehart & Winston, Inc.

de Saussure, F. 1959. *A Course in General Linguistics,* New York: Philosophical Library.

El Guindi, F. 1972. "The Nature of Belief Systems: A Structural Analysis of Zapotec Ritual." Ph.D. Dissertation, University of Texas, Austin, Texas.

_____. 1973. "The Internal Structure of the Zapotec Conceptual System." *Journal of Symbolic Anthropology,* 1, 15-34, The Hague: Mouton.

_____. 1977a. "The Structural Correlates of Power in Ritual." In *The Anthropology of Power*. R.N. Adams and R. Fogelson, eds. Academic Press.

_____. 1977b. "Lore and Structure: Todos Santos in the Zapotec System." *J. of Latin American Lore* 3, 3-18.

_____. n.d. *The Myth of Ritual: Zapotec Ethnography of Life Crisis Rituals*.

_____, and D. Read. 1979. "Mathematics in Structural Theory." *Current Anthropology* 20, 761-790.

_____, and H. Selby. 1976. "Dialectics in Zapotec Thinking." In *Meaning in Anthropology*. K. Basso and H. Selby, eds. Albuquerque: University of New Mexico Press, pp. 181-196.

Jakobson, R. & M. Halle. 1956. *Fundamentals of Language*. The Hague: Mouton.

Kearney, M. 1972. *The Winds of Ixtepeji: World View and Society in a Zapotec Town*. Holt, Rinehart, & Winston, Inc.

Levi-Strauss, C. 1963. *Structural Anthropology*. Basic Books, Inc.

_____. 1964. Mythologiques I: *Le cru et le cuit*. Paris.

_____. 1966. Mythologiques II: *Du miel aux cendres*. Paris.

_____. 1968a. Mythologiques III: *L'origine des maniéres de tables*. Paris.

_____. 1968b. Mythologiques IV: *L'Homme Nu*. Paris.

Nader, L. 1964. *Talea and Juquila: A Comparison of Zapotec Social Organization*. Berkeley and Los Angeles: University of California Press.

_____. 1969. *The Zapotec of Oaxaca. Handbood of Middle American Indians 7,* Part One: Ethnology, 329-359. Edited by Evon Z. Vogt. Austin: The University of Texas Press.

Paddock, J. (ed.) 1970. *Ancient Oaxaca*. Stanford: Stanford University Press.

Parsons, E.C. 1936. *Mitla: Town of the Souls*. Chicago and London: The University of Chicago Press.

Pickett, V. 1960. The Grammatical Hierarchy of Isthmus Zapotec. *Language Dissertation 56.* Baltimore.

_____. 1967. *Isthmus Zapotec. Handbook of Middle American Indians* 5, 291-310. Edited by Norman McQuown. Austin: The University of Texas Press.

Ravicz, R. 1967. "Compadrinazgo." In *Handbook of Middle American Indians,* Vol. 6, 238-252. Edited by M. Nash. Austin: The University of Texas Press.

Selby, H. 1974. *Zapotec Deviance.* Austin: University of Texas Press.

Whitecotton, J. 1977. *The Zapotec: Princes, Priests, and Peasants.* Norman: University of Oklahoma Press.

PART THREE

REVISING AND EXTENDING
THE STRUCTURAL PARADIGM

11
The Meaning of Nonsense
(Structural Analysis
Of Clown Performances
And Limericks)[1]

Paul Bouissac

> *"De même que l'alliance matrimoniale est perpétuellement
> menacée 'sur les bords' du côté de la nature par l'attrait
> physique du séducteur, du côté de la culture par le risque
> d'intrigues entre alliés vivant sous le même toît, la cuisine
> elle aussi s'expose, par la rencontre du miel ou par la con-
> quête du tabac, à basculer tout entière du côté de la nature
> ou du côté de la culture, bien que par hypothèse, elle dût
> représenter leur union.'"[2]*
> Claude Levi-Strauss
> *Du Miel aux Cendres*

When ethnologists are confronted with recurrent phenomena which appear to them as being *oddities* in the cultures they study, it is relatively
easy to reduce this difficulty by investigating the underlying logic of such
oddities. The mere labelling of a phenomenon as an *oddity* is already a
semi-formalisation and a first step toward the formulation of the problem. If ethnology can be rightly considered as a progressive reduction of
the oddness of other cultures, starting from the amazed description of
thoroughly strange behaviour and ending with a "naturalisation" or

"rationalisation" of such behaviour through the mediation of a "structure," the acknowledgement of *something odd* is in fact the acknowledgement that the system of relations which was constructed in order to account for all aspects of the given culture is not powerful enough. This stumbling block, which does not fit into the logico-semantic representation set forth as "expressing" this culture, appears indeed as belonging nevertheless to this culture as a whole. Ruth Benedict's concept of "compensatory daydreaming," for instance, is an attempt to integrate "archaic elements" in the system of the contemporary Zuni culture.[3] It could be said that the situation is a figure-ground type of relation at the level of the system: elements which can be both described and accounted for versus elements which can only be described. Therefore the oddity quality presupposes a latent logical processing of experience on our part; it is a construction or an effect of this very processing. It is indeed a sort of system hiatus which is, or should be, attributed to the weakness of the theory and not to a property of the culture considered. Good examples of this attitude and subsequent treatment are found in J.C. Faris' study on the lexicon of "occasions" in Cat Harbour[4] and in R. Bulmer's paper on the taxonomy of the Cassowary among the Karam of the New Guinea Highlands.[5] It is noticeable, however, that the taxonomies with which both were confronted were not considered as abnormal by the members of the cultures studied.

It is far less easy to perceive oddities whenever we engage in an auto-ethnological analysis because if there are any, with respect to a certain level of representation of our own system, they are "naturalised" by two expedients which fallaciously account for their presence. Indeed, as any society seems to construct permanently a "natural" theory of itself in order to legitimate all aspects of its experiencing of its own system (i.e., explicit or implicit ideologies), the two main devices through which phenomena sensed as being alien to the assumed logic of the system become acceptable, are the categorization of such phenomena as *traditional* (e.g., "E antico") or *comical*. Even though it would seem that these two categories sometimes overlap, they appear to be in fact mutually exclusive. In the case of clowns, for instance, which are *alternatively* labelled as both, we observe in actual instances an "either–or" categorisation — as signs of tradition they are not laughable, and as signs of humour they are not respectable. Of course this way of dealing with systemic difficulties within the culture has no explanatory value from without. Unless we accept the idea that a culture is made of bits and pieces put together by chance (or history) somewhat as a collage, we conceive of the necessity of discovering the underlying logic which would account for these apparent systemic hiatuses.

In this respect, the works by M. Déteinne[6] are exemplary because, against a pervading view of the ancient Greek society for which recorded odd cutoms and tales are "les débris d'un folklore où il n'ya rien à comprendre,"[7] he showed that a large corpus of the oddities put together forms a consistent system. After so many generations of fostering the idea that the most sophisticated aspects of our own culture relate through filiation to ancient Greece, such an attempt requires a great effort of objectification of phenomena which would otherwise remain protected by the fallacious transparency of "familiar things." On the other hand the structuralist literature[8] has accustomed us to incidental allusions to our own cultural system through the identification of similar behaviour under apparent differences or the pointing out of oddities within our own system. But the approach is quite ambiguous in the absence of a genotype theory, because once it has been pointed to the fact for instance that the Hadjerai women of Chad perform fundamentally the same function as our psychiatrists, it is not clear whether the oddity of their behaviour is equated to a "natural" one by setting forth identical relevant features, or whether the behaviour of our psychiatrists is conversely transformed into an ethnological problem. The comparison in itself, albeit legitimate and objective, causes a certain intellectual excitement but does not yield any specific knowledge. The "pleasure" which is so produced seems to come from the oscillation between the discovery of alterity within ourselves and identity without; "excitement," "oscillation" are expressions of this movement or operations of the mind generated by ambiguity, switching alternatively from one program to another, and mistaking sometimes the awareness of the identity of two problems for their solutions. It is true, however, that the perception of similarities is a first step toward formalisation and structural discoveries, as it presupposes that the consciousness of relations has overcome the fascination with the terms.

Clowns and Limericks

A methodological phenomenon of this type occurs frequently with respect to the clowns. Ethnologists who deal with ritual clowning allude usually to circus clowns,[9] and essayists writing about circus clowns do not fail to mention the "savage ones."[10] In both cases the "rapprochement" is purely decorative. The aim of this chapter is to outline a theory of clowning, provisionally restricted to contemporary circus clown performances, and using synchronic data for comparative purposes, namely the limericks. Clowns and, to a lesser degree, limericks are indeed two institutions whose manifestations are not negligible in contemporary Western societies. Superficially they have in common a direct or indirect relation to sexual behaviour, and they are in part connected with children; but they also share the quality of being categorised as nonsensical cultural "objects." They are sometimes considered as mere survivals from another age; their presence is accounted for through tradition and their assumed meaninglessness is explained accordingly by the absence of their original context which deprives them of any obvious relevancy. This attitude cannot be accepted for the simple fact that both "traditions" show a remarkable creativity, i.e., new "objects" are produced constantly and the interest and laughter which they trigger demonstrate that their "non-sense" is paradoxically endowed with a great amount of pertinence: they are culturally alive.

Both can be analyzed as messages or texts in a communication framework; even though they differ greatly in their forms (a short linguistic message on the one hand, a complex unit involving dialogue, acting, and props on the other), they both imply senders and receivers, message structures, and codes at least partially shared by the senders and the receivers. However, at the same time, they are considered as nonsense. This might mean that either the codes are not adequately shared or there is no code. But the evidence contradicts these hypotheses: first, the messages are obviously enjoyed, hence somewhat understood by the participants; second, they are not erratic occurrences but strictly patterned events from the point of view of both their intrinsic qualities and the socio-cultural context in which they are performed. They are at one and the same time *nonsensical* and *necessary*, i.e., non-contingential. Our cultural competence enables us to tell a clown act from insane behaviour, and a limerick from a haphazard sequence of words. This leads us to attempt to explain them at the synchronic level, i.e., to relate them to other observable data of their contextual culture through the explicitation of a structure.

Hypothesis

The basic hypothesis developed in this chapter is that clown performances and limericks are meta-cultural phenomena, i.e., discourses through which fundamental categories and relations constitutive of the contextual culture are denoted and manipulated. These fundamental relations can be viewed as tacit conditions which determine the meaningfulness of "normal" behaviour, i.e., sensible utterances and acts. It seems impossible to refer to these relations and categories per se as long as one stays within the field determined by the cultural norms, i.e., through sensible discourse. In other words, if it is impossible to describe adequately a system from within, the only way to engage in a meta-discourse, when the system to be described is the set of conditions for the "sensibility" of any discourse, is to produce a nonsensical discourse. It is, therefore, legitimate to attempt to set forth the rules of this nonsensical discourse and to assume that they are necessarily related to the structure which articulates the cultural system of their context.

Having outlined a general hypothesis regarding the "meaning" of nonsense, the analysis of a clown act and some limericks will be attempted. The act examined is known as *"the bees"* or *"the honey."* A close examination will enable us to relate this act to three limericks in which bees have a part, and to develop the hypothesis that these "nonsensical" instances are dealing with crucial categories and relations constituting our present culture.

The Clown

The clown scenario known as "the bee" or "the honey" is one of the classics of the circus repertoire. We find numerous allusions to it during the last hundred years. It has been, and still is performed both in small circuses and by famous clowns. During the summer of 1974, it was part of the program in at least two major European circuses.[11] I have recorded both of them for the purpose of this analysis, and witnessed the positive response on the part of the audience every time I have attended a performance of this clown act. In addition, there exist two written documents in which this scenario is described and its dialogues transcribed. The first one is the work of J. and M. Vesque, two professional artists who devoted most of their free time to the gathering of first-hand information on circus performances, during the first half of the twentieth century.[12] The second document was published in a selection of clown scenarios recorded and edited by Tristan Remy,[13] a circus historiographer. Both documents are from about the same date (1922 for the former, 1920 for the latter) but they concern different clowns.

The existence of these four recordings is entirely due to chance. There are only minor differences between the four versions which form the corpus. As in the case of myths, it would be pointless to look for the most authentic one; there are no valid criteria of comparison with an assumed source. As long as this act is performed it means that it "works" on the public. A clown act, indeed, which does not trigger interest and laughter in the regular audience is automatically dropped from the program. It should be added that this scenario is known, if not performed, by all professional clowns who have had access to the European tradition.

We shall refer in this study mainly to the performance of Dédé Gruss, which I have been able to observe and record several times during the summer of 1974, in Paris. But before attempting to describe summarily this act, it should be remembered that clown performances involve basically two participants and occasional assistants or extras. The two main actors are systematically contrasted in their outward appearance and behaviour. On the one hand the white-face clown is an overdetermined sign of culture (make-up suppressing natural colours of the face and introducing elements of dissymmetry, suppresssion or strict control of the hair, sophistication of the costume made of precious fabric and glittering material, elegance of manners, authority and perfect articulation). On the other hand, the tramp-looking clown can be viewed as an overdetermined sign of nature through the systematic inversion of the above features (make-up emphasizing natural colours and symmetrical elements of the face, shaggy hair, ridiculous aspect of the costume made of rough material and ill-fitted; unrefined manners, awkwardness and poor articulation). Extra characters may be duplication or triplication of the latter type, or neutral elements, i.e., "normal" appearance, in which case they belong to the side of the former.[14]

The Performance

As interpreted by Dédé Gruss (the tramp) and Alexis (the white-face clown) the act runs as follows:

1. After two minor sketches which will not be taken in consideration here, because it does not seem that they co-occur regularly with the scenario of "the Bee" but function independently in other combinations as introductory sequences, Alexis asks his partner, Dédé Gruss, if he likes to work.

2. Dédé Gruss answers that he dislikes work immensely.

3. Alexis announces that he has found a way to get basic food without working. Dédé is enthusiastic and wants to learn about this method.

4. Alexis replies that it suffices to imitate the bees. He will transform Dédé through hypnosis into the queen bee, and himself will play the part of the worker bee and will go in the countryside collecting the substance from the flower from which he will make honey in his mouth; then he will come in front of the queen bee, will bow three times and will give him the honey when he will have said: "give me your honey."

5. While Dédé is sitting on a chair, waiting for the honey, Alexis dances around and on his way back fills his mouth with water from a bottle. When asked to give the honey, he spits the water on Dédé's face, who becomes angry and says that he does not appreciate the joke.

6. Alexis convinces him that he can have fun by doing the same thing to someone else.

7. Just at this moment a man from the circus walks across the ring and tells them goodbye; he declares that he is sick of working and has quit his job. Dédé explains to him the new method he discovered, but phrases the words wrongly and is corrected each time by Alexis. For instance he says: "I found a way to work without ever eating or drinking," or "I will come back and spit the water on you," or "I will hypnotize you and transfrom you into a camel," or "I will go in the country side and will gather honey from all the flowers, such as, potatoes, cabbages, carrots, turnips, etc."

8. Eventually the third person accepts, but, four times in a row, Dédé fails to carry the water in his mouth from the bottle to him. First he spills the water on himself because he cannot help laughing. Second he falls down on his way. Thirdly, he has to swallow the water because the "queen bee" does not ask for the honey. At last, he has to spit the water

aside and angrily tells the "queen bee" that he must say "give me the honey,"

9. At this point, the "queen bee" who has filled his mouth with water through the help of Alexis, spits the water on Dédé face.

10. Alexis gives Dédé a trumpet as a consolation and as a transition for the concluding musical sketch.

Confronted with such an institutionalized behaviour, rigorously patterned, orally transmitted, showing a remarkable resistance of form over at least sixty years and likely many more, it is legitimate to formulate a series of questions: what does account for the obvious gratification of the public which attends such performances? What is the relation of these odd actions with our culture as a whole? If we want to go beyond mere summaries of such performances and raise the problem of "what it is all about," which dimensions or which level of abstraction should be selected as relevant in the analytical process?

Indeed if we consider a distanced description of one of these performances, which day after day repeats itself with only minor variations, in front of a new public with more or less the same effect of intense participation and laughter, we find ourselves in the presence of a strange object: two adult males dressed as nobody else in the audience, and another one who could be a member of this audience judging from his outward appearance, are pretending that they are insects and spit water on each other from their mouths, while a crowd, which has been admitted to witness this event for a set fee, is focusing its attention on it, both emotionally and intellectually mobilised, bursts into laughter at some expected time and eventually produces a noise by clapping of hands to make manifest enjoyment and approval.

A first approach could be to dissociate the form from the content and to analyse this act as a narrative structure, using Gleason's[15], Labov and Waleski's[16] or Greimas' model;[17] in the latter case, for instance, the main *Actant* (Dédé Gruss) could be defined as the subject of the quest of an object: food in the first part, then completion of a practical joke in the second; the other two actors could be viewed as representing the Actant opponent in the guise of the Actant helper, i.e., the deceiver. The relations between the "hero" and the "opponent" take the form of successive contracts which are completed in a systematically detrimental way for the "hero," who is subsequently transformed into an "anti-hero" as he fails all the tests. But Alexis could as well be seen as the "hero" whose object is the ridiculing of Dédé with the help of the third person, in which case the first sequence is for Alexis a qualifying test because the practical joke is a fairly simple one, whereas the following sequence is a glorifying test because the practical joke is more sophisticated: the victim being the one who thinks that he is performing the joke. In such an approach the interest of the audience is accounted for by the clear understanding of the tasks undertaken and the successive stages of the completion of these tasks, regardless of their specific content. Undoubtedly a dramatic articulation of this type is at work at the syntactic level of the performed actions. But, as we have seen earlier, such a structure applied to the analysis of this instance generates an ambiguity; moreover it definitely does not account for the specificity of the clown performances. Its degree of abstraction makes it useless for our purpose.

A second type of approach could be to focus our attention on the two main actors and to analyse the "act" in function of their well-established complementarity in the code of the circus. An average European audience expects to see such a basic pair of characters whenever "the clowns" are announced in the program. Before they start performing it is anticipated that the tramp will be victimised by the white-faced clown. If the dichotomy culture/nature which has been proposed above for explaining their contrast is relevant, the actual content of their actions ccould be de-emphasized as merely sustaining the antithesis. Such an attitude is overwhelming in the sub-literature which developed around the clowns. They do not take into consideration the fact that the tramp-type performs more than often successful tricks and gags in which he has the dominant role. For instance in the two sketches preceding the bee scenario, Dédé Gruss outsmarts Alexis twice, and in the concluding sequence Dédé displays the qualities of a virtuoso in a trumpet solo. Moreover it would be impossible to contend that as long as they conform to their assumed part, they could do anything. In fact some attempts to develop a new scenario prove occasionally to be failures (i.e., there is no response on the part of the public), whereas other ones are very successful. On the one hand, there are obviously precise constraints or rules the existence of which is empirically sensed by the clowns themselves but are not explicit; on the other hand, the system at work in the act of clowning is much more complex than it appears in the straight-forward dichotomy of two characters. The mere display of their opposition could hardly explain obvious deep relevancy in the culture where they belong.

As opposed to pure formalism and over-individualisation of the characters involved, the third approach, which will be used in our analysis of the "bee," consists of emphasizing the content which is articulated in the performances of clown scenarios. This does not mean that the narrative structure and the string of features which determine the characters are excluded from the analysis, but that they are only a part, as contributing factors or simple effects, of the logico-semantic operations that are constitutive of the clown performances. These operations manipulate selectively the rules of the contextual culture. Our hypothesis is that the clown act which was described above constitutes a metadiscourse on the culinary code in its greater generality. There are indeed other scenarios that deal, it seems, with specific sectors of the culinary code as operation on a particular rule. If one accepts indeed the thesis developed by C. Levi-Strauss in *From Honey to Ashes,* every detail of the performance, even the most seemingly gratuitous and nonsensical, appears to be necessary, i.e., motivated by the complete system. Moreover it becomes easy to account for the intense participation of the public if indeed the fundamentals of the contextual culture are the very object of the operations that take place in the ring.

We have a man, whose distinctive features situate on the side of nature, who denies the necessary connection between working and feeding. This means, in addition to the economical implications, a denial of cooking, but also a refusal of the whole social system. In the version recorded in 1920, the dialogue runs as follows (translation mine):

> Dario (white-face clown): *Now we are going to work.*
> Bario (tramp): *To work? I am fed up with working, it is useless... I do not want to work.*
> Dario: *Oh! This is serious... unless you become wealthy suddenly.*
> Bario: *No, nothing like that!*
> Dario: *Well, then how do you manage to survive?*
> Bario: *How I manage to survive? Well, I wait for someone to give me something.*
> Dario: *But,* **this is not a system** (emphasis mine. Literally translated from the French: "Ce n'est pas un système.)
> Bario: *So what!*
> Dario: *Listen, I will teach you a way to drink and to eat without working. Did you hear of the bees?*

The man who is going to "teach him a lesson" is an overdetermined sign of culture, and he will use water instead of honey. There are several indications that make the identification of this water with tobacco possible. It is of course well known that tobacco can be consumed in liquid form, without relying on South-American examples, the habit of chewing tobacco was well spread in Europe, and we could hypothesize that at a time when spitting out the tobacco diluted in saliva was common practice, the white-faced clown was just spewing that on his partner's face. Moreover, without even relying on a hypothetical source, it has been pointed out by Norbert Elias that in the evolution of European manners, the general habit of spitting out saliva with or without tobacco was progressively replaced by exhaling pipe or cigarette smoke.[18] Therefore if the identifications can be accepted, this "discourse" would consist of the following operations:

(1) Negation of culture through denial of cooking.

(2) Deceiving affirmation of nature through production of infra-cooking.

(3) Real affirmation of culture through production of super-cooking.

The transgressor is enticed into a detrimental contact with the over-affirmation of the very thing he attempted to deny through the bait of the gratification of the negation.

The second sequence of the act displays elements which follow logically the first one. The transgressor will learn the lesson from within, but significantly he tends to invert all the excesses which had determined his initial transgression. For instance, he says: "I have found a way to work without drinking or eating," then he reveals the trick instead of enticing the victim-to-be with the bait; later on he substitutes names of vegetables exclusively linked to cooking for the names of flowers that he is supposed to visit in order to gather the honey; eventually he spills the water *on himself* or he *swallows it* before being *again* spewed on by a character whose outward appearance and manners situate on the side of the culture and who is *d'intelligence* with the white-face clown.

In the light of this approach, some elements of the two sequences, which might have appeared to be secondary and gratuitous, become narrowly integrated into the whole scheme. Firstly, there is the hypnotic scene; a consequence of the refusal of cooking is the rejoining of animals; this operation may be represented conversely by a transformation into an animal as a condition for enjoying a "natural" food. Therefore the hypnotic scene is the sign of a necessary disjunction. When Dédé Gruss, in the second sequence, transforms the third person "into a little animal" and is asked "what animal?" he replies: "a camel." In the 1920 version, Bario says: "I will transform you into a beast...into a camel" and after the protestations by his mentor, he adds "no, into a cow," then: "into a mother-in-law," the latter joke, soon corrected in "no! into a queen bee," introduces another element which will be considered further.

Another interesting aspect of the scenario is the ambiguous status of the bees. It should be noted that in the 1920 version Bario states at the beginning of the act that he did not know that it was the bees who were making the honey. This remark is important because it introduces a disjunction which accounts for the fact that on the one hand the honey is the temptation or the seduction of nature that implies the denial of culture and on the other hand the bee is instrumental in the correction of the transgression. There are indeed numerous evidences of a tradition which considers the bees as the guardians of the well-ordered culture. M. Détienne has shown their value in Greek myths, in which they are the epitome of puritanical life.[19] In recent European folklore the custom of "telling the bees" whenever an important event occurs in the family is well attested for instance in England[20] and in the Basque country,[21] and demonstrates their close connection with the institutionalised family life. Moreover the bees are presented in elementary schoolbooks as a model of well-organized and hard-working society. All this makes the bees particularly well qualified for the role of repressing the transgressions.

The two opposite "values" of the bees which are enacted in this scenario are logically understandable as they are situated on the borderline of nature and culture, if they do not even constitute this borderline. They are congruent to nature as producers of an "infra-cuisine," but they are congruent also to the "ultra-cuisine" represented by tobacco inasmuch as they appear as an ultra-society. It suffices to remember the innumerable warnings of our humanist philosophers against the dangers for human society of becoming similar to the social insect, i.e., ultra-social.

Undoubtedly, there are more dimensions and many more details which should be taken into consideration in an analysis of this clown act. However, it seems that our hypothesis regarding the underlying operations at work in the act accounts for an appreciable number of elements as well as for the deep meaning produced by these "non-sensical" patterned and institutionalised behaviours. Moreover, it supports the idea that non-sense or odditities are the categories through which a cultural meta-discourse can display itself.

The Limerick

The history of the limerick is interestingly parallel to this history of the clowns: the night of oral tradition until the nineteenth century; then a few historical landmark contributions to the art and finally the recent recording and compilation which make a structural analysis of these phenomena possible. We shall limit ourselves in this chapter to the study of three non-sensical limericks which involve bees and honey in order to investigate any possible similarities with the clown scenario that was tentatively analysed above.

The first two are from Edward Lear's *A Book of Nonsense*,[22] the third one is an anonymous one provided to me by a colleague. They will be successively quoted and commented upon. The first one reads as follows:

> There was an old man in a tree
> who was horribly bored by a bee
> When they said, "Does it buzz?"
> He replied, "Yes, it does!
> It's a regular brute of a bee!"

Since Lear has illustrated all of his limericks, it seems necessary to describe the drawings which most of the time contain more information than the poems, or at least emphasize some aspects of them. In this case we are presented with a man sitting in a tree and showing an apparent discomfort as a bee, bigger than he is, faces him in an aggressive manner. On the ground two characters, made much smaller through perspective, display signs of aggressive excitement.

The fact of withdrawing in a tree for no apparent useful or technological purpose can be considered as an anti-social behaviour. Moreover, animals live in trees, not humans. Therefore this initial move is a disjunction from culture to nature, formally similar to the initial refusal to work found in the clown scenario. The rest of the limerick describes the aggressive behaviour of a bee who can be viewed as a retaliation on the part of culture and can appear instrumental with respect to the concern of society represented by "they" in the poem and by the two characters in the drawing.[23] The repression of the transgression is made by way of noises and the buzzing can be interpreted here as a form of "chivari."

The second limerick resembles more precisely the first sequence of the clown act:

> There was an Old Person of Dover
> who rushed through a field of blue clover
> But some very large bees
> stung his nose and his knees
> So he very soon went back to Dover.

If we note indeed that the blue clover is a flower particularly appreciated by the bees and therefore entertains a metonymic relation with honey, the man appears to be irresistibly attracted by nature; in this case, we can consider that this limerick is "played" in the culinary code and consequently "Dover" would relate to culture not only because it is a city but also because of a sophisticated dish known as "Dover sole." As a result of this immoderate attraction towards honey, the bees retaliate less as owners of the clover than as guardians of the culture. Significantly the parts of the body which are stung are the nose (instrument of the seduction) and the knees (instrument of the transgression).

The third limerick is a subtle demonstration of the congruence of the bees with social order in general, i.e., the respect of the rules constitutive of a given culture. Indeed the absence of the word "bee" disrupts the poetic rules and transforms the limerick into an irregular one; poetic order is here a metaphor of social order.

> There was an old man from St. Knee
> who was stung on the arm by a wasp
> When asked "Did it hurt?"
> he replied, "No, it didn't.
> I'm so glad it wasn't a hornet."[24]

It should be noted that wasps and hornets are in the popular imagination considered to be wild bees. They are credited for feeding on raw or rotten meat and for being asocial insects. With respect to an assumed transgression, they are not qualified to correct the transgressor, hence the fact that "it didn't hurt." It is noticeable that the expected rhyme in the last line is "bee."

Considered individually, some of the interpretations expounded so far in this study may appear to be arbitrary. However, their consistence or confluence reduces considerably this arbitrariness and contributes to set forth a system of relations which account for each partial actualisation such as a clown scenario or a limerick. In the absence of such a logico-semantic system, these instances not only would not have any relevance, but simply would not exist. In the first limerick studied, the determination of the bee as a "regular brute" enacts precisely the non-contingency of this oddity of our cultural environment: the nonsense.

Very complex operations must be inferred from such evidence. With respect to the fundamental dichotomy between culture and nature, their crucial position make the bees a rich logical tool in the development of the meta-discourse without which culture as a code could not be thought, or rather, could not think itself. The fact that the bees are seen as over-socialised individuals, a sort of ultra-society, can account for their congruence to tobacco in some of the examples studied in this paper (the spitting out of water in the clown act and the smoking bee in the first limerick). If we are indeed confronted with systematic inversions, it can be expected that a given relation will be transformed both ways, so giving the well known impression that the extremes meet. From this comprehensive point of view the inclusion of the mother-in-law theme as an item in the list of the transformations in the clown scenario recorded in 1920, makes sense, inasmuch as she represents the guardian by excellence of the regularity of the matrimonial life and at the same time is the very symbol of the dangers which threaten this delicate balance on the side of the culture.[25] This list displays a complex paradigm which includes the two dimensions, or the two directions in which a harmonious culture can be disrupted: animality and excessive socialization. Therefore, the paradigm is contradictory in appearance only because the categories which it includes have in common that they negate the same rule and manifest its meaning through their nonsense.

Conclusion

In conclusion to this outline of a hypothesis regarding nonsensical "objects," the question of humor and laughter should undoubtedly be raised. In which respect is the social behaviour which qualifies some phenomena as comical related to the operations described in the above analysis? Psychologists have often, and somewhat unconclusively, tried to account for it. But although laughter has been considered for centuries a distinctive feature of humankind, it is generally acknowledged that there does not exist as yet a satisfactory theory which would accurately describe and explain this eminently human characteristic. One might be tempted to object that the audience laughs during the clown scenario of "the honey" for reasons quite independent from the semiotic operations which have been set forth, the make-up of the actors, their faces, gait, gestures, intonation, etc. But it is a fact that such "pieces of behaviour" never occur independently from a scenario of some sort, even if it is reduced to the bare minimum of a gag or a joke. It seems that the difficulty encountered here comes from the incompatibility which exists between, on the one hand, the meta-semiotic approach which reveals some systematic relations and construct the set of conditions that account for the meaningfulness of some instances and, on the other hand, the empirical level of the performances in which such instances can be experienced only as non-sensical. Therefore, as laughter would be part of this latter domain it would be unaccountable in structuralist terms, although it would signal the occurrence of a particular type of "meta-discourse," i.e., some operations upon the rules as such of the contextual culture. It will be the task of pragmatic semiotics to bridge the gap between the structure we can only think and the performances we can only experience, although the former condition depends on the latter, at least as much as they are revealed by them. If such is the case, the effect of oddness would be the first symptom that the empirical level is being transcended in the direction of the structural level.

Notes

[1]This research was supported by a fellowship of the J.S. Guggenheim Foundation 1973-1974. It belongs to a book length study of contemporary circus clowns (forthcoming).

[2]Cl. Levi-Strauss, *Du miel aux cendres,* Plon, Paris, 1966. Translated into English by J. and D. Weightman, *From Honey to Ashes,* Harper and Row, New York, 1973. "Just as matrimony is perpetually threatened at its edges by the natural physical attraction of the seducer, and by the cultural phenomenon of internecine conspiracies, cooking as an institution also runs the danger of falling entirely on the side of nature (through the seduction of honey) or conversely on the side of culture (through the abuse of tobacco) whereas it should represent an harmonious union of nature and culture." (translation mine)

[3]R. Benedict, *Zuni Mythology,* A.M.S. Press, New York, (1935), 1969.

[4]J.C. Paris, "Validation in Ethnographical Descripton: The Lexicon of 'Occasions' in Cat Harbour," *Man,* New Series, Vol. 3, No. 1, March 1968, pp. 112-124.

[5]R. Bulmer, "Why is the Cassowary not a Bird? A Problem of Zoological Taxonomy among the Karam of the New Guinea Highlands," *Man,* New Series, Vol. 2, No. 1, March 1967, pp. 5-25.

[6]M. Détienne, *Les Jardins d'Adonis,* Gallimard, Paris, 972. Translated into English by Janet Lloyd, *The Gardens of Adonis,* Harvester Original, European Philosophy and the Human Sciences Series.

[7]L. Robin, *La pensée hellénique des origines à Epicure,* (The meaningless remnants of an ancient folklore) Paris, 1942, p. 35.

[8]Cl. Levi-Strauss, *op. cit., passim;* J. Pouillon, *Fétiches sans Fétichisme,* Paris, Maspero, 1975.

⁹L. Makarius, "Ritual Clowns and Symbolical Behaviour," *Diogenes,* 69, 1970, pp. 44-73.

¹⁰J. Starobinski, *Portrait de l'artiste en saltimbanque,* Skira, Geneva, 1970.

¹¹Circus Gruss, Paris (Dédé Gruss and Alexis) and Circus Benneweiss, Copenhagen (Toto Chabri and Company).

¹²This collection is the property of the Musée des Arts et Traditions Populaires (Paris). The documents are presently being processed for publication. See *Ethnologie Française* Vol. VII-2, pp. 111-120. The item referred to here consists of two sketches, one of the hypnotist scene and the other of the white clown miming the flying worker bee. The comment reads: "l'abeille, Miche (name of the clown), 1922 Janvier, Cirque de Paris."

¹³T. Rémy, *Entrées clownesques,* Paris, L'Arche, 1962.

¹⁴This aspect is fully developed in my book, *Circus and Culture: A Semiotic Approach* (chapter IX), Indiana University Press (1976).

¹⁵H.A. Gleason, Jr., "Contrastive Analysis in Discourse Structure," *Monograph Series on Language and Linguistics,* Vol. 21, ed. by J.E. Alatis, Georgetown University School of Languages and Linguistics, 1968, pp. 39-63.

¹⁶W. Labow and J. Waletsky, "Narrative Analysis: Oral Versions of Personal Experience, "*Essays on the Verbal and Visual Arts, Proceedings of the 1966 Annual Spring Meeting of the American Ethnological Society,* Seattle, University of Washington Press 1967.

¹⁷A.J. Greimas, Sémantique structurale, Paris, Larousse, 1966.

¹⁸N. Elias, *La civilisation des moeurs,* Paris, Calmann-Lévy, 1973.

¹⁹M. Détienne, "Le mythe, Orphée au miel," in *Faire de l'histoire,* J. Le Goff and P. Nora (eds.), vol. 3, Paris, Gaillimard, 1974 (pp. 56-75).

²⁰E.g. G. Winter, *A Country Camera 1844-1914,* Penguin Books, 1973 (p. 63). F. Thompson, *Lark Rise to Candleford,* Oxford University Press, 1945 (pp. 65 and 71-73).

²¹J. Caro Baroja, *La vida rural en vera de Bidasoa,* Biblioteca de Tradiciones Populares, Congejo Superior des Investigaciones Cientificas, Madrid, 1944 (pp. 77-78), et P. Veyrin, *Les Basques,* Paris, Arthaud, 1955 (p. 268).

²²E. Lear, *A Book of Nonsense,* London, 1863.

²³Both the man in the tree and the bee appear to smoke a pipe.

²⁴This limerick was kindly communicated to me by Professor E. Walker. Other sources confirmed that it is a classic of the oral tradition.

²⁵See quotation by Cl. Levi-Strauss at the beginning of the article.

12
A Semiological Analysis of Self-Decoration in Mount Hagen, New Guinea

Roger Neich

Introduction

Many of the peoples of the Central Highlands of Papua New Guinea are famous for their pre-occupation with personal decoration. The Gawigl and Melpa speakers living about Mount Hagen in the western Wahgi Valley are typical Highlanders in this respect. Their elaborate self-decoration with feathers, wigs, furs, shells, beads, plants, paint, oil and charcoal is described by Andrew and Marilyn Strathern in their book *Self-Decoration in Mount Hagen* (1971). The quality of the ethnographic observation in this work is excellent, but the analysis tends to be vague (Gell 1972). Believing that an explicitly linguistic model can produce a more coherent analysis, I will attempt a semiological analysis of Mount Hagen self-decoration, based mainly on the Saussurean model outlined by Barthes (1967).

Ethnographic Background

Hageners, both men and women, decorate themselves for formal and informal occasions. Formal occasions include the large pig and shell exchange festivals (moka), warfare compensation payments, and performances of the two main religious cults. The decorations worn for formal occasions are the most elaborate of all, serving to transmit their "messages" with the greatest intensity. One further context is also important as an opposition to the occasions above. This is the funeral, where the lack of decoration, or even self-abasement and mutilation are highly significant. Actual warfare forms an ambivalent situation between these two extremes.

The political unit most often involved in payments and cult performances is the clan, about 50-100 men who live with their wives and children within a common territory. The clans, and the big men themselves, are continually competing for temporary advantages over each other. Since the cessation of warfare, the moka ceremonial exchange system provides the main arena for this competition and, as decoration is intimately involved with competition, also for the display of self-decoration.

Many of the items used for self-decoration are also valuables used in exchanges. Success in acquiring ornaments is felt to parallel and to indicate the general prosperity of the individual and his clan. Different decoration sets are appropriate to different formal occasions and categories of participants, but Hageners have no verbal usages which refer to sets as a whole. Rather they conceive of an outfit as a combination of elements, only some of which are diagnostic of a particular occasion or dance, while within the overall combination there is room for individual variation. The Stratherns regard wigs, feathers and aprons as the major diagnostic items for decoration sets, with face-painting as a major accessory item. These main items exert a certain constraint on the accessories, depending on the overall effect aimed at in the decoration. Decisions as to what will be worn are firstly the result of the process of deciding what festivals to hold and what dances to perform, then the cultural code which defines what decorations and what scale of decoration are suitable for the particular occasions, and finally the aesthetic code which determines the most favoured items to make up the chosen decoration set. For formal occasions performers will standardise their decorations over the course of several practises and dress-rehearsals. Dancing groups are praised for the consistency among their individual decorations, although men with sufficient prestige and status can vary their outfit up to certain flexible limits.

The Stratherns' Analysis

The "general" message conveyed on informal occasions is personal wellbeing, and on formal occasions it is group prosperity and health. The content of messages, that is the "meaning," seems to be contextually determined to a high degree. As the Stratherns say (1971: 142):

It is hard to tell, in fact, whether colours derive their meaning from, or impart their meaning to, the occasions when they are worn. Hageners imply, however, that achieving such a general effect as "brightness" is an end in itself, and hence we are led to think that "brightness" is a concept which carries meaning to them; our problem becomes why it should be a desired end.

They proceed to try and show why the qualities of brightness and darkness in decorations are so highly valued. This leads to a treatment of the three basic colours—red, white and black—in terms of their substantive meanings and associations. Appeals are made to the two major religious cults, exchange festivals, warfare, funerals and the male/female opposition to construct a scheme of symbolic meanings of decoration colours. These have been summarized (Stratherns, 1971: 168) as follows:

> In the context of decoration we have suggested that dominant meanings can be identified for the three colours, two of which are linked together as bright, in contrast with the third, which is dark. White stands for health, fertility and attractiveness, and through the equation between health, grease and semen it comes to be most clearly associated with male fertility and clan continuity. Red, which like white is regarded as bright, also stands for fertility and especially for powers of attraction, but through its latent equation with blood, it is most closely linked with women and thereby gains a tinge of ambivalence which parallels the ambivalent nature of affinal ties between groups. Black stands unambiguously for male strength and aggressiveness, and in that sense is opposed to red. It represents the internal solidarity and external competitiveness of groups, which are counter-balanced by individual links of friendship between them.

The Stratherns make explicit comparisons between Hagen and Ndembu colour symbolism as described by Turner (1967), but their analysis becomes more sophisticated as they distinguish between levels of meaning for brightness, going beyond the simple oppositions of colour. However, since the Hageners (Stratherns, 1971: 163) do not associate particular colours as unequivocally with psychobiological universals, as Turner would lead us to expect, the Stratherns' analysis also has more scope for ambiguity.

After a very full and suggestive description of Hagen decorative symbolism, the Stratherns reduce the formal part of their argument to the multiple meanings and associations of colour and brightness for the Hageners. However, because of the substantivist, "atomistic" approach to each colour symbol and the unsystematic appeal to contexts for essential meanings, the range of referents and associations for each colour are lost in ambiguity. On the same page as the summary quoted above, the Stratherns write (1971: 168) that each colour taken as a category could be said to be ambiguous, but this only becomes ambivalence in certain contexts. Because of the interpenetration of ambiguity and ambivalence, connotation and denotation, and contextual meaning, no real system emerges. The concepts of contextual intrusion, suppression and reversal are introduced to compensate for the confusion of subsystems and contexts, but they are not sufficient to produce order out of the ambiguities. The Stratherns attribute their difficulty to the problem of distinguishing between a folk system and an analytical system. Rather, I would see it as a result of failing to first define self-decoration as a system in itself, with its own grammatical rules, then as a subsystem in relation to other subsystems, before trying to place it in a welter of detailed situational information.

Although I have criticised them for bringing in too many unsystematic associations, I still agree with Gell's comments (1972: 684) that the man:bird relationship and the symbolism of the plain human body have been undervalued by the Stratherns. Clearly, the Hageners do attach great importance to body symbolism (Stratherns, 1971: 78, 113; Strathern, A., 1972: 187-193). Douglas (1970: 65, 159) has indicated that, relative to the elaborate code of New Guinea art, the body itself is a highly restricted medium of expression. This suggests that a semiology of the unadorned body may be systematically connected to the system of self-decoration through rules of aesthetics and style, in the same way that a restricted linguistic code may be related to an elaborated code.

Similar systematic connections in the man:bird relationship can be expected. For the nearby Karam, Bulmer (1970) has indicated the nature of the relationship between bird classification and behaviour, and human ritual behaviour. Despite our limited knowledge of Hagen ethnozoological principles it is clear that Hageners make similar analogies. Some specific associations are mentioned, such as eagle feathers, which make the wearer successful in obtaining wealth in the same way that the rapacious bird hunts its meat, and red bird of paradise plumes, which associate the dancer with the graceful movements of this bird when it is in display before females (Stratherns, 1971: 141). But the analogy is more systematic than this, as the Stratherns themselves (Stratherns, 1968) demonstrate. Operating on an opposition between wild/domestic domains, Hagen men attempt to transcend women (with their weakening effect) by becoming like wild birds. The men explicitly and systematically compare their own ceremonial exchange activities to the behaviour of birds (Stratherns, 1968: 198).

I have outlined the possible nature of the connections between self-decoration and two other subsystems, the unadorned body and bird classification, but I envisage similar interrelations with many other systems (Fig. 1). Each subsystem is regarded as a semiotic or a system of signs. Connections between systems may be of many different kinds. What is denotation in one system may become connotation when it extends into another. Connotation itself forms a system and thereby may provide for a systematic relationship between semiotics, rather than links given by associations, penetrating haphazardly through several subsystems. The associations of Turner and the Stratherns, which mix denotation and connotation indiscriminately, are very different from the systematic paradigmatic associations of Saussure (Barthes, 1967: 58, 59).

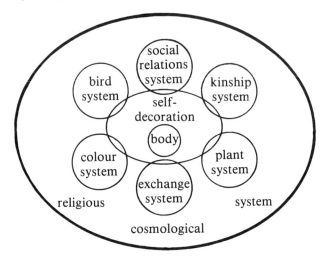

Figure 1.

Douglas (1966: 69) has suggested that a major difference between primitives and modern men is that "we do not bring forward from one context to the next the same set of ever more powerful symbols: our experience is fragmented. Our rituals create a lot of little subworlds, unrelated. Their rituals create one single, symbolically consistent universe." On the other hand, Barthes (1967: 46), speaking of modern Europe, foresees a total ideological description, common to all the subsystems of a given synchrony, based largely on the overlapping signifieds of different systems. This impasse can only be resolved after a careful examination of the systems involved.

Hagen Self-Decoration as a Semiotic

The question now arises as to whether self-decoration in Mount Hagen is in fact a semiotic, and if so, what is the place of meaning in such a semiotic? Forge (1966: 23) phrased these questions in New Guinea terms when he asked,

> How far is the art of the Sepik a means of communication, and if it is what sort of communication does it make? By what means can we find out what it communicates? Underlying these questions is the bigger one; How far does the art form a system *sui generis* or, in other words, to what extent can we take carvings and paintings as

things in their own right relating to each other and the beholder, and not as mere manifestations of some other order of cultural fact such as mythology or religion. Does the plastic art of a group have its own rules, not just of style, but also of meaning and interpretation, or is its apparent unity illusory being based only on style, while "meaning" can only be discovered by relating each individual piece to a rite in which it has a function, a myth that it illustrates, or a decorative purpose it fulfills?

For the Abelam, Forge found that if there is any system of symbols in the art, it does not lie at the level of overt symbolism.

Any systematic symbolism must be at the level of the relation between symbols, and at this level may not be consciously perceived by either the artist or the beholder. For this sort of analysis the overt meaning of any symbol is not of great importance. What matters is the arrangement of symbols and the significance of that arrangement (Forge, 1966: 25).

He concluded (1970: 288-90) that:

Abelam painting could be regarded as a form of language operating on its own rules and communicating things that are not communicable by other methods. The art communicates some fundamental values of Abelam society and this communication is not fully conscious to anyone concerned. Abelam art is about relationships, not about things. One of its functions is to relate and unite disparate things in terms of their place in the ritual and cosmological order. It does this, I would suggest, directly and not as an illustration to some text based on another symbolic system such as language.

Most of these findings can apply equally well to Hagen self-decoration. The Stratherns note (1971: 140, 172) that self-decoration carries its own symbolic load and transmits messages that are not explicitly duplicated in other media, verbal or otherwise. People may not themselves be fully aware of the statements about social values that their decorations are making. Furthermore, while the cultural code is explicit and consciously applied at one level of meaning, that of the appropriateness of a total set of items, at the level of item details attributed values are vague or unformulated. In other words, both the rules for generating the statements and for "reading" the message have a large unconscious component. In Saussure's terms these constitute *langue,* a social institution and a system of values. For the Hageners, it is the arrangement of elements as a total set that conveys the meaning, not the separate items alone.

In spite of the fact that the intermediary of language is needed for eliciting the native exegesis of these sign systems, the works of Forge and the Stratherns indicate that, even when dealing with minor iconic systems, we will encounter semiological systems without a linguistic admixture or duplication. This is contrary to the expectation of Barthes (1967: 10) and agrees with Ardener (1971: x1).

Levi-Strauss (Charbonnier, 1969: 108, 125) suggests that art as a signifying system always remains halfway between language and object. In this view the aesthetic emotion is simply the way we react when a non-significant object is promoted to the role of signifier. Therefore, treating Hagen self-decoration as art, this raises the question of the degree of motivation in the self-decoration sign. For while the object as object can only signify itself, simple linguistic signs, according to Saussure, have no material relationship with what they are intended to signify. Saussure himself wondered whether his new science of semiology could include modes of expression based on completely natural signs. He decided that since every means of expression used in society is based on collective behaviour or convention, the use of such analogical signs is still governed by social rules, not by any intrinsic value of the sign.

Along with Barthes (1967: 53, 56-7) we accept the co-existence of the analogical and the non-analogical in a single system, while noting that it is articulation, the double phenomenon of signification and value which ultimately generates meaning. At the level of the most general semiology Barthes detects a complementary tendency to naturalize the unmotivated and to intellectualize the motivated. The signs of Hagen self-decoration vary between more and less motivated, from the predatory eagle feather denoting success in obtaining wealth, to the long netted dance apron with almost no independent denotation. Some signs in the self-decoration system appear to be motivated because of the position of their signifier in another system, for example the Saxony feathers and pearl shells which carry over their denotations from the valuables system. Thus the degree of motivation will be intimately linked to the relation between denotation and connotation, and will have consequences for the relations between semiotic systems.

Hagen self-decoration seems to fall between the extremes of the linear, discursive nature of language and the immediate presentational forms of visual symbolism (Langer 1942). It is involved in a simultaneous integral presentation forming a non-discursive system, but by the nature of the tightly-bounded, highly structured medium on which it is presented, self-decoration has some of the qualities of discursive form. The procedures for building up the presentation have a discursive character, involving successive paradigmatic choices in the filling of each tightly defined "body slot." Instead of being progressive through time like language, self-decoration is progressive through space from head to foot of the body medium. This is not to say that receivers of the message "read the body sentence" in this way, but the linear structure is there. For Saussure also, linearity was the criterion by which language was to be distinguished from other sign-systems. The linearity of language makes possible the division into paradigmatic and syntagmatic planes. I believe that the self-decoration system is progressively structured enough for a linguistic-type of paradigmatic/syntagmatic division to be applied to it.

Description of the Semiotic

All the actual self-decoration sets in the corpus provided by the Stratherns constitute *parole* (speech), the result of individual acts of selection and actualization. In building up his set of decorations, the individual works with a systematized set of signs and rules, that is the *langue*. Where performers standardize their decorations, we see a speech which is partly institutionalized. During the preliminary practices, performers are made aware of the norm or ideal for this performance and attempt to conform to it. Nevertheless, their individual *paroles* will still display variations. As Barthes says (1967: 18), the norm determines usage and speech, but also at the same time usage and speech have an effect on the norm. There is a dialectical relation between the language and speech here, as in verbal language, resulting from the interplay of social convention and individual choice.

In the Hagen self-decoration system the threshold between language and speech does seem to be rather precarious. At the level of language there are some fixed syntagms (Barthes, 1967: 19) because of the strongly determining effect of the main items on some of the accessories, for example the donor decoration set is virtually a sentence that the individual no longer has to combine himself. This semiotic, by the nature of its substance of expression, seems to have no double articulation. Instead it is built up on minimal units of meaning (comparable to phonemes). Writing of the film as language Mruklik (1970: 443) demonstrates that a lack of distinctive articulation is compatible with the existence of *langue*. A single articulation may prove to be a characteristic of iconic visual semiotics.

The body can be regarded as providing three main paradigmatic slots corresponding to the main items of decoration: feather headdress, wig and apron. Within the headdress slot, commutation tests will reveal up to about four subsidiary slots, as for example in the donor's feather headdress which consists of about four syntagmatic units (Fig. 2). If the *kói wal* feather plaque is replaced by larger and more numerous red bird of paradise plumes, the outfit still signifies that the wearer is a donor with respect to the other participants in the *moka*. But relative to the other donors, the lack of a *kói wal* may indicate that this man is poor, because of the high value attached to the *kói wal* King of Saxony plumes. This meaning therefore depends on the place of the *kói wal* in the exchange system. As Barthes says, meaning is given by signification and relative position. No one single unit of the donor's outfit designates him as a donor. It needs them all in a certain configuration. The sign *kói wal* is a relationship in itself between signifier and signified, but it also has a value in the system. It can be exchanged for the idea of "donor" or "high status," but it can also be compared with red plumes or Sicklebill tails. As suggested, value as relative position within the syntagm may not be that important in determining meaning, but value generated on both the syntagmatic and associative (paradigmatic) planes (Barthes, 1967: 55, 58) is vital. *"Køi wal"* (denoting donor) derives its value from its co-existence with, say, Princess Stephanie feathers (denoting recipient) as

Syntagmatic plane ⎯⎯⎯⎯⎯⎯⎯⎯⎯⎯⎯⎯→

Denotation	Feathers	Wig	Apron	Connotation
Donor	Saxony Red *Køi wal* Blue	Enga	Netted	Dark (good)
Donor	Red *Køi wal* Blue	Enga	Netted	Dark
Donor	Saxony Red Red Blue	Enga	Netted	Dark
Donor's helper	Red Eagle Cockatoo	Hagen	Netted	Dark
Recipient	Princess Stephanie, Sicklebill	Enga	Netted	Bright-red
Donor's wife	Sicklebill Red Eagle Parrot	—	Netted	Bright-red
Warrior	Red Cassowary etc	Hagen	Netted	Dark (bad)
Donor (pig *moka*)	Saxony Red Red Blue	White cover	Pig-tail	Bright-white
Female Spirit cult	White eagle	White cover	Netted	Bright-white
Male Spirit cult	Saxony Red *Køi wal* Blue	White cover	Netted	Dark (good)
Male Spirit cult-woman	Ribbon-tail Red Eagle	Hagen	Cordy-line	Bright-red

(*Paradigmatic plane* is labelled vertically along the left axis.)

Figure 2. Examples of Self-decoration

worn by other participants. Using Hjelmslev's stratified approach (Barthes, 1967: 40, 56) it is seen that the signification of *kói wal* and Stephanie plumes partakes of the substance of the content, while value partakes of the form of the content, for example, recipient cannot exist without the complement of donor. Therefore the meaning of *kói wal* in its configuration comes not only from its reciprocal situation vis-a-vis the other signs worn by donors, but also vis-a-vis the other signs worn by all the other participants, and even vis-a-vis all the signs that could have been worn but were not.

The problem has been raised of how a paradigmatic series can be established when the signifiers are analoga. Figure 2 shows that, while self-decoration may have a degree of analogy and a certain presentational character, the discontinuous nature of the signs and their discursive deployment along the body enables sets of paradigmatic terms to be distinguished. This process of grouping the minimal significant units into paradigmatic classes is essentially one of classification. Barthes (1967: 73) foresaw a problem here in maintaining Saussure's stress on the *langue* as nothing but a system of differences. For languages with a very restricted speech, Barthes (1967: 33) postulates a third presignifying element, a matter of substance providing the support of signification. The Hagen semiological sign has a substance of expression consisting of the material objects used in the self-decoration, such as feathers, furs, hair, grease, paint. When the essence of such elements of the substance of expression is not to signify but to have a utilitarian function, Barthes talks about sign-functions. The sign-function is supposed to be important as the unit where the relations of the technical and the significant are woven together. However, the substance of expression in the Hagen system is solely for signifying; the elements have no utilitarian, presignifying function. Since the sole purpose of the elements is to signify, and the system is not relayed by the intermediary of language, each element is immediately significant and cannot be decomposed into an inert and semantic element. For example, the Enga wig *(Enga peng),* the short "judge's wig" *(peng kukinga)* and the long "judge's wig" *(peng koem)* are all immediately significant as items of the self-decoration semiotic. It is only when we deal with the metalanguage which Hageners impose on their self-decoration, that a third, pre-signifying substance, *peng* (wig) seems to exist. The substance, wig, cannot exist without being one of the significant types, nor are there gradations between the types. The same applies to the striped, netted apron *(mbal omb)* and the pigs' tail apron *(kng oi mbal). Mbal* cannot exist as an inert support without at the same time being one of the significant varieties of apron. True, some of the substances are also valuables in the exchange system, but this is part of their signifying function. Barthes falls into this confusion because of his belief that objects can only form systems in so far as they pass through the relay of language, thereby mistaking the metalanguage as the primary system. Accordingly, he held that in semiological systems, the paradigmatic oppositions can only apply to the differential, qualifying element and not to the positive support. He proposed (1967: 75 ff.) a classification of paradigmatic oppositions based on a typology of the relations between the similar element and the dissimilar element of the opposition.

I suspect that the difficulty arises from a confusion of the signifier as external object, as the mental image of that object, and as the verbalisation of that image in a metalanguage. Saussure's observations on the purely differential nature of *langue* apply explicitly to the mental image only. As external objects there can be no non-significant feather or wig; they can only exist as the immediately significant Saxony feather or Sicklebill feather, and Enga wig or Hagen wig. But as mental images, we can classify and group them into paradigmatic series. The abstract conceptual categories of the paradigmatic series only receive a metalanguage verbal label after the selection and categorizing of the object system.

The Combinative Constraints

Even considering only the main paradigmatic slots with their possible fillings, the total number of combinations would run into the hundreds. However, the strong combinative constraints of this system reduce the number of permissible sentences drastically. The limited length of the body sentence itself is a strong limiting factor. Bilateral symmetry is one combinative constraint. Other constraints can be grouped into colour matching preferences, rules of arrangement, and type selection, which restricts specific colour to specific types or items of decoration.

These combinative constraints are fixed by the *langue*. Based on the same *langue*, Hagen self-decoration can be divided into a male and female speech. On certain occasions women and girls may wear male speech but they parade as women wearing male speech, not disguised as men. Similarly, young adolescent boys may wear female speech in the form of bright face paint.

Denotation and Connotation

It is essential to distinguish denotation from connotation. Most agree that denotation is necessary to the existence of the sign, and connotation is an optional, selective extra. But in visual art, which is continuous, there is a certain unsteadiness of denotation. In this case, the secondary connotation to attributes and qualities becomes more important. If self-decoration transmits meanings which are not duplicated in verbal language, we have to be careful when describing the signifieds in our metalanguage. In linguistics, denotata can be obtained through an informant asked to give statements of fact. Connotata require that the investigator be exposed to social context, and are difficult to handle. In semiology, especially with an isologic system such as Hagen self-decoration, even the denotata require that the investigator be exposed to the social ethos.

The distinction could be based on the fact that whereas denotation is situationally determined by the context, connotation is not. Connotation finds its reference in the total cultural ideology of each society. The different systems which go to make up a society are all "denotators" tied to particular contexts, but as "connotators" they adapt to and refer to the total cultural reality. As Barthes says (1967: 91), the signified of connotation is at once general, global and diffuse, a fragment of ideology.

Hjelmslev's strict division into superimposed layers of denotation and connotation is difficult to maintain for Hagen self-decoration. I find it more useful to conceive of whole paradigms of connotations which are hierarchized into several levels (Levy, 1970: 555). The denotative meaning of a sign or group of signs governs a wide paradigm of connotative meanings. Through the influence of context, one of these connoted meanings may take on the denotative function, that is, the function of a definitional instruction for a more limited paradigm of connotative meanings. Denotative meaning can take up different connotations with different "readers," but the more the connotation is tied to context, the more conformity there will be in meaning.

Within the context of the *moka* there are levels of signifieds. At the first level are such concepts as big man, donor, recipient, helper, person planning a future *moka*, and so on. At a second, more complex but still situationally defined level, self-decoration can express subtle distinctions of political relations and competition between groups and individuals. These denotations will define and support a wide range of connotations which have been grouped under brightness or darkness in Figure 2. They include concepts of attractiveness, fertility, aggressiveness, solidarity, arranged in hierarchial paradigms along with the qualities of colour, freshness, goodness, coolness and their opposites (Fig. 3). Now in another situation where self-decoration is worn, such as the Female Spirit Cult, one of these connoted meanings — in this case male fertility — takes on the denotative function and governs a diminished paradigm of connotative meanings. In major warfare decorations, male aggressiveness becomes the governing denotative meaning, and so on for each context in which decorations are worn.

Hagen culture is considered here as a set of symbolic systems in the front ranks of which are language, marriage rules, kinship, economic relationships, art, and religion. As denotators these systems aim at expressing certain aspects of physical and social reality. Also as denotators, the systems of a society all lead towards the existential paradoxes of trying to know the unknowable, to control the uncontrollable and to communicate with the incommunicable (J. Pouwer, pers. comm. 1972).[1] The Hageners' Female Spirit Cult leads to the paradox of stressing male fertility, which in fact cannot exist without female fertility. The major warfare self-decoration system stresses male aggressiveness and impending death, which is the greatest paradox of all. In the attempt to overcome these paradoxes, society typically moves from denotation to connotation. Men participating in the Female Spirit Cult are asserting that their own male fertility is sufficient to perpetuate the clan. But the Spirit that the men are worshipping has connotations of both male and female. She is like a woman in that she is female and links groups together by marriage. Yet although she comes to men as a bride, she is closed, virginal, non-menstrual and does not bear children. She is associated with white, which has connotations of male fertility, and she protects men against the menstrual threat of their true wives. By seeing her as female, the men are covertly admitting the importance of their wives as bearers of fertility. By combining all these connotations at a higher level, Hagen men attempt to overcome the supposed contradiction between the life-giving and death-giving powers which their wives possess (Strathern, 1970: 583).

In the process of relating his paradoxes to an overall universe of connotation, man in his religion attempts to transcend the paradoxes and make his world ultimately meaningful. It is in the nature of connotations to be ambiguous and ambivalent. System will only emerge from this amorphous, ambivalent universe of meanings whenever connotation is called upon to help man surpass his limitations. However, there is always an inadequacy between denotations and connotations which results from the existence of a superabundance of denotations in comparison with the connotation on which it can rest (Levi-Strauss, 1950). The paradoxes can never be overcome permanently. At best, they can be mediated for a time, then new paradoxes and the old ones are produced again. Man's continuing attempt to overcome the inadequacy between denotation and connotation gives rise to a dynamic, changing system.

Self-decoration for the *moka* exchange has been shown to have the widest and deepest range of connotational paradigms. Other evidence (e.g. Strathern, 1972) indicates that the *moka* is a central value for Hagen society. In Mauss's terms it is a total social fact with social, religious, economic, magical, utilitarian, sentimental, legal and moral significance for the individual Hagener. With its range of connotational paradigms, the *moka* provides the main arena where Hageners strive to overcome their existential paradoxes, to communicate with the Sky Spirits and to contact the source of knowledge and life. Religious cults and other systems of signs also govern connotations linking with the major concepts informing Hagen society (level VI of Fig. 3), but as the central value, the *moka* is paramount. New religious cults have often diffused rapidly through the Hagen area displacing older cults, but if their arrangements conflict with the moka they will be rejected or discarded.

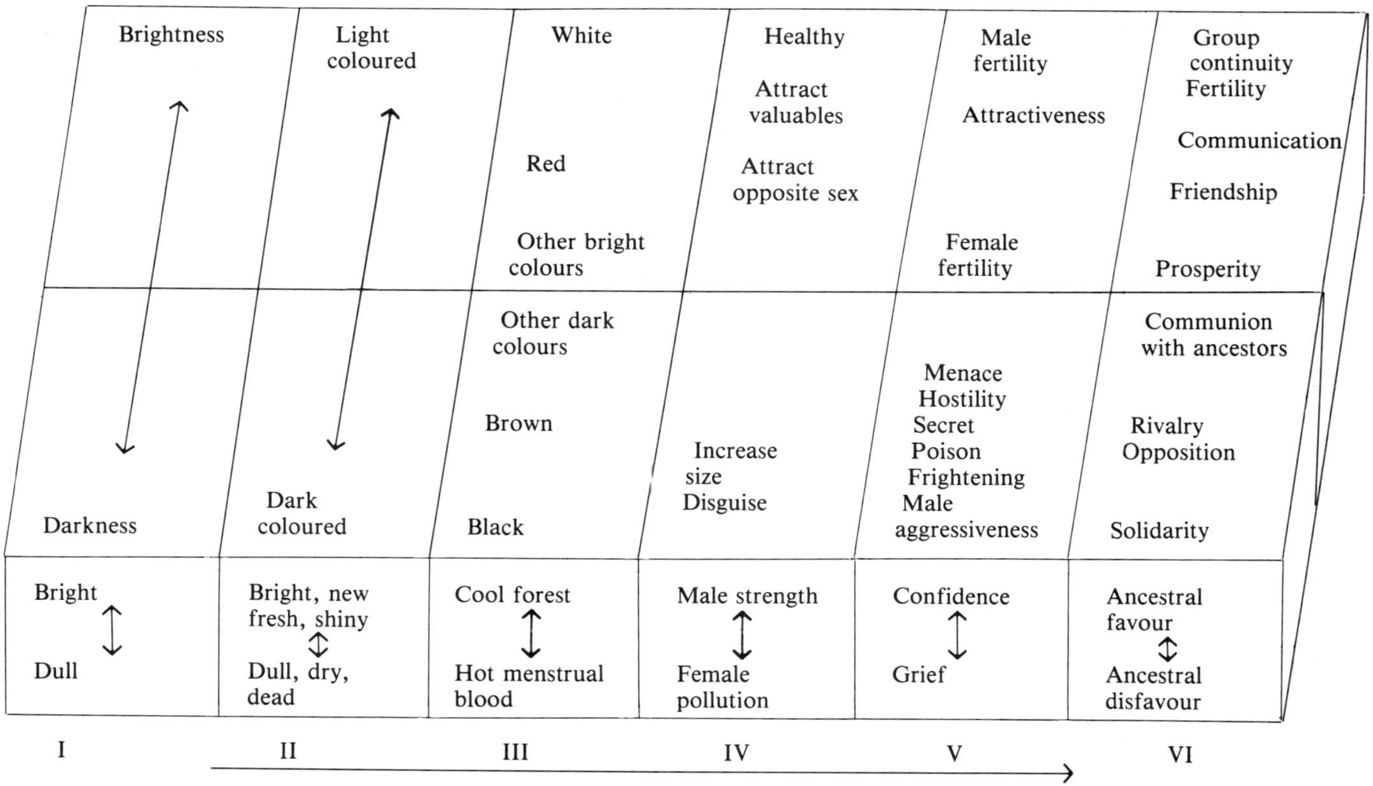

I	II	III	IV	V	VI
Brightness	Light coloured	White	Healthy	Male fertility	Group continuity Fertility
			Attract valuables	Attractiveness	Communication
		Red	Attract opposite sex		Friendship
		Other bright colours		Female fertility	Prosperity
Darkness	Dark coloured	Other dark colours	Increase size	Menace Hostility Secret Poison Frightening Male aggressiveness	Communion with ancestors
		Brown	Disguise		Rivalry Opposition
		Black			Solidarity
Bright ↔ Dull	Bright, new fresh, shiny ↔ Dull, dry, dead	Cool forest ↔ Hot menstrual blood	Male strength ↔ Female pollution	Confidence ↔ Grief	Ancestral favour ↔ Ancestral disfavour

Figure 3. Tentative Schema of Connotational Paradigms.

Articulations between Semiotics

Having defined self-decoration as a system in its own right, the nature of its connections with the other systems of signs constituting Hagen culture must now be considered.

Levi-Strauss has demonstrated that the articulations between systems will not necessarily all be of the same kind. We can conceive of relations of reflection, homology, correlation, discrepancy, contradiction, mutual independence, dialectical interaction, inter-dependence, or projective representation between the systems of a culture. One common denominator of these systems, according to the semiological approach, is that they are all systems of communication, even though on very different scales. Semiology posits that the material out of which language is built is of the same type as the material out of which the whole culture is built; logical relations, oppositions, correlations and the like. However, these semiotics are expressing different things in different ways. Hagen self-decoration is expressing meanings that are different from most other systems of Hagen society; it is not just a reflection of society. Furthermore, the self-decoration signifieds contain elements that are not expressable in the linguistic semiotic, although there is some overlap of self-decoration signifieds and linguistic signifieds. In the special case of the relation between the body semiotic and the self-decoration semiotic, it was suggested that the signifieds of self-decoration encompass the signifieds of the body in the same way that an elaborated linguistic code is related to a restricted code. Relations with the bird system were of a different type. Many of the signs in the self-decoration semiotic appeared to be motivated because of their overlap (both as signifiers and signifieds) from the bird system. Alternatively, the same object can give rise to a mental image that links with different signified concepts in different systems and final meaning is given by articulation and value within each system.

Some degree of translation between these different semiotics is possible but there will usually remain some inadequacy. Assuming that culture is somewhere between a juxtaposition of irreducible systems and an homology of equivalent systems (Levi-Strauss, 1963:84), the analysis of the different features of social life must proceed to a deep enough level to be able to cross from one to another. At this level we are approaching Levi-Strauss's order of orders, by which he means the formal properties of the whole made up of sub-wholes (1963:333). By setting content aside, the different orders of structure can be related to each other as transformations of an ideal homologous relationship. For Levi-Strauss, the unconscious nature of the language means that it is not the contents which are unconscious but the forms — that is, the symbolical function. Therefore the unconscious structure underlying each system of symbols and providing a common basis for comparison and connection is to be looked for at the level of the form of content in the self-decoration system. This is the formal organisation of the signifieds among themselves (Barthes, 1967:40). Behind the readily evident compositional features there are structural principles linking this system with the broader intellectual order of Hagen society.

Hjelmslev's stratification of the semiological sign now enables the conflicting views of Barthes and Douglas to be reconciled. Douglas is referring to an overlap in the substance of content in primitive society and a lack of overlap in modern complex society. Barthes's comment explicitly relates to the form of content, which — in an unconscious manner — provides a common structure for all the symbolic systems of a society, by passing through various transformations. This would be true for both traditional New Guinea and modern Western society.

Applying this insight to the articulation of Hagen systems of symbols, a diagrammatic cross-section through Figure 1 can be produced (Fig. 4). In relation to self-decoration some systems — such as the bird system — will show overlap in the substance of content, while others — for example the kinship system — appear to be independent at the level of substance but can be related, through transformation, at the level of the form of content. Because of the integrating function of self-decoration, nearly all systems of Hagen society have some overlap with

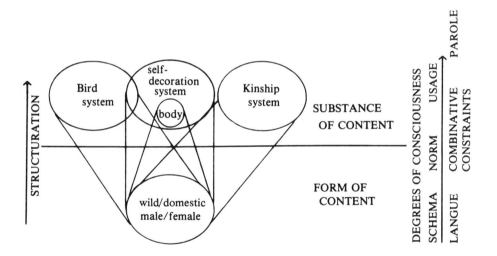

Figure 4. (Section through Figure 1)

self-decoration at the substance level. The nature of this overlap, whether dialectical, complementary, or the like, needs to be determined for each case.

Pure form cannot be discussed without immediately giving it some content (i.e., substance), but in their work on Hagen spell symbolism, the Stratherns (1968) have been able to outline a formal structure of Hagen society depending on a general categorization of the world into wild/domestic and male/female. By a hierarchy of transformations, these basic oppositions structure the form of content in all Hagen systems of signs. This process of structuration in each system is paralleled by an increase in the degree of consciousness of the working of that system. At the deepest level the *langue* of a system is unconscious, but this *langue* gives rise to a set of combinative constraints which can become conscious to varying degrees in different participants. Thus, Hageners can quote the combinative constraints when making judgments on the appropriateness of particular self-decoration outfits.

The Semiotic as Art

In structuralism, the transition from the conscious to the unconscious is associated with a progression from the specific to the general. Perhaps Hagen self-decoration, in its conscious specific denotations, is acting merely to express the orders of other cultural systems such as religious cults or the exchange system. But art not only expresses meaning, it produces meaning by creating new combinations. As well as serving as a medium to communicate ideas, art actually reveals what cannot be translated adequately into terms different from its own. Therefore in its connotations, which largely work at the unconscious level, Hagen self-decoration serves to "relate and unite disparate things in terms of their place in the ritual and cosmological order" (Forge, 1970:290). Deriving its connotational signifieds from all the other systems of Hagen culture and subjecting them to a new generalised synthesis, self-decoration seems to provide a similar type of integration to that which Forge found for painting among the Abelam. It follows that instead of being an ornament, an accessory or a social superstrucutre, Hagen self-decoration fulfils a fundamental function in this society.

Notes

[1]This chapter was written at Victoria University in Wellington, New Zealand. For his teaching there, and for much of the unreferenced theoretical capital in this chapter, I am deeply indebted to Professor Jan Pouwer. However, I alone am responsible for the interpretations presented here.

References

Ardener, E. 1971. "Introductory Essay." In *Social Anthropology and Language,* edited by E. Ardener. ASA Monograph 10. London: Tavistock, pp. ix-cii.

Barthes, R. 1967. *Elementes of Semiology.* London: Cape.

Bulmer, R.N.H. 1970. "Which came first, the chicken or the egghead?" In *Exchanges et Communications,* edited by J. Pouillon and P. Maranda. The Hague: Mouton, Vol. II, pp 1069-91.

Charbonnier, G. 1969. *Conversations with Claude Levi-Strauss.* London: Cape.

Douglas, M. 1966. *Purity and Danger.* London: Routledge Kegan Paul.

_____. 1970. *Natural Symbols.* London: Cresset.

Forge, A. 1966. "Art and Environment in the Sepik." *Proceedings of the Royal Anthropological Institute of Great Britain and Ireland for 1965:* 23-32.

_____. 1970. "Learning to See in New Guinea." In *SocializationL the Approach from Social Anthropology,* edited by P. Mayer. ASA Mongraph 8. London: Tavistock, pp. 269-91.

Gell, A.F. 1972. Review of Stratherns (1971). *Man* 7(4): 683-4.

Langer, S.K. 1942. *Philosophy in a New Key.* New York: Mentor.

Levi-Strauss, C. 1950. "Introduction á l'oeuvre de Marcel Mauss." In Marcel Mauss, *Anthropologie et Sociologie.* Paris: Press Universitaires de France.

_____. 1963. *Structural Anthropology.* New York: Basic Books.

Levy, J. 1970. "Generative Poetics." In *Sign, Language, Culture,* edited by A. J. Greimas, R. Jakobson et al. The Hague: Mouton.

Mruklick, B. 1970. "The Film as Language." In *Sign, Language, Culture,* edited by A. J. Greimas, R. Jakobson et al. The Hague: Mouton.

Strathern, A. 1970. "The Female and Male Spirit Cults in Mount Hagen." *Man* 5(4): 571-85.

_____. 1972. *The Rope of "Moka."* Cambridge Studies in Social Anthropology 4. Cambridge University Press.

Stratherns, A. & M. 1968. "Marsupials and Magic; A Study of Spell Symbolism among the Mbowamb." In *Dialectic in Practical Religion,* edited by E.R. Leach. Cambridge Papers in Social Anthropology 5. London: Cambridge University Press, pp. 179-202.

_____. 1971. *Self-decoration in Mount Hagen.* London: Duckworth.

Turner, V. 1967. *The Forest of Symbols.* Ithaca: Cornell University Press.

13
Myths, Infrastructures and History in Levi-Strauss[*]

Maurice Godelier

I. Levi-Strauss and the "Primacy of Infrastructures"

Is Levi-Strauss a Disciple of Marx?

In *The Savage Mind,* Claude Levi-Strauss assumes as a general hypothesis and accepts as "law of order" ... "the undeniable primacy of infrastructures."[1] For him, it is "as fastidious as it is useless to work out arguments to prove that all society is a part of history and in the process of change. The evidence is overwhelming."[2] History is not only a "cold" history at the heart of which "societies which produce extremely little disorder ... have a tendency to maintain themselves indefinitely in their original state." It is also made of those "chains of non-recurrent events whose effects accumulate to produce violent economic and social upheavals."[3] It is Levi-Strauss himself who warns us not to misunderstand the meaning of his work on myths and primitive thought, which he presents as a contribution to the "theory of superstructures scarcely sketched by Marx."[4] His intentions should be continuously mentioned

[*] The translation of excerpts from "The Savage Mind" has been at times made directly from the French. The editor of this volume has made sure that the translation of this essay is as close as possible to the original and has given a secondary priority to the stylistic form. The translation of this paper has been edited by Ino Rossi.

because some authors invoke Levi-Strauss to develop a more "mentalistic" and "idealistic" theory of symbolic representations and practices; Levi-Strauss himself challenges them.[5]

> It is of course only for purposes of exposition and because they form the subject of this book that I am apparently giving a sort of priority to ideology and superstructures. I do not at all mean to suggest that ideological transformations give rise to social ones. Only the reverse is in fact true. Men's conception of the relations between nature and culture is a function of modifications of their own social relations. But, since my aim here is to outline a theory of superstructures, reasons of method require that they should be singled out for attention and that major phenomena which have no place in this program should seem to be left in brackets or given second place."[6]

These propositions are clear. Everybody can verify that Levi-Strauss has never included in "his current program" the *systematic* study of these "major" social phenomena, the infrastructures of societies, whose thought and myths were being studied and he has not, therefore, really explored these "laws of order" which constitute the necessary linkage between ideological transformations and socio-economic transformations. But he has explicitly recognized the decisive importance of such research which he has left to others to carry out. There should be no question of reproaching him, as many do for having chosen his part in the intellectual division of labor. Just concentrating on myths and thought is an immense job in itself. Levi-Strauss has not only discerned and categorized with utmost detail all the elements of the ecological, economic and social realities which are present* in the myths of the American Indians, but especially he has demonstrated the presence and functioning, in the course of this mode of social thought, of a rigorous logic of the imaginary which orders and interprets the prime matter of these manifold concrete representations through the constraining role of the symbolic principles of metaphor and metonomy. These are unconscious continuities which cannot operate but unconsciously and which manifest through their recurring effects something like a "structure of the human mind," something like a complex of properties immanent to the thinking matter, and form among them the necessity of a signifying order. This leaves a great deal to be desired, and one should question the positive or negative effects on the works of Levi-Strauss of the absence of any systematic analysis of the infrastructures left outside of his program of study for reasons of convenience, because these are "major" phenomena which are referred to every time one has to analyze the myths of any society. The most important consequence seems to us that he is incapable of revealing, or exploring more deeply, the internal

---

* Rather than "present," I should say "represented" in their thought, which is made by them, the thought of men living in determined material and social relationships. (Author's footnote.)

relationships of "causality" which, in the footsteps of Marx, he supposes to exist between *forms and contents* of the ideological representations and the *forms and contents* of the infrastructures that these "represent." He seems to reveal more the relationships of *"expression"* than the relationships of "structural causality" between the two orders of social phenomena.

To make the point clear, we must spend some time on the text of *The Savage Mind,* where Levi-Strauss explains what he understands by "the primacy of infrastructures." He explains this concept when he analyzes the mythical representations of the Murngins, a people living in the land of Arnhem in Australia. These people had already furnished him the opportunity in *The Elementary Structures of Kinship*[7] to prove the existence of systems and to unravel the internal mechanism of their functioning.

In What Does "The Primacy of Infrastructures" Consist?

Levi-Strauss first makes an inventory of the contrasts and oppositions which exist in the local ecological environment between a dry season and rainy season, and on the level of economic and social organization, and between men and women, old and young, initiated and uninitiated, etc. He then shows that all these data confront fourteen Murngins with "contradictory situations," which are precisely "in what the primacy of infrastructures consists." These are the data elaborated by the thought of the Murngins, and one perceives that

> The mythical system and the mode of representation it employs serves to establish homologies between natural and social conditions or, more accurately, it makes it possible to equate significant contrasts found on different planes: the geographical, meterological, zoological, botanical, technical, economic, social, ritual, religious and philosophical.[8]

But Levi-Strauss also shows that the "canon of the Murngin logic" which establishes these equivalences hides a contradiction.[9] In fact the men who in this society personify all that is powerful, pure and sacred—and therefore good—find themselves associated with myths in the bad season, which in the territory of Arnhem is the wet season. At this time of the year, water covers a large part of the land. The bands have to break up into small groups, which find refuge on the dry areas of land.

This season of the year is consequently one of social isolation, dangers and risks of famine. In the dry season, a luxurious vegetation springs up, the game reappears, abundance reigns, collective life and rituals recommence. This season is associated with women, in virtue of their natural fecundity, because of their vital power—although on all other planes (economic, political, ritual, cosmic) women are considered inferior to men and thus ought to be associated with the bad season. But this season connotes sterility and death, and this would deny women their fertility. Men consequently are incapable of "being the rulers and, *at the same time,* personifying the happy side of life" that is the dry season. Levi-Strauss states that they must "choose the meaning" to give to this contradiction. They do this by establishing the principle that in the society of men, the superior society, "the non-initiated are to the initiated in the same relationship as women are to men in the general society."[10] Consequently, the class of the masculine age of the initiated is a "snake element"[11] and is associated with the Great Python which is simultaneously the master of the rains and the one responsible for the dry season and also the civilizing principle and therefore master of all which is pure, sacred, powerful. Consequently, the mythical thought of the Murngins succeeded in unifying "the heterogeneous semantic fields" by building around the contradiction, which has to be thought, a succession of equivalences referred metaphorically to the serpent: "the wet season literally swallowed the dry season just as men possess women and as the initiated dominate the non-initiated, as famine destroys abundance, etc."[12] But this unification pays the price of other contradictions "which the ritual has the function of overcoming by acting them out."

We can thus agree that the relationships between mythical thought and the infrastructure established by Levi-Strauss are much more relationships of *"expression"* than relationships of *"structural causality."*

These terminologies should not be misinterpreted, for the relationships of expression are not those which exist between a thing and its passive reflection in a mirror. In fact, thought is never passively subjected to the facts of history and nature—rather it always actively *"interprets"* them by building a conceptual system which makes them intelligible. In showing that the thought of the Murngins should "choose the sense" to give the contradictions it deals with, Levi-Strauss has shown, as many others have done, that the "ideologies" are not "just copies" of the social relations but simultaneously their expression and an internal component. Ideologies represent directly or indirectly social relationships in the consciousness, but this is a re-presentation of their social "meaning." That is, of something which thought elaborates and which is, at the same time an internal condition, necessary to the functioning and reproduction of these social relationships.

Later on, we will return to the issue of the role of ideology in the reproduction of societies, but we have already stated that we will not follow certain Marxists who perch ideology on the vertex pyramid of "instances," as the superstructure of superstructures which "mirrors" economic infrastructures. To get back to Levi-Strauss, what he calls the "primacy of infrastructures" reduces to the fact that history serves "primitive thought" as a pretext to free and exercise itself by imposing situations and "structures of contradiction" to think about.

Two Complementary Theses on the Matter and Form of Contradictions

According to Levi-Strauss, history would serve as a pretext for the development of primitve thought because:

> the substance ["matter" in the French original] of contradictions is much *less* important than the *fact* that they exist ... Now, *the form* contradiction takes *varies much less than their empirical content.* The poverty of religious thought can never be overestimated. It accounts for the fact that men have so often had recourse to the same means for solving problems whose concrete elements may be very different but which share the feature of all belonging to—structures of contradiction.[13]

If the matter of contradictions is less important than their existence, and if their forms are less rich than the matter, Levi-Strauss would be largely justified in not having included in his program the systematic study of the content and of the logic of the infrastructures which impose these contradictions. However, if we consider the example of the Murngin themselves which led Levi-Struss to such an affirmation, we realize that it is the matter of contradictions in their society which oriented their thought towards a solution which "would give them a sense." For if the Murngin in their myth treat the uninitiated men "as women," it is because in social and economic practice, the initiated men who are aged adults or even old men control the circulation of women among the sections and consequently the reproduction of social relations of kinship, which function equally as relations of production. By the same token, they also control the rituals which "action" the reproduction of the vegetal and animal species which serve as their means of subsistence, etc. Briefly, they *alone* fully and really embody the *general* interests of the community, and draw from it all kinds of privileges and benefits (including sexual ones). Therefore, in reality, the uninitiated men as well as the women are excluded from all social power and from this prestigious status, the women and the men provisionally. In adopting the principle that the uninitiated men are to the initiated as women in general are to men, mythical thought is then a definite part of the content of the economic and social relationships—content which gives a form analogous to the two relations of dependence which exist *vis a vis* the old men. As a solution given from such a point of departure "legitimizes" in myths the sovereignty and the real privileges of the old men, we can state that the content of the relations of production has imposed not only the direction to look but also, on a much larger scale, the manner of finding an imaginary solution to the difficulties encountered in the working out of a coherent representation of their natural environment and of their social organization.

Does Ideology Interpret and Legitimize Social Reality?

But there is a danger of making believe that mythical ideology legitimizes, after the fact, a dominance already existing in reality. In fact, this dominance would not exist without this ideology because this ideology is not only a "reflection," an elaborate expression, but one of the *internal* components *essential* for this dominance. *This complex relation is not analyzed by Levi-Strauss,* who puts in evidence the "relation of expression" existing between the economic and social structures and mythical thought. It is necessary to go further, and investigate what makes mythical thought a necessary and internal element of the relations of men among themselves and with nature. To say it more concretely, it is necessary to go deep enough to get an explanation of the reasons why the Australian aborigines represent in a phantasmatic form of a big python serpent the causes which control the reproduction of plants and animals, the fertility of women, the cycle of the stars and of the seasons. It is necessary, therefore, to explain the conditions of appearance and the internal machinery of these phantasmatic and anthropomorphic representations of the invisible powers which seem to regulate the visible order of the world. The explanation usually given is that the level of development of the productive forces, thanks to which primitive hunting and gathering societies appropriate for themselves the nature which surrounds them, is weak, despite the immense wealth of empirical knowledge which they produced through a millenary transaction and familiarity with nature. This low development of productive forces would not allow them to represent anthropomorphically the necessary relations between things which are not observable on the level of perception and of the concrete and direct relations with nature. Certainly, this explanation is sought in the content of the infrastructure of these societies, but as it is presented it quickly falls short and at times it takes the form of a paralogism. Instead of analyzing the real effects on the level of the development of productive forces really present within these societies, they are compared to the effects by other productive forces in other places and in other times. As a result, we end up explaining the effects of one level of development as the result of the *absence* of another level of development. This is like saying that a fact is what it is because it is not something else. It is not necessary to interpret this critique as a refusal to compare societies and eras, but as a simple reminder that every comparison is not a "reason" or explanation.

Therefore, to explore the effects introduced by the "tranformations of infrastructures," we should build up a true theory of the processes by which the relations of men among themselves and with nature necessarily assume a phantasmatic character, not only in their form but also in their context.

This theory, which Marx suggested more than a century ago and whose development he desired, does not exist yet. However, without it we cannot hope to make any serious progress in the explanation of the disappearance in history of the ancient classless societies, and the appearance of many forms of societies with ranks, castes and classes. Why is this so, and from whence arises this link between problems and domains so diverse?

We must start with the fact that, in their depths, these phantasmatic representations of the powers that rule the invisible order of nature at the same time function to represent the society itself. By the same logic, mythical thought anthropomorphises nature in endowing it with human attributes (consciousness, will, intentions) and, at the same time, necessarily endows man with a power and effectiveness comparable (and for this reason illusory in our eyes) to these natural phenomena. We call this power and effectiveness "supernatural" when for "primitive thought" it is part of the nature of men and testifies to the imaginary continuity, to the organic unity which links society to the cosmos, culture to nature. For mythical thought, the *social,* the human, do not appear as separate, distinct from nature and still less as being opposed to nature. On the contrary, mythical thought makes "society" appear as a part of nature, it naturalizes the human and the social from the very fact that it humanizes and socializes natural phenomena.[14]

But the analysis cannot rest on these conclusions, arrived at long ago, since the processes are not reducible to the production of mythical "representations" but generate at the same time "social matter," that is, relationships *among* men. If we admit the hypothesis that the phantasmatic representations of nature (and therefore of society) are linked to a certain content, to a certain level of productive forces (and we understand by this material as well as intellectual forces), we must go further and show through what mechanisms this content generates not only the social representations but also social relationships, not only forms of thought but also forms of action and organization, that is, social institutions. For it is of crucial *social* importance for men to make themselves understood and perhaps even obeyed by exterior imaginary powers, from whom the *reproduction* of the order of nature and society depends. It is no longer a question here only of abstract representations and of an effort of intelligibility and coherence, but of concrete practices — those of prayer, sacrifice, magic, initiation — which permit communication with this invisible world and act on the will of these imaginary powers which inhabit it. Throughout the stages of mythical thought and its conscious or unconscious elaborations, we find "engendered," "instituted," a specific realm of social relations, a realm of imaginary powers and duties, illusory in our eyes, which divide among each other or deny to each other individuals and groups. This strategic domain is open to social competition, and is unequally accessible to men and women, young and old, initiated or non-initiated, related by blood or related by marriage, natives or strangers, etc. The forms and reasons of this unequal access must be explained.

To return to the Murngins, we understand that this is the reason why older and initiated men appear as the only ones "pure" enough to communicate with the great serpent Python and other imaginary persons, who hold in their power the alternation of seasons, famine and abundance, etc., and only they appear as guarantors of interests common to all the members of their society. They are the only ones to "represent" their society fully and to personify it. They govern because they "embody" the general interest, and consequently they represent — *more* than any other social category — their society. They are therefore at the *center* and on the *top*. Therefore the other members of the society *owe* them for what they *are* and for what they do. All the more, the sacred magic power demands food, sex and other restraints, that is, *constraints* on the individual. The reverse of a right is always a duty. Every religious, imaginary action on the secret forces who direct the world implies a real and symbolic action of a man on himself to communicate with these forces, to reach them, to make oneself heard and obeyed. The taboos, prohibitions, constraints imposed on the future initiated are not really restrictions but ways of accumulating powers, social power. But they create debts and just as great duties for those who are not (yet) initiated (the younger ones), and for those who will never be initiated (the women).

Here we come to the link which connects this analysis to the problem of birth and to the development of social inequalities, which ought one day to transform the structures of most classless societies. We will return to this theme many times, but from now on we wish to suggest that the monopolization of imaginary powers by certain lineages and certain hands is not on every occasion the effect or the reflection of the monopolization and of the direct control of the material conditions of social life, of the material means of production.

The processes which have enabled certain factions and certain individuals in primitive societies to directly control the land, the work force, the tools and the products of other members of the society had perhaps been started by the monopolization of illusory powers and of the access to the imaginary conditions of reproduction of societies. This monopolization came about without physical coercion and without police violence, lies or mystification. The majority of the members of a society agree to give — more importantly, *to offer without being asked* — their services and a part of their personal property to those beings whose existence and exceptional powers are imagined *to be responsible* for their will being and even their own survival. The reverse of a recognized dependency is an accepted obligation. This offers us for the first time the opportunity to say that neither violence nor calculated lies can explain the *original* and primary forms and the conditions of the appearance of the dominant classes and of the state. To explain the *appearance* — the *social necessity* of these classes — we must reject the idea that in the heart of classless societies, minorities had *wished and were able to directly seize* the *material conditions* of existence of the other members of their societies, and had kept these other members by force or by lies, in subjection. On the contrary, all anthropological knowledge suggests that the state is born and could be born only legitimately. This means that the principle force of the state does not reside in the *force* but in the *structures* of the society it dominates.

This is a fact that Marx and Engels had already recognized, after Hegel, when they pointed out the limits "Of the Role of Violence in History."

The analysis of what Levi-Strauss understands by "the incontestable primacy of infrastructures" has taken us very far, but it already permits us to appreciate the immense difficulty of the research concerning the forms and the role of economy in "primitive" and "peasant" societies and also their great importance. However, we are not finished with this thesis of Levi-Strauss and if we delay on it, it is because we have made progress by starting from it. In fact, we have shown that *more* than one relationship of expression existed between mythical thought and the infrastructure of the hunting and gathering societies whose myths Levi-Strauss analyzes. We resume the last part of our analysis concerned with the effects of that component of the infrastructures which consists in productive forces, that is, the material and intellectual relationships of the members of a society with nature. We have seen that the content, the level of these productive forces, entails two things: on one hand, the dominance of the mythical forms of representation of the powers and invisible relationships which explain the order of nature and of society; and, on the other hand, the necessity of a realm of social relationships, of institutions destined to organize the relations of men with these imaginary powers and, therefore, also their own relations.

Therefore we see that, even reduced to the content and to the limits of the productive forces which compose it, the *matter* of the infrastructures does not serve only as a "pretext" for the "savage" mind to exercise itself by offering the form of its contradictions. It equally determines, through the mediation of the representation of nature and of society, the necessity and social importance of religious institutions, that is, of other social relationships, another form and level of social organization, another part of the first matter of social relationships. But here religious phenomena are not separated from the political ones, since they define one part and some essential forms of the authority of certain members of the society over others.

Now we see appear, alongside the "relationships of expression" which exist between infrastructure and ideology, other relationships which we have called by the vague term "of causality." By this term we do not mean that we can "reduce" the ideology to the infrastructure or "deduce" it mechanically from it, but that its forms, functions and, in the long run, its reproduction depend quite largely on the evolution of the social matter of the infrastructure. It depends just as much on the content of the productive forces as on the nature of the social relationships which bring them into play.

By relationships of "causality," we mean, therefore, the *internal* relationships which are probably more than relationships of functional and structural "compatibility" between what either functionalists or structuralists or Marxists usually understand to be distinct "levels." We assert this because these so-called "levels" designate some articulate aspect of one and the same social process and are related to the unique and complex logic of this articulation or structure or order among the social structures which compose the whole society. This structure or order is the foundation of reciprocal transformations which are possible among social structures. By relationship of "causality," we therefore mean an order of priority, not chronological but of structural linkage, a hierarchical order of functions all of which are simultaneously necessary for a society to exist but which have an unequal importance in the reproduction of this society. Therefore, there does not exist *first* an infrastructure and *then* a superstructure which would more or less "correspond" to it. What we must discover is an order of internal linkages in the matter itself of the social relationships as well as their form, explaining the laws of the processes of production and reproduction, of diverse social *organizations* of distinct (or similar) societies.

One can perhaps indulge in the dangerous pedagogical game of representing in the form of a diagram the order of structural linkages which at first appeared to us in a very abstract manner. The idea that the content of the productive forces determines at the same time the dominance of the mythical representations of nature and society and, through their mediation, a realm of distinct original social relationships, can be graphically expressed as follows:

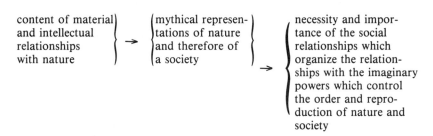

We will recall that productive forces never *exist* alone, but always within a complex of social relationships which put them in use. However, we will also recall that the unity of these two social realities "does not suppress their difference" and therefore the difference of their specific effects. Our diagram is an abstraction which has only the merit of "visualizing" the role of the necessary mediation of the mythical ideology between the infrastructure and religion (which does not necessarily operate here or anywhere else only as a "superstructure").

Mythical ideology "expresses" the limits of the productive forces — that is, something like the negative properties of their content — and at the same time elaborates an imaginary world beyond the experience of men. It also serves as the positive justification of religious institutions and other social relationships, of which it constitutes, in a way, the ideal internal framework. Ideology here is not a "reflection" of these institutions, since it is somehow the condition for their existence and their development and since it is "lodged" inside of them by constituting simultaneously their reason for existence and their internal kernel. Hence, the institution becomes a real body, the social realization of the imaginary, that is, of a recognition which cannot but fail to recognize itself. Ideology is simultaneously the *expression and interpretation* of the productive forces and the *mediation* necessary for the appearance of the social relationships whose *finality* it defines.

Perhaps, in distinguishing between praxis and practices, Levi-Strauss attempted to surmount the narrow, mechanical and false character of the usual empirical and mechanical conception of the relationships between infrastructure and the superstructure and to move towards the formulation of what he called a "dialectic of superstructure." Be it as it may, as soon as a materialist begins to recognize and investigate the fact that the ideology is not a reflection and not just an "interpretation" and "expression" of the social relationships but one of their internal components, as an ensemble of conceptual schemes which define and govern practices and institutions, he immediately runs the risk of being accused of intellectualism and idealism by vulgar materialists (and idealists). Both enjoy believing that the author is no more than, or never was, the materialist he believed and asserted he was. Levi-Strauss perceived this danger, and cleared himself beforehand of the accusation in asserting his materialistic stance.

> Here again we do not wish to say that social life, the relationships between man and nature are a projection, if not indeed a result, of a conceptual game of the mind.

But we must agree that it does not suffice to reassert a materialistic thesis to have produced an explanation which verifies the primacy of the infrastructures, that is, of the social process of production of material life. Levi-Strauss does not produce this explanation because he is caught between two theses, between two materialisms. For he definitely asserts, alternatively, that social practices are not the result of projections and caprices of the mind, and that the practices are "defined and governed" by conceptual schemes which are the necessary mediations to realize social relationships as "structures." Myths are simultaneously fantastic representations of social reality and of nature, as well as their necessary mediation, and finality. It seems that Levi-Strauss had begun to consider these problems when he wrote, a little further on in *The Savage Mind*:

> Without questioning the undoubted primacy of infrastructures, I believe that there always is a *mediator* between praxis and practices,

namely the conceptual scheme by the operation of which matter and form, neither with any independent existence, are realized as structures, that is entities which are both empirical and intelligible. (p. 130, translation revised, ed.)[15]

Or again:

> The conceptual scheme governs and defines practices. . . (These practices) which the ethnologist studies as discrete realities placed in time and space and distinctive in their particular modes of life and forms of civilization, are not to be confused with praxis which constitutes the fundamental totality for the sciences of man. (*Ibid.*)

The problem is, therefore, considered, but with the help of distinctions and a vocabulary which leaves it obscure. The distinction between praxis and practices remains evasive. On the one hand, it seems to correspond to the distinction between infra and superstructures, but on the other hand it is more than this since the praxis is designated as the "fundamental totality," the object of human sciences and, therefore, ought to contain in itself in some way all practices, all kinds of life and all forms of civilization. Levi-Strauss continues to conceive even the distinction between infrastructure and superstructure in the usual, empirical, banal way as a distinction between institutions, between the levels of social organization, and not as the distinction of an hierarchy of social functions which is found in every society, whatever may be "the matter" and "form" of social relationships assumed by the internal functions of religious and political practices. It is this double nature of the mythical representation, its form and its functions, which must be explained simultaneously by the same materialistic explanation, and not by combining the usual reductive materialism — which we take as the thought of Marx — with a Marxist materialism which in these issues is barely beginning to see the light. The question then, can legitimately be asked whether myths "produce" social realities.

Do Myths Produce Social Realities?

Ideology is the expression of an element of the infrastructure and the necessary mediation for the institutionalization of a superstructure of which it becomes the internal finality. Ideology is not, therefore, the superstructure, the "instance" which comes afterwards and registers more or less passively all that happened in the inferior stages. Myths "produce" social reality which is entirely embedded ("nourished") with phantasmatic idealities. But myths themselves depend on the real relationships of man with nature, which according to Marx are "relationships which generate myths." Such would be the first loop of the structural links between economy and society, between an infrastructure, here again cut off from the relationships of production, and of the superstructures, here reduced to religious practice. Levi-Strauss seems to lend himself to an equivocation, as he defends a slightly reductive materialism when he writes about mythical thought: "We only study shadows whose profile appears at the back of the cave, without forgetting that only the attention we give them confers on them a semblance of reality."[16] In fact, the attention given to these shadows by the thought of primitive men has conferred on them more than a resemblance to reality. The reason is that they have become the *internal reason* and *support* of social realities and institutions which were extremely important to the eyes of primitive people and had an immense role in human history, and which are not yet quite ready to disappear.

One can guess, therefore, what would be the contribution of a "programmatic" study of the *content* of infrastructures. Without this study we would never be able to discover the social effects entailed by "the matter of infrastructural contradictions." We will never be able to study history as it is, a largely unconscious progress of production of new social realities. Since the study of these "major phenomena," the infrastructures, did not figure in his program of studies, Levi-Strauss sees in history only a pretext for primitive thought to manifest itself, and by manifesting itself, to manifest "the Architecture of the Mind."[17] He does not have the proofs to show that "the *matter of* contradictions is of less importance than the fact that contradictions exist." But this does not mean that he is wrong when he asserts that the "forms of contradictions are less varied than their empirical content." On this point we will not contradict him, since we know that mythical thought elaborates symbolic "explanations" and that symbolic thought has the property of interpreting many situations with the aid of a same code which serves as a support for many messages embodying opposite contents with the aid of the same signs. Besides, it is on this excess of possible meanings that all reinterpretations reside, including heresies. In a more general way, apparently similar forms of thought or social relationships can "cover" very different contents and really "function" in an opposite manner. This is one of the reasons why we have to go beyond a structural morphology of myths or social relationships, and not separate the analysis of the "form" of these relationships from the analysis of their "functions."

Therefore it is a fact that, due to the properties of symbolic thought and to the properties of the forms of social relationships, there is a relative autonomy of ideologies in relationship to the social structures which they interpret. But it is equally a fact that this autonomy has its limits, whose existence and necessity must be explained. Levi-Strauss should have met this problem from the moment he states that "the mind of savages is not the mind of primitive or archaic humanity, but rather the mind in its untamed stage, as distinct from mind cultivated or domesticated for the purpose of yielding a return."[18] The definition of this other form of thought "domesticated for the purpose of yielding a return" remains, at best, vague and enigmatic, as is the allusion to the fact that it "appeared in certain areas of the world and at certain moments in history."[19] However, in the last pages of *From Honey to Ashes* the same problem returns, this time at a precise time and a precise place, when he makes reference to the upheaval "at the frontiers of Greek thought, where mythology yields in favor of a philosophy which emerges as the preliminary condition for scientific reflection."

History as Primacy of Contingency—History as Catalyzer

We find again the famous theme of the "Greek miracle" where Levi-Strauss only sees "a historical occurrence which means nothing but that it happened at that place and that time; the transition is necessary, not more here than there, and if history keeps its place of priority, it will rightfully be because of its irreducible contingency."[20] Levi-Strauss, however, captioned *The Elementary Structures of Kinship* with this sentence of Tylor: "If there are laws anywhere, they ought to exist everywhere."[21]

It is the way by which Levi-Strauss defines in *The Savage Mind* the "incontestable primacy of the infrastructures" which leads him to reduce an "historic" event to the role of an eternal catalyst which releases the possibilities "lying dormant in the seed" of mythical thought. From the start, the primacy of infrastructures is reduced to offering the savage mind the occasion to exercise itself by delivering the "structures of contradictions," whose matter is less important than the form. Because of this, historical changes, defined as "those chains of non-recurrent events whose effects cumulate to produce economic and social upheavals" and what Levi-Strauss calls "hot history," are for him merely the "initial flick" necessary to draw out of mythical thought the possibilities lying "dormant" within it — that is, "states of thought" already "enmeshed into each other."

Therefore, history offers the occasions which permit some of these states of thought to "disentangle themselves," that is to become part of human experiences, whereas the other states of thought remain in the "latent" state of possibilities. Therefore, these occasions of history are both *necessary,* because the possibilities of thought "could not be realized" without them, and *contingent,* because they are simply nothing in their existence as possibilities and, therefore, in the nature of the principles of thought. We are reaching here a difficult theoretical stage, where we can only measure our uncertainties and recognize that any theoretical position is as good as any other because every hypothesis remains suspended until it is not verified. We are facing at least three problems: the relationship (1) between the possible and the real; (2) between structure and event; (3) between the structure of thought and the structure of historical reality. Apparently, these problems are philosophical in nature. But their essential solution cannot come from philosophy nor exclusively from the efforts of the anthropologists.

II. Beyond Levi-Strauss

The Missing Concept[22]

In the case of the Australian aborigines, we have started to show that the concrete relationships that they entertain with nature leave them only the alternative of mythical thinking for getting a coherent and "totalizing" view of the forces that govern the universe. But we have only scarcely mentioned the nature of their relationships of production. This gives us the opportunity to clarify what we mean by *social relationships of production*. They are the social relationships which determine the use and control of the means of production and of the social product, and the distribution of the social labour among the different productive and nonproductive activities. However, it has been noticed that for the Australian Aborigines, it is the kinship relationships among the groups and individuals that serve as the framework for the use and control of the territory and the natural resources, for the organization of the process of labor based on the division of sexes and generations, as well as for the redistribution of products. These kinship relationships *therefore function as* relations of production and belong both to the "infrastructure" and to the superstructure of society, of which they somehow constitute the general organizational framework, the dominant feature.

Productive forces and social relationships of production never exist separately but rather they exist only as articulated and united in one complex. Although they have distinct effects the productive forces of hunting and gathering societies provide a partial explanation for the division and unequal value attributed to the productive tasks of men (hunting) and women (collecting), of the elders and of the youngsters. But the aged people do not work any longer as they enjoy all of the forms of social power. On the one hand, they control the circulation of women among the kinship groups they *represent,* and control the reproduction of the social relationships of production. On the other hand, they are the only ones to have access to supernatural powers that are supposed to control the conditions of reproduction of nature and society, and it is *as* representatives of their own kinship groups (moieties, sections, subsections) that they *cooperate* in all the rituals and ensure by their symbolic work their own survival and that of all the members of the tribe. The nature of productive forces and the relationships of production explain, therefore, that here social power is both inseparable from religion, and from kinship, and is also a male privilege.

If we take the example of a Greek city, like Athens in the fifth century B.C., we notice that after the reforms of Solon and Clisthene, the political power thereafter existed largely dissociated from the functioning of old kinship groups and from priestly and religious privileges which some "well-born" families continue to preserve. We have previously referred to the little we know of the development of productive forces that could have taken place in Iony and in continental Greece in the seventh and sixth centuries B.C., but we notice that the social relationships which thereafter functioned as relationships of production were political relationships between citizens and non-citizens and between the free men and the slaves. To be a citizen was to be an owner of a part of the land of the city. Reciprocally, only owners were citizens. When real estate was made accessible to the foreigners of the city, it was always as an exception and as a privilege. To be a citizen, in other words to be somebody enjoying *all* the rights related to freedom, meant to be a real estate owner, to have access by right to political and judicial responsibilities, to participate in the cult of the gods of the city and to have the honor to defend it with arms in hand. A specific division of labour was thus determined by this functioning of politics as *relationships of production*. The free people who were foreigners to the community, and to the *politeia* (and, a fortiori, the slaves) were excluded simultaneously from agricultural activities, political responsibilities, ritual activities and from the protection of the assets of the city. To the Mestizos were therefore reserved the activities of handicrafts, commerce and banking. That was a primary feature of the economic, social and intellectual development of a Greek city. But to this first opposition another one should be added, because every free man — whether he was a citizen or a Mestizo — could, according to his wealth, exploit his resources himself or give them over to the slaves, in other words, do the work himself or get the work done by the slaves. That was a second feature of the functioning of a Greek city. Mestizos and slaves — excluded in various degrees from the direction of the affairs of the community, of the *politeia* — were nonetheless essential to the functioning and to the prosperity of Greek *society*.

It seemed, therefore, that something emerged and existed like an economic "system" of the city-states of classical Greece whose original characteristics, whose specific "logic" had to do with the features of the two constitutive parts of their infrastructure. These two parts were, firstly, the fact that the basis of production was a rural economy, more and more open to commercial production and to monetary economics and secondly, above all, the fact that the social relationships that organized and oriented this material basis were, from the inside, political relationships. It was because of the original of these relationships of production that Greek economy was neither "primitive" nor "modern," and that it had the capacity of reproducing itself like a "system," like a whole, but to the very extent that political relationships were reproducing themselves. This is a challenge to modern thinking, which can consider only in an anachronic and ethnocentric manner politics, economics, kinship, religion as distinct institutions (as they "appear" in our industrial capitalist society), and not as distinct functions that could be undertaken by the same institutions and the same social relationshps.

Levi-Strauss holds this habitual ethnocentric view of the relationships between the infrastructure and the superstructure as if it were a relationship among distinct institutions. For this reason, he can do nothing else but unceasingly *state* the primacy of infrastructures without illustrating the *internal mechanisms,* therefore *without really demonstrating* it, without *making* it a *scientific* truth. This is the case because the concept of infrastructure is borrowed from Marx, without borrowing the other concepts developed by Marx to transform the empirical concept bearer of a reductionistic and vulgar materialism (the "economics" of bourgeois economists) into an instrument of scientific analysis of the complex logic of societies and their history. The *word* "infrastructure" was borrowed, but not the concept of productive forces and relations of production.

> By the way, let us recall that for Marx the concept of infrastructure means the combination — specific in each case — of three aspects of reality: (1) the ecological and geographic conditions in which and through which a society extracts the material means of existence; (2) the productive forces that are the material and intellectual means that man invents and sets up as the framework for various processes of work to act on nature and extract from it his means of existence; (3) the relationships of production — that is, according to our definition, the social relationships, whatever they are, that have the triple function of determining the access and social control of productive forces and resources, distributing the social force of labour among various processes of labor and of determining the social distribution of the products of labor.

Let us stop for a moment and examine this brief summary of the concept of infrastructure to draw attention to an important fact that unfortunately has not up to now been the object of in-depth theoretical analysis. Forming part of the infrastructure are all the intellectual representations of the ecosystem (or ecosystems) and the productive forces, the rules governing their making and their use, as well as all the linguistic means that are necessary for their expression and communication. No process of work (even if it is accomplished on an individual basis) can exist without these common representations being communicated in a language and transmitted from generation to generation by a culture. *Thought and language* here function as elements of the productive forces, as "infrastructures."

A Distinction of Functions and Not of Institutions

This observation is fundamental because it enables one to immediately perceive that the distinction between infrastructure and superstructure has nothing to do with a distinction among institutions but points out a distinction of the functions and of the structural causalities that regulate the logic of the functioning and reproduction of societies, of every society. That leads to the methodological consequence that a rigorous Marxist *cannot* and *should not* have any prejudice regarding the nature of social relationships that can perform these functions, nor on the number of functions that could be assumed by what appears to us as kinship relationships, or political relationships, or the like.

Our analysis seems to us to radically transform the various usual ways of formulating what could be called in vague and confused vocabulary the problem of the relationships of "economy" and "society," or what Marxists call the problem of "causality in the last instance" of the mode of production. Empiricist non-materialistic historians and anthropologists (and this is true as much for Evans-Pritchard as for Polanyi) notice that in the society they study kinship or politics or religion plays a major role, and conclude that in all these cases "the economy" only plays a role subordinated to social relationships which are dominant in all societies, and thus in no case and in no way can fulfill the role of "determinant cause in the last instance" that the Marxists dogmatically attribute to it. This is equally the position of Louis Dumont in his analysis of the foundations of the caste system in India, even though his method of analysis is structural in character. But what he analyzes structurally is nothing else but the ideology, the system of religious and political *representations* which governs the conscious relationships among the castes and gives them legitimacy.

For the empiricist anthropologists who defend a certain materialism (like Marvin Harris, who defends cultural ecology or cultural materialism), and even sometimes for Marx, the economy is reduced to ecology plus technology, and the causality of economics (cut off from the relationships of production, which are confused with the forms of organization of labor) boils down to a mechanism of "adaptation" of social relationships to a determined ecological environment and technology.

Althusser and his disciples in anthropology — namely Terray, Meillassoux, and Rey — who develop a new dogmatic Marxism, are confronted with the difficult problem of explaining at the same time the determination in the last instance of the economy *and* the domination, depending upon particular cases, of kinship or politics or religion. They interpret the causality of economy as a process of *selection* by the economy among all the superstructures of society, one of which is thus *put somehow in a dominant position,* called upon to *dominate* the others. Again, this Marxism, which claims to be "rigorous," sees the distinction between infrastructure and superstructures as a distinction among distinct institutions. Despite a new name, it is the old empirical distinctions and the positivist approach that it fights which underlies the "new" theory of "instances."

However, what we have shown by the analysis of the Murngin and Greek examples is altogether a different thing. We have shown that the relationships of kinship on the one hand and the political relationships on the other hand function simultaneously as relationships of production and as superstructure. But in each case it was the *same* social relationships, the same social "institution" that performed these two functions. The distinct functions were thus not supported and expressed in distinct institutions.

But most of all, this analysis has enabled us to unravel the reasons and foundations of domination, in different cases, of kinship or of politics. In each case, it is only to the extent that they function as relations of production that kinship relations or political relations play a dominant role. This radically refutes both the theses of the empiricists and those of the neo-dogmatic Marxists.

For the first group, it is because of the fact that they are pluri-functional that the kinship relationships dominate and they dominate because they are pluri-functional. These circular and tautological statements explain nothing. Social relationships in effect assume many functions, but that *is not sufficient* to make them dominate the logic of the functioning, the mode of development and the systems of collective representations of a society. *They have necessarily to assume the function of relations of production.* Hence it is no longer possible to say, like the neo-dogmatic Marxists, that the infrastructure determines which one of the superstructures shall be dominant, since a superstructure becomes dominant because it assumes *in itself* the function of relation of production and of social matrix of the infrastructure.

These two points are crucial because they demonstrate the *universal* validity of the Marxist thesis regarding the primacy of the infrastructure, while accounting for the dominance according to societies and according to the historical period of a particular "superstructure." As a matter of fact, when kinship functions as relations of production, it is no longer kinship as it exists in our society; it is the same when religion, the temple, and God constitute the dominant social relations — it is no longer religion as it exists within our society. In each case, parenthood, religion, or politics requires a new definition. But in each case *what appears through the domination* of one or another of these structures is the *same hierarchy of functions* as the one that exists in our society, because the structures play a dominant role in these societies exactly because they function at the same time as economic infrastructure.

This is the way we understand, after revising it, the hypothesis of Marx of the "causality" in the last instance of the social modes of production, an hypothesis that Levi-Strauss brings back as well in his own way, at least at an abstract level, when he recognizes the "primacy" of the infrastructures. Far from contradicting or eliminating it, every serious analysis of the foundations of the dominance of one or another superstructure in one or another society, at one or another period, reaffirms this primacy in all cases. For this reason, it appears to us as the most rigorous starting point for any analysis in the human sciences.

Then we can see clearly what is lacking in the analyses of the human sciences, and this is true for political economy as well as for history and anthropology: what is *deficient* in the *work* of researchers in these fields, what prevents the resolution of crucial problems, prevents our making progress. Up to now, in effect, these researches have not enabled us to discover the reasons and conditions that have brought about, throughout history, the changes of place of the function of relations of production in various human societies — and with the changes of place, the metamorphoses of their forms and the transformations of their mode of development. Researchers have not found them because they have never looked for them, because the question has never been raised in these terms.

According to us, it is to provide answers to this type of question that anthropologists, historians, and economists should work henceforth, and among them — above all — those who explicitly are supporters of Marx (and feel more obliged than others). The Marxist perspective is a crucial part of the future of the human sciences, and this future should not be confused with the task of developing an anthropology and an "economic" history of mankind. That was our thought ten years ago when we wrote *L'Objets et méthodes de l'anthropologie économique*, but one can see clearly now in what way and why we have changed our view.

It is thus much easier to appreciate with precision Levi-Strauss's theoretical position when he speaks of the infrastructure and reaffirms its universal primacy. What does he mean, in the final instance, by infrastructure? He defined its character when he wrote in *The Savage Mind* that he leaves it to "History — assisted by demography, technology, historical geography and ethnography — to pursue the study of the infrastructures" (p. 130).

He reserves for himself "ethnology which is first of all a psychology," a formula which for us ambiguously designates both the theory of the invariable structures of the human mind (thought in its untamed state) and the theory of mythical thought (which, to us, is as much "tamed" and historically determined as any other).

And Levi-Strauss gives further precision of his views when he writes the following with regard to the mythological thinking of the Murngins:

> One verifies, in a way, the primacy of the infrastructure: the geography, the climate, their impact on the biology, creates for the indigenous thought a contradictory situation: there are two seasons as there are two sexes, two societies, two degrees of culture (the initiated and the non-initiated). (p. 93-94, our translation)

What he takes into account in the infrastructure are the natural and ecological conditions, and he correctly writes:

> The natural conditions are not passively accepted. Moreover, they do not exist in their own right, because they are functions of the techniques and way of life of the population which defines them and gives them meaning, developing them out in a given direction...to the historical and technical form that such and such activities assume. (p. 93-94, our translation)

We see here Levi-Strauss starting to unravel the *links* or order within the elements themselves which constitute the infrastructure of the Murngins. He shows that the impact of natural conditions is taken as the nature of productive forces. But one must refine his formula because, even if they are not perceived, the natural conditions have their own existence which always acts on society through the objective constraints that they carry alone. What is lacking in the analysis is the area of relations of production and the study of relationships or order between productive forces and relations of production. Besides, Levi-Strauss does not use the term "productive forces" but makes use of usual and trivial empirical distinctions of "techniques" and "ways of life."

In the final instance, while borrowing from Marx the concept of infrastructure, Levi-Strauss fills it with all kinds of domains which are distinct, or at least empirically distinguished by the terms "technology," "demography," "geography," "history," and "ethnography" without analyzing these distinctions, without questioning their validity, without trying to build up their specific articulations. He thus uses for a while the vocabulary of Marx, but he immediately cancels its original content by substituting in its place, spontaneously and probably unconsciously, common empirical definitions that he uses as a *real starting point* for his analysis of the primacy of infrastructures.

Hence, the structural analysis is condemned in its inability to analyze and therefore verify the causality in the final instance of infrastructures, which was presented at the beginning as "the law of order" of social realities, hence as a first epistemological principle needed to build up the knowledge of these realities. And this internal contradiction of the theoretical practice of Levi-Strauss has the consequence of always postponing the analysis of an "order of orders," which is postulated but which will never be reached. This concept comes in fact to take and hide the missing place of causal analysis in the last instance of the modes of production and the lack of real analysis of the primacy of infrastructures.

In conclusion, we shall indicate briefly how a transformation occurs equally with regard to the problem of the relationships of ideas and social realities, the forms of thought and the forms of society, when one advances the hypothesis that a superstructure plays a dominant role in society only if it assumes at the same time the role of relations of production — that is, if it functions as infrastructure.

III. Structural Transparency and Opacity: Relations of Production and Illusory Forms of Conscience and Action

When we say that in some cases religion (or at least what we *call* religion) can function as relations of production, some and not only "orthodox" Marxists could object that we have abandoned the area of science to revert to pre-critical forms of history, sociology, or anthropology criticized by Marx back in 1846 in the *German Ideology,* and are mistaking for reality "the illusions that each society and each period have about itself."

However the opposite is true, as our way of conceiving the distinction between infrastructure and superstructures as a distinction of functions within the *process* of life enables us equally to unveil the basis and machinery of the illusions that each society has of itself. For example, in a society in which kinship functions as relations of production, and where this dominates the overall logic of that society, all the social relationships appear necessarily as many diversified *aspects* of kinship relations among individuals and groups, and as many varied but complementary *effects* of *kinship* relations. Therefore, the relations of production do not appear as conditions and social forms of a process of the *material production,* a process which itself depends upon a certain level of productive forces, but only as aspects and effects of a *process of exchange of women and filiation.* The way in which the relations of production appear causes the partial disappearance of their content. However, to the extent to which these appearances constitute the starting point of the *spontaneous* representations that individuals and groups have of their own relationships and relationships with nature, these individuals and groups are from the very beginning in a *theoretical and imaginary relationship* with themselves and with nature. These illusions are not only illusions about what their relationships are, but also illusions regarding the reasons for the existence of these relationships.

The spontaneous representations cannot go further than the appearances from which they originate, enabling one to see that the appearances do not *allow* to see: namely, that the dominance of kinship relations is itself determined by their function as relations of *material production* and not their function as relations of alliance and filiation. Spontaneously, on the contrary, things appear the inverse of what they are. Therefore, the nature of social relationships of *all* social relations remain *opaque* or, to be more precise, become falsely intelligible, falsely *transparent.* In fact, it is not only the material basis of social life which disappears in the form under which it appears but it is *kinship* itself — as relationships of alliance and filiation — which assumes a content that it does not have.

What is spontaneously "evident" to the individuals and groups of a society where kinship dominates is thus to a great extent "illusory," because these evidences hide the material content of social relationships by transferring it into an imaginary reality and by presenting in reverse the order of links among the different functions of social relationships. But at the same time these evidences have a real basis, because they start from a real fact, the fact that the family dominates the functioning of society, not only in the thinking of individuals but also in their action, behavior and life.

If we consider the example of Athens, another form of spontaneous illusion of the social conscience appears, related this time to the fact that there political relationships functioned as relations of production, and therefore dominated the thinking and action of the Greeks. This was true of the citizens who were full members of the city, because the free men who were foreigners to the city, i.e., the aliens, were automatically excluded from access to land and to political responsibilities. The slaves — upon whom rested more and more the material and social existence of free men, either citizens or aliens — were not only excluded like aliens from the *politeia* but were also rejected from society, the human community, and classified with the working animals and other instruments of work, with nature domesticated by man.

Contradictions that opposed them to each other — especially the rich to the poor and the aristocrats to the democrats — could appear directly at the political level and dominate the conscience and action of Greek citizens. On the other hand, contradictions between free men and slaves could not directly appear at the political level, as slaves were unable to lead directly political struggles to put an end to their slavery and exploitation. The social relations of production between free men and slaves were thus concealed even in the political context, although they were present there since the beginning, and governed in the long run its outcome. For the contradiction between citizens and slaves did determine the very mode of development of productive forces, among which one — servile work — became little by little the essential productive force. But these *fundamental* contradictions among men, and therefore among their relations of production and the productive forces that these relationships *allowed* to develop, could not be recognized as such and appear as the *main* contradiction of that social system. On the contrary, for the Greeks the main social contradictions could be only the political contradictions which divided and opposed free men and above all the citizens of the city-states. One can see, therefore, why the fundamental contradictions of their mode of production could be resolved neither by the masters, for whom these did not have a priority character, nor by the slaves, who were subjected to them but who had no means to bring them to the political arena and to fight to abolish them to their advantage. However, although located outside the thinking or the reach of masters and slaves, these fundamental contradictions were not going to cease to operate; on the contrary because of their opacity and their indefinable character they influenced more inevitably the evolution of Greek society.

Little by little, the society was falling back upon itself, going into stagnation and offering less and less resistance to the effects of its internal antagonisms and to the assaults of neighboring societies which were more dynamic. A few centuries later, Rome was also to experience the same fate.

The analyses of these two examples (Murngin and Greek) show that the illusions that each society and each period has of itself proceed from the same mechanism, have the same root, and are distinguished from each other to the extent to which the relations of production of each society and each period differ. This mechanism is unconscious, which means that it works, *permanently* and *simultaneously* upon *all* the individuals who belong to a society characterized by specific relations of production, and that no individual can become conscious of it at the level of the spontaneous immediate consciousness of social relationships. From this fact, the illusory forms of consciousness entailed in particular relations of production cannot disappear except with the disappearance of these relations.

We can thus conclude by summarizing the theses we have developed in the previous pages.

(1.) To the extent that social relations function as relations of production, they dominate the whole functioning of society.

(2.) When the social relations which function as relations of production function as well as superstructures, in the spontaneous consciousness of the individuals and groups of which society is composed everything looks as if the dominant characteristics of these social relations come from their *explicit* functions, that is from their superstructural functions. Reality thus appears in reverse.

(3.) The order of structural linkages among the various functions of social relations finds itself thus reversed, and therefore the causal relations among the various forms of social practice find themselves metamorphosed and transformed into *imaginary relationships* with the material conditions of the process of social life. These imaginary relationships constitute for the spontaneous social consciousness "evidences" which, although illusory in character, have a real basis because they spring from real fact, that is, from the dominance of a particular social relationship.

(4.) As a result of these inversions and metamorphoses, what disappears is precisely the real relationship of individuals to their material conditions of existence. This relationship becomes thus opaque, forever indefinable at the level of the spontaneous social consciousness. From the start it is deprived of the "evidences" of that consciousness. Therefore, the material conditions of existence and the real relationships which the individuals have with these conditions exist outside the realm of the spontaneous social consciousnesses of individuals, and cannot be the object of a practice of an action that takes them directly as an object. Hence, the influence of these conditions and the real relationships of these conditions to the social life and the evolution of society are as much more constraining as they remain indefinable and opaque to social conscience. It is this permanent constraining, this unintentional intervention on the social evolution of the complex of material realities and of real relationships to these conditions, which is called "determination in the last instance" of infrastructures. This notion belongs to the domain of "structural causality," which means that this intervention is considered as the ultimate content of misintentional necessities of history or "historical necessities."

(5.) But these historical necessities did not realize themselves through the impossibility of men to *conceive* and set up certain forms of *direct* intervention on their real relations of production. Rather, they realize themselves as much through multiple illusory actions undertaken to intervene upon imaginary realities, but which modify nothing of the real data of the problem. The necessities of history do not act only in the negative but also in the positive, not only in the absence of efficient actions but also in the presence of inefficient actions. We shall give three examples: Confronted with a situation of excessive drought that threatened the reproduction of the material conditions of their life, the Indian peasants of the Inca empire responded, among other things, by an intensification of religious sacrifices. They burned a variety of precious and ordinary cloths upon the *huacas* or in the temples to get the help of ancestors and of gods, they sacrificed llamas, they poured beer made of maize upon the altars. Thus, given the nature of their relations of production and the fact that their material conditions of existence appeared in the form of kinship relations (ancestors) and politico-religious relations (the gods, the sun and its sons, the Inca) they tried to reproduce these conditions of existence by spending an enormous amount of symbolic work, which took up a substantial part of the material wealth and time available to the society. But, *by themselves alone*, these actions could not affect the objective situation.

One could mention another example of the "fantasmatic" response of a society to a contradictory situation that threatened its reproduction. In the middle of the nineteenth century, after the systematic destruction by the whites of the herds of bison which were the major resources of the mounted hunting tribes of Northern America, there appeared a cult of the sun that spread little by little to all the tribes of the prairie. They placed in the gods their hopes to see the bison "blacken again the plains," but that was in vain.

Finally, to add a last example, this time from antiquity, Marcel Détienne (1965) has well pointed out in his book *Hesiode: Crise Agraire et Attitude Religieuse en Grèce Au XVIIIème Siècle* that Hesiode explained the agrarian crisis in Greece as the result of a flight of gods to heaven. *The Works and the Days* is not a treatise of agronomy but a religious poem. It is by the observance of a ritual of work that one becomes virtuous and that the gods listen to one. In following this advice, Hesiode was believed to have found the best form of conscious action for the development of society. But the unknown properties of social relationships will always produce their efforts. This is the working of the unintentional in history.

One can, then, misunderstand why Morrison is necessarily opposed to empiricism and positivism in social sciences and constitutes their radical criticism. Different from spontaneous thinking, abstract theoretical thinking can *accept* or *reject* getting involved in the direction indicated by the dominance of particular social relationships, a dominance which is endlessly reiterated by spontaneous ideologies and the immediate evidence of people. However, when it gets involved in that direction, abstract thinking will end up sooner or later taking for solutions what constitutes a problem, or exhaust itself solving problems in a field where there are no solutions. It is condemned to understanding as *facts* replies already formulated and out of the question, which constitute rather many *implications* guiding it in advance and preventing it from seeing other than what appearances show. Yet, in the name of empiricism, abstract thinking believes it is following without prejudice, humbly and step by step, the shapes of facts all along as they are discovered.

In conclusion, one can put forward the general hypothesis that in the course of history, up to one time, each type of production has determined various illusory, but always specific, forms of spontaneous social conscience which consisted in imaginary representations of the social process of production. This process disappeared as a process of *material production* within the confines of these representations, and appeared under another form with a different content, imaginary in character. Spontaneously, all the individuals and groups involved in these various historical forms of the social process of production found themselves living in imaginary relationships with themselves and with the particular nature upon which their social process of production was carried out. In each period, and in forms that were specific in each case, men found themselves unconsciously, spontaneously and necessarily alienated. At this level of our analysis — where the theory of the various forms of the exploitation of men by man and of the relations of classes was not yet developed — this means that they are represented in a different way from what they really were and acted.

Our analysis has nothing that is idealistic, because the illusions which men had of themselves and about nature depended not upon their conscience but upon the character of social relations of production, and could not really disappear except with the disappearance of the social relationships which produced them. It was thus not their consciousness that was mistaken and alienated, but appearances misled and alienated them.

This analysis of relations between the forms of thinking and the content of the relations of production is connected with the Marxist analysis of the "fetishism of the commodity," and develops it in directions which Marx himself had foreseen and suggested. It is known what Marx meant by the expression "fetishism of the commodity," namely the fact that individuals, living in societies within which there exists a marked production, imagine spontaneously that the exchange value of commodities is a property which belongs to them as things and not as a social relation among persons who produce and exchange them. Thus, in the spontaneous consciousness of individuals, the commodities and their value have a "fantastic" character. But in pre-capitalist societies market production often did not exist, or when it existed, played a very different role — at times very important, as in ancient Rome or in China — without ever becoming the dominant form of production, the general way of producing all the material means of social existence.

In pre-capitalist societies, production was above all directed toward the creation of use values within the framework of social relations of production, which would be kinship, political, or religious institutions. Consequently, these institutions seemed to dominate society and gave rise to fantastical representations, each time different, of the relationships between individuals and their material conditions of existence. The illusions proper to the forms of market production had, then, only a secondary importance.

However, with the emergence of the capitalist mode of production — which is the most developed form of market production because the whole material basis of society rests upon the production and exchange of commodities — the illusions brought about by the "fetishism of commodities" have their most complex development. As stated by Marx:

> All forms of society that have market production and circulation of money participate in this hoax. But in the capitalist mode of production and for the capital which is its predominent category, the determining relationship of production, this magical and upside down universe, knew yet other developments (Marx, *Capital III*, t. 3, p. 205).

These new developments spring from a new social reality. Henceforth the labor force, a direct producer itself, has become a commodity, and the only one that workers can sell because they are deprived of the ownership of the means of production and of money. In the spontaneous and fetishist representation of the *agents* involved in the capitalist process of production — be they capitalists or workers — things happen as if the value added in the production process and circulation of commodities, the sur-value, created by the capital itself and not by labor, was a mysterious, autonomous, enigmatical property of capital and not the product of a social relation of production between the class of those who have the monopoly of the ownership of means of production and money and the class of those who have only their labor and are compelled to sell it to capitalists who combine it with the other factors of production to produce social wealth. Wealth is produced within units of production which are no longer organized on the basis of kinship or politico-religious relations, as in the pre-capitalist societies.

There is, then, the following difference between the illusions born of the various types of relations of production which have existed within the various forms of *pre-capitalist* societies on one hand, and the imaginary representations of material conditions of social life and relationships of individuals to these material conditions within the *capitalist* mode of production on the other hand. In the first ones, the relations of production do not exist *separately* from kinship or politico-religious relationships, and the production itself is to a great extent oriented toward the production of use values. The spontaneous illusions which the individuals have of themselves lead to the metamorphosis of their real relationships to their material conditions into *inter-personal* relationships and into imaginary relationships among the real persons (in the case of kinships and political institutions) or among imaginary persons (religion). In the forms of market production — and in the capitalist mode of production, which is the most developed and complex form — the infrastructure exists as a distinct state of institutions to regulate kinship, political and religious relationships. Production is essentially oriented toward the production of exchange commodities whose fate escapes the control of producers. Consequently, the spontaneous illusions which the individuals have of themselves lead to the metamorphosis of their real relations to their material conditions, not into other interpersonal relationships but into relationships among *things*, the products of labor being among them.

To the extent that bourgeois political economy makes of the exchange value of commodities a property of things exchanged, it consolidates and make more complex the spontaneous — that is, non-scientific and false — representations which the individuals involved make of the conditions of production and of the production process itself. While pretending to follow the indications of common experience, political economy prevents itself at the very beginning from being a science, and limits itself to function more often as an ideology in the usual sense of the word, that is, as a set of representations that impress the appearances of social relations in a way that gives them legitimacy. But one must not fall into the simplistic functional explanation and take the consequences to be the reasons, the effects to be the causes. Because of the fact that an ideology legitimizes social relationships while occulting its content, one cannot conclude that it was born to legitimize and occult that content.

According to us, it is from such an attitude that one should understand why Levi-Strauss, on the one hand, has recognized the solid foundation of the Marxist thesis of the primacy of infrastructures and, on the other hand, has found himself unable to draw the implications of that thesis. Here also, the answer must be sought in what for him has remained opaque, undefinable in the thinking of Marx which he has intended to follow.

Notes

[1] C. Levi-Strauss, *La Pensée Sauvage*, Paris, Plon, 1962, p. 173.

[2] *Ibid.*, p. 311.

[3] C. Levi-Strauss, *Entretiens avec Georges Charbonnier*, Paris, Plon, 1961, p. 38.

[4] C. Levi-Strauss, *La Pensée Sauvage*, p. 173.

[5] Let us remember that in the introduction of *Le Cru et le Cuit*, that opens the four books of *Mythologiques*, C. Levi-Strauss has rejected without any ambiguity this idealistic and formalistic use of his own thinking:

> ...the structural thinking (...) defends today the colors of materialism (...). We thus succeed in showing that the structuralism finds on its way an idealism and formalism, it is sufficient that the structuralism finds on its way an idealism and true formalism so that its own inspiration, deterministic and realistic, manifests itself fully. (*Le Cru et le Cuit*. Paris, Plon, 1964, p. 35).

[6] C. Levi-Strauss, *La Pensée Sauvage*, p. 155.

[7] C. Levi-Strauss, *Les Structures Elémentaires de la Parenté*, Paris-La Haye, Mouton, 2e ed. 1967, chap. 12, pp. 144-225.

[8] C. Levi-Strauss, *La Pensée Sauvage*, p. 124.

[9] *Ibid.*, p. 123.

[10] *Ibid.*, p. 123.

[11] *Ibid.*, p. 125.

[12] Lloyd Warner, *A Black Civilization*, New York, 1958, p. 387; cited by C. Levi-Strauss, p. 124.

[13] *La Pensée Sauvage*, p. 127 (underlined by C. Levi-Strauss).

[14] *Cf. infra*, chap. 4.

[15] *La Pensée Sauvage*, p. 126-127 (underlined by Rossi).

[16] See the critique by Claude Levi-Strauss of the unilateral character of the thesis of Auguste Comte on the religion of anthropomorphism of nature:

> The mistake of Comte, and of the majority of his predecessors, was to believe that the men could, with some likelihood, breed the attributes of this nature in which he recognized himself. (*La Pensée Sauvage*, p. 291).

We put together this text that Marx, contemporary of Auguste Comte, had written on the relations between society-mythology and Greek art, and where he states that the mythological representation of nature was at the same time that of society:

All mythology masters, dominates the strengths of nature in the field of imagination and through imagination, and gives them form; it disappears when these forces are really dominated.... Greek art supposes the Greek mythology, in other words the artistic but unconscious elaboration of nature and social patterns themselves by the popular imagination. Here are its materials. This does not mean whichever unconscious artistic elaboration of nature (*this word as understood here means all that is objective, including society*). Never could Egyptian mythology have provided a favorable field to the blooming of Greek art. But anyway one needs *a* mythology. Thus, in no case does society arrive at a stage of development excluding all mythologic connection with nature, *all connections generating myths*, thus calling for an *independent* imagination of mythology. (*Contribution to the Critique of Political Economy*, 185 Social editions, p. 174 stressed by M.G.)

However, let us add that Greek thought was already partly rendered "independent" from mythology by the arrival of philosophy.

[17]*Du Miel aux Cendres*, Paris, Plon, 1965, p. 407.

[18]*La Pensée Sauvage*, p. 289.

[19]*Ibid.*

[20]*Du Miel aux Centres*, pp. 407-408.

[21]Tylor, *Primitive Culture*, Londres. 1871, p. 22. C. Levi-Strauss cites this sentence of Tylor, that he had put into the frontispiece of *The Elementary Structures of Kinship*, again in 1964 in the Overture of *Le Cru et le Cuit* (p. 18), when he affirms "to have obtained the conviction that when the human spirit appears determined up to its myths, then *a fortiori* it must so be everywhere."

[22]Due to the length of this chapter, the author has agreed to omit eight pages where he has discussed Levi-Strauss' notions of event, structures, and the relationships among structures and between thought, society and history.

PART FOUR

CONCLUSION

14
On the "Scientific" Evidence for the Existence of Deep Structures and Their "Objective" and Mathematical Nature

(A Training Session for Rodney Needham, Ronald Cohen, Peter Caws and Paul Chaney)

Ino Rossi

At the end of this journey it is quite obvious that semiotic structuralists and structural Marxists share the fundamental notion that the "scientific" object of analysis consists in deep or meta-empirical structures, although they hold different conceptions of the nature and roots of the deep structures. Both Levi-Strauss and Althusser (and Godelier tries to make a link between the two) attribute a priority to structure over history and hold an antiempiricist conception of structure. For both thinkers structure consists of a set of basic elements which can be combined and recombined in an indefinite number of ways to produce empirical structures. Levi-Strauss defines structure as the "content itself, apprehended in a logical organization conceived as property of the real" (1976:115), and he links this logical organization to the combinatory activity of the human mind. On the contrary, Althusser links structure to an autonomous social process (social formation) which is explained in terms of social interaction and is ultimately based on the mode of production.

265

For Althusser each social formation is reducible to five invariant elements: (1) labour power; (2) the means of production; (3) the non-worker appropriating the surplus labor; (4) property relations of production; and (5) the material appropriation of productive forces. It is the notion of invariant constants which is crucial to both Levi-Strauss and Althusser and which qualifies their approach as meta-empirical. Far from perceiving the importance of the meta-empirical and mathematical thrust of structuralism, many critics have objected to the notion of deep structure as a mentalistic notion not germane to the scope of "empirical" social science. In their view, social scientists should select hard core or "objective" data as objects of analysis and make use of "rigorous" and replicable procedures of data collection and interpretation.

Whereas social scientists have long since accepted the notion that ideology can be a hidden motivating force of social phenomena, many empiricist social scientists hold fast against the notion of a deep logic of ideology and, especially, against Levi-Strauss' notion of universal mental structures as the ultimate foundation of cultural phenomena. We have already seen (in the second chapter of this volume) that this notion has been recently labeled as a useless "mumbo jumbo" (Cohen, 1977) and has been implicitly rejected by the overall thrust of Needham's recent "pronouncement" (1978) — a pronouncement of a highly questionable scientific nature (see Rossi 1978a).

Far from being original critics, Cohen and Needham are imitators of a long list of anthropologists who before them have summarily dismissed structuralism either as a form of mentalism (Harris 1969:480-481, 513) or because it fosters "a cavalier attitude towards the facts of ethnography" (Leach 1961:77), and produces unverifiable explanations (Maybury-Lewis 1969:119). Other authors have argued that the controversy between structuralists and anthropologists of prestructural orientation amounts to a confrontation between two epistemic paradigms (Scholte 1966), or between a Baconian, positivistic and inductivist conception of science, on the one hand, and a Newtonian, deductivist and post-Einsteinian conception of science, on the other hand (Nutini 1970). However, the controversy surrounding structuralism cannot be easily disposed of by simply stating that social scientists are free to choose between the structuralist and the empiricist conception of the scientific method. On the contrary, one must clearly state the theoretical foundations and methodological implications of such a choice.

I have explained elsewhere why Levi-Strauss has firmly rejected the accusation of mentalism (Rossi 1974:69-70) and has shown that his approach is based on a "scientific" definition of the object of analysis, one possessing procedures for prediction, interpretation and verification (*Ibid*:80-100). One task, however, remains: one must show that the structuralist definition of the object of analysis — the notion of "deep structure" — is not a mere by-product of an arbitrary and questionable notion of "science," but has its foundations in the contemporary research trends of experimental sciences. In fact, for too many critics the acceptability of structuralism stands or falls with this notion.

In this concluding chapter I will first discuss the scientific foundations of the notion of deep structure (Part One), and then the "objectivity" of Levi-Strauss' notion of deep structure (Part Two). Finally, I will show the mathematical nature of the notion of deep structure and the mathematical level of analysis entailed by such a notion (Part Three).

I.   The Scientific Basis of the Notion of Deep Structure

Germane to (or perhaps a preliminary aspect of) the discussion of the "scientific" nature of the object of analysis of a given approach, is the question of whether that approach claims to be a "scientific" or a "humanistic" approach. Levi-Strauss stated in 1964 that only hard sciences can properly be called "sciences," but later on he hinted at the possibility that future scientific progress may one day render hard sciences and human sciences indistinguishable (Levi-Strauss 1964, in 1976:294, 311). In the last volume of *Mythologiques,* Levi-Strauss claims:

> If the structural analysis of myths prepares the advent of scientific anthropology, it must as any science set up experiments to control its hypotheses and deduce, on the basis of its guiding principles, unknown properties of reality: that is it must predict what, under given experimental conditions, must necessarily occur" (Levi-Strauss, 1971:133-134).

Levi-Strauss claims that in the *Mythologiques* he met the two-fold criterion of science, — prediction and experimental control of the hypothesis. (*Ibid*:134). However, in Levi-Strauss' opinion, basic differences remain between exact and human sciences. Both the exact and the human sciences reach their object through symbols formulated by the mind independent of the constraints and threshhold of sensory organization. However, *physical* and *natural* sciences work with symbols of "things," and, therefore, they can verify the adequacy between symbols and their referents through experimental consequences. On the contrary, *human* sciences work with symbols of symbols and do not possess yet a method of determining the adequacy of representing symbols to represented symbols. This kind of verification can be accomplished only by exact sciences if they will ever be able to reach the "true objects" of which we now see only shadows (*Op. cit.*:574-575).

Levi-Strauss mentions the possibility that the ideas presented by structuralism in psychological terms are "tentative approximations of organic and even physical truths" (*Op. cit.*:616). He also claims that structural analysis can emerge in the mind because its model is already in the body: studies in visual perception show that the "first matter" of perception does not consist of raw data or objects perceived as isolated entities but rather of binary approaches of the type "simple/complex, light/dark, high/low, right/left." Far from being purely mental production or "mumbo jumbo," for Levi-Strauss deep structures bring to the *surface* of consciousness deep and organic truths (Levi-Strauss 1971:619). He has recently reinstated his hope that one day we will be able "to verify or falsify structural hypotheses when the natural sciences are able to reach those organic foundations for progress which we can now perceive only as undefined and distorted reflections" (Levi-Strauss 1976:ix).

Far from being a vague and elusive statement, Levi-Strauss' repeated references to the organic foundations of truth represent a direct challenge to the associationist and atomistic conception of science, and a direct claim that structuralism, and not empiricism, is in line with the most recent and pioneer trends in natural sciences. I have examined some recent research in physics, neurophysiology of perception, biology and linguistics which documents the existence of binary and discontinuous processes within physiological, biological, psychological, and linguistic phenomena (Rossi 1978). Neisser and Bower have summarized as follows the state of scientific research on the neurophysiology of perception in the 1960's, — research from which Levi-Strauss has drawn in *L'Homme Nu*.

> The eye and brain do not act as a camera or a recording instrument. Neither in perceiving nor in remembering is there any enduring copy of the optical input. In perceiving, complex patterns are extracted from that input and fed into the constructive processes of vision, so that the movements and the inner experience of the perceiver are usually in good correspondence with his environment. Visual memory involves the same kind of synthesis. (Neisser 1968:214; see also Bower 1966:92). Bower has defined the process of perceptual development as the development of "information-processing capacities" (*Ibid.:*91).

The scientific research of the 1970's added further support to this line of reasoning. In this section of this chapter I will examine some recent research in the field of visual perception. The eye is the most studied organ and the most direct avenue to understanding the structure of the brain. The scientific research of the 1970's has revealed more precise features of the information process operative in visual perception: "The human viewer is a fantastically competent information processor" (Harmon in Held and Richards 1976:195). Based on the fact that man can recognize an amazing large number of faces, Held and Richards conclude that the perceptual system somehow manages to define a small set of features that allow it to perform the recognition" (*Op. cit.*:139). In cases where the perception of depth is ambiguous — for instance in the dimensional drawing — the perceptual apparatus can select one orientation "out of the infinite number of legitimate possibilities that exist" (Attneave in Held and Richards 1976:147). "The power of the visual system to perform perspective transforms during depth alternation is impressive. Clearly, there are laws operating in this system" whose nature is not known to us (Held and Richards 1976:138). The correct identification of disoriented figures "depends on certain mental processes such as description and correction" (Rock, 1974:182). The "complicated process of correction is one more example of processing by a cognitive factor — actually a rule-determined process intrinsic to the visual system" (Held and Richards 1976:138).

The existence of such mental mechanisms is documented also by studies on the perception of speech.

> Observations...for the perception of auditory sequence indicate that special perceptual treatment of the sounds of speech (and music) allow us to extract order and meaning from what would otherwise be a world of auditory chaos. It is curious that in studying illusions and confusions we encounter mechanisms that ensure accurate perception and the appropriate interpretation of ambiguities. (Teuber, 1974:182).

This makes Held and Richards conclude that "the perception of speech depends greatly on the listener's linguistic knowledge" (1976:138). Experiments in reading show that the perceiver does not need to perceive each letter before he can get the meaning of the sentence. Otherwise, he could not read at a fast speed.

> What appears to happen is that the reader knows much about the properties of what he is reading before he begins to read...From a consideration of the errors made by readers, Kolers concludes that the reader constructs an internal grammatical message that is then matched with the written text by sampling at certain points. (*Op. cit.*:139).

This means that

> A reader proceeds not by perceiving letter by letter.... but rather by generating internal grammatical messages.... A reader formulates messages to himself that are based on clues in the text at hand.... The activities take place as part of the unconscious work that the reader's perceptual and linguistic machinery carries out...(This is) an internal — perhaps more cerebral — process of generating language. (Kolers 1972:202).

Misreadings by readers, often left uncorrected, show that the readers are "paying more attention to the internal message they were generating than to the surface features of the text" (*Op. cit.*:203). These conceptualizations in terms of internally generated messages and surface features is, of course, very congenial to Levi-Strauss' notion of mental and deep structures:

> It is in the process underlying what we call attention that we find the most important controls on the amount of information that undergoes perceptual processing. The process that we know by such names as "expectations," "set," "internal schemata" and other synonyms, selects among partially processed sensory inputs and also produces completed percepts from fragmentary stimuli. (Held and Richards 1976:139).

In general "the great facility with which man perceives such things as human speech and writing suggests that he has innate capabilities for both generating and perceiving them" (*Ibid.:*140).

Gunther S. Stent, a molecular biologist from Berkeley, has drawn an explicit connection between neurophysiological studies on cellular communication and "the latter-day philosophical view" called structuralism as represented by Carl Jung, Wolfgang Kohler, Noam Chomsky and Levi-Strauss (Stent 1972:24). The advent of structuralism, Stent argues, represents the overthrowing of "positivism" and its psychological counterpart, "behaviorism" (*Ibid.*). There are two crucial tenets of positivism, according to Stent: (1) the exclusion of innate knowledge; and the assumption that sensory experience is the only source of knowledge; and (2) inductive reasoning from raw sensory data is held to be the method by which empirical scientists can know the world in terms of patterned features of experience and causal connections among events. Positivism holds that both of these principles must be true also for the empirical study of psychological and social phenomena. Stent argues that these two positivistic criteria did not have a profound consequence on the scientific research of physical scientists, because the latter don't need philosophers of science to justify their methodology. They can also empirically verify their explanations. Stent is certainly right in stating that matters are different when we consider the influence of positivism in social sciences. He argues that the two above mentioned positivistic canons have forced social scientists to investigate only "factual observations" — observable patterns of overt behavior — and to formulate only those kinds of propositions which can be justified on the basis of a direct induction from raw sense data. The consequence is that human sciences have remained taxonomic, producing only descriptive propositions and very little genuine explanation. As a result, human sciences do not possess a theoretical framework for understanding man (Stent 1975:1052-1053). Stent argues that two structural principles permit the construction of a framework more appropriate to the study of man: (1) structuralism admits the possibility of innate ideas, in harmony with Kant's position that mind structures reality by processing sensory experience through innate (a priori) categories; and (2) structuralists argue that surface and observable structures of behavior are not self-explanatory but rather they are generated from deep structures. As a result, structuralism permits the formulation of propositions about behavior which are not directly deducible from observable behavior and cannot be submitted to direct and empirical verification (*Op. cit.*:1053). To these two principles mentioned by Stent we should add the systemic, elementarist and transformational principles which make of structuralism a truly deductive approach. Firstly, deep structures are composed of a finite number of elements. Secondly, these elements are the ultimate principles from which we can deduce the structure of larger and observable entities. Thirdly, the large units are composed through rules of combination and recombination of basic elements. The systemic, elementarist and transformational principles of explanation derive from as many properties of the notion of deep structure. From this it follows that the acceptability of structuralism as a deductive — hence "truly scientific" method — stands or falls with the scientific tenability of the notion of deep structure.

Stent has argued that contemporary neurophysiological research on visual perception supports the notion of deep structure, which is a fundamental notion of structuralism.

> In any case the findings on the nature of nervous communication...have some important general implications, in that they lend physiological support to the latter-day philosophical view that has come to be known as "structuralism." In recent years the structuralist view emerged more or less simultaneously, independently and in different guises in diverse fields of study, for example in analytical psychology, cognitive psychology, linguistics and anthropology. The names most often associated with each of these developments are those of Carl Jung, Wolfgang Kohler, Noam Chomsky and Claude Levi-Strauss. The emergence of structuralism represents the overthrow of "positivism" (and its psychological counterpart "behaviorism"), which held sway since the late 19th century, and marks a return to Emmanuel Kant's late-18th-century critique of pure reason (1972:24).

The neurological communication network of the higher vertebrates consists of three parts: (1) a sensory part (input), which informs the animals about the external and internal environment; (2) an "effector," (output) which imparts commands to muscles and contributes to the production of motor behavior; and (3) a connecting link between the sensory and effector components. The brain is the most important part of the connecting mechanism, as it processes the information received in the sensory part and imparts commands to the effector on the basis of perceived meaning. The process of information largely consists of abstracting among the large number of sensory stimuli. "In order to abstract, the brain destroys selectively portions of the input data, and this transforms these data into manageable categories, or structures that are meaningful to the animal'' (Stent, 1975:187).

The presence of innate structures in the perceptual apparatus of animals was demonstrated a long time ago.

> Lowly chicks as well as lofty primates perceive and respond to form without experience if given the opportunity at the appropriate stage of development. Innate knowledge of the environment is demonstrated by the preference of newly hatched chicks for forms likely to be edible and by the interest of young infants in kinds of forms that will later aid in object recognition, social responsiveness and spatial orientation. This primitive knowledge provides a foundation for the vast accumulation of knowledge through experience (Franz, 1961).

> Specifically, the position now is that basic neuroanatomic structures and physiochemical processes underlie color vision and that these have a determining influence on how humans respond to color, code it through language, and retrieve it in memory. Related but not identical uniformities in neurological structures and functions characterize infrahuman species so that one can say that among them also organic factors serve to categorize or impose color boundaries (Fabrega, 1977:435).

On the basis of neurophysiological studies, Stent makes inferences about the structure of human mind.

> Neurological studies have indicated that, in accord with the structuralist tenets, information about the world reaches the depth of the mind not as raw data, but as highly processed structures that are generated by a set of stepwise, preconscious informational transformations of the sensory input. These neurological transformations proceed according to a program that pre-exists in the brain (1975:1055-1056).

Stent uses interchangeably the terms ''preexisting brain program'' and ''preexisting mental structure'':

> Any set of primary sense data becomes meaningful only after a series of such operations performed on it has transformed the data set into a pattern that matches a preexisting mental structure (1972:25).

For Stent, this kind of experimental research supports the assumption of structuralism as a philosophy.

> The neurological findings thus lend biological support to the structuralist dogma that explanations of behavior must be formulated in terms of such deep programs and reveal the wrong-headedness of the positivistic approach which rejects the postulation of covert internal programs as mentalism (Stent, 1975:1055-1056).

Or "mumbo jumbo," according to the latest professional insights of Ronald Cohen (1977). Elsewhere Stent argues:

> Structuralism admits, as positivism does not, the existence of innate ideas, or of knowledge without learning. Furthermore, structuralism recognizes that information about the world enters the mind not as raw data but as highly abstract structures that are the result of a preconscious set of step-by-step transformations of the sensory input. Each transformation step involves the selective destruction of information, according to a program that preexists in the brain. . . .
> These conclusions of structuralist philosophy were reached entirely from the study of human behavior without recourse to physiological observations. As the experimental work discussed in this article shows, however, the manner in which sensory input into the retina is processed along the visual pathway corresponds exactly to the structuralist tenets (Stent 1972:24-25).

Stent concludes his article as follows:

> Apparently a beginning has now been made in providing, in terms of cellular communication, an explanation for one of the deepest of all philosophical problems: the relation between reality and the mind (*Loc. cit.*).

Stent's reasoning is based on the assumption of isomorphic relations between neurophysiological and mental structures, an assumption we had discussed in the first chapter of this volume.

Charles D. Loughlin and Eugene G. D'Aquili have also made an extensive review of neurophysiological research.

> The species distinguish relevant from irrelevant patterns of constructing models of their environment against which they match sensory input for relevance, from which they generate expectations of the state of their environment, and that they modify as the sensory input requires. . . . models for most organisms are located in sensory association areas. At least some, if not many, of the associative structures are programmed genetically, are passed from generation to generation through genetic material (1974:78-79).

In so far as the neurological structure of human beings is concerned, Loughlin and D'Aquili argue that there is

> . . . the strong possibility that all men everywhere process sensory input in more or less the same fashion. . . . Neurognostic models are inherited through the recombination of genetic material in the gametes and are later modified and ramified in reaction to feedback from the external world. . . —These models are being continually tested for accuracy of fit by formation of probability expectations — expectations that are homologous to deductive hypotheses and that are matched to empirically perceived outcomes. . . . Men are conscious of only a minor fraction of this process (*Loc. cit.*:148).

Shortly, Loughlin and D'Aquili concur with Stent that there exist preconscious programs or neurological models which are, at least partly, innate.

We can argue for the scientific tenability, or at least plausibility, of the notion of deep structures or "programs" within the cognitive apparatus of humans and, to a certain extent, of non-humans also. We can also agree that this review of the literature on the neurophysiology of perception clearly supports Levi-Strauss' contention that contemporary research trends back up his epistemological attitude (1971 Finale). However, what I have said so far does not directly clarify the issue of the "objective" character of Levi-Strauss' notion of mental structures. Obviously this issue is of crucial importance to Levi-Strauss because mental structures are the building blocks of culture: "to understand the common basis of political, religious, marriage life, inquiry must be directed to certain fundamental structures of the human mind" (1969:75).

II. Objective Nature of the Deep Structure of Culture

From the existence of deep neurognostic models Laughlin and D'Aquili do not infer the existence of mental structures as entities differentiated and separate from cerebral or neurological structures. On the contrary, they argue that "from the biogenetic structuralist's point of view social institutions are behavioral exemplars of an underlying neurophysiological structure that regulates human social behavior in a biologically adaptive manner" (1974:150). They accuse Levi-Strauss of relying on such metaphysical notions as "apprehension, primitive thought" and of being "a Neo-Platonist who conceives of structures as 'ideal forms' having in some sense an existence apart from prehending minds" (*Op. cit.*:151). For them, the Platonist position of Levi-Strauss is evident from the already quoted statement that "cross-cousin marriage and dual organization correspond to different stages in the growing awareness of these structures" (Levi-Strauss 1969:101). For Laughlin and D'Aquili,

> the structures are neither ideal nor imperfectly prehending. Furthermore they have an ontological status as "real" as the left ventricle or cornea. In short, they are the neurognostic models discussed at length earlier in this book (1974:153).

In their view biogenetic structuralism makes structures instantly amenable to empirical verification. Culture, cognition, mythologizing and so on are nothing but

> behavioral manifestations of universal structural models. These models are probably phenotypic expressions of dendritic-synaptic connections located within the brain. Structural configurations are initially totally, and later partially, determined by genetic coding and are susceptible to the pressures of natural selection (*Op. cit.*:196).

According to biogenetic structuralism, "human behavior is the result of a dialectic between the central nervous system, primarily the higher cortical functions, and the environment. All other asserted or posited levels of reality have analytic status only" (*Op. cit.*:195). Laughlin and D'Aquili buttress their argument with recent ethological research showing that non-human primates possess certain traits previously considered the landmark of humans — the culture bearers. If one day we possess "the technology by means of which we can trace 'holographic' models and connecting traits in the human central nervous system,...accurate prediction of behavior would follow" (*Op. cit.*:205).

I fail to see the analytical power produced by such a reductionistic position: "For whether we like it or not, science is committed to reductionism" (*Op. cit.*:12). The thrust of this kind of argument is to deny that psychology, sociology, anthropology and linguistics have a distinct object of analysis, and to assert that they all deal with "reifications." By the same token, one can argue that biogenetic structuralism is dealing with reification also. In fact, what do the terms "environment" and "central nervous system" connote but concepts, and what status do these concepts have other than the analytic status accorded by Laughlin and D'Aquili to the notions of culture or mental structures?

It is incumbent upon structuralists to show where the deep unconscious structures spoken of by Levi-Strauss are located. I shall first briefly examine Levi-Strauss' position and then will discuss some recent essays which have appeared in anthropological journals on this very issue.

Levi-Strauss' position can be summarized in the following two propositions: (1) the unconscious structures discovered through structural analysis are "real" — that is, they refer to an "objective," "extramental" aspect of culture; and (2) the deep structures of culture have an existence independently of the neurological structures of the anthropologist and of the culture bearers. Both points have been explicitly made by Levi-Strauss himself. In so far as the "objective" reality of unconscious structures is concerned, Levi-Strauss has argued as follows:

> Structure has no distinct content; it is content itself, apprehended in a logical organization conceived as property of the reality (1960 in 1976:115).

> Music and mythology appeal to mental structures that the different listeners have in common. The point of view I have adopted involves reference to general structures that the serialist doctrine rejects and whose existence it even denies. On the other hand, these structures can only be termed general if one is prepared to grant them an *objective* foundation on the hither side of consciousness and thought (1969b:26).

In *L'Homme Nu* also Levi-Strauss has unequivocally stressed the real and absolute character of unconscious structures.

A myth is never reducible to its appearances. As diverse they might be, these appearances hide structures which are undoubtedly less numerous but also more real. Without claiming the right to add or substract anything from these structures, they exhibit the character of absolute objects. (1971:33, my translation).

As to the independence of deep structures from the neurological structures of the anthropologist and of culture bearers, Levi-Strauss has stated that the brain can be considered the "external referent" of structural explanations. By "brain" Levi-Strauss means "a network whose properties (or some of them) are translated by the most different ideological system into particular structures" (*Op. cit.*:561). However, Levi-Strauss cautions that "authentic structuralism attempts to assess the intrinsic properties of certain types of orders; and these properties do not express anything which is external to these orders" (*Loc. cit.*). In one of the passages of the 1969 preface to *The Elementary Structures of Kinship* which we have already quoted in the first chapter of this volume, Levi-Strauss claims that culture can be considered as a "synthetic duplication" of a biological mechanism already present in the animal kingdom — a duplication permitted by the complexification of the brain (Levi-Strauss 1969:xxx). These two quotes clearly exclude the notion that Levi-Strauss' mental structures are identical to brain or neurological structures.

Then where are the deep or unconscious logical structures to be located? Do they have an existence independent of the scientific activity of the structuralist? Recently, Peter Caws has explicitly addressed "the question of the relationship between structure and model as it arises in the work of Levi-Strauss and Leach" (Caws 1974:2). Caws has argued that the "unconscious set of determinations" which the anthropologist reconstructs to account for the complexity of events and implausibility (or contradictions) of natives' explanations "may be thought to be an explanatory model" or "an objective structure embodied unconsciously in the social group. Levi-Strauss seems to choose the latter alternative, since what he means by 'social structure' is just the model that the anthropologist succeeds in establishing by his variational analysis of data from different groups" (p. 5). Caws has argued that "the explanatory model is a mental structure in Levi-Strauss' head" (*Ibid.*), which "raises the question of the possible objective existence of a structure that is modeled by the anthropologist's explanatory model and which is neither the representational [the way people think things are (p. 3)] nor the operational model [the way people practically respond or act (p. 3)] found among the mental structures of the natives" (p. 6). Having taken cognizance that neither the representational nor the operational model adequately represents the objective social structure, Caws states that

it is the scientist's representational (i.e., explanatory) model, the theory he constructs to account for the data and their interrelation, that confers objective structure on the system. And the use of "confers" is deliberate, since it would be quite accurate to say that until the explanatory model was constructed the system had no objective structure (p. 7).

Hanson (1976) and I (1977) have argued that the notion that the scientist projects structures into the data is not acceptable. I now clarify further that such a conception is not acceptable either from the traditional or from the structural point of view.

How does Caws define the term "objective"? As a skilled philosopher he considers that "the question of whether (theoretical understanding) ever arrives at anything like final objectivity is an empty one" (1974:7). He distinguishes between "objective relations (such as) those attested by the natural sciences independently of the opinions of those who enter into them" and he admits that "in the matter of kinship there are objective relations" understood in this way (pp. 6-7). He then proposes "an unproblematic relative use of the term, according to which, roughly speaking, a view is more objective the more comprehensive the framework within which it is held." For him, the task of scientific theory consists in providing the "rectification of experience" by including into the framework of judgment the context and other situational and non-situational elements (my interpretation) of the experience. I accept this concept of scientific theorizing, and I can also accept this definition of the term "objective." Caws then goes on to compare the way physical and social sciences see the issue. In physical sciences the "facts" of causal relations are independent of their formulation so that "in the natural sciences the final authority in disputed questions is conceded to the empirical data" (p. 7). In the social sciences the matter is different; for instance, in the case of kinship, people are related according to their conception of kinship (representational model) and not according to biological (causal) laws, as the latter are differently conceived by people of different cultures. However, "relations of duty, of sentiment, of permissible conjugation, may be different in practice from their specifications in indigenous theory." Since social structure is not adequately represented by the representational nor the operational models, Caws argues that it is the anthropologist's model to give the objective structure to the system. This last statement is highly questionable, and untenable both from an empiricist as well as a structural point of view. Caws supports his statement by arguing that social sciences deal "with mind-dependent entities" because "the causal sequences studied by social sciences always pass through heads;" "this leads to a self-referential dimension in the social sciences that is quite lacking in the physical sciences." (p. 9).

The statement that there is no meaning in phenomena "without passing through the heads" is acceptable to structuralists, with the qualification that the mediation of mind can be either conscious or unconscious. Caws argues that "a society is, in the last analysis, nothing except what is said and thought about it, by those who observe it as well as by those who compose it" (pp. 9-10). Consequently, "the structure is dependent in one way or another on these models, since without them the relations that constitute it would not exist. Priority goes, in the end, to the explanatory model, as the one that is in a position to reflect all the relevant relations and to get them right" (p. 10).

This mixture of "explanandum" and "explanans" is totally unwarranted and confusing. In an earlier rejoinder to Caws, I called the attention of the reader to the distinction made by Levi-Strauss, Chomsky, structural linguists and structural Marxists between the deep and surface level of structure, and to the fact that both of these levels are considered "objective"; by the latter term I mean they are thought to exist independently of and prior to the formulation of respectively statistical and mechanical models by the anthropologist (Rossi 1977:914-916). Caws has replied that what is important to him is "the fact that the actual state of affairs in the societies in question consists only of people's doing or saying things in accordance with their operational or representational models; I, therefore, challenged the additional postulation of an objective social structure that fills out, as it were, a comprehensive scheme of relations only partially instatiated by what is actually done and said" (Caws 1977:916).

Caws' reply makes clear that in writing his original article on "the question of the relationship between structure and model as it arises in the work of Levi-Strauss and Leach" he intended to side with Leach against Levi-Strauss. As far as one can deduce from his statements published in the *American Anthropologist,* Caws' position is not substantially different, at least on the issue in question, from Leach's and Needham's positions. Caws' position is well summarized by his statement that the actual state of affairs in the society in question consists only of what people actually say or do. This statement, combined with the dismissal of the "postulation of any objective social structure," is equivalent to saying that in society there "actually" exists only what the anthropologist can directly and immediately observe people saying and doing. Such a programmatic statement betrays an empiricist, mentalistic (hold and behold) and undialectical attitude. Caws' rejection is, first of all, an empiricist one because to argue that in society there exists only what people are "doing or saying in accordance with their operational or representational model" is the same as arguing that the only legitimate data for the social scientist consists in the immediate and obvious content of people's verbalizations and behavior. As I have explained in the first chapter, this is exactly the position of the empiricists.

Secondly, Caws' position is by implication a mentalistic one because he bridges the discrepancies between representational models or between operational models and representational models with relationships introduced by explanatory models—the latter having the task of rectifying experience (1974:7). This is the same as saying that the actual state of society is what the anthropologist conceives it to be, a position consistent with Caws' statement that it is the anthropologist's theory to "confer objective structure to the system" (*Ibid*).

Finally, Caws' position is an undialectical and uncritical one, because he seems to accept contradictions and discrepancies among verbalizations and behavior of people as genuine data; gaps or unintelligible aspects of data must be remedied ("rectified"), not through more accurate observations and understanding of deeper or "objective" relationships, but by projecting mental intuitions into the data. This interpretation seems consistent with Caws' statement that "a society is in the last analysis, nothing except what is said and thought about it by those who observe it as well as by those who compose it" (1974:10).

On the contrary, structuralists argue that apparent contradictions and discrepancies are the occasion and justification for searching, and not inventing, underlying relations which make apparent contradictions and discrepancies intelligible. Levi-Strauss hopes to reach unconscious categories

> by bringing together domains, which, at first sight, appear disconnected to the observer; on the one hand, the social system as it actually works; on the other hand, the manner in which, through their myths, their rituals and their religious representations, men try to hide or to justify the discrepancies between their society and the ideal image of it which they harbor (1976:80).

Levi-Strauss, however, cautions that to assume such a distinction from the beginning would mean to beg the question. On the contrary, there must be ethnographic evidence to make the anthropologist recognize discrepancies. It is the task of scientific analysis to show that the two realms are not

> as heterogeneous as it seems. To some extent, they may correspond to codes whose functions and fields of application are permutable. Herein lies one's right to deal with social segments and symbolic representations as parts of an underlying system (*Op. Cit.*:81).

The underlying relationships are an "objective" part of the social structure because they are shown to be the causes of the existence of apparent conflicts in people's verbalizations and behaviors.

Caws fails to prove why the dialetical conception between the two levels of reality has to be abandoned after a long tradition of contributions by the Marxist, Freudian, linguistic and Piagetian, not to mention Levi-Straussian and structural Marxist[1] approaches. All these schools of thought have made invaluable contributions to the understanding of the real structure and dynamics of social, linguistic and cultural phenomena.

One must concede at least as much as this: that the enormous number of substantive analyses and controversies that these schools of thought have generated abundantly prove that the dialetical conception of social and psychological reality is useful, at least, as a methodological hypothesis, and that such a conception has forced competitive modes of explanation to refine their positions.

The plausibility of a dialectical conception of culture can be shown also by considering the absurd consequences entailed by the opposite attitude. Unless one concludes from the existence of discrepancies in cultural data that culture is unintelligible, one must postulate the existence of a level of intelligibility (and hence logic) beyond mere appearances and the surface level. At the same time, unless one is a mentalist, he cannot state that the missing intelligibility can be "just projected" into the data through the elaboration of explanatory models. Hence, one can see the soundness of Levi-Strauss' assumption that the universe is intrinsically rational (see my introductory chapter); from this assumption it follows that the real task of the anthropologist is to search for the deep logic of culture.

As Pierre Maranda reminds us in his chapter in this volume (see his footnote 8), for Levi-Strauss anthropology is an ethno-science, in the sense of an "ethno-logic." According to Maranda, Levi-Strauss' view is consistent with Piaget's notion that "structure" refers to the structural properties inherent in the operations which mind performs on objects (see the end of Maranda's chapter). As far as I can see, this is true in the sense that culture derives (but is not totally produced) from the structuring activity of mind, and that structural analysis attempts to discover "the algebraic" of the structuring minds. Because the "algebraic" is found to be the same in different cultures, we can state that the deep structures (or logic of cultures) are objective (and universal).

I disagree with Caws on another point. He states that this issue is a philosophical and not an anthropological one (1977:916). I maintain that this is both an anthropological and an epistemological issue, and that it is an anthropological issue *because* it is also an epistemological one. The issue is an "anthropological" one because we do need deep structures to account for heterogeneity and apparent contradictions, and these structures must be considered the "objective" foundations of cultural data. The need for deep structure has been demonstrated not only in Piagetian psychology and structural and transformational linguistics, but also in the neurophysiological research on perception, in physics and in biology (see Rossi 1978). No one would argue that the mathematical relations governing the atomic composition of physical matter or the mathematical rules according to which the elements of the genetic code are combined have an "objective" existence — that is, that they are operative before they are discovered by scientists. This is what Caws concedes for geographical relationships such as "south of Mexico," or "north of the U.S." "The geographical entities in question embody the relationship objectively, even though if nobody had ever thought of directionality in this way there would have been no relationship of this sort to embody" (Caws 1974:8). By the same token, no one can deny that grammatical and phonological rules are embodied within language use before they are discovered, and nobody would deny that such rules govern our language usage, even though we might have forgotten about them. The same kind of objectivity is attributed by structuralists to mental structures as building blocks of cultural data.

The issue of the objectivity of structure is also an epistemological one because, as Piaget argues, we need to postulate deep structures to avoid the inadequacy of both empiricism and a priorism. In fact the necessary and universal character of scientific propositions cannot be adequately explained on the basis of inductions or of predetermined and innate ideas. Rather, it is the equilibration or self-regulatory aspects of the construction process (of knowledge) to explain the necessary (and universal) character of logical structures. What is innate is the self-regulatory mechanism, whereas the programming of cognitive development is learned—except perhaps the programming of very few logical operations (Piaget 1969:184).

However, the notion of deep structure is not just a mere question of epistemological preference; it receives support from modern mathematics: "In general a social network contains more than culturally codified relationships, perceived by the individuals connected by them, but also numerous objective relationships which are no less real although they are not necessarily perceived by the people involved in them" (Lorrain 1975:13, my translation). I will come back to this mathematical notion of deep structures at the end of this chapter.

Having revenged the objectivity and autonomy of deep structures, someone might still encounter objections against the intellectualistic — and therefore immutable and predetermined — character of deep mental structures.

> Behind dual organization, regarded as an institution limited in its forms and in its distribution, there are certain number of logical structures the recurrence of which in modern society, and at different ages in life, proves it to be both fundamental and universal (Levi-Strauss 1969:151).

To be sure Levi-Strauss has clarified that he is not an intellectualist in a reductionist sense. He has never proclaimed that culture is a mere product of mind, nor apparently does he hold that "ideas as such (are) fundamental to social life." Rather, he holds that "both ideas and action derive from qualities of mind, and that neither activity nor ideas have any particular priority" (Schneider 1965:79). Whereas this position inequivocably attributes a priority to the human mind, it does not clarify whether such a priority must be attributed to the affective or the cognitive functioning of mind. It is well known that Levi-Strauss finds in universal logical structures the ultimate foundation of culture. In *L'Homme Nu,* he entered into an explicit polemic against V.W. Turner and E. Leach, "who pretends to place affectivity at the center of ritual" (1971:598). In polemic with Caws, Paul Chaney has expressed his strong opposition against the intellectualism of structuralism (1978). However, Chaney *assumes* rather than *documents* such an intellectualism, which he counters by attributing an analytic priority to affectivity — the latter being vaguely defined. In the wake of "a new wave of historians and philosophers of scientific inquiry" such as N.R. Hanson, S. Toulmin, T. Kuhn, he rejects Hempel's notion of scientific explanation based on the "symmetry between explanation and prediction" (1972:1008). Together with N.R. Hanson he argues that a "'retroductive' procedure of thinking back from data details to pattern statements is fundamental to theoretical physics" (1974:42). According to Chaney,

> theories put phenomena into systems. They are built-up-in-reverse — retroductively. A theory is a cluster of conclusions in search of a premise. From the observed properties of phenomena the physicist reasons his way towards a keystone idea from which the properties are explicable as a matter of course (1972:1008).

This concept of science well fits the first phase of structural analysis. In fact, Levi-Strauss proceeds retroductively from an infinite variety of details back to a few key logical structures. However, on the basis of basic symbolic structures, Levi-Strauss makes predictions about kinship or mythological systems. Structuralism, then, integrates inductive and deductive procedures, although the analytical specificity and power of structural models consist in their deductive and predictive quality.

Even more antithetical to structuralism is Chaney's over-interpretation of Sapir's principle of linguistic relativity, which is said to imply a relativity of forms of thought. Chaney quotes Peirce as saying: "nothing is safe from change, not even the classification of the sciences themselves...Sciences (are characterized by a) radicalism that tries experiments" (1976:753). One, however, does not see how this arbitrary and undemonstrated principle can lead to the conclusion that "an explanation is once an obstacle to reconceptualization" (1974:242).

To be sure Chaney rejects historical relativity and value relativity — and presumably relativism, which amounts to agnosticism. The specificity of positivism, however, consists in stating that there is a "multitude of local distortions in the space-time-mode-meaning-significance frame to expose potentially creative imaginations diversely interlocked in humanly created values" (1978:594).

The end product of this continuously imaginative process of local distortions and local understanding is for Chaney a "potential diversity of semi-autonomous and conflicting notions, trends, and aspirations" which supplant each other and which cannot, therefore, be explained "in terms of universal properties" (*Ibid*). Structuralism has the fault of assuming that "human nature is uniform" whereas it is "variable" (*loc. cit*:593).

> Structuralism has indicated that human minds have structured our understanding of a natural manifold. It has masked from view, however, the extent of this humanly created asymmetry in the semantic manifold which has led to profoundly diverse inference channels for human comprehension (*loc. cit*:594).

It is true that Levi-Strauss has tried to reckon with the multiplicity of semantic fields and human creativity. However, Chaney argues that "the idea of structure as transformation is one level of variation — kind of variation on a theme" (1976:753). This implies that the oppositional method of structuralism reduces the variety of cultural themes to a basic theme or to immutable universal structures. What is the alternative proposed by Chaney against the presumed determinism and immutability of Levi-Strauss' intellectualism?

> An additional explanatory idea of transformation is needed in discussion of semantic reticula in order to recapture the quality of diverse patterns of linguistic usage, experiencing and understanding that are not translatable (mutually unintelligible themes and/or conceptual tools) (1976:753).

The idea of "transmutation" is taken from V.W. Turner, who uses it to express the notion that symbols are saturated by emotions. Chaney emphasizes that emotions provide the connecting links among various semantic fields, and he quotes Durkheim and Mauss in support of this notion (*Ibid*). He then continues:

> Our task in understanding psychohistorical phenomena in human beings is an analogous one of searching for the characteristics of a "potential circuit breaker" to explicate both regularity and variability in human exploitation, emotion, action (Chaney 1974:243).

The emphasis is, again, placed on emotion, action, cognitive element. Somewhat echoing Levi-Strauss and Chomsky, Chaney posits a "circuit breaker" within the deep structure "in the form of a potentially creative energy" (Chaney 1973:1370). However, he emphasizes the notion of "energy," emotion; this leads him to state:

> the present discussion is not addressing itself to variations within a syntactic structure but rather to additional aspects of variation in semantic networks that are exposed in an examination of recorded culture histories of meaning (Chaney 1974:243).

One must make two points clear. Firstly, the interest in the semantic level does not authorize one to reject the syntactic level of analysis as a useless formalism and universalism. Secondly, structuralists recognize the need for developing a grammar of semantics, whereas Chaney does not offer any suggestion on how to charter such a study. Instead he offers generic statements such as the following: "there is a multitude of local distortions in the space-time-mode-meaning-significance frame," "an enormous diversity of semiautonomous notions and aspirations" (1978:594), and "a synergetic flow of human feelings as a result of a shape of a given morality" (*Ibid*). No precise analytic dimension of this semantic multiplicity is suggested or a methodological approach formulated to charter such a multiplicity. On the contrary, we are left with an uneasy sense of relativism, and perhaps agnosticism, as apparent in his statement that anthropology must attempt to

> capture the quality of diverse patterns of linguistic usage, experiencing, and understanding that are not translatable, mentally unintelligible themes and/or conceptual plots (1976:753).

The weakness of attributing a primacy to affectivity has been clearly pointed out by Levi-Strauss, when he stated that affect cannot be the most fundamental datum. The ritual is not a spontaneous reaction to lived situations, as naturalists and functionalists contend. Anxiety can be generated in this way only by physiological situations, whereas in ritual the anxiety is generated by the way thought conceptualizes reality (1971:608).

There is an apparent cogency in the objection that Levi-Strauss' structuralism is vitiated by an intellectualistic bias. Given the assumption of the immanent rationality of the physical and cultural universe,[2] and its origin from the structuring activity of mind (which is supposed to have the same laws of physical reality), one issue immediately arises to the mind: are the structures of mind innate, universal and immutable structures? If so, how can contingent and changing institutional arrangements be explained in terms of universal and immutable principles? In his 1949 volume Levi-Strauss asserted that the structure of human mind is permanent, and is repeated in its entirety in each individual thought (Levi-Strauss 1969:491). The laws of primitive and civilized thought are the same and, as a matter of fact, the laws of thought are the same as those expressed in physical and social reality (*Op. cit*:451). These assertions do not imply that the great heterogeneity of contingent and historical phenomena are a priori reduced to immutable logical entities. To begin with, Levi-Strauss is correct when he claims that historical and particularistic explanations cannot account for universal phenomena. Levi-Strauss states that the mental schemata of adults vary according to various cultures and time periods, but that each culture and historical period retains and develops only a few possibilities out of a "universal resource" (*Op. cit*:193). In another passage of the same work, Levi-Strauss considers the cross-cousin marriage and dual organization as two different stages of growing awareness of basic structures (p. 101). Elsewhere, he states that a number of logical structures are recurring in modern society and at different ages of life, and, therefore, they prove to be fundamental and universal (p. 151).

Under the impact of Piaget, Levi-Strauss admits that reality is in permanent construction rather than being made by an accumulation of already made structures.

> Unconscious structures are more real and absolute than the appearances; they are generative matrices by successive deformations of types which can be ordered in series and which can permit to find the smallest nuances of each myth considered in its specificity (Levi-Strauss 1971:33).

> Human nature is not a totality of immutable and already made structures but rather a set of matrices from which other structures originate; structures never remain identical from birth to adulthood during the life time of individuals, nor do they remain the same in all places and times in human societies (*Op. cit*:561).

We must remember that it is structured content which varies in time and space, whereas the structuring principles are governed by combinatory and grammatical rules of mathematical or quasi-mathematical nature. We have seen that for Levi-Strauss a cybernetic notion of homeostasis can take the place of the notion of deep mental structures. In this sense, the mathematical thrust is more crucial to structuralism than the notion of mental structures. Consequently, when Chaney denies the usefulness of the syntactical level of analysis and universal propositions, he rejects (perhaps overlooks?) the most crucial contribution of structuralism.

III. The Mathematical Nature of Deep Structures

We have seen in the first two chapters of this volume that structuralists are concerned with identifying the relational constants underlying observable phenomena. The structure consists in "invariant propositions (rapports) among the amazingly diversified terms which are the appearances, or raw data" (Levi-Strauss 1968:176-177, my translation). The notion of invariant proportions is, of course, a mathematical notion. In Levi-Strauss' words, the task of structuralism is "to define and circumscribe the phenomena, to reduce the number of variables, and to enucleate constants which can be expressed in the form of ratios and combinations" (1968a:10, my translation).

Levi-Strauss implies that mathematics could provide the ideal tools for structural analysis because "mathematics unveils the properties intrinsic to the functioning of the human mind in their greatest purity" (*Ibid.*, my translation). In fact, "mathematical thought reflects the free functioning of "the mind, that is the activity of the cells of the cerebral cortex, relatively emancipated from any external constraint and obeying only its own laws" (Levi-Strauss 1966:248); (see also Levi-Strauss 1971:578). After 1950, Levi-Strauss emphasized for a long time that the task of mapping the logic of mind falls within the domain of qualitative and not quantitative mathematics — that is, "a mathematics which teaches us that the domain of necessity is not necessarily the same as that of quantity" (quoted in 1963:330). In 1965 Levi-Strauss stated that "the mathematics designated as qualitative has broadened our logic by making the concern for rigor prevail over the concern for measure" (reproduced in 1976:65). In 1950 Levi-Strauss had stated that it was the usage of mathematics which enabled Troubetzkoy and Jakobson to lay the foundations of structural linguistics:

> there also the question was to distinguish between a purely phenomenological datum, which is beyond the competence of scientific analysis, and a simpler infrastructure, from which all the reality of phenomena derive. Thanks to the notion of "facultative variants," "combinatory variants," "terms of group," and "neutralization," phonological analysis has permitted a precise definition of language through a small number of constant relations, whose possible range of authorized combinations is illustrated by the diversity and apparent complexity of the phonetic system (1966a/1950:xxxv).

In the last volume of *Mythologiques,* Levi-Strauss expressed his dismay at the facile objection of those who dismiss logical and mathematical typographical symbols as invalid (1971:566-567), whereas in the first volume of *Mythologiques* he had explicitly stated that these symbols were meant not as tools for rigorous proofs but as a kind of shorthand writing (1969:30-31). There, he had also auspicated the advent of a "genuine logico-mathematical analysis" of which he had "naively attempted to sketch the outlines" *(Ibid.).*

Does Levi-Strauss' advocacy of qualitative mathematics imply a rejection of statistical techniques? And if so, why? Structural and transformational linguists appraise us about the limitations of statistical and quantitative techniques. The structural conception of language as a form composed of invariant relationships among discrete elements permits a quantitative description and a distributional analysis of linguistic units. By applying the principles of information theory, one can show there is a constant and inverse relationship between the frequency of a given unity and the information it carries. However, the probabilistic model based on Markovian processes permits one to study language only as a closed system of signs, but not to study the signifieds, the subject, the situation and—importantly—the generativity of the system in the Chomskian sense. According to L. Hjelmslev, linguistic theory consists of establishing a non-quantitative calculus based on the logical properties of the classes of elements which can be detected in the text. By rejecting the probabilistic model of information theory and by assimilating linguistic description to an algorythm, Chomsky seems to fulfill Hjelmslev's dream for an algebraic of language (see Corneille 1976:195-206).

The mathematical notion of class (or more precisely "category") is singled out by Levi-Strauss as a key notion of future mathematical developments in structural theory. In *L'Homme Nu* he expressed the hope that the recent development of the "theory of category" and the "notion of morphism" may permit us to approach myths as systems composed simultaneously of terms and relationships among terms (1971:568). Levi-Strauss also referred there to two manuscripts of Francois Lorrain on the formal study of networks—and Lorrain has subsequently published the already quoted volume (1975). Lorrain distinguishes his mathematical approach from the traditional "vulgar" sociometry of social networks, the latter being limited to the statistical study of relationships among individuals. The mathematical approach proposed by Lorrain is built on the notion that a society consists not only of a collection of terms or a set of relations, but also of relations among systems of relations. The thrust of this mathematical procedures is to assess the "systematic global properties of social networks." These

> indirect social relationships are particularly important and one of my fundamental hypothesis is that each chain of social relations constitutes by itself a social relation, which is an integrant part of the social process under consideration. I will attempt to develop a calculus of implications and equivalences among the structural properties of these global social networks, whose reality is largely beyond the domain of individual or collective representations (*op. cit:* 13).

Lorrain applies his mathematical concepts largely to the study of kinship, but he argues that they can be applied also to the study of myths (*op. cit:* 54, 105),—the latter application falling outside the plan of his book.

Lorrain gratefully acknowledges his own intellectual debt to Levi-Strauss, Jakobson and Harrison C. White. Having argued that the logic of binary oppositions is basic to all aspects of social life, he states:

> If binary opposition truly holds a privileged place within the human mind, one must conclude that at the heart of this human mind lie the structural seeds of the social and cultural architecture which order human activity . . . . The deep rooting of this logic of binary oppositions within the human spirit is for me a guarantee of reality, providing the certitude that I am not involved in the labyrinth of an arbitrary formalism (*op. cit:* 54).

We can see that mathematicians are not at all afraid of relating their mathematical tools to the structure of the human mind.

The importance of structural mathematics in social sciences has been recently stressed by Paul A.Ballonoff, a population geneticist. He makes a systematic distinction between statistical treatments and statistical theories, on the one hand, and structural treatments and structural theories, on the other hand. Statistical treatments are largely descriptive and aim at discovering "significant correlationships." Statistical theory implies a more advanced step, as it can make predictions on the basis of axiomatic propositions. Structural treatments are mathematical descriptions usually carried out through algebraic matrices. Structural theories describe all the possible forms of a given type and can predict expected ranges of values or the external parameters of statistical models. Ballonoff argues that statistical models have been the first ones to be discovered in the history of sciences, followed next by structural models and theories. As of now, only particle physics possesses an established structural theory, whereas in kinship theory one can find some incipient formulations of it (Ballonoff 1975:184).

Being already familiar with empiricist misunderstandings of structural position (see Chapters one and two), the reader will not be surprised that empiricists ignore—or, worse—misunderstand the mathematical value of structural models. For instance, Francis Korn maintains that the mathematical studies of kinship carried out by Andre Weil, J.G. Kemeny, J.L. Snell, G.L. Thompson, P. Courrege, and H. White are primarily a mathematical translation of marriage rules into a formal notation. Korn argues that such translations are useless because they do not "add anything to the ethnographical facts known" (1973:131). Korn concludes his chapter on permutation models by stating that he fails to see what "properties not immediately apparent at the empirical levels" are brought out by the algebraic treatment of prescriptive systems (*op. cit:* 139). The last sentence refers to a passage of a famous article written by Levi-Strauss in 1960:

> If a distinction is made between the level of observation and symbols to be substituted for it, I fail to see why an algebraic treatment of, say, symbols for marriage rules could not teach us, when aptly manipulated, something of the way a given marriage system actually works and bring out properties not immediately apparent to the empirical observer (1960 in 1976:80.)

Levi-Strauss refers to structural properties of kinship systems, whereas Korn refers to empirical properties and "ethnographical facts" as immediately observable.

Buchler and Selby have a different understanding of what modern branches of mathematics such as graph theory, matrix algebra, theory of games and theory of groups of permutations can contribute to the study of marriage systems. They argue that these mathematical models, to be distinguished from "probability models" (1968:151), permit one to see "formal relationships between the properties of structures that are neither obvious nor trivial" and provide "interpretations for results that are deduced from equations, allowing us to go beyond the information given" (*op. cit:* 164). It is not so much a question of additional ethnographic data, although this is a possible outcome of structural hypotheses, but rather that the theorems of graph theory produce assertions which apply to empirical structures. By showing that empirical structures match the axioms of graph theory, we show structural properties of empirical data which were previously unknown. It is intelligibility, more than factual information about empirical structures, which is enhanced by graph theory.

Empiricist shortcomings similar to those propagated by F. Korn are also evident in George Homans' criticism of Boudon's "effective" definition of social structure. Boudon's "effective" definition of social structure consists of a threefold element: (1) a set of axioms, (2) a set of rules specifying the assignment of people to different groups, (3) a set of rules specifying which close relatives can or cannot be chosen as marriage partners (1968). The second element is called by Boudon the "structural description" of the system, and the third element—which is derived from the axiom combined with the structural element—predicts the "apparent characteristics of the system." Homans' criticism that he does not see the difference between the second and third element (1975) amounts to a confession that he does not understand the structural position. As I have explained in the second chapter here, structuralists predict marriage choices in terms of one's position within the system and not in terms of psychological and other particular reasons, such as liking, wealth, etc. From this failure to understand the structural perspective derives another miscriticism of Homans'—that structural models do not predict the exceptions to the systemic tendencies, nor do they explain why people conform to norms. I have explained in the introductory chapter to this book that the reasons for the exceptions must be searched in empiricial contingencies and interferences with the tendencies of the system as a system; these reasons are, of course, the same reasons why some people do not conform to the structural tendencies of the system. Briefly, Homans' criticism does not affect the mathematical aspect of the structural models, but rather the structural approach as a theoretical perspective.

Fadwa El Guindi and Dwight W. Read have provided an excellent ethnographic application of mathematical models for the study of ritual (1976). They argue that the mathematical formalization is not just a parsimonious language ("translation" in Homans' terms) but it is a direct expression of the characteristics inherent in the cultural system. Moreover, mathematical formalizations generate ethnographic descriptions and explanations. El Guindi and Read distinguish between stochastic models, based on probability, and the deterministic framework underlying stochastic models. It is the deterministic framework which expresses the structure of the ritual in terms of conceptual categories and a set of relations among the categories. The structure of the ritual can be represented as an algebraic structure, which is the logical principle organizing the ritual events; this shows that beliefs and ritual are inherently mathematical in nature. El Guindi and Read argue also that mathematical analysis provides a form of verification of structural analysis, in that it confirms the conclusions which are previously reached on the basis of ethnographic data. Anyone familiar with the endlessly repeated criticism about the presumed unverifiability of structural analysis (see Chapter two) will appreciate the importance of this point.

Before closing this chapter, we have to dispel the notion that statistical and structural models are in direct and total antithesis to each other. On the contrary, Ballonoff has argued that the mathematical study of marriage systems and population genetics has shown that certain problems can be identified only when we attempt to make compatible the results of structural and statistical theories (1975:198).

Mathematicians are perhaps better equipped than epistemologists to demonstrate the complementarities of the statistical and structural levels of analysis, and to show that the experimental level of analysis is not contradicted but refined by structural analysis. At the same time, we must credit structuralists for stimulating mathematical thinking and challenging mathematicians to produce more appropriate tools for the study of belief systems. It is perhaps ironic to realize that mathematicians, on the one hand, and structuralists and structural Marxists, on the other hand, are both concerned with the logic of combinations. As we mentioned at the beginning of this chapter, Levi-Strauss emphasizes the combinatory logic of mind and Althusser emphasizes the process of social formation as a combination of five invariant elements. "Both believe that structures are based on a limited number of elements which may be combined in a finite number of ways to produce different but related empirical social realities" (Glucksmann 1974:163). For both thinkers, structure consists in "the syntax of transformations which pass from one variant to another and is known as the 'combinatorics' " (*op. cit:* 35). Insofar as mathematics is concerned there is currently a great need to develop a "combinatorics," a mathematics of discrete phenomena; whereas classical mathematics was indispensible for the study of continuous phenomena, a combinatorics is needed for the study of discontinuous processes which occur in network analysis, molecular evolution and in computer science. However, there is no unified theory of combinatorics yet. For instance, the problems in the area of computer algorithms have been approached on an individual basis. However, more and more mathematicians believe that "combinatorial theories are necessary to the future of the mathematical, physical, and life sciences" (Kolata 1974:883).

One can see that structuralism is directly connected to the development of a new branch of mathematics; in fact, the structuralists' need for more precise and predictive tools foster the refinements of new tools in the area of qualitative mathematics. In this sense, structuralism must be considered a pioneer scientific thrust which may considerably expand the analytical and methodological apparatus of human, sociological and linguistic sciences. It has already done so in the physical sciences.

Notes

[1]Maurice Godelier has proposed a sophisticated conceptualization of the distinction between infrastructure and superstructure. In his view the distinction is not a distinction between levels or aspects of social reality, but between functions of a same institution or between "positions within those activities necessary to the reproduction of social life." (1978:764).

[2]This notion is in line with the structural Marxist approach of Althusser based on the "rational materialism" of Gaston Bachelard. Bachelard maintains that an essential step in developing any scientfic knowledge is to provide a scientific definition of the object of inquiry by formulating concepts which refer not to what is immediately observable, but to "hidden" aspects of reality. The term "rational materialism" seems also apt for expressing Levi-Strauss' notion of the "intrinsic rationality of the universe."

References

Ballonoff, Paul A. 1975. "Structural Models and Correspondence Problems," *Social Sciences Information* 14(3/4):183-199.

Boudon, Raymond. 1968. *A Quoi Sert La Notion De "Structure"?* Paris: Gallimard.

Bower, T.G.R. 1966. "The Visual World of Infants," *Scientific American* 215(6):80-92.

Buchler, Ira R. and Henry A. Selby. 1968. *Kinship and Social Organization: An Introduction to Theory and Method.* N.Y.:The Macmillan Company.

Caws, Peter. 1974. "Operational, Representational and Explanatory Models," *American Anthropologist* 76(1):1-10.

_____. 1977. "More on the Ontology of Social Structure: A Reply to Rossi," *American Anthropologist* 79(4):916.

Chaney, Richard Paul. 1972. "Scientific Inquiry and Models of Socio-cultural Data Patterning: An Epilogue," in *Models in Archaeology*. David R. Clarke, ed. London: Company Ltd. 991-1031.

Chaney, Richard Paul. 1973. "Comparative Analysis and Retroductive Reasoning or Conclusions in Search of a Premise," *American Anthropologist* 75:1358-1375.

_____. 1974. "On the Precepts of 'Culture Area' and 'Language Culture'," in *Comparative Studies by Harold E. Driver and essays in his honor,* edited by Joseph G. Jorgensen. New Haven: Human Relations Area Film Press:237-245.

_____. 1976. "On Z Factors," *Current Anthropology* 17(4):749-756.

_____. 1978. "Structures, Realities, and Blind Spots," *American Anthropologist* 80(3): 589-596.

Cohen, Ronald. 1977. "The Emperor's Clothes: Review of a Review, *American Anthropologist* 79(1):113-114.

Corneille, Jean-Pierre. 1976. *La Linguistique Structurale: Son Portee, Ses Limites.* Paris: Librairie Larousse.

El Guindi, Fadwa and Dwight W. Read. 1979. "Mathematics in Structural Theory," *Current Anthropology,* 20(4):761-790.

Fabrega, Horacio, Jr. 1977. "Culture, Behavior, and the Nervous System," *Annual Review of Anthropology* 6:419-455.

Franz, Robert L. 1961. "The Origin of Form Perception," *Scientific American.*

Glucksmann, M. 1974. *Structuralist Analysis in Contemporary Social Thought.* Boston: Routledge and Kegan Paul.

Godelier, Maurice. 1978. "Infrastructures, Societies, and History," *Current Anthropology* 19(4):763-771.

Hanson, F. Allan. 1976. "Models and Social Reality: an Alternative to Caws," *American Anthropologist* 78(2):323-325.

Harris, Marvin. 1969. *The Rise of Anthropological Theory.* N.Y.:Thomas Y. Crowell.

Held, Richard and Whitman Richards, eds. 1976. *Recent Progress in Perception.* San Francisco: W.H. Freeman.

Homans, G.C. 1975. "What do We Mean by Social 'Structure'?" in *Approaches to the Study of Social Structure,* edited by Peter M. Blau. N.Y.: Free Press, p.53-65.

Kolata, Gina Bari. 1974. "Combinatorics: Steps Toward a Unified Theory," *Science* 183 (No. 4127):839-840, 883.

Kolers, Paul A. 1972. "Experiments in Reading," in Held and Richards 1976:196-203.

Korn, Francis. 1973. *Elementary Structures Reconsidered: Levi-Strauss on Kinship.* Berkeley: University of California Press.

Laughlin, Charles D. and Eugene G. D'Aquili. 1974. *Biogenetic Structuralism.* N.Y.: Columbia University Press.

Leach, Edmund. 1961. *Rethinking Anthropology.* London:Athloue.

Levi-Strauss, Claude. 1963. *Structural Anthropology,* translated by Claire Jacobson and Brook Grundfest Schoepf. N.Y.: Basic Books.

_____. 1966. *The Savage Mind.* Chicago: University of Chicago Press (French original 1962).

_____. 1966a. "Introduction a L'Oeuvre de Marcel Mauss," in *Sociologie et Anthropologie* by Marcel Mauss. Paris: Presses Universitaires de France, pp. IX-LII (original 1950).

_____. 1968. "Broadcasting," in Michael Treguer's series *"Un Certain Regard."* Reprinted in Catherine Backes-Clement - Levi-Strauss. Paris:Seghers 1970:172-188.

_____. 1968a. "Hommage aux Sciences de l'Homme," *Social Sciences Information* 7(2): 7-11.

_____. 1969. *The Elementary Structures of Kinship,* translated by J.H. Bell and T.R. von Sturmer under R. Needham's editorship. Boston: Beacon Press (French original 1949; revised French edition 1967).

_____. 1969b. *The Raw and the Cooked.* N.Y.: Harper and Row (French original 1966).

_____. 1971. *L'Homme Nu.* Paris: Plon.

_____. 1973. "Reflexions sur l'Atome de la Parente," *L'Homme* XIII(3):5-30.

_____. 1976. *Structural Anthropology,* Vol. II, translated by M. Layton, N.Y.: Basic Books.

_____. 1976a. "Structuralisme et Empirisme," *L'Homme,* XVI (2-3):23-39.

Lorrain, Francois. 1975. *Reseaux Sociaux et Classifications Sociales: Essai sur L'Algebre et la Geometrie des Structures Sociales.* Paris: Hermann.

Maybury-Lewis, David P. 1969. "Review of Claude Levi-Strauss' *Mythologiques: Du Miel aux Cendres,"* *American Anthropologist* 71(1):114-120.

Needham, Rodney. 1978. "Pronouncement vs. Competence," *American Anthropologist* 80(2):386-387.

Neisser, Ulric. 1968. "The Processes of Vision," *Scientific American* 219(3):204-214.

Nutini, Hugo G. 1970. "Levi-Strauss' Conception of Science," in *Exchanges et Communications,* edited by J. Pouillon and P. Maranda. The Hague: Mouton, p.543-570.

Piaget, Jean. 1969. "Discussion" of "On Voluntary Action and its Hierarchical Structure," by Jerome J. Bruner in *Beyond Reductionism: New perspectives in the life sciences,* edited by Arthur Koestler and J.R. Smythies.

Rock, Irvin. 1974. "The Perception of Disoriented Figures," in Held and Richards 1976: 175-182.

Rossi, Ino. 1974. *The Unconscious in Culture: The Structuralism of Claude Levi-Strauss in Perspective.* New York: Dutton.

Rossi, Ino. 1977. "Reply to Cohen." *American Anthropologist* 79(1)114-115.

_____. 1978. "Toward the Unification of Scientific Explanation" in *Discourse and Inference in Cognitive Anthropology,* edited by M. Loflin and J. Siverberg. The Hague: Mouton.

_____. 1978a. "On theoretical and technical incompetence; the case of Rodney Needham" *American Anthropologist* 80(3):675-76.

Schneider, David M. 1965. "Some Muddles in the Models: Or, How the System Really Works." In *The Relevance of Models for Social Anthropology,* Bantom Michael (ed.) N.Y.: Praeger.

Scholte, Bob. 1966. "Epistemic Paradigms: Some Problems in Cross-cultural Research on Social-Anthropological History and Theory." *American Anthropologist* 68(5): 1191-1201.

Stent, Gunther S. 1972. "Cellular Communication." in *Communication,* A "Scientific American" book. San Francisco: W.H. Freeman and Company, p. 17-28.

_____. 1975. "Limits to the Scientific Understanding of Man." *Science* 187 (4181): 1052-1057.

Teuber, Marianne L. 1974. "Sources of Ambiguity in the Prints of Maurits C. Escher." in Held and Richards 1976:153-167.

INDEX